TRADE SECRETS

TRADE SECRETS

A MEMOIR

Pat Carney

KEY PORTER BOOKS

Canadian Cataloguing in Publication Data

Carney, Patricia, 1935-
    Trade secrets : a memoir

ISBN 1-55263-163-X

1. Carney, Patricia, 1935- . 2. Canada – Politics and government – 1980-1984.* 3. Canada –
Politics and government – 1984-1993.* 4. Cabinet ministers – Canada – Biography. 5. Women
legislators – Canada – Biography. 6. Women consultants – Canada – Biography. 7. Women
journalists – Canada – Biography. I. Title.

FC631.C37A4 2000   971.064'7'092   C00-931500-4   F1034.3.C37A3 2000

The Canada Council | Le Conseil des Arts
FOR THE ARTS | DU CANADA
SINCE 1957 | DEPUIS 1957

The publisher gratefully acknowledges the support of the Canada Council for the Arts and the
Ontario Arts Council for its publishing program.

We acknowledge the financial support of the Government of Canada through the Book
Publishing Industry Development Program (BPIDP) for our publishing activities.

Key Porter Books Limited
70 The Esplanade
Toronto, Ontario
Canada   M5E 1R2

www.keyporter.com

Design: Peter Maher
Electronic formatting: Heidi Palfrey

An excerpt from the song "Penny-pinching Bastards" is reprinted on p. 298, courtesy of Kent Fiddy.
© 1997, British Columbia Music, Kent Fiddy.

Excerpts from *Vancouver Sun* articles by Pat Carney are reprinted in Chapters 7, 10, 11, 12, 17
and 20 with the kind permission of Pacific Press, a Division of Southam, Inc.

The publisher has made every effort to contact the copyright holders of material reproduced in
this book. We would be pleased to have any additional information regarding this material.

Printed and bound in Canada

00 01 02 03 04 6 5 4 3 2 1

This book is dedicated to:

Jane, my gift
John, my joy
Jim, my blessing
And Paul, my love.

Contents

Introduction

People know I am writing this book. When I leave my keys in the door of the truck in a parking lot, when I walk past friends with a bemused stare instead of a friendly hello, when my best friend slams down the phone because I don't recognize her voice, when I leave half the mail on a table in the Saturna General Store and have to phone postmistress Flo House to put it back in our mailbox, people know Pat has something on her mind.

But when they ask what my book is about, and I answer "my life and times," they look bemused. Whose life and what times, and why now? This is a challenge; as a former journalist and present politician I understand that everyone's life and times are stories worth telling. But mine has been—and continues to be—a grand adventure, and I want to share it, because the experiences I've had and the lessons I've learned are worth sharing.

Only in Canada, one might argue, could anyone, particularly a woman, live a life of such variety and opportunity. From Shanghai to Saturna Island, via southern Ontario, British Columbia, the Northwest Territories, and Ottawa, which has its own geography. From veterinary assistant to journalist, MP to cabinet minister, adjunct professor, and senator. Often the first in my field of endeavour, with stories to tell other women.

Our Canadian mobility across professions, geography, and social barriers is an unacknowledged asset. Once, in Europe, I arranged to interview a high-ranking businessman, and was amazed at the scramble among my colleagues to accompany me in order to gain access to the Personage. In Canada, access to jobs, political positions, and important people can be had through a classified advertisement, phone call, or encounter at the local ski hill. In a global age of security gates, political corruption, and assassinations, may it always be so.

While this book has been produced over the last year, I have been writing it for the past 40, recording interviews in my journalism notebooks; marking events and my reactions in my journals; saving family letters, manuscripts, and scrapbooks; and savouring scraps of handwritten comments from my political colleagues that future historians will find illuminating; they have not been reproduced here, but in time they will be available. The illegal destruction of my ministerial papers when I left the department of International Trade—by law they must be archived—effectively wiped the slate on my ministerial performance in the Trade post. The events described here are drawn largely from my journals, or "black books," and parliamentary papers.

My favourite question to anyone is: What have you learned? In writing this book I learned the importance of the written record in preserving our voices from both the past and the present. My father's World War I letters to his sister changed my view of him; his children never knew him as a young man. The stories of South Africa in the early 1900s, and of Toronto in the 1920s, culled from the unpublished manuscripts of my mother, her sister Byrne Hope Sanders, and their brother Wilfrid Sanders, portray a world we will never see again—a world fresh and colourful to them.

Even my own voice changes when heard through the scribbles in my journals, from the young businesswoman living and working in Canada's northern territories, to the elected MP, a new political penny shining with purpose, to the worn and wiser cabinet minister. Readers will also notice how my view of politics and people, including my boss, Brian Mulroney, changes focus as events unfold. While time alters perspectives and may produce a more balanced view, the fresh responses recorded in my journals, unlaundered by the rue of hindsight, provide a snapshot of events at the time they occurred, and their effect on me. Whether scrawled in a diary or stored on computer disks, write down the details of your life—now!

I needed the help of many people to produce this book, including author Barry Broadfoot, who kick-started the writing of it; my researcher, historian Tammy Nemeth, who organized my political archival papers; UBC Special Collections librarian George Brandak, who has stored boxes of these papers for the last 10 years; Susan Mayse for friendly advice; Janice Whitters, who produced the manuscript; Susan Folkins, who edited it; Anna Porter, who published it; my longtime political photographer Kent Kallberg; my agent and friend Perry Goldsmith; my twin Jim and my cousins Len Neave, Eileen O'Keefe Giuliani, and Adrian Higham for family information; Martin Green, Emile Franco, Ian Smyth, and Diana Lam, who provided political information; Senator Nick Sibbeston, who read parts of my manuscript; Rick Tipple, Saturna photographer; and finally my husband Paul White, who floats in and out of these stories as he has my life for the past 47 years, for his unflagging, if sometimes supperless, support.

And finally, a special thanks to my friends and neighbours on Saturna, who have unfailingly protected my private life during my public-service years. It is amazing how journalists, arriving at our wharf, can't find anyone who knows where I live; is it the Gulfside, or maybe East Point? Nor, shaking their collective heads, can they recall my telephone number. Here is an example. When our friend and great cook Janet Comstock operated her Poppy Hill Bed and Breakfast on Saturna (she has since moved to Victoria), my buddies Jean and David McLean and I would go over to her house after her guests left to have coffee, gossip, and gobble up the leftover muffins. Once, when I was doing the dishes there after breakfast, the phone rang and I answered it, cheerfully giving the caller information on the B & B and taking his reservation. When he called back to confirm the arrangements, the caller said to Janet: "Your hired help sounds a lot like Pat Carney."

"Everybody says that," said Janet. Now that's privacy!

PAT CARNEY
SATURNA ISLAND
JUNE 2000

CHAPTER 1

Shanghai

TRADE SECRET:
*One pace begins a journey
of a thousand miles.*
—Chinese proverb

I was in the Senate reading room behind the Red Chamber in the Parliament Buildings, idly flipping through the pages of the Vancouver newspapers, when a Liberal Senator approached me and said: "I guess you'd like to be Canadian Ambassador to China." It was in the mid-1990s, I was deputy chair of the Standing Senate Committee on Foreign Affairs, and China was in the news.

"Oh, no," I protested. As a former Minister of International Trade, I knew Beijing was considered a hardship post, albeit a senior one, in the Foreign Service. With all that dust blowing in from the Mongolian desert and the polluted air, I always found it hard to breathe in the capital of my beloved Middle Kingdom.

"What I would *really* like to be is Consul General in Shanghai, my birth city," I explained. "I opened our consulate office there in 1988 and it is one of the most exciting cities in the world—very commercial, pulsing with energy, very historic. I love it," I added.

The Liberal Senator looked thoughtful, but I thought no more of it. A few weeks later during the Christmas break the Senator called me in my Saturna Island kitchen. "I was talking to André Ouellet at a Christmas cocktail party and your name came up," she said, calling from *her* kitchen on the other side of Canada. Ouellet was the Liberal Minister of Foreign Affairs[1] at the time. "I told him of your interest in Shanghai. He said that if you were interested in the Consul-General position he'd like to talk to you about it when he returns from Geneva

13

in the New Year. But you would have to decide quickly because he's due to announce changes in diplomatic postings abroad."

I was taken by surprise. Shanghai! What an intriguing thought! I could envision the humid, crowded city on the muddy Huangpu River located a few miles upstream from its junction with the Yangtse River; the spires and huddled brick buildings, the Victorian-Gothic buildings on the Bund, that former towpath used when coolies pulled boats upstream with ropes; the cheerful, cheeky people, considered the most entrepreneurial in China.

What should I do? While posting politicians abroad in place of career Foreign Service officers was typically discouraged, I had earlier been informed that, given my background in international trade and particularly in China, no objections would likely be raised.

But I was attached like a barnacle to my new home on the shores of Saturna, the southernmost Gulf Island anchoring the Strait of Georgia between the mainland and Vancouver Island. As Senator for British Columbia, I was deeply absorbed in the economic problems of the valiant coastal communities, with their depressed forest and fishery resources and their struggles with distant Ottawa. And I was Mom or Granny Pat in my extended family.

Plus, I had arthritis. I was well aware of how hard our diplomats worked abroad, under often difficult conditions. Could I physically do the job? Most of our senior appointees in China had some basic knowledge of the language; unfortunately, however, I had forgotten the Shanghainese dialect that my twin brother Jim and I had spoken as children and my Mandarin consisted of basic cocktail-circuit phrases.

"I'm going to Maui with my family for the winter break and I'll think about it," I informed the Liberal Senator, whom I liked and trusted. "Please ask the Minister to call me when he returns and I will let him know."

After our conversation, I reflected that maybe it was fate, ending my political career in Shanghai, our first Canadian trade office in Asia. Maybe I could live in our old house there. Maybe it was meant to be.

Maybe.

My family's former home in Shanghai is a modest two-storey house situated on a lane off Yu Yuen Road in an area known to my parents as

West End Gardens. This neighbourhood is located outside the boundaries of the International Settlement, the financial and social heart of the most exciting city in Asia until Mao Zedong founded the Communist party in Shanghai and chased most foreigners out. Under the 1843 Treaty of Nanking, which concluded the opium wars between Great Britain and China, the former fishing village had become a "Treaty Port," open to trade with foreigners. In 1844, France and the United States gained the rights to foreign trade in treaty ports such as Shanghai, and the International Settlement was created, downriver from the Chinese settlement, since the Chinese did not want to live near the whisky-drinking, hairy, smelly foreigners, who were allowed to bring their families with them.[2]

Our house in West End Gardens is the only home in China I remember.

Across the lane is the birthday-cake-styled structure of the Children's Palace. When we lived there in the late 1930s the children's playground was the home of Wang Ching Wei, the puppet governor recognized by the Japanese as head of the Nationalist Government. Guns installed on the high stone walls tracked us as we played in our tiny garden. Barbed-wire fences barred the streets and machine-gun fire rattled the night.

In 1998 a restaurant was located at the end of the lane and tourists thronged the Children's Palace to watch Chinese children sing and play on cue. "It's a lot noisier than it used to be," sighed Shen Jiang Xie, whose family has owned the house for most of the last 60 years since the recurring bloody conflicts between the Japanese and Chinese finally drove my father home to Canada after 20 years in China.

We were sitting in the front sunroom where my twin brother Jim and I had once played with our younger sister Norah and eaten our meals together. In the darkly panelled dining room beyond, an Amah in a white jacket prepared tea, just as our Amah had done 60 years earlier. It was my first visit to China since I had regretfully declined Foreign Minister Ouellet's offer of the Consul-General post in Shanghai.

Shen Jiang Xie is the daughter of former tea merchant Shen Zhen. I had met them both 10 years earlier, in 1988, when I entered the house for the first time since that night in 1939 when we left on the ferry to Nagasaki and a Canada that we children had visited only once. In 1987, on another visit to Shanghai, my son John Patrick and I had located the house in the lane, following a map drawn by my mother. Two old "aunties" answered our knock, but since I spoke no Shanghainese and they spoke no English we only smiled at each other and I left my card.

Shortly thereafter my office in Ottawa received a letter from Shen Zhen written in impeccable French, apologizing for his absence in Hong Kong on business and inviting me to visit. When I returned to Shanghai as Minister Responsible for Asia Pacific in the Mulroney government to open our new consulate, Mr. Shen greeted me at the airport and briefed me on new reforms taking place in my birth city.

The next day, at his invitation, our modest cavalcade of five official cars swept down Yu Yuen Road and turned down the lane to No. 30. The house had hardly changed from my childhood. The painted shutters guarding the paned windows still peeked over the walled inside entrance and the yellow plaster showed years of resigned neglect from lack of money and materials for repairs.

Mr. Shen, his son-in-law Cheng Yi Gang, and his daughter Shen Jiang Xie waved me through the door into the narrow hall and invited me to explore the house. The only room I did not recall was my father's study; children were not encouraged there. Everything else was as I remembered, racing room to room: the beamed living room with its varnished wood floors and fireplace, the dining room with its inset buffet, the kitchen where I had once watched with interest the cockroaches on the wall under the sink, to the disgust of Amah.

My front bedroom with its balcony and Jim's bedroom with the same-coloured blue wash on its walls. My parents' bedroom next door (I still have the curry set that Mother found on a closet shelf when we moved in) and the small bedroom where the baby, Norah, slept. The two bathrooms where we played with the faucets, splashing water on the tiled floors with gleeful satisfaction.

After my tour, Mr. Shen and I took tea in the sunroom, eating *zhongzi*—sticky rice steamed in banana leaf—to mark the fifth day of the fifth lunar month, traditionally the day of the dragon-boat races, and discussed the history of our house over the previous half-century of war, turmoil, Communist takeover, and the Cultural Revolution. Cheng Yi Gang, a senior engineer with Shanghai Cable Works, Shen Jiang Xie, and their young son Daniel joined us, the men talking, the daughter listening, her peach-tinted face like an old Chinese painting.

Sitting in the sunroom, looking out at the tiny garden where, as children, we had made a submarine out of our sandbox—the sand had been hastily removed when Amah discovered its usefulness to kitty—I felt that my childhood, removed by time, distance, and silence, had somehow been restored. There were three tiny wicker chairs on the porch—surely they could not have been ours?

Over the years, the Shens became my Shanghai family. We exchanged brightly figured Christmas and Chinese New Year cards. During the Tiananmen Square crisis in 1989, when Chinese students had been mowed down by Chinese tanks and Shanghai students were rioting in the streets, discreet letters were exchanged. Was Daniel, an engineering student, okay? Involved in his studies, came the oblique reply.

Mr. Shen's younger daughter Jeannie visited with our family in Vancouver and immigrated with her husband and son to California. She told me how, as a rebellious teenager, she had "reported" her father and mother for their bourgeois behaviour and had been transported with other students to the countryside to plant cabbages, working in the fields in her bare feet. Older and wiser, she studied English and French for the opportunity to study in a foreign country.

She told me how the Shen family, parents and four children, had been crowded into Amah's cramped quarters during the Cultural Revolution and how 12 families moved into our house in their place. Mrs. Shen became ill and never recovered. Shanghai was overcrowded and housing for its 14 million people was at a premium. It took the Shen family until the early 1980s to reclaim their house, whose patched and plastered walls and darkly varnished floors had housed the history of modern China.

When I returned to the house on Yu Yuen Road in 1998, this time in a modest consulate van, it was as I remembered. The family crowded the narrow doorway, smiling their greetings, but sadly without Mr. Shen, who had passed away. As I sat in the sunroom next to a stack of letters and cards I had sent over the past 10 years, Shen Jiang Xie explained, her eyes misting, that they are presented to Mr. Shen's portrait over the fireplace so that he can read them too. The wicker chairs had vanished from the porch.

Daniel Cheng entered the room, no longer the teenaged engineering student but now a mature young executive with a freight-forwarding company exporting Chinese goods to North America. Then through the sunroom door came another grandson, Hong Kong–raised Henry Shen, whose father Peter I had visited in Hong Kong. Jeannie called from California, laughing and homesick, to welcome me back to Yu Yuen.

We settled in for a good gossip, joined by my guide from the Canadian consulate, Chen Ying, who, like other consulate staff, has adopted an Anglicized name, Helena, chosen when she was still in high school. Shanghai-born and -raised, she is married to a civil engineer who designs power systems.

After answering inquiries about other family members, I asked the question that fascinated me. What was Henry, who had lived in the United States and Hong Kong, doing in Shanghai? And why hadn't Daniel emigrated to Canada or the United States like his cousins?

"There is more opportunity in Shanghai," explained Henry, whose consulting firm advises on strategy management, market-entry strategy, and other business trends. Daniel noted, with a hint of resentment, that his visa application to study in America had been rejected at the time of Tiananmen, but he agreed that Shanghai was the place to be even if some young people had trouble finding a job.

To me, nothing could be more illustrative of modern Shanghai, the fastest-growing city in the history of the world, according to former Canadian Consul General Ted Lippman, also China-born. More than a thousand new high-rise buildings have pierced the squatting brick neighbourhoods of the old city since 1990 and another five hundred are under construction, making Shanghai the hottest construction site on earth.

As I walked down the Bund, with its Victorian and art deco facades, I could see across the river the futuristic towers and spheres of Pudong, Shanghai's new business district, which is planned to be the financial centre of the world in the twenty-first century. For the first time the Bund's grim grey buildings, those former citadels of trade and finance built on a marshy bog granted to Europeans under nineteenth-century treaty rights, appeared to me to be squat and shabby compared to the shining office towers across the river.

Henry Shen agrees that Pudong's towers may be half-empty but he calls them half-full, waiting for the city to reclaim its position as the commercial heart of China; before World War II, two-thirds of China's total foreign trade flowed through the international concession of Shanghai. Henry came back to Shanghai from Hong Kong, the former British colony returned to China in 1997 in a blaze of fireworks and flags. "Shanghai is built to last," he informed me over tea. "Built for the future."

Hong Kong-style optimism, maybe. But today's Hong Kong was largely built by yesterday's Shanghainese, fleeing the Communist conquest of the Chinese mainland and seeking refuge in the British colony, helping to build the basis of its entrepreneurial economy that is enshrined in the Basic Law reuniting it with the People's Republic of China.

Shanghai's destiny as the financial centre of the world will be fulfilled in the twenty-first century, in the eyes of its proud young citizens.

Our house is not my only interest on my Shanghai visits. As an archaeologist might sift through sands searching for lost cities, I am absorbed in the hunt for the world of my parents, who lived in the International Settlement in the years before World War II—glittering jazz-filled nights and days, oblivious to the Depression dust bowl sanding the gears of the American economy, the war clouds over Europe, and Mao Zedong's Long March to Liberation, when Shanghai was the Sin City of the Orient and where, my father told me, one really did part the beaded curtains and plunk one's foot on the brass rail of seedy bars.

Much of this Shanghai is lost forever, buried under the weight of the Cultural Revolution, when the classical Chinese and western influences were rooted out and destroyed, eventually replaced by the bamboo scaffolding of new buildings, Maoist dictums, and the millennium's construction boom. The new Chinese museum stands in the middle of the old racetrack, social centre of the International Settlement and later an execution ground under Mao.

Searching for clues to the Shanghai of the Thirties on every visit, I have wandered through streets jammed with bicycles, horns blaring in the humid air, thinking that if I turn my head fast enough, I can see my parents holding hands over there, on the corner. I can hear their voices echoing through the Chinese chimes and traffic noises in the wind-cooled, tree-shaded boulevards of the former French Concession.

My father Jim Carney came to China in 1920. Raised on an Okanagan homestead and bored with the prospect of returning to teaching after his experiences in the trenches of World War I, he returned to Vancouver and signed on as a stoker, fuelling the coal-fired engines of the freighter *Canadian Inventor*, bound for China. Having signed on for the two-way trip, my father arranged with the captain to jump ship when the freighter reached Shanghai in return for foregoing his pay. This highly unusual entry caused his China-born children some problems years later when we were classified by immigration officials as "white Orientals."

He joined the Shanghai Police Force, studied and became fluent in the Shanghainese dialect, and switched to the Shanghai Municipal Council as a public health officer and meat inspector, working in the slaughterhouses along the Huangpu and similar locales that brought him in daily touch with ordinary Chinese and provided a treasure chest of stories and experiences far removed from those of many Caucasians, living within the comfortable confines of their European clubs and culture.

He met my mother Dora in 1933 on the *Empress of Russia*, one of the famous Canadian Pacific White Empresses that crossed the Pacific from Canada to Asia every two weeks before World War II. Dora was a 29-year-old South African-born journalist who was en route to Hong Kong to marry a cousin. Enchanted by Jim and his stories about Shanghai, she did the unthinkable for young women of her generation: she decided to leave the ship at Shanghai, where she knew no one.

Several months later, in March 1934, my parents were married in the green gardens of the British Consulate on the Bund. My twin brother Jim and I were born in 1935, my sister Norah in 1937. For six years my parents explored the city and the countryside; my mother's journalistic curiosity and my father's language skills taking them places few foreigners ventured. "Every day I am thankful that Jim is in the Municipal Service," Mother wrote her family in Toronto.

It isn't a fashionable job—Dad's friend Society isn't rushing after us—but it leaves us so free!

The pay isn't much but it is ENOUGH and for the time being anyway, sure. If a bust-up happens—a real war, or anything like that—we'll be in the soup, and that is why we are building up a savings account in Canada. If the Municipal Council goes phutt we'll lose the superannuation, etc. but any way it would be heavenly to come back to Canada, wouldn't it?[3]

In the margin of her letter she added in pencil: "There is little chance of it—could only happen if all the nations went to war and Shanghai was given back to China." The nations did, and Shanghai was, and we were evacuated back to Canada in 1937 when the Japanese attacked the city, my father staying behind to help defend the Settlement.

We returned to China and moved into the house off Yu Yuen Road a few months later, but my father, wise in the ways of China, took us back to Canada in time for the birth of our brother Tom in 1940, escaping the internment by the Japanese that took the lives or harmed the health of so many of our Shanghai friends.

But I did not know any of this on the last night of my Chinese childhood, faced with my first big decision. The day we left, we twins, then four years old, had been flower girl and ring bearer in a posh wedding in the Anglican Trinity Cathedral. Afterward, as my exhausted mother finished her last-minute packing, she said we could each take one favourite possession on the night ferry to Nagasaki.

I stared at my reflection in the bureau mirror in my bedroom overlooking the front garden, a serious little girl with dark brown pigtails, torn by the choice between my wedding party flower basket and my teddy bear. Teddy won, and the beautiful basket was left in all its glory on the bedroom bureau.

When I recounted that memory to the Shen family on my first return visit to our Yu Yuen home, standing in the same bedroom then occupied by Shen Jiang Xie and her husband, their son Daniel went to his room, once occupied by my twin, and returned with a small black-and-white toy panda bear. I took it home with me to Canada as a replacement for my old teddy bear, long since lost.

On my first two return visits, I tried unsuccessfully to find the cathedral where I ended my Chinese childhood. Many of the old icons of the International Settlement vanished with the lease, and the cathedral appeared to be one of them. Once or twice when I asked my Chinese hosts about the Anglican Cathedral, I was taken to the American Community Church whose brick building had been restored and used for church services.

Armed with my parents' maps and pictures, reasoning that the cathedral would be centrally located, I would recruit legendary Chinese interpreter, French-Canadian Jean Duval, to scour the Shanghai cityscape with me. Sorbonne-trained, Jean was so expert in Mandarin and knowledgeable about Chinese history and culture that even Chinese tour guides would stop and listen when we explored a Chinese museum or landmark. He even looked Chinese with his mandarin-style moustache.

He told me about the Chinese lord Qi (200–300 BC), the tiny mounted figure on the roofs of the Imperial Palaces, who must ride a hen for eternity as punishment for tyranny. He took me to the bird market in Beijing, where old men buy their caged canaries and reports of local executions are posted on the low stone walls. During my several ministerial trips with Jean I only once caught him by surprise when he did not know that only the Imperial family could use a five-clawed dragon as a symbol; mere mortals must settle for four or less.

He rescued me once when, in a ministerial speech, I referred to a decision as a kind of "King Solomon's choice," realizing even as I spoke that my audience would likely be unaware of the biblical reference. Duval hesitated briefly, then continued his interpretation. "What did you say?" I asked him later. "I referred to a similar Chinese legend," he smiled.

We eventually found the cathedral by its architecture. Walking down a street, we recognized a church bell tower, the same the world over. We tiptoed up the steps and peered through chained doors into the interior. It was being used for a meeting place, but on the columns were the wooden plaques where the numbers of hymns had once been posted. There was no ghost of a little girl in a blue dress with a basket of flowers.

My memories of China are the random images of childhood. Our house and garden. Amah, our nurse. Riding in a car through flooded streets. A refugee family camped under a yellow beach umbrella. My father in his tropical whites, and my mother in silk prints and bobbed hair. The rickshaws and beggars in the crowded streets. The Japanese sentry at the end of the lane.

Among these memories is one of Jim and me sitting in a dark theatre watching a brightly lit stage where a hunter danced with ladies dressed as white swans. Sitting in the balcony, we were enthralled. Later I learned the ballet was *Swan Lake*.

Setting off with our maps, Jean and I looked for the theatre. The probable site was masked by a storefront and pavement filled with racks of cheap dresses. It was only when we turned the corner into an alley that we recognized the fluted corners signalling a theatre stage. We pushed open a back door and entered a dark hall obviously being used as a warehouse.

But—look! There! On the left! A stage! And over on the wall, the art deco light fixtures! On the ceiling, the outline of a floral decoration! And up there—a rubble-filled balcony! The elegant outlines of a small, perfect hall emerged through the dust and boxes and fallen plaster. It looked like a scene from Dickens' *Great Expectations*.

A woman worker approached us and Jean recounted our story. She was all smiles, gracious to the foreign visitor. I wished we had brought our cameraman, despite the rain. But the next day when we returned with our photographer, it was a different story. The stage door was firmly shut and bolted. Finally the woman appeared and shrilled that they had been reported and punished with the threat of lost wages for showing a rubble-filled building to a foreigner. Dismayed, we apologized profusely. In China only restored buildings, no matter how garish, can be displayed to foreign eyes. Jean Duval and I decided to suspend our explorations for the lost world of my childhood.

On my first trip back to China in 1979, I stayed in the Jin Jiang Hotel, known to my parents as the Cathay Mansions. On the night of our arrival I had excitedly explored the halls, barging into rooms allocated to our tour group, wondering whether my mother came to tea here, what liaisons whiled away the hot, humid afternoons, whether in his bachelor days my father's French mistress entertained him in the hotel that now serves as the official residence of the Canadian Consul General in Shanghai.

Through the trees below shone the white domed roof of the French Club, where my parents and their friends had played and swum and danced on the famous cushioned floor of the oval ballroom while the band played "As Time Goes By" and other standards. The French Club closed in 1979 and later reopened as an entertainment centre for Shanghai's youth; 50 years after his grandparents had waltzed around the oval floor, my son John Patrick twirled my assistant around the dimly lit ballroom.

On my 1998 visit to the Shens, I found that the French Club had been skilfully integrated into the modern Garden Hotel Shanghai. My consulate guide and fellow Shanghainese Chen Ying stopped the consulate van at the entrance to explore it.

Chen Ying, as cultural officer with the Canadian consulate, was as fascinated by my memories of Shanghai past as I was by her experiences in Shanghai present. We poked through the public rooms, eventually attracting the attention of a middle-aged Japanese hotel executive. Smiling when he heard my story, he offered to be our tour guide. He explained that the bowling alley is now a restaurant, although the swimming pool remains, and is used regularly by our Consul General. An exquisitely dressed bride posed for her wedding photographs on the handsomely carved staircase.

We arrived at the oval ballroom. The balconies remain, but the polished dark floors have been covered by thick carpets since the room is now used mainly for meetings and media conferences. The original cushioned or floating floor remains in place under the carpets.

"Have you ever danced on this floor?" I asked our guide. "No," he replied, surprised. Then I took the impeccably suited executive by the hand and before he could object I had twirled him halfway round the room. "You have now," I said, bowing to the affronted Japanese.

Her hand hiding her mouth in a traditional Chinese gesture, Chen Ying giggled. There are still lingering Sino-Japanese resentments in my birth city. We were coldly escorted to the door.

It was time to say goodbye to my Shanghai family. We knew I might never see the house again. Cheng Yi Gang and his family could not afford to maintain it on their pension income and earnings and it was up for rent, possibly to an American who was starting a public relations business and who had promised to renovate the house under the terms of the lease.

As I went down the front steps into the garden, a real estate agent who was photographing the house recognized me. "Pat Carney!" she exclaimed. "What are you doing here?"

"What are *you* doing here?" I asked the smartly dressed young woman. Her name, she smiled, was Emily, and she had studied business administration at the University of Victoria. She had returned to Shanghai because of job opportunities. "Why don't you buy the house?" she asked.

For a moment I was tempted. Certainly China remains my first home—the place of my birth, the place I return to in my dreams, where I hear the silky, sibilant sounds of a young willow tree's leaves rustling in the wind, and the cool song of a stone water fountain, and see the serene image of Kuan Yin, Goddess of Mercy.

Maybe it *is* meant to be.

CHAPTER 2
Mei Mei

TRADE SECRET:
Life is a Great Harmony:
Look for the colours, listen for the music.
—Dora Sanders Carney

I was relaxing in my claw-footed bathtub in my old cottage on Saturna Island one autumn evening when suddenly the lights went out. Panic! I gingerly stepped out of the tub, felt my way to the wall phone, and called my mother in her cottage less than a mile away. "Are you all right, Mom?" I asked. "Of course, darling," she replied. "I have the fire on in the fireplace, some candles lit, and am as cozy as can be. How about you?"

"Just fine, but I think I'd better drive over and check on you," I lied. Her eldest daughter was unwilling to admit she was too afraid to stay in her dark cottage alone, particularly when she couldn't remember where she had stashed the gas lanterns for such emergencies. I arrived at my mother's place to find her sitting by the fire in her flannel nightie, brushing her long snow-white hair in the flame-licked darkness.

"I was writing a piece on clouds," she explained. Earlier that day I had driven her over to the cliff side of the Island to view the storm clouds piling up over Plumper Sound and Pender Island. She had hobbled out to the cliff's edge on her cane and had carefully studied the cloud formations in order to describe them in her weekend column for the Victoria *Times-Colonist*. No reader would ever imagine that the author was in her eighties.

"I finally think I have got it right," she proclaimed, her face lit up like a young girl's in the firelight. "I think, finally, I know how to write the way I want to."

It had taken her 70 years of apprenticeship as a writer to make that statement, from the 12-year-old who published her first poem, "Song of the Trees," in the *Globe* in 1915. Earlier, unpublished works from the age of five are among her papers. Published or unpublished, my mother wrote: magazine articles, poems, newspaper columns, radio and television scripts, and finally her memoirs of my parents' years in Shanghai, where three of their four children were born. Her children and grandchildren called her Mei Mei. She originally thought it meant Grandmother, but in fact it means Little Sister. In many ways it was a more accurate description; a strong woman, a caring mother, a romantic wife, but in the bosom of her tightly knit family, we protected her as we do our little sisters.

In her youth my mother wrote for the now-defunct *Mayfair* and the newly launched *Chatelaine*, edited by her older sister Byrne Hope Sanders, and for *Maclean's* and other periodicals. She was one of the first female advertising professionals, writing copy for T. Eaton department stores. She took her small portable typewriter to China and filed for newspapers during the 1937 evacuation of foreigners from Shanghai during a Japanese attack, travelling downriver to the British destroyer *Rajputana*, holding her baby with one arm and typewriter with the other, two fingers extended to us twins to clutch.

Back in Ontario during the war we were lulled to sleep in our unheated bedrooms, our feet warmed by hot bricks stuffed in old socks, by the sound of her typewriter as she tapped out stories for *Saturday Night*, *Family Herald*, and other periodicals. Her earnings augmented first my father's part-time income while he studied at the Ontario Veterinary College in Guelph and years later our summer wages as students at the University of British Columbia. That typewriter is still in my possession. In a family of writers—her younger brother Wilfrid was a reporter for the *Financial Post* and *Toronto Star*, and all her children at some point have written for a living—her style was the freshest, her images the clearest.

My mother wrote until the day she died at age 83. I read her last column about beach pebbles, featured on the second front page of the Victoria *Times-Colonist*, on the ferry when returning for her Saturna Island funeral. On the tombstone that she shares with her beloved husband Jim, we wrote simply *Dora Sanders Carney, Writer*.

She was born on September 12, 1903, near Cape Town, South Africa, the second of four children and a fourth-generation South African. Family legend is that her great-grandmother Susan O'Byrne, daughter of an Irish Catholic diplomat, ran off with a Prussian Protestant, emigrating to South Africa to escape angry relatives. Her husband fell on hard times (there were rumours of gambling losses and a hint of suicide) and the young woman, then widowed, supported her three daughters by her exquisite embroidery, her Irish harp muted.

The family lived in a small cottage next to a larger estate owned by retired customs officer Fred Bing. One day an inmate escaped from the local asylum and showed up at the cottage when the youngest daughter, Laura Cassandra, was alone. With great presence of mind she locked him in a bedroom and ran next door for help—and into the arms of Captain Bing who was in his orchard. A few months later they married and my grandmother Lucy Emma May was born, the first of eight children.

Lucy Bing grew up in a large family, in the free and easy life of the Cape, riding her horse along the wide beaches of the Indian Ocean, sailing on the Cowie River, and revelling in the flowers that embowered gardens and countryside. "Mother was merry, tender, and humanitarian,"[1] wrote Byrne. She never had to learn housework because there were always plenty of black servants.

Miss Bing was musical, an organist in the church and known for her fine soprano voice. Her thick brown hair was brushed smoothly back from her temples and coiled in a big glossy bun. Her Victorian upbringing was typical of that of a young lady in comfortable circumstances: riding, shooting, playing tennis, and swimming in the surf of the Indian Ocean with her younger brothers. Known for her beauty, she was nicknamed Queen. Despite her mother's strong opposition, who had heard of his violent temper, she married a crippled schoolteacher, Harry Sanders.

Harry had arrived from England as the new master at a boy's school. They married in St. Paul's Church, Port Alfred, on December 18, 1900, during the Boer War. Lucy's bridal wreath was woven from lilies-of-the-valley to mark her May birth month. She wrote a lively account of the wedding in the stone church by the sea, the morning tea with the traditional family tea service (the little blue teapot I inherited from her may be the one she used), and their honeymoon trip by train while the Boer War raged around them—a metaphor for the life she would lead with her new husband.

Twenty years later she confided to her youngest daughter Dora the details of her honeymoon. That first night, in a strange hotel's double bed, was miserable. Neither of them knew anything really about sex. Each was accustomed to sleeping alone. They lay awake and uncomfortable, trying not to disturb each other, not to touch each other. In the morning, haggard and weary, they prepared for breakfast. My grandfather said solemnly, "We might as well begin as we intend to continue," and his bride burst into tears. "Are you going to beat me?" All he wanted was family prayers.

Lucy told her daughter: "After three weeks, I don't know just how, suddenly it just happened."[2] They must have got it right, for the union produced four children: Minnie Byrne Hope, my mother Dora, John, and young Wilfrid.

Harry was tall, fair, and attractive. But he was often melancholy and his rages were frightening. "Knowing what was to come, I am haunted by the picture of their wedding—the bride surrounded by her family and friends, the groom, so alone, and so far from his natural setting,"[3] wrote Byrne.

My grandfather was a controversial figure to those who knew him. His children either loathed him, as Mother did, or firmly believed he was brilliant, as Uncle Wilfrid did. Some of my cousins adored him. Reflecting my father's dislike and my mother's anger at his frequent jowl-shaking, chin-bobbing temper tantrums, I thought he was an awful man. As an 11-year-old in Victoria, I spent my Sunday afternoons in front of his fireplace in my parents' home while he taught me the basic precepts of communism, catechism, and chess. He was an avowed Marxist Leninist and one-time member of the Communist party, handing out his pamphlets to the distress of my father, a civil servant in the provincial—and conventional—capital of Victoria at a time when the Red Menace was not politically correct.

He was born in 1872, the youngest son of Mary Wilde and Frederick Frances Sanders, an affluent builder and estate manager in Cheshunt near London, in an era when career choices included the army or navy, the church, or the civil service. All such career options were closed to Harry because of polio, which had crippled his entire left side. His mother Mary dedicated herself to her wounded wee lamb, often referring to him as "poor, dear Harry"—an epithet he loathed.

According to family tradition the youngest son must always join the navy. Harry's great-uncle, Commander John Harry Sanders, had fought at Trafalgar in 1805 under Admiral Nelson on the *Swiftsure*, which he later commanded, harassing the French fleet until he was captured by the enemy, surviving despite his wounds to the age of 90. But the navy still trained on sailing ships and this was impossible for young Harry. Instead, he became a teacher, graduating from Trinity College, Dublin, with first-class honours, and later becoming a reluctant and not very successful lawyer.

Although it is unclear why Harry travelled to South Africa, Byrne wrote in her memoirs that his brother-in-law Charles Higham had asked Harry to accompany him on an assignment to a parish in Port Elizabeth as a tutor to Charles's children. Charles, a young and impoverished vicar, had met Harry's sister Emily while on a visit to Cheshunt. In Victorian England the young ladies of the household made breakfast. Charles spotted Emily rising from the fireplace after toasting the bread in the open fire and fell in love with her because of her flushed cheeks.

When Charles and Emily returned from Africa to England, Harry chose to remain. An unflattering entry in his cousin Richard Higham's journal states: "Old Mrs. Sanders came out to the Cape, also Harry Sanders. He failed to make a living and with four children dogged Charles [Higham] there and back."[4] There is a picture of Harry and Charles playing chess in a relaxed and friendly mood in June 1899, with Grandfather's crippled arm carefully camouflaged.

Harry used a small legacy to return to Cape Town to qualify as a lawyer. But for most of their life in South Africa, the family lived in isolated black communities in the Transvaal. There were no other white children, as there were no schools. So Lucy taught her four children to read and write.

Once, the family crossed the veldt to the village of Willowdale in a cape cart (covered wagon), a journey of several days. Willowdale was at the centre of a large rural area with a population of about 80 whites and 10 000 blacks. The railway stopped about 30 miles away and Lucy thought it would be interesting to travel across the veldt as the

Boers had done in the mid-nineteenth century, fleeing from man-made government and obeying only God's word. This group were known as the Voortrekkers.

The family's rented wagon was pulled by 16 oxen. Byrne, the eldest, describes the scene: "The cape cart has been fitted with a double-bed spring halfway up the interior. Mother and Dad travel and sleep on the top shelf, while we children stretch out like sardines on the lower, or sit with our legs dangling over the back."[5]

Dora wrote:

It had four big wooden wheels, rimmed with iron, and metal hoops arching over it, covered with canvas. In the front half was stacked our basic furniture, including Mother's piano, which made us different from the Boers, who considered a piano to be an instrument of the Devil. To Mother it was the door to the magical land of great harmonies and tempos devised for us by Gounod, Strauss, Beethoven, and so many others. A big rocking horse, a gift from English Granny, hung on the back of the cart.

We also had with us Father's four boxes of books which again made us different from the Voortrekkers. They allowed only the Bible. Actually, Dad's four boxes contained several bibles. Dad's own favourite leather-upholstered reading chair was well up front, carefully wedged so that Mr. Williams, the driver, could sit in it as he drove. He was not full Kaffir but "coloured" and wore a felt hat as well as the Mister to emphasize his status.

Four servants travelled with them to build the fires and cook. Their African home was beautiful.[6]

Byrne recounts:

We walk in single file through tall grasses of the veldt, so brown and dusty in the dry season, so transformed with instant beauty in the rainy months. Then maidenhair ferns mass the fissures of the earth and there are pale green orchids twisting on tree branches.

Memories come like snapshots on a home projector. Click! We are in Willowdale, named, surely, by a homesick settler for there was never a willow in sight. Our living room is an immense round hut with a high pointed roof thatch, its only entrance the door. I can see the Kaffir women, cleaning the earthen floor with pails beside them from which they scoop handfuls of a thick mixture—mainly cow dung—which dries to a hard finish, on which our mats are spread.

Beside it is a narrow row of bedrooms, made from corrugated iron; in front a fence-enclosed tennis court. Alongside it is Dad's hut in which he meets his clients. A narrow path runs to it and alongside sit a row of blanket-wrapped Kaffirs, legs stretched out in front. Still further are the Kaffir quarters and the outbuildings. We like to linger there at day's end, watching the groups around the cooking fire, centred with its high black iron pot, set on a tripod.

Someone starts to hum and soon our friends are in full voice, with haunting minors of native melodies. They are particularly fond of the little boys—Jack whose yellow curls are dazzling against the dark skins, and roly-poly Wilf, so likely to fall into the fire.

We take our Kaffir world for granted. They are handsome people with very dark skins and thick heads of hair. They move with dignity, aloof but kindly. Most of them wear blankets, draped over their shoulders or folded about their waists. Although we were always under the care of a native woman, I have no recollection of Ol' Black Mammy's southern style.

The women seemed to do most of their chores, at home or in the fields, with babies clamped on their backs or on their hips with blankets; they carried immense bundles on their heads as well as a baby, striding swiftly with ramrod stiff backs. I remember our delight in a staging of Snow White, with complete black cast, and Mother's annoyance with the missionaries who insisted that converts wear sloppy-looking Mother Hubbards instead of Grecian blankets.[7]

But troubles and a cattle plague decimated both the herds and Harry's clients. The children found themselves on a white ship in a steerage cabin, sailing away from Table Mountain, their 29-year-old mother crying in the next cabin.

They were returning to England to stay with Uncle Charlie and his family until Harry found work. Much later Byrne learned that the first news the Highams had of their arrival was a cable sent by Harry when they were halfway home, so there was some truth in Cousin Richard's acid comment in his journal entry.

Charles was the vicar of the Seaman's Orphanage in Liverpool. The ivy-covered red brick orphanage already housed English Granny, the five Higham children, Annie the cook, and Isabel the housemaid, so feeding the Sanders flock was very hard. It was particularly difficult since Harry and Lucy left the children behind when they went to Canada to seek work in response to the immigrant-enticing posters of the Canadian Pacific Railway and the Salvation Army. But the children never detected any hint of the strain, and formed a merry and inventive crew with their cousins.

"NEWS OF THE MOMENT," reported the August 24, 1911, edition of *The Jolly Slasher*, the family newspaper produced by the young Higham cousins. "Latest intelligence from Near and Far. ARRIVAL of the South Africans in England is already announced. The Slasher Club has sent them a p.c. [postcard] of welcome with the Club's usual forethought and good taste. [Cousin] Maude is learning Swedish."

The *Slasher* gives an intriguing glimpse into Edwardian middle-class childhood, before television, radio, movies, or video games. One section entitled "Queries without Answers" asks: "Haven't you got an umbrella? Was Grannie NEVER known to fuss? What's the use of Girl Guides? What's the matter with the Town Crier's voice?" *The Jolly Slasher*'s motto: "If you can't be funny, be rude." Their mother's recorded rejoinder: "There is no funny rudeness, my dears." Another of Emily's sage comments, after half a century of life: "I am old enough to know that when a man's married he has a wife."

Another edition reports:

Boating intelligence. On Tuesday morning at 9 o'clock E. Hamilton, noted for his love of airships, yachts, etc. took Dora Drefinia for a row on Lord Haggles' estate. They spent a most enjoyable hour, the artist handling the oars in a masterful manner. E. Hamilton lounged in the stern and steered "No. 16" with much skill proving his knowledge of hidden shoals and bays.

A crowd had collected to see the famous Slasherites disembark. They were greeted with ringing cheers. After acknowledging the reception E. Hamilton and his companion strolled back to Lord and Lady Haggles' residence at Newsham Park where for the present the Slasher Club are staying. [Newsham Park was across from the orphanage, a green haven in grimy Liverpool.][8]

An early hint of romance here, since Dora Drefinia (our mother) was on her way to Hong Kong to marry Cousin Tony (E. Hamilton) when she met our father on board ship and disembarked at Shanghai instead. There are Dora and Tony, snuggled up together in a faded photograph of the cousins in their bathing costumes circa 1912, smiling, healthy, vibrant. Nearly all would become writers, artists, or publishers. The *Slasher* reports that 10-year-old Minnie (Byrne), the future editor of *Chatelaine*, returned from a run in the rain to declare: "Oh, I am wet with rain and inspiration!"

It was the last happy time for the Sanders children. After nearly two years in Canada, Harry and Lucy finally sent for their four children and they settled into a life of genteel poverty in a series of small Ontario towns such as Paris, which they enjoyed, and Norwich, a flat, ugly town from where the previous lawyer had absconded with a significant amount of money.

Uncle Wilfrid described the difficulties the family faced in the strange, often alien world of small Ontario villages where a foreign accent (including an English one) was completely unknown and where their manners, speech, habits, and point of view were incomprehensible: "No band of palefaces, in the centuries before, attempting to establish an outpost on the Red River, or the hinterlands of Upper Canada, faced a stranger, more alien world,"[9] he wrote.

A generation later we Carney children faced the same alienation when we returned to Canada from China and settled in the Ontario village of Morriston, with our odd ways and Chinese vocabulary. One of my earliest memories is the chant of the skipping girls at the two-room school near the village: "Chinky-chinky Chinaman/sitting on the fence/trying to make a dollar out of fifteen cents," or the even nastier "Chinky-chinky Chinaman/sitting on a wall/trying to make a dollar out of nothing at all." Another acid memory is of our neighbour, a Scot, snarling at me: "Why don't you go home, you dirty little Chink?"

At least the Sanders children could enthrall villagers with embellished tales of South Africa, such as frantic leaps into trees to escape lion attacks at picnics, snakes coiled in children's beds, and menacing spear-carrying black men. Unfortunately the Carney children's accounts of Japanese air attacks lacked the same panache since, by the 1940s, Canada was at war.

Harry had a small if unsuccessful law practice, even though his violent temper scared away some clients, but for Lucy, far from the warm shores of the Indian Ocean, the isolation and poverty were very tough indeed. Her blithe spirit gave way to an aura of sadness that she carried with her until her death on another shore in the Gulf Islands, a world away.

Shortly after settling in Norwich, Lucy called at the office of the *Norwich Gazette* to order engraved visiting cards. The local newspaper, more accustomed to printing handbills about auction sales, stallions standing at stud, and church bazaars, was unable to comply with her request but offered instead to print them with the essential information: Mrs. Harry Sanders, 22 Light Street, At Home on Thursday Afternoons. These cards were then distributed to the wives of the local ministers—with the exception of the Baptist minister's wife—the two doctors, the reeve, the local MP, and a few others deemed suitable for a lady of her station. The first Thursday was preceded by a flurry of activity, cleaning, baking, and preparing cucumber-and-watercress sandwiches and other mouth-watering confections.

The Spode and the linens were set out, the tea wagon loaded. But, of course, nobody came. Tears on her cheeks, Lucy distributed the largesse among her four hungry children. A few days later one of the invitees asked Lucy: "Did you stick a card with your name and address on it under our door the other day?"

"Yes," said Lucy softly.

"We couldn't figure out what you were selling."

"Goodness," said Lucy, mortified. "I wasn't selling anything!"

And that was the end of the calling cards.

At home the code words were duty, discipline, self-denial, and devotion to God. The children, accustomed to their own company, invented their stories, performed their home-grown theatricals, produced their magazines with bylines like Gussie Goose and Dickie Donkey, and played their charades; ironically, noted Byrne, their best companions were the rollicking family in the Baptist minister's house.

Laundry day was traumatic; as youngsters the boys wore English sailor suits cut from heavy cotton while Lucy, Minnie, and Dora wore cotton dresses on top of white cotton petticoats, camisoles, and drawers frilled with eyelet embroidery. But unlike their homes in England and South Africa, there was no household help in Canada.

The result was the Royal Washing Corps. "On Monday mornings, Dad blew the Coxswain's whistle at six to rout us out of bed and down to the kitchen, pronto," wrote Byrne.

We each wore navy blue jackets emblazoned with gold braid and signifying our rank; mine was Major Buzz-fuzz.

Dad had filled the boiler and set it on the range the night before. The washing machine, on a metal base, could be swung from side to side and, in turn, we grabbed its wooden handle to shove it back and forth while we sang what Dad called our Sea Shanties. "Slosh, Slosh, Slosh the clothes are washing" to the tune of "Tramp Tramp Tramp the boys are marching" or "There's a RIGHT way to do the washING by the Royal WASHing Corps" to "Tipperary."

While the water was emptied down the sink and fresh supplies poured back for the rinsing, Dad served us Hot Grog (weak tea), then carried some up to Mother. By 8:30 the clothes were on the line, the kitchen dried out, the machine rolled into a corner, breakfast gobbled, and the Sanders off to school.[10]

The family heard their first radio broadcast in a small concert hall owned by Hezekiah Forsythe, the local undertaker, who sold phonograph records and sheet music in his coffin-stuffed show-room. The hall was used for town meetings, medicine shows, and local productions. The broadcast was played around 1919 and the performance was heralded in the local *Norwich Gazette*. "To a capacity audience, Hezekiah explained that the device on stage was a radio," reports Dora.

He had, he said, a few in stock in his store and could order more. Then he switched it on. For a brief time there was silence, then a crackling sound like rifle fire.

Soon into the hall ebbed a sound that was recognizable as music. It faded, ebbed, faded again, ebbed again, for half an hour. We heard a voice announcing that we were listening to Station KDKA, and that the music was that of a group called the Ipana Troubadours. Everyone was vastly impressed. Hezekiah stepped forward, turned off the amazing machine, and asked if there were any questions.

There was only one question and it was at the forefront of everyone's mind. It was aptly voiced by Irv Uren who owned the hardware store: "Where in Hell does the noise come from?" "All the way from Pittsburgh," replied Hezekiah with pride. "How does it get in there?" asked Irv, pointing to the box on stage.

Hezekiah realized his audience wanted technical details, so he gave them to us. "The sound comes a hurtling through the air, only its kinda a silent sound, and it gets caught in the wire up there on the roof. Then it comes down this here wire, into the box and out again," he explained.

The listeners then shuffled out into the night and stared hard at the copper wire, which was barely discernible against the night sky.

Irv Uren asked Hezekiah to turn the thing back on and open a window so we could hear it outside. Hezekiah did so. We must have been there for half an hour, staring at the wire, trying to correlate it with the sounds emanating from the hall.

Once more, Irv summed up the feeling of all. "No Sir!" he said. "No Siree-ee!" and he walked home, as did we all.[11]

The four Sanders children grew up. Minnie prepared for her Ontario College of Music exams and wrote young people's columns for the *Mail & Empire* and *Toronto Star Weekly*. She was eventually hired by the *Woodstock Sentinel Review*, mainly for her typing skills, which were the entry point for so many women reporters, and she sensibly dropped Minnie from her byline for the simpler Byrne Hope Sanders.

Dora entered Trinity College at the University of Toronto, and majored in mathematics. When young Wilfrid was due to enter college, however, the two sisters knew their duty; their studies ended and they both found work at an advertising publication for the T. Eaton Company, then the largest department store in Canada. Eaton's had pioneered the five-day work week on the theory that having two days a week for personal affairs would encourage employees to attend church on Sundays.

The sisters' earnings helped support their younger brother as a student at the University of Toronto. They recognized that he needed an education in order to eventually support his wife and family, whereas they would have husbands to support them. Years later, however, when my brother and I were ready for university, Dora ensured that I received the same opportunities as my brother, despite strained budgets.

But the sisters were happy in their new setting. They shared a sunny, big-windowed apartment on College Street opposite Toronto's main library. They bought their first lobster and first champagne and their favourite croissants. Toronto in the 1920s was an exciting place for budding writers and artists; the Group of Seven held their first show in May 1920 in Toronto, and proved to be tremendously appealing to Dora and her friends. Years later Dora's children met their mother's early friends in almost every sector of the arts, an unexpected and welcome legacy.

The Eaton family, the department-store owners and the girls' original employers, were strong supporters of the arts. The sisters were invited to attend private showings of art exhibitions at the Grange, a great house built on the edge of the early settlement of York. The sponsor was the Art Gallery Association, R.Y. Eaton, patron and president. The imposing entrance faced the lake and was approached by a short driveway, lined with elms and horse chestnut trees, from high iron gates opening from a country road called John Street. The private showings were formal affairs: "Mr. R.Y. Eaton seemed to be the centre of it all, tall and impressive, with twin expanses of bald head and white shirt front."

Margaret Eaton, Timothy's daughter, founded a School of Drama beside the Conservatory of Music at the corner of College Street and University Avenue, which provided small halls or rooms with podiums where students could stage individual recitals and performances. Dora went to hear soprano Lily Pons in Massey Hall with her irrepressible friend Charles Comfort, later a famous war artist and director of the National Gallery in Ottawa. There were Twilight Symphony concerts, so named because the orchestra players were also the pit band musicians for the silent movies, which were screened at night.

A streetcar shivered its way beyond the city limits on Yonge Street, as far north as Richmond Hill, where the sisters skied in winter. There was also horseback riding and snowshoeing in High Park, where Minnie and Dora went on winter Sundays if they had the necessary two streetcar tickets and 20 cents for tea and crumpets.

The sisters fed the squirrels in Queen's Park, attended writers' workshops in Caledon, and were invited away for weekends in Muskoka and

Georgian Bay. Dora eventually left Eaton's to work for a small advertising agency housed in the old Harbour Commissioners building, whose waterfront pier for small boats was eventually replaced by landfill created by the excavation for the Yonge Street subway. Wilf worked for the *Toronto Star*; his beat included Holland Marsh, a stretch of country located north of Toronto. When it was drained and cultivated the marsh grew fine vegetables for the old St. Lawrence market; then, however, most of it was covered with dense willow bush and shrubs.

The sisters were earning a handsome $25 per week, a rate that was no longer a wage but a salary. Byrne was eventually hired by Colonel Maclean's company to edit *Chatelaine*, a job she would hold for the next 22 years. *Maclean's* was Canada's first national consumer magazine, offering political and financial articles and some roistering stories aimed at men, who held the country's purse strings, and one or two pages at the back offering recipes and cushion-cover designs for their wives.

Chatelaine was to be an expansion of those pages—a magazine for women and about women. Initially, however, the magazine would not necessarily be written by women, who were notoriously unreliable, as Byrne proved to be by seeking permission to keep her job when she became engaged to *Maclean's* art director Frank Sperry. *Maclean's* finally gave her permission on condition that she retain her maiden name, keep the wedding highly secret (not a hint of it in the newspapers), and not have children. Byrne's subsequent early pregnancy then caused a crisis for the organization and for the family, fearing the loss of income. In the end, her beloved boss Victor Tyrell said: "Let's look at it this way, Miss Sanders. Now you'll be a married woman with a child. Most of your readers have children. It may prove even better for you in your work for them."

Dora similarly switched to the advertising department of another *Maclean's* magazine, the high-end *Mayfair*, a fashion and society book printed in elite typeface on heavily coated paper. She was responsible for writing personal letters to prospective clients in advance of the sales pitches made by the cigar-smoking, male salesmen.

For nobody was rich anymore. Nobody was buying "comforts and pleasantries," so few companies were buying space to advertise them. Something had happened on Wall Street in New York City, and savings had vanished. Until then, everyone had believed that the way to get rich was to buy stocks on margin and sell them when they increased in value. The sisters had taken the plunge with $100 of their savings and had watched their investment drop to $20 the following day, eventually dropping to $4. They did not repeat the experiment.

"Now the two big words that hung in the sky like heavy storm clouds were Unemployment and Relief," wrote Dora.

> Anybody could be unemployed. Until then it had been unthinkable. You grew up and you went to work. The only questions were what kind of work and how much you were paid. The quality of your work was your security.
>
> Now the good workers were unemployed as well as the not-so-good, and for many the shame of it was unbearable.

Dora eventually moved to *Maclean's* to help her sister Byrne edit *Chatelaine* when Byrne appalled her male bosses by becoming pregnant for a second time. This time her superiors were not as forgiving. So Byrne stayed home by the phone and Dora sat in her office chair and between them they produced the magazine.

In 1933 Dora returned to England to visit the Higham cousins and came back full of happiness about her childhood boating companion, cousin Tony. She agreed to marry him and set off for his home in Hong Kong, typewriter in hand—a daring endeavour for a 29-year-old woman to do during the 1930s. She left Vancouver aboard the *Empress of Russia*, one of the famous Canadian Pacific White Empresses that plied the Pacific to the fabled Orient before World War II.

During the voyage, Dora noticed a tall young Irish Canadian with copper-coloured hair among the other passengers. Jim Carney was returning home after a long leave from the Shanghai Municipal Council, where he had worked in police and public health work. The two avoided each other for the first three days, each aware of the other but loath to become involved in a shipboard romance.

But by the time the ship reached Shanghai, Dora had made the most daring decision of her young life. Jim Carney wanted her to abandon her fiancé and stay in Shanghai, where she knew no one, and where the only single women were White Russian refugees and prostitutes, according to Toronto standards. But Jim had entranced her with tales of life in the International Settlement, where people from 55 countries lived in an enclave surrounded by the largest city in the world in 1933.

"Suddenly I knew I did not want to go to the well-regulated colony of Hong Kong and the suitable marriage the family approved," Dora wrote. Poor cousin Tony, abandoned in Hong Kong. "Instead, I wanted to explore this unique international experiment, the only community of its kind in the world. I fled to my cabin and sat on my bunk and thought about it." She had her trunk, one suitcase, and her portable typewriter. She rang for the cabin boy and disembarked.

For the next six years, Shanghai would be her home. And for the rest of her life, despite the terror and the troubles, it was her magical place.

She gave each of her four children a blue Buddha, a small symbol of our China roots. In my house, there is always a statue of Kuan Yin, the Chinese Goddess of Mercy. My mother's affection for China and her voice, audible in her manuscripts, are her gifts to me. She also bequeathed me her courage, her independence, and her unfailing belief that life is an adventure, to be explored and enjoyed. Her philosophy, she wrote to a friend, was that all the arts formed a Great Harmony, and we should "look for the colours, listen for the music." She is always with me.

CHAPTER 3

The Home Place

TRADE SECRET:
Buy the best land you can afford;
God isn't making any more.
—Dr. J.J. Carney

One autumn day in the early 1980s I was in my West Block MP's office in Ottawa when a security guard phoned from the entrance door to say there was a Mary Hilda Kelly to see Pat Carney. I thought for a moment and surmised that it must be one of my grandmother Bridget Casey's relatives; her mother was named Mary Kelly. "Send her up," I said.

Mary Hilda turned out to be Bridget Casey's niece. We had tea and a good visit. I was particularly excited to learn that she had attended Ottawa's Rideau Convent school with my father's sisters, Elizabeth and Catherine, around the time of World War I. Rideau Convent was famous and when it was torn down to make room for an Ottawa steakhouse, the chapel was restored and enshrined in the capital's National Gallery. Whenever I visit I say a prayer to the ghosts of the giggling little Carney girls and their O'Keefe cousins, all 3000 miles away from their Okanagan homes.

And now here was Mary Hilda Kelly, who apparently had not seen nor heard from Catherine Carney since. Although the Caseys then lived at Twin Elm near the parish church of St. Patrick's at Fallowfield, 16 miles east of Ottawa, and the Kellys lived only a few miles away at Bells Corners, cousinly visits between families were rare due to the volume of work on the small Ottawa Valley farms in the early 1900s.

Thrilled, I called Aunt Catherine in the Okanagan Valley line and connected the two cousins. It was a short conversation. "Mary Hilda

Kelly," mused Catherine. "I remember you. What have you done with your life?" Not much, it seemed. Mary Hilda had kept house for her brother Tom. She trained as a nurse, as did Aunt Elizabeth and several O'Keefe girls, two of whom had quit their convent after 28 years, disheartened and discontented with the religious life. Instead, they bought a red Mustang, permed their hair, and left for California. When I met them at the O'Keefe Ranch in the 1970s, the only outward sign of their convent career was the way they folded their hands on their tummies, as if they were holding rosaries.

"I wish I'd known Bridget Casey," Mary Hilda told me wistfully, speaking of the aunt she never knew but admired, who about 1890 had braved the journey on the new transcontinental railway that ran by Twin Elm across the new country of Canada to the legendary O'Keefe Ranch at the head of Okanagan Lake in British Columbia. It was here that the young seamstress sewed for the many children of another family originally from the Ottawa Valley, Cornelius O'Keefe and his first wife, Mary Ann McKenna.[1]

Cornelius O'Keefe, who had come west from Fallowfield, once owned a hotel in the Cariboo, site of the 1858 gold rush that opened up the interior of BC to settlement. Following the historic Okanagan Brigade Trail first used by the North West Company fur traders in New Caledonia, O'Keefe and his partner Thomas Greenhow drove 178 cattle north from Oregon to feed the hungry gold miners. When they discovered the wide valley at the head of Okanagan Lake, they sold the hotel for a poke of gold nuggets and acquired land in 1867, the year Canada was born, and four years before British Columbia joined Confederation after acrimonious debate in the young British colony's legislature in Victoria.

The O'Keefe holdings covered 15 000 acres at their peak and included a general store, post office, original log homestead, blacksmith's shop, and a 17-room mansion where Cornelius entertained Canada's governor general, the Marquess of Lorne, and his wife in 1882.

My father's family is entirely Irish, and their story is typical of the Irish who immigrated to Canada in the nineteenth century. For decades Canada was a prime destination for Irish immigrants. From 1825 to 1845 at least 450 000 Irish landed in Canada, by far the largest migration from any country, and outnumbering the number of Irish immigrating to the United States during that period. The earlier immigrants were small farmers who paid their own way or worked as labourers on farms, lumber camps, docks, and canals. The flow increased during the early years of the Great Famine, although after "Black '47" the flood of immigrants to Canada slowed as hundreds of thousands poured into the United States.

"They arrived less like emigrants than refugees from terrible disaster," records historian Donald MacKay in his book, *Flight from Famine, The Coming of the Irish to Canada*. "Of these, up to 20 000 died in the worst year of all, 1847, on the ships, in the quarantine stations of Grosse Isle, Quebec, and Partridge Island, New Brunswick, or out in the towns and roads of Quebec and Ontario."[2]

By 1870 there were almost 900 000 Irish in Canada. They were the largest ethnic group in the country, outnumbering the English and the Scots two to one, changing the nature of provinces such as Ontario, where United Empire Loyalists had been the majority. By the time of Confederation the Irish accounted for one-quarter of Canada's population, although declining Irish emigration and increasing arrivals from England, Scotland, and other countries in the late nineteenth century lessened their impact on Canada's mosaic; by 1961, the last census that identified them as a separate group, Canadians of Irish descent had dwindled to 10 per cent.

How did my grandmother, a tiny, pretty woman with dark, bouncy curls and eyes the colour of bitter chocolate, ever summon the courage to make the gruelling trip from Ontario to British Columbia? Was it the momentum of the flight from famine back in Ireland that forced so many of our forefathers and mothers to set out across the unknown ocean for Canada?

Bridget Casey was born on February 23, 1862, in Twin Elm, Carleton County, in the Ottawa Valley, one of the first generations of our family to be born in Canada. Her mother, Mary Kelly, was born in 1836 in County Donegal, Ireland, and her father, Patrick Casey, was born in County Tyrone, Ireland, in 1840. Mary had survived a voyage from County Donegal on one of the infamous coffin ships, arriving at the age of nine at the beginning of the Great Famine in 1845. Mary later told her granddaughter Catherine Carney that three sisters had died on the sea journey. By what stroke of fate had my great-grandmother survived the direct effects of the famine when her sisters, my great-great aunts, had not?

The Caseys owned a blacksmith shop at Twin Elm on the Jock River, near the location where in 1819 the Duke of Richmond, Governor General Charles Gordon Lennox, beached his boat, ran through the Casey property, and died in the barn from rabies caused by the bite of a domestic fox.

The hamlet of Twin Elm was named by Bridget's brother, Patrick Casey, when a group of local residents gathered around his forge to debate the naming of a new post office for the community. According to a newspaper account, until then, Bob McRae, who pioneered the mail stage between Richmond and Ottawa, simply tossed the mail off at Casey's blacksmith shop. "Someone asked just where the proposed post office was being located and Mr. Casey with the roguish eye of his mother from Donegal and the brogue of his father from Tyrone made answer and said: 'Shure it's to be down beyant on Philip Green's farm, near the twin elms,' a landmark on the River Jock. Storms have since washed them away."[3]

I first learned about Twin Elm in 1980 as a new MP from the West when Justin Durgen, a driver of one of the green buses that ferry MPs and staff around Parliament Hill, shifted gears and said to me: "Carney, eh? I know your cousin, Eileen Casey." Well, that's possible, I thought, since the Caseys came from the Ottawa Valley and Eileen is a family name. I had heard the name Twin Elm from my father, Bridget's first-born son.

So I accepted Justin's invitation to visit St. Patrick's Church, established in the early 1860s on Piety Hill in Fallowfield, where the Catholic, Anglican, Methodist, and United churches jostled for the position closest to God in the pretty Ontario village where farmland has replaced the original pine forests and the graveyards are filled with early pioneers.

As a youngster Justin had taken horses to blacksmith Patrick Casey, Bridget's brother, a tall, mild-spoken man who played the fiddle, as did Bridget, slinging the instrument low on her shoulder or hip. I checked her birth entry in the church records, and at Justin and his wife Flo's kitchen table I leafed through the printed accounts of that era. These records generally ignored the Irish, many of whom were employed to build the Rideau Canal from the Ottawa River to Kingston to buttress the young colony's defences against the American invaders. The Irish labourers lived in swampy, mosquito-ridden Lower Town, where I bought my first Ottawa home within earshot of St. Brigid's bells. Although the early records provided the names of the British settlers, often army officers retiring on their land grants, my forefathers and their friends were mere footnotes, which mentioned how the Irish families clustered around their Roman Catholic churches.

Our kinsmen and our friends came with us, according to the gravestones in churchyards from Castleconnell on the River Shannon near Limerick to the Ottawa Valley in Ontario and the Okanagan Valley in British Columbia—Carneys and Caseys and Tierneys and O'Keefes and McKennas and Monaghans and Troys and Kellys and others.

In my heart I can see them—young friends and kin who joined forces to escape little food and no future by leaving their small, crowded mud and stone homes to risk the cholera-infested "coffin" ships for an unknown future in an unknown land. If they survived, they would likely arrive at Grosse Isle in the St. Lawrence and then make their way up the rivers to forest camps and farms hand-hewn out of the wilderness, the next generation moving on via the rivers and then the railway to the West, marrying and working together, baptized and buried together, keeping family ties intact within the comforting bosom of their church.

My father explained to me how his grandfather Patrick Kearney had landed broke and barefoot in Montreal, making his way into the Upper Canada bush in the late 1840s or early 1850s. In 1856 he married Mary Keouh Kelly, a widow with two daughters and a sawmill.

Patrick Kearney was born in County Limerick in 1828. Clearly famine was the driving force behind his emigration to Canada. In the earlier famine of the 1820s, Reverend Michael Fitzgerald reported that half his parish was starving, "seldom able to provide more than one meal a day of oatmeal gruel and it is not always that this miserable meal can be procured."[4] Priests who were normally reluctant to lose their flock of parish faithful actively promoted emigration to ease violence and hunger.

Little is known about our early Irish ancestors. Probably many of them were illiterate, and their efforts to avoid starvation by clearing forests and planting crops in stump-strewn fields left them little time and energy to record their emotions. Our family history comes from church records, letters, and oral accounts handed down through generations.

The records of Castleconnell in County Limerick show that another Patrick Kearney married Catherine Casey in 1874 in the local Catholic church (which took 20 years to build, from 1843 to 1863, because of the Famine). My Irish cousin Tom Kearney in nearby Stradbally regularly sends me a postcard of the church. So it is no wonder that in 1894 my grandfather John Joseph Carney, probably Patrick's cousin, married brown-eyed Bridget Casey when he met her at the O'Keefe Ranch, where he was foreman.

John Joseph was one of the seven surviving children of Patrick and Mary. He was born in Woodstock, Ontario, on May 29, 1859, the year the Okanagan Mission was established by Oblate priests. The first white settler in the Valley, Roman Catholic priest Father Pandosy planted the first apple seeds that evolved into the great orchards that hug the fertile side hills and valley flat lands today.

Family legend records that Jack, as he was sometimes called, ran away from home, stealing his father's milk cow to raise the money to ride the new railway west to British Columbia in 1891. He worked on the Sicamous-Armstrong construction of the railway, which took him to the O'Keefe Ranch, where he found work as a cowboy. The ranch accounts still show his purchase of a bandanna, which cowboys wore over their mouths and necks.

John Joseph proposed to Bridget in the dairy, which still stands outside the old kitchen at the O'Keefe Ranch, now a historic site and museum capturing the pioneer era of small homesteaders with their log cabins, cattle barons with their buffalo sleigh robes, and Chinese cooks with their iron cots. Bridget Casey's sewing machine, which she packed on horseback over the mountain trails, is among the exhibits.

Kearney is the name on their marriage certificate, which states their residence as Head of the Lake, as the ranch was known in an era when white settlement in the Okanagan Valley was just beginning. The area had a population of 1000 to 2000 people, and Indians still rode their ponies down the dry gulches and sage-spattered side hills. Bridget cared for the altar embroideries used in St. Ann's, the small wooden church on the ranch and the first Roman Catholic church in the Vernon district.

Jack and Bridget then moved to the Simpson Ranch, one of the best-known ranches in the Ellison District, where Jack was foreman and Bridget was housekeeper at the time of my father's birth. John

James (Jim) was born in 1894, while Jack and Bridget were living in a cabin on a pre-emption, or homestead, on Black Mountain. When labour began, Bridget made her way down the mountain to the midwife's home. Dr. Benjamin de F. Boyce, Kelowna's first doctor, went there with Jack, who had never mentioned that his wife was pregnant, possibly because the records show that they had a shotgun marriage.

The Simpson Ranch was one of two or three large ranches in the Valley. It was founded by George W. Simpson, whose wife was a sister of Chief Pantherhead of Westbank. Their daughter, Eliza Jane Swalwell, gives us a great description of life in the Valley at the time in *Girlhood Days in the Okanagan*.

> I remember this Valley when everything was in a wild state, before there was a wagon road, and everything had to be brought in by pack train. All our dishes were on tin, and we baked bread and pies in a Dutch oven. There was great rejoicing when the first wagon road was completed to the Mission. I was grown up and married before the first buggy arrived. It caused quite an excitement amongst us girls who had been born here, and never been out of the Valley.

Cattle were the backbone of the economy:

> Where ever you looked over the hills and ranges you saw cattle, and the sight of them coming out of the timber where they had been resting in the shade trees, and scattering over the ranges in droves to feed with the little calves jumping and skipping wherever you looked, was a sight never to be forgotten.

Eliza Jane wrote about the cowboys:

> Some of them were as vain as schoolgirls. When rigged up in full regalia, with a silk handkerchief around their neck, they fancied themselves. They thought they were "some spuds" all right. Most of them I knew as rascals.[5]

The Carney family bought the Joe Brent homestead, a 320-acre preemption with a two-storey, four-room loghouse that became the Home Place—the centre of the Carney family, no matter where we lived—until

47

it was dismantled and the logs stacked sometime during the 1980s. There they raised their four children: Jim, Catherine, Tom, and Elizabeth.

After John Joseph and Bridget took over the Home Place with its poor range and alkali-rimmed lakes, he branded his cattle with the Box 2. On the wall of my study is mounted a piece of siding from the old house with the Box 2 seared on its grey surface with John Joseph's own branding irons.

When the railway ran through the homestead in the early 1900s, the house was in the way. So Jim and his younger brother Tom jacked the house up and moved it farther up the hill while Bridget worked in the kitchen making her famous wild strawberry jam. The Old Man was in Ottawa enrolling daughters Elizabeth and Catherine in the Rideau Convent school to show the O'Keefes that the Carney girls were as good as the Head of the Lake crowd. Their brother Jim wrote stern letters to his sisters, urging them to study hard at the convent "or there will be trouble." He explained: "Mama is very anxious that you girls stop there. She would do anything to have you stay there in the convent."[6]

Bridget spoke with an Irish lilt: "Did you now!" she'd say, or answer, "I did that!" She always referred to her husband as Mr. Carney, even in his presence. She was famous for both her buttermilk and her strawberry jam. So I think of her every year as I make my ritual wild blackberry jam at my own Home Place on Saturna Island. Bridget was self-effacing and a strong Roman Catholic. There were no stories or reading books or singing songs, but she enjoyed playing the fiddle and at age 76 she was still playing jigs at dances.

Life was hard on the Home Place, however. Dry farming yielded poor returns and survival was uncertain, particularly after John Joseph failed to apply for the water rights to a vital water source, a large, clear spring known as the Punch Bowl, located in a thicket of willow next to the log home. John Joseph rode into town to apply for the licence, but fell into a drinking session with his buddies. He reached the government offices too late, and one of his neighbours snapped up the licence instead. The right to use scarce water was a life-and-death issue in the arid Okanagan, with its alkali-ringed lakes, and my grandfather's drinking spree changed his family's life.

There were five gates between the Old Vernon Road and the house. Bridget would plough through the deep, uneven snow to listen for her children returning on horseback from the school at Ellison across the valley, following the route she had marked by tying white rags to the jack pine trees. "I used to think I heard them crying on the wind," she told my mother, Dora.

When Bridget's pregnant daughter-in-law later visited her in November 1937, after we were evacuated from Shanghai, she was horrified to find Bridget in the old log house with tin tub baths and without electricity. "The Old Man was afraid of it," Mother told me later. "He said it caused fire." The house had a big wood stove—Bridget bought Dora a new set of flat irons—and a rough, uneven plank floor. The water pump was outside so that it was easier to water the horses.

Mother loathed her father-in-law. When Bridget was sick, the Old Man bought bay rum with dollars earmarked for food. He had started drinking when he became road foreman, she said. Bridget was 75 then and still carrying in her wood from the woodpile, which Dora found disturbing, even though she herself would carry in her own wood until her death at age 83.

Since Bridget was sick, Dora was responsible for cooking dinner. The Old Man told her she would find the meat stored in a tent outside. There she found half a calf hanging, blanketed in flies. She had no idea what to do in the situation. Her husband was still in China, serving in the International Settlement's defence force, and Mother and we three children were supposed to stay on the Home Place for three months. Instead, Dora ran away, staying one week with my father's brother Tom and his wife Maggie, and then heading for familiar Toronto and family and the comforts of electric light and hot water.

When John Joseph died in November 1943, at the ripe old age of 84, the *Kelowna Courier* noted the passing of the "oldest settler in the Ellison district" at a time when cattle-raising and wheat-growing were the backbone of the Okanagan economy. "A large gathering of old friends were present to pay their last respects to the deceased, who was known and loved by all the early citizens of Kelowna and district," the *Courier* noted. "His death marks the passing of another of the pioneers who saw the birth of Kelowna and its growth into a modern city with diversified industries and rich farming and fruit growing areas in the surrounding districts."[7]

I discovered both Patrick and John Joseph's obituaries in an envelope among my father's papers. His sister Catherine had written on the front: "To whom it may concern—Kindly treat the enclosed tenderly—We owe them our existence after all—Two of the world's finest."

After John Joseph's death, Bridget told her children, "I'll never have to sleep next to the Old Man again." Ironically, however, she did, because in the old Catholic cemetery you were buried in the order in which you died, and since she was next—on January 27, 1944—she must lie beside him for eternity.

It was fortuitous that they died within months of each other, considering John Joseph's will left his wife of 49 years an income of only $200, which the Home Place could not produce. In a letter to her father, lawyer Harry Sanders, Dora worried: "How is Mother [Bridget] going to get her $200? We don't think the place will yield it."

The letter lists a lifetime's accumulated assets: "Offhand, the value of the property is about $5,000. As for the implements, there aren't any to speak of. Livestock $1,000 to $5,000. Furniture nil. No life insurance. Possible small bank balance. Liabilities, the last time I heard there was an $800 or $900 mortgage on the place. He usually owes about two years taxes, which amount to about $100 in all. There is no grain, no nothing."

The letter recounts the source of so much heartbreak, so many family dramas and family feuds of the fighting Irish. The Old Man had left his second son, Tom, out of the will, although Tom had stayed home to farm while his older brother Jim went off to see the world. Neighbours reported that "the Old Man was drunk when he made this will," the letter stated. My father Jim added: "This is an indication of what the Old Man was like all his life. He only messed things up."[8]

After old John Joseph died, his daughter Catherine bought out her siblings' shares and took over the Home Place. Grandmother Bridget worried about her daughters, particularly lively Catherine who, Bridget confided in a letter to a sister-in-law, Mary Monaghan, was "no better than she should be."[9] But Catherine settled down, married orchardist Percy Neave, and produced three children, Irma, Betty, and Len, the last two of whom have been among my closest Carney cousins.

In her old age Catherine reverted to type, becoming according to her own account "the best pig woman in the Okanagan" and carrying on a longtime feud with her brother Tom. That was after she ended her longtime feud with my father Jim—who had said that six-year-old Betty was a spoiled brat, incurring 30 years of silence—who then didn't talk to Tom, either. "Not speaking" is one of our family traditions; except at family funerals or weddings, I haven't spoken to my brother Tom in nearly 30 years. Or maybe he's not speaking to me.

Uncle Tom raised Black Angus cattle on his spread, now the site of Kelowna's airport. You can see the trees ringing his old farmhouse where his grandson Don and his wife Betty still live and where the initials TC are painted on the shed door by the highway. Tom had a sign on the gate to his cattle range: "Trespassers Please Leave Name of Next of Kin at Ranch House."

When his prized Black Angus bull wandered into the Home Place, where Catherine farmed, Tom thought it was a great laugh. Let Catherine feed the bull for a while, he told the neighbours. But when she took out an advertisement in the Kelowna paper, "WANTED. New Home for Big, Black Bull," Tom sent someone down to collect his prized animal.

Catherine later settled the score when she arranged with then BC Highways Minister Phil Gaglardi to divert his planned new highway towards Tom's range. Gaglardi visited Catherine after she stood off highway construction crews with her shotgun when they attempted to build an overpass across her land. She then took the Highways Minister up the side hill and indicated the route she would agree to, in the general direction of Tom's place. After that she contented herself with unleashing a few blasts from her shotgun, aiming in the general direction of Tom's ranch each New Year's Eve. The two never made up.

When I last went to visit Uncle Tom there was a shotgun by the front door, which framed little Aunt Maggie wringing her hands in her apron, saying she didn't want any trouble. The brothers, Tom and Jim, weren't speaking because Tom had charged his costs for babysitting his Black Angus to Aunt Elizabeth's funeral expenses. Elizabeth had shown up late for her own funeral in Olympia, Washington. Her body had been sent to the wrong Catholic church, creating much confusion and a new family legend. The brothers never made up, either. We cousins made a pact that we would never not speak, which we have honoured, with the exception of my brother Tom and me.

Once I drove the stretch of road between the Home Place and the O'Keefe Ranch at Vernon with Catherine, who was wearing an Indian fringed, tanned leather jacket. We were going to visit her daughter

Betty, who had married Tierney O'Keefe. At regular intervals she asked me to pull over to the side of the road, ostensibly to view the landscape but in reality to take a nip from the mickey of rye she had secreted in her jacket pocket.

At the ranch, a visiting Catholic priest had undone his white collar, parked his statue of the Virgin Mary on the kitchen counter, and settled down for a good ranch meal. Three sheets to the wind when she got to the ranch, Catherine staggered to the door of the kitchen, saw the statue on the kitchen counter, and fell to her knees. "Father, forgive me my sins," she prayed, clutching her mickey as we tried to hoist her to her feet.

Catherine adamantly refused to leave the Home Place, although her children tried to persuade her to move to more comfortable quarters.

Late in life, she and my father resumed the close friendship of their childhood, when she was his constant companion, riding over the tan hills and forest-green valleys of the Okanagan. I was pleased for them. Although Catherine remained a challenge for my mother, who had little in common with her convent-educated, rural-rooted sister-in-law, their reunion healed a wound in the family.

The last time I visited Catherine we drank rye whisky in her kitchen, surrounded by freshly scalded milk pails and stacks of old *Vancouver Sun* newspapers. Later we went out to the barn and I stacked bales of alfalfa in her hay loft while Aunt Kate, wearing a World War II pilot's helmet with ear flaps and goggles, her keys pinned with safety pins to the front of her leather bomber jacket, used a ski pole to break the ice in the water pans for her chickens.

I looked at her quizzically. In family pictures of her as a young girl, she looked very attractive, with an oval face, dark brown hair, hazel eyes, and black eyebrows. Just like me. Scary thought!

My brother Tom was born in Vancouver in February 1940 after our second and final return from China. My mother was pondering names, in the way of new mothers, wavering between David (her girlhood nickname) and Daniel for the Irish connection. "Which do you prefer?" she asked Bridget. "I prefer Thomas," Bridget said firmly in her lilting voice, following the family tradition of generally limiting names to John, Joseph, James, Patrick, and Thomas for boys and Mary, Elizabeth, Bridget, Catherine, Kathleen, and Patricia for girls.

So the second son was named Daniel David Thomas. And the tradition continues. When my sister Norah and her husband daringly named their son Jeremy, our father simply called him Joe, his family name to this day, after John Joseph. Peace was made when the Casey family tree yielded a Jeremiah. My own son is John Patrick and Jim's daughter Natalie is called Trish to mark the Patricia in her name. The O'Keefe cousins have even grander names—John Kevin Carney O'Keefe and Sean Casey O'Keefe. The Neaves have Thomas Carney Neave and John Patrick Joseph Neave. My niece Jennifer Jill Carney, whose name reflects the family initials JJC, married a Japanese Canadian and called two of their three sons Colin and Liam. "They look like you," blonde Jill told her husband Tom Sakata. "So they can be given Irish names."

The Irish names are like totems recounting the family history. Even in the next generation, where intermarriages have added new genes to the Irish ethnic mix, Eileen has become Ileana, to mark her mother's Guatemalan heritage, and the newest girl cousin, Casey's daughter, is McKenna O'Keefe, after old Cornelius O'Keefe's first wife.

The labyrinthine ties continue. Cornelius' second wife was Elizabeth Tierney, whose youngest son, Tierney O'Keefe, married my cousin Betty Carney Neave, the granddaughter of Bridget and John Joseph. Their marriage joined two pioneer Okanagan families and maintained the Irish family ties. Carney, Casey, and O'Keefe cousins still congregate for dinners, weddings, funerals, and good times into yet another century, although the families have added Japanese, Guatemalan, Chinese, Italian, British, German, and American spouses for the first time in their entwined history.

Tierney and Betty O'Keefe, who restored Cornelius O'Keefe's mansion to its original glory as their own personal 1967 Centennial project, lived in the house with their five children until it was designated a heritage site in 1977.

My children used to play with their cousins on the Victorian furniture in the rose-and-green drawing room. We celebrated our final New Year's Eve dinner there with Elizabeth Tierney's 14-foot-long linen damask tablecloth and her 258-piece set of sterling silver, the heaviest set ever made in Montreal, and toasted the ranch's past and future around the great table under the exquisite crystal chandelier in the panelled dining room. Some traditions die hard!

When I first visited Ireland in 1996, nobody asked me where I came from or what I was doing there. Everyone knew where Pat Carney came from—Ireland, of course—and naturally I was back there searching for relatives. A Dublin billboard screamed: "Is Ireland Racist?" How would I know, with a good Limerick name like Carney?

It took me a while to realize this unquestioned acceptance and to experience the blessed relief it bestowed. In Canada, when we meet someone, there are the inevitable polite questions: Where does your family come from? When did they arrive in Canada? In Quebec, of course, there are the original "pure laine" French-Canadian families and in northern Canada you can usually identify an aboriginal Canadian's home village by her family name. But in general, we expect that a family named Greba from Two Hills, Alberta, came from somewhere else at some other time.

Before I met my cousin Tom Kearney in Castleconnell, on the River Shannon in Limerick, neither of us knew the other existed, but we weren't surprised to find one another. My father had told me that the Caseys and Kearneys came from Limerick, although the Kearneys originally came from Cashel, where there was actually a Kearney Castle, which has now become a pub. Records in the area show that a Kearney was hanged as a martyred priest and Elizabeth Kearney was Keeper of the Keys.

During my time there my guide Ray McGrath and I checked gravestones in the cemetery to record various dates (cemeteries are valuable sources of information). McGrath, a sprite of a storytelling man, had worked as a public servant in Ottawa for years before returning home with his wife, an Ottawa Valley girl. We asked the priest if any Carneys still lived in the area. "There's old Tom Kearney in Stradbally up the hill," said the harried-looking priest. "At least you're not a Ryan," he said. (The cemetery was thick with Ryans.) "But he doesn't like people with the Carney version of the name," he warned.

Since it was suppertime, I was loath to visit, unannounced and uninvited. But McGrath insisted, locating the small cottage and explaining, when the door opened: "We're here on a mission of history." Next thing I knew Tom's home-care worker, Margaret Joyce, was hustling me into a tiny living room, making tea and bologna sandwiches while Tom and I examined each other like two wary cats.

At age 65 he was older than me, but had the same Black Irish look. His mother was a Casey. He was a widower—his wife Bridget had died childless—and Tom was the last of the line. His brogue was so thick I could hardly follow him. He and Margaret were great step-dancers, taking a taxi into Limerick for the dances, 16 punts there and back, since neither owned a car. I asked Margaret if she and Tom were a couple. "No," she explained as she poured the tea. "I'm taken."

Tom then retrieved some photographs of Patrick Kearney, who had gone to America, but the dates didn't fit my great-grandfather Patrick Kearney, who had left much earlier and was probably an uncle instead. The exact relationship didn't much matter. Finally I said: "You don't seem surprised to see me." Tom answered: "No—that I'm not." When I asked him why, he proceeded to explain.

"Years ago, a man came," he said. I realized it might have been my father, who had visited Castleconnell in 1968. "I was that angry because I wasn't here," said Tom. "I had gone over to Waterford that weekend for the first time in 20 years. But the man told Mother: 'Don't worry. Someone else will come.'" And almost 30 years later someone did.

I leaned toward Tom and said: "Do you think I could buy you and Margaret a Jamieson's at the pub to celebrate my coming?" So we went down the hill to his favourite pub, the Shannon Inn, where he ordered Guinness for himself, rum for Margaret, and Irish whisky for Ray and me, introducing me to the pubkeeper: "This is my cousin Pat Carney from Canada." When we left the pub and took him home, he gave me a kiss and I gave him a hug. "Now he will clean himself up and go back down to the pub for the closing round," explained Margaret, as we drove her home. "And he will tell his Burns cousins the Great Event. A cousin from Canada came home."

CHAPTER 4

Ya Ya

TRADE SECRET:
The wild goose never laid a tame egg.
—Irish proverb

I f Mei Mei taught her children how to look and listen, our father taught us how to use language. Watching someone ineptly handling an animal on a back-bush farm in the Kootenays, Father would comment, "He's as useless as tits on a bull." If someone was slow to get his meaning, he'd say, "It's like talking to a goose about God."

Father would inspect some young man foolish enough to date one of his daughters and ask, to our mortification, "What breed of cat are you?" He could remember his Latin from his high school classes and, from his years in a Russian boarding house in Shanghai, he could swear in several languages, including Russian.

He spoke fluent Shanghainese and would hurl "ice-cream brain" in Chinese at anyone who made a soft-headed comment. Or to describe a stingy person he would say in Chinese: "He's so mean he can do somersaults in the eye of a cash [coin]." His grandchildren called him Ya Ya, Chinese for Grandfather.

My father also taught us other lessons. Look after your mother. God broke the mould when he made her. Write when you find work. Check the survey posts before any property purchase. Buy the best land you can afford; God isn't making any more. Water rights may determine your survival. Always muzzle an animal before you work on him. Keep the woodpile filled. Point a gun away from you; never aim at any per-

56

son. Eat what game you kill. Turn the handles of pots on the stove inwards so they don't spill on you.

When I was a child, I knew I was my father's favourite. When my parents met on the ship to Shanghai, he told her that one day he would have a dark-eyed daughter called Pat. I also knew that I would become a rancher like my Carney relatives. I even knew where I would ranch— either on the Sunset Ranch, which topped the forest-covered side hills on the other side of the Okanagan Valley from the Home Place, or at Gold Creek in East Kootenay. Gold Creek was the dry, sun-baked valley across the Kootenay River from Flagstone, the saw-milling village where my father had taught school before the World War I. I dreamed that I would run Herefords; ranching and love for the land were in my Irish blood.

Okanagan Valley pioneer Eliza Jane Swalwell wrote:

> It was nice to ride over the range in the morning and see the bunch grass, sunflowers and lupins springing up so abundantly, and to feel your horse springing under you at every step, as if he too were enjoying it, as no doubt he was. To me it was an exquisite pleasure as a girl to ride over this green and gracious pasture land in the mornings, and see it stretching for miles with the sand roses scattered on the ground as if a fairy princess had passed that way at dawn, and children had strewn flowers in her path, and to see the sunlight on the hills.
>
> On such occasions I have sometimes seen things, or rather sensed something, so serene and beautiful that it left me weak and weeping, as I sat in the saddle.[1]

Did the land seem that way to my father Jim and his sister Catherine and later Elizabeth and Tom as they rode their horses over the valley floor to the elementary school at Ellison? It did to me, as a leggy nine-year-old riding in the back of Uncle Tom's pickup truck over his range to view his prized Black Angus cattle, while my older cousin Anne Carney rode her horse through the sagebrush in her fearless tomboy style.

John James wanted more than a cowboy's life. He worked his way through high school in Kelowna, living in a tent during the school week through the winter and cleaning horse stables for Dr. William John "Bill" Knox for a nickel a week. Even so, he found the time and energy to attend the local dances and baseball games with the Monford and Conroy kids, sometimes leaving the homestead through the bedroom window at night to meet up with his friends or to escape the Old Man's drinking rages.

Teaching was one option open to both bright young men and women, although it was discouraged by my grandfather, who viewed his sons as a kind of crop whose strength was to be used on the farm like the strength of horses. My father was probably the first member of his family to complete high school and certainly the first to earn a university degree.

In 1913 he went to Vancouver and rented a room for $20 a month over a grocery store owned by his roommate's uncle. He often walked the 44 blocks on wooden sidewalks to the Normal School at the corner of 11th and Cambie to save the nickel streetcar fare. One could do a lot with a nickel: attend the Vaudeville in the old Pantages Theatre on Hastings Street; take a ride to New Westminster on the Interurban, two electric cars in tandem, which rocketed along with a fearful clatter; or buy a pack of cigarettes.[2]

Broadway, now a major thoroughfare, ran through bush land and vacant lots full of old burned stumps. At Normal School the 140 girls and 20 boys studied geography, history, art, arithmetic, singing, and physical drill (the girls in full blue bloomers and long black stockings). The students also studied primary teaching, since most of them would eventually teach in one-room schools where four- and five-year-olds were enrolled to keep the schools open. Outings for the students included picnics on Bowen Island, and once as far away as Sechelt. A group climbed Grouse Mountain on a dark, rainy day, building a fire and making tea at the top. Since Father walked to and from the North Vancouver ferry on the Vancouver side, the whole day's outing cost him just 20 cents.

In January 1914, armed with his three-month diploma, Dad was sent to Flagstone, a logging settlement on the Kootenay River with a big sawmill. Average pay in a one-room school was $60 a month, more if the conditions were difficult. His salary was $83 a month, since the school was reported to be rough and several teachers had fled. Officials in Victoria had chosen my father, six foot tall and red-haired, believing he could establish order.

Flagstone was built on the banks of the Kootenay River as it swung down into the United States. Since the village was short of baths, Father rode the railway, which ran from the Fernie area coal fields, to have a bath in the barbershop at Eureka, Montana. Flagstone was a ghost town when Father eventually took us back to visit—its weathered grey houses and stores were still standing, as was the one-room school with its abandoned desks where he had once strapped a tough teenager who had put gunpowder in the stove, using the same leather strap that he would caress, standing at the bottom of the stairs, while asking his four quarrelling children upstairs, "Anyone want a little love tap?" and commanding instant silence.

Now Flagstone lies under water flooded by the Libby Dam. But when I went down the path to the gravelled beach I could almost glimpse the young lads and ladies at their picnics under the chattering aspens shading the swirling green river, so real were they to me in the fresh water-scented air. I have photographs of my father, barely older than his students in their rough serge pants and pinafores. My nephew Joe is a mirror image of our father at that age. But then he was born on my father's birthday, August 31.

In August 1914 war was declared and, although he took a cadet instructor's course, Father failed to pass the medical test for the Army for reasons never discussed in his letters home to his sister Catherine. Instead he returned to his school at Flagstone and contented himself with drilling his students in saluting the flag and at night accompanying a friend in the police force to catch Germans and Austrians sneaking down the railway track into the United States to escape internment in Canada.

As the war dragged on, and casualties consumed Canada's young men, whatever ailed my father no longer barred him from military service and in 1916 the *Kelowna Courier* listed J.J. Carney among the Kelowna contingent of the Rocky Mountain Rangers, which later joined the 72nd Seaforth Highlanders and were shipped overseas.[3]

My father fought his war in a kilt, serving 18 months in the muddy, rat-infested trenches including the hell on earth that was Passchendaele, earning a Military Medal in the battle of Amiens and a commission in the field as an officer. Despite being wounded in the knee, he spent four years overseas, part of it on embarkation duty after the Armistice.

Yet his faded brown letters to his sister Catherine rarely refer to the bloodier aspects of the war except to record the fates of other Okanagan boys killed or wounded.

From France he pencilled:

> I got your letter shortly after coming out of the line and I am still out and may be out for some time—one never knows does one—especially in la belle France . . . I hope the good weather stays with us. Of course the roads are a bit muddy but that's nothing over here. We would be surprised if there was no mud.
>
> At present, we are staying at a farm, only this is a real one as it has never been shelled as yet. We reside in the barn. We got a pretty good billet this time. . . . Yes, I had a swell Easter. I went into the line on Good Friday night—a new draft were with me and we stayed in for a long time. Yes, I don't think the Germans had their Easter the same day as they carried on just the same, so did us, and there were no Easter eggs in the rations either.
>
> We got an orange apiece in our rations last night—we surely must be winning at that rate—there are a couple of Fritizies less since last fall that I know of—I claimed one for myself in case I should get scratched up sometime and the other goes to make up for George Monford's death . . . I remain the same as b4. Jimmy.[4]

I have never heard of my father being called Jimmy, but then again I never knew he loved dancing until I read his letters to his sister. Unfortunately, his war injury left him with a limp.

Another letter to "Dear Sis" and signed "Jimmy," dated 21/10/18 from "Angleterre" where he was in hospital, refers to his fellow soldiers in their kilts and the women volunteers in their breeches: "People look at the Land Army girls in their khakis and then look at us Jocks and look puzzled. They can't figure it out somehow."

Clearly riled at the attention the air force was receiving, he wrote: "Where do you get that 36 hour notion about airmen—Bishop[5] has lasted longer than that, hasn't he? And he takes chances and lots don't—Look here we have some good airman and some duds—Don't believe all that stuff about our brave airmen holding the air supremacy on the Western—they do some days and some days Fritz does. Ours give me a cramp in the neck sometimes—they often seem to be away at tea when they are wanted. Meanwhile Fritz is over firing machine guns into our trenches and dropping bombs around as careless as can be. . . ."[6]

"XMAS DAY IN PARIS: New Year in Trenches; J. Jas Carney Tells about Festivities Near the Front," reported the *Kelowna Courier*, quoting from Jim's letters to Catherine, who was Valley correspondent. "Have you ever forgiven me for all the articles in the *Kelowna Courier* for which I was responsible?" she wrote him years later. "I got $1 a column and boy! Could I ever elaborate."

The Christmas letter records Father's 14-day leave with five others in 1917. "Paris must be grand in the summer time without a war on, but even now it surpasses expectations and has London faded." There were innumerable theatres, lots to eat, no "Reveille"—even breakfast in bed, consisting of hot chocolate or coffee and hot rolls. "Not many kilts have been seen there so they are a scream in Paris. The Parisians are fond of the Canadians because they prove to be good troops and the Canadian Scottish are just it."

After outlining the sights, including Napoleon's tomb, Versailles, Notre Dame, midnight mass at the Church of St. Roche, the Eiffel Tower, the Champs Elysees, and *Romeo and Juliet* played in the National Opera House, Father reported: "On Xmas Eve we had a Zeppelin scare; sirens sounded, lights went out and people went indoors into the underground trains, all except the soldiers, and such an assortment of soldiers British, Canucks, Ansees or Australians, New Zealanders, all kinds of British and French colonial troops such as Soudanese, Zouaves, Hindu cavalry, Algerians, Russians, heaps of Belgium soldiers, and of course, lots of French and tons of Yanks; saw all kinds except Fritzies, Austrians and Turks."

He went on to describe the Christmas turkey dinner, the present of an electric flashlight, cigarettes, and chocolates, and a performance by the Seven of Spades, "who were seven American coons and had a coon band and sure could play." His account concluded: "Well, we sure hated to leave Paris, to come back and soldier again. It is very cold now for France and the ground is covered with snow, but we are supplied with leather coats and pants till spring," presumably to replace the kilts. He described New Year's Eve in the trenches: "Everyone was glad to see 1917 go. Just about 12 o'clock the big guns were going pretty strong and we could hear that old familiar sound of bursting shells."

The *Courier* commented dryly: "The letter (by Lance-Corp. J. Jas Carney) will certainly create the feeling that the recompenses are almost greater than the hardships. However, it's due to the boys. It is a certainty, too, after a few weeks in Paris and London such as Carney spent, many of the boys will return to Kelowna with a widely different opinion of the world than that gained in British Columbia and the Far West."[7]

That was certainly true for Jim Carney. When he finally returned to Vancouver in 1920 he took another course at Normal School and was assigned a school in South Vancouver. Family legend holds that he was walking along a beach one day when, attracted by a large crowd, he went over to a wharf to investigate. A large man came out onto the loading dock and said, "I'll pick you, you, and *you*," pointing to red-haired Jim, who found himself hired as a stoker on a freighter, the *Canadian Inventor*, stoking coal into the gluttonous ship's engines across the Pacific to China. The truth, which I later discovered when I was researching his letters, is more mundane. A week or so before school opened he met an army friend who was a fire fighter on the ship. The call of adventure was too strong; he abandoned teaching and jumped ship in Shanghai.

Whatever his plans were then, he never returned to the Okanagan. He stayed in China for nearly 20 years.

Father's greatest legacy to his children was the fact that he brought us home to Canada from China, while most of our friends stayed, oblivious to the threat of war clouding Shanghai's sunny outlook. After the war, with our family safe in Victoria, we watched some of those friends return, gaunt and ill, from the internment camps in China. Unfortunately, some never made it home.

My twin brother Jim and I were particularly excited by the move because we were nearly five and eager to start school. My first views of Canada when our ship, the *Heian Maru*, approached land were the cars travelling along Dallas Road in Victoria and then the lights of Lions Gate Bridge arcing across Burrard Inlet in Vancouver. We stayed with our Aunt Elizabeth in her Holly Lodge apartment in Vancouver's West End awaiting the birth of our brother Tom.

One night I listened to my parents debate whether they should use their small savings to buy the Sunset Ranch in the Okanagan or to finance my father through veterinary college in Guelph to meet Canadian specifications for the public health work he had been performing in Shanghai. They sat on their bed holding hands as my father opted for Guelph. The cowboy, teacher, and soldier would now become Dr. J.J. Carney, doctor of veterinary medicine. A few months later we took the transcontinental train to Ontario to enrol Father in the Ontario Veterinary College.

It wasn't until I reached adulthood that I realized the enormity of Father's decision to enter veterinary college at that point in his life. He was 45 years old, with a wife and four children under the age of five, and very little money in his Canadian savings account. He was the first member of his family to attend college. He had graduated from high school in the Okanagan Valley during the Edwardian era and survived World War I. It was now World War II, the era of Churchill, Roosevelt, and Stalin. After nearly 20 years in China, his own country was foreign to him. He would be age 50 when he graduated and entered the workforce seeking a job.

Father could not have done it without Mother's support, but it was among the worst experiences of her life. She was transported from a life of relative comfort and excitement to that of a penny-pinching college student's wife in a small, insular Ontario town that was suspicious of the strangers from the home of the Chinamen, with their foreign accents and customs. It must have reminded her of her family's experience when they arrived in Canada from South Africa and England. She chronicled her unhappiness in an unpublished manuscript entitled "Merrily, Merrily."

Our parents chose the town of Morriston in which to live, population 206 with six Carneys included, because it was only nine miles from the college town of Guelph and housing was available and cheap. The village was little more than a crossroads, with the general store on one corner and a garage, a converted blacksmith shop, across the street. A pond was situated below the crossroads, and along the highway was the school, a red-brick, two-classroom building with a bell tower, with pictures of King George and Queen Elizabeth in each classroom. When Jim and I revisited the school 20 years later, our grade one records were still stored in the filing cabinet and the janitor remembered us.

Our house was a crumbling plaster-covered dwelling, set in a garden, with fruit trees and a henhouse. A verandah sagged across the front. Inside the house, the wallpaper hung in strips from the walls, and the few electric light bulbs hung from the ceiling on cords. There was no indoor plumbing, but an outhouse out back. We bathed in a galvanized round washtub in front of the wood stove. Water was pumped by hand at the kitchen sink and stored in buckets; we kids used to peer at the white worms at the bottom of the pail. It was so cold in winter that ice formed on top of the water bucket. The rent for the house was nine dollars a month.

Mother set to work, decorating orange crates with dyed flour sacking to make dressing tables for the girls' bedroom upstairs. Orange crates also served initially as our dining-room table, set with good linen and rice china tableware. We had very little furniture, mainly a studio couch used as our parents' bed, iron cots for the children, two violins, a huge thermometer, three lovely Chinese chests, and a desk, which remains in the family to this day. An ancient Chinese rug woven in wine, gold, and purple covered the worn living-room floor.

Our father dug up the garden and planted corn, peas, and potatoes, although our neighbours loafing around the gate told him that vegetables planted on Sunday would be smitten with rot by God. They never were, thank Heavens, because with little money and limited wartime supplies we relied on the garden and the Old Girls in the henhouse for much of our food. Mother collected dandelions and lamb's quarters from the lawn for our "greens" long before it became fashionable to do so.

Father bought an ancient Model T Ford, much admired by his children, to travel back and forth to college. When the Model T broke down, Father took the bus to classes. Occasionally we drove to the Big Smoke—Toronto—to visit The Relatives and outfit Norah and me in Cousin Dodie's outgrown clothes. A trip that today takes less than an hour was an all-day adventure then.

We did not mix much with the other children in the village outside the schoolyard, since Mother had deemed them "not our kind of people," after her early attempts to help with Red Cross teas and such were rebuffed by the village women. Unfortunately, Mother did not even have the comfort of her Anglican church, since only Methodist and Presbyterian services were available in the village.

But we played in our garden, fishing for leaves in water-filled buckets, using bent pins tied to string; walking with Mother to the village dump to rescue pretty blue saucers for flower pots and other treasures; looking for the first trilliums in the woods by the pond in spring; swimming in the leech-infested mill pond in nearby Aberfoyle in summer; fighting off bees to eat the warm ripe pears, dripping juice, which hung like golden goblets from the fruit trees in the fall; and buying black jawbreakers at the general store with our pennies. In winter there was the novelty of snow, and snowsuits, and huge snowdrifts created by the snorting snowplough, and sleigh rides to school when the roads were closed. There was tobogganing down the hill behind the school, and hot cocoa by the school's coal stove, and the inevitable school concerts at Christmas. Jim remembers the snow blowing through the keyholes of our house, so we used to sleep with our clothes tucked under the blankets so that they would be warm enough to crawl into when morning came, rimming the bedroom windows with frost.

Mother befriended the doctor and his wife across the street, and a highlight of our young lives was the rare opportunity to stay overnight at the Doctor's House. That's what the sign outside the grey stone house said: "The Doctor's House." It had big beds that we needed a stool to climb up into and real indoor plumbing. The doctor, a frail man, was a relative of Olive Diefenbaker, second wife of John Diefenbaker.

Mother found life with four children exhausting. "There were wash days and ironing days, days for sweeping and washing the linoleum floors, days for mending and days for baking—and every day the meals and dishes and baby routine, the carrying of clean water in and dirty water out, the gathering of vegetables and fruits and preparing them, some to be cooked and some to be canned," she wrote in her manuscript, which in reality was her journal.

Our father was a remote figure to us, as he was all his working life. In Shanghai, he had followed the local custom of leaving for work at 6:00 a.m., returning home for a noon lunch and siesta, and then working until late at night. At veterinary college, in addition to his studies he worked part-time in a war-weapons plant on weekends and holidays to augment the family income. After his soldier's life and his career in China he found it hard to return to his studies. "Then, too, his classmates were fresh from high school, with knowledge at their finger ends, which he had never even heard about. Their brains were trained and quick to catch the salient points of any lecture, while his assimilated slowly," our mother wrote.

Years later I appreciated Father's difficulty with resuming studies when I returned to the University of British Columbia at age 40 to study for my master's degree in regional planning, 15 years after earning my bachelor's degree in economics and political science. I performed so poorly in the first semester of the two-year course that the school director called me into his office and asked me gently if there had been a death in my family. But I eventually graduated with first-class marks.

Mother recorded Father's schedule:

When he finished his dinner, he carried out the ashes, brought in the wood and water, and went to bed. At midnight the alarm aroused him and pulling on his heavy gown over a couple of sweaters, with extra socks on his feet and a blanket wrapped around him, he stoked up the fire in his study and went to work.

In this way he found quiet hours which were impossible for him when the family was astir, for the little kitchen was too small and the other rooms too cold and the study was the only room in which the children could play. At half past four or five he went to bed again, setting the alarm clock for half past six.[8]

In Father's final year of studies, my parents found a house on River Road in Guelph itself, a narrow two-storey brick building with real plumbing, which rented for $24 a month. In a state of high excitement, we moved to a comfortable home and a city school, ballet classes, and buses. Jim and I, now aged eight or nine, were allowed to visit the veterinary college to wash out the test tubes in the laboratories and ride the dead horses, which were held upright by wires strung up to the ceiling.

When Father finally graduated, he sold the Model T for $25, picked up a new car delivered fully wrapped in brown paper, packed his four children in the back seat with Mother in the front, and headed west.

Finally, at last, the Carney family was going home. Not to the Okanagan Valley, but to Victoria, where Father had been offered a job as Commissioner of Milk, responsible for producing new legislation dealing with pasteurizing and cleaning up the milk supply in British Columbia. His office was in the Legislative Buildings, which impressed us, as did the Legislative Assembly, although Mother said the language used by the MLAs when the legislature was in session was far too rowdy for children.

The four years we spent in Victoria were among the happiest of our childhood. We learned to swim in the Crystal Pool behind the Empress Hotel. We joined Girl Guides and Boy Scouts and Jim discovered soccer. We bought a three-storey house with five fireplaces at 3579 Quadra Street in Saanich, which we called Odd Numbers, below a hill of gorse and Gary oak where we practised our semaphore and played hide-and-seek. We attended Cloverdale School and took music lessons.

Our Sanders grandparents came out from Toronto to live with us, to my mother's delight and my father's reservations. They took over the table-setting and dishwashing chores, and Granny taught us how to set a formal table, each knife and fork and spoon lined up in its correct place; since we had started our lives with chopsticks, this was a new concept.

My father's experience as a veterinarian with a background in tropical public health was greatly in demand during the post-war period and he received many job offers, one from Hong Kong. When trouble flared up again in southeast Asia, however, Mother sat on our suitcases and refused to return. Father was also offered a position as Chief Veterinarian of Hawaii, which tempted him, but he refused upon learning that he would be expected to become an American citizen— hard for a man who had fought under a Canadian flag.

My siblings and I, who all love the Hawaiian island of Maui, often dream of what our lives would have been like if Father had accepted the job. We would probably have owned a cattle ranch somewhere. Been expert surfers. Married different people. And the boys would have faced the Vietnam War draft, Jim reminds me.

Father ultimately settled for a posting in the Kootenays, the region next to the Okanagan. He may now have been a doctor of veterinary medicine, but the ranch boy in Father was determined that his children would not be lily-livered, artistic layabouts allegedly like some of my mother's family. So he purchased a stump farm in the Kootenays, dumped chickens in the henhouse, tied a milk cow to an apple tree and left town, forcing us back to our Carney roots. For years, our Home Place was the Blue J on the Kootenay River.

CHAPTER 5

The Blue J

TRADE SECRET:

*To skin a dead porcupine, turn the animal on its
back and gingerly skin it as you would a rabbit by
making an incision up, down, and across.*

—Jim Carney

Most politicians, like many people, have at least one skeleton rattling away in the family closet. And I am no exception. There is one aspect of my past that my campaign managers implored me to keep secret, never to reveal to the media or the public, on pain of embarrassment or worse.

My secret is that I can talk to animals. Really!

I first confessed this to my handlers in Vancouver Centre when I ran there as the Conservative candidate. They were horrified. Never admit that, they advised. "Why?" I asked indignantly. I had just exhibited my skill at muzzling a pet cocker spaniel, by inserting two fingers between its legs and turning it on its glossy side.

"Because people will think you're crazy," said the lead handler, lifting the family pet back on its feet, eyes rolling and sides panting. "One log short of a load. Not the sharpest knife in the drawer. We have enough troubles in this campaign."

"Why not?" I asked. "I mean, it's not as if I served time in jail, or committed fraud or ran off with a teenage lover. But if you have to help sew up the conservation officer's dogs when they've been torn up by a cougar, and you have to get near enough to them to muzzle them, raise a vein on their leg, and insert a syringe full of sedative so you can swab out and sew up their wounds, you better bloody well learn how to talk to them. And it might get out the animal lovers' vote."

"Not a word," reiterated the handlers. And then they warned, "Do you want campaign contributions to dry up?"

So I've never had the opportunity to campaign on my skills as a veterinary assistant, which I learned in my father's surgery in the Kootenays. It was also unlikely that I could exhibit my proficiency at milking cows, given that Vancouver Centre is one of Canada's most densely populated urban ridings, although I once threatened to challenge former Liberal Agriculture Minister Eugene Whelan to a milk-off. But those high-rise apartment buildings in the West End were filled with budgies, pet kittens, small dogs (legal or not), goldfish, and the odd hamster. No wonder I lost my first election.

Milking cows and planting potatoes are necessary life skills, according to our father, a homesteader's son. So is peeling fence posts; good fences make good neighbours. To this day I make my own blackberry jam and apple chutney and plant Yukon Gold spuds in the garden. Naturally there is a woodstove, Miss Emily, in my kitchen to provide heat and food on those winter days when the power is out on Saturna Island.

Unnecessary life skills, in Dad's view, included playing musical instruments, writing, painting, and most of the artistic endeavours enjoyed by our mother's relatives in Toronto. Such indulgences were guaranteed to lead to the life of a starving artist in a garret. The fact that most of Mother's artistic relatives lived in posh places like Rosedale or Leaside seemed to escape his attention.

The Blue J consisted of 54 acres of mostly rock cliff at the tail end of Elephant Mountain across the lake and was situated three miles from Nelson. It had been an orchard before the earlier Okanagan season had crippled the West Kootenay fruit industry, and apple and cherry trees bloomed in the two pastures.

The shingled and stone house itself had been built in grand style around the turn of the last century with building materials reportedly barged up the lake. Although it had no bathroom or inside plumbing, it had stained-glass windows, French doors opening onto wide verandahs, and a huge staircase that swept up from the front hall to a landing where it split into side stairs leading to the upstairs bedrooms.

The place had been empty for years when my parents bought it in 1950, gingerly walking through the fallen plaster and old newspapers that littered the derelict living room. During the first night in our new home a packrat stole my socks. The next day I retrieved them from the packrat's nest in the attic and turned out with my siblings to plant potatoes in the freshly tilled garden. Inside plumbing soon followed.

I loved the Blue J, every grey granite rock, every black spruce tree, the mountain creek where gold dust glinted in the sand. Jim stoically endured it, Norah ignored it, preferring to play with her friends in town, and the animals were largely gone when younger brother Tom was old enough to help. Mother put on blue jeans before they were popular, but she remained terrified of cows. When she met our cow tossing her head on the path to the barn in winter, it was Mom who stepped into the snow bank.

Ah, the animals. The first was a Jersey cow named Blondie, a seductive creature with a languid way of chewing her cud, culled from some Doukhobor herd in the nearby Slocan Valley. Jersey cows gave milk with a high cream content, which was important because Dad insisted that we make our own butter. Churning butter was another necessary life skill.

Blondie wasn't actually producing milk when we bought her because she was pregnant, explained Dad. But she was due to "freshen" after she gave birth, providing milk for both her calf and us. But Blondie never freshened, to the embarrassment of our veterinarian father. She simply chewed her cud while Dad and the local farmers stood around and shook their heads in wonder, since she certainly looked pregnant, her tummy sticking out like that. Finally it was off to the butcher for her.

Molly was milking when she arrived, the femme fatale of the local herd with her long-lashed, white-rimmed eyes, and shapely legs marked like black stockings. Since we didn't have a barn, Dad tied Molly to an apple tree and left for Cranbrook, leaving Jim and me responsible for milking her. This was similar to throwing someone into the deep end of the pool to learn how to swim. Mom, working at the kitchen sink, watched us milk in relays, the inside of our jeans stiff with misdirected streams of milk.

We learned to milk and walk Molly on a rope up the highway to a neighbour's bull for servicing when she came in heat, producing a fine little Jersey calf some months later. Mom found an old one-room schoolhouse, which she bought for $28 and moved to the Blue J to serve as a barn.

Normally I milked Molly in the morning and Jim milked her at night. I savoured the early morning ritual: scalding the milk pail and the cloth to wipe her udder; walking the snowy path to the barn in the winter dark while coyotes howled on the rockslide below Elephant Mountain; heaving the sweet smelling alfalfa into her manger; pushing the steaming manure out of the barn, and replacing Molly's bed of fresh wood chips in her stall; and, finally, curling my fingers around her warm teats and drilling the milk into the pail, with the odd squirt at a mouse or two that showed up for company.

Molly enjoyed being sung to while being milked. I invented new words to the old favourite *Once in Love with Amy*. "Once—squirt—in love—squirt—with Molly—squirt—always—squirt—in love—squirt—with MOLLLLY," I sang, while Molly flicked her ears back and chewed her alfalfa, swishing her tail across my face to indicate her interest. Or "MOLLLLY, I'm always thinking of you, MOLLLLY," I sang.

Norah refused to learn to milk, showing up in her bobby socks, plaid skirt, and twin sweater set, seating herself as far away from Molly as possible and ineffectually squeezing her teats until Jim and I, in Molly's defence, banned Norah, to her great satisfaction, from the barn. Norah made us green omelettes for breakfast instead; Jim and I preferred steak and eggs.

Dad banned Mother from milking lessons on the sensible grounds that she would not be left to do the milking if she didn't know how. One rare evening Jim and I were out on the lake in front of the Blue J fishing, when we watched Mother march up the hill to the stanchion in the Upper Pasture where we often milked Molly in the summer. She managed to guide Molly on a rope to the stanchion, lock the cow's head in the device, and start milking. Like members of an audience watching a stage performance, we saw Molly swing her leg back and kick the milk bucket down the hill. We abandoned our fishing trip and rowed back to shore and the milking chore.

Our friends loved Molly, who was featured in several of our high school parades in Nelson, wearing floral hats and stepping daintily along the old streetcar tracks while we played in the school band, swinging along smartly in our blue-caped uniforms. Spoiled, petulant, and productive, Molly had only two major faults: she loved to escape from the Blue J and head down the highway, and she loved to eat the apples in the orchard until she became bloated.

News that Molly was AWOL usually came from the ferry crew who operated the cable ferry across the West Arm between the North Shore and Nelson and regularly relayed reports to the Blue J about truant horses and cows and sometimes dogs from our boarding kennel. Since the road ended at the ferry then, they couldn't escape any farther. Generally Jim and I would climb into our family's 1938 Nash and drive to the ferry, roping the truant animal to the bumper. Once Molly realized she was headed home to her dinner, she would normally move out in front of the Nash and trot briskly toward the Blue J, giving the impression that she was, in fact, towing the car, and us. Animal rights advocates in passing cars would wave their fists and shout threats at our motley cow-and-car procession, sometimes enhanced by a calf, another partner in crime, tied to the back bumper.

Molly's penchant for eating ripe apples was more serious, however, since she could die from bloat or more likely from the knife thrust Dad showed us how to make in an emergency. Such a cut would be made at a point identified by the position of her hip bone and thus would enter her stomach, if we were lucky. Instead, we opted for a "Molly cocktail," a mixture of mineral oil, ginger ale, and a dash of kerosene, pepper, or anything else guaranteed to make her belch, and served in a bottle stuck through her clenched teeth at the side of her mouth. We inserted the bottle by grabbing her under her snout and pulling it up until she finally unhinged her jaw. When enough of the mixture had been poured down her throat, we would take turns kneading her side to promote belching—a job that could take up to the midnight hours, aided again by music. "Once—knead—in love—knead—with Molly— knead—always—knead—in love—knead—with MOLLY," we sang in the heavily odoriferous barn.

Molly also taught us many necessary life skills. Unfortunately, we did not teach her necessary survival skills, because when Jim and I left for university we had to find her another home on a small farm above Kaslo. Years later we learned that Molly did not take kindly to the belled lead cow in the herd and was expelled, as the nuns said about Carney family members, for being a "disruptive influence." Although no one would tell us her eventual fate, I suspect she eventually went off to the butcher.

Dad's work as a government veterinarian took him to all the small farms tucked away in the benches and valleys of the Kootenays, and people unloaded their sick and psychotic animals on him to bring home. Even the Greyhound bus drivers stopped at the sign of the Blue J, swinging on its chain by the steps heading down to the highway, to drop off unwanted puppies and kittens found en route.

Our horses were generally such castoffs. The first two, an ancient pack horse named Belle and her almost-as-ancient daughter Lady, had some definite psychological problems as I discovered when I tried to ride Lady, who attempted to scrape me off her back by rubbing against the apple-tree branches while Belle used her hind legs to try to kick me off her daughter. Since we had no saddles and rode bareback with bits and bridles only, this was an alarming experience.

All our animals had to contribute to the Blue J in some way, and Lady and Belle were expected to earn their keep by ploughing the potato patch. All efforts to convert them into workhorses ended with an unsuccessful attempt to plough a neighbour's field. Harnessed as a team, they broke away and headed over the hill for home and oats, dragging the plough through gardens and fences behind them. Sigh. Another call to the butcher.

Our next horse was Daisy, whose contribution was a tax write-off. Her presence ensured the Blue J its farm tax status. To earn this, Jim and I hitched Daisy up to the stoneboat on winter days and coaxed her into dragging logs out of the mountain bush and down to the woodpile. The rest of the year she snoozed under the big fir tree in the Upper Pasture, sharing Molly's barn if the weather dropped to around 20 degrees below zero.

Since Daisy was a large logging horse, riding her bareback made one seasick. Another problem was the lack of any places to ride to, since riding on the highway was forbidden and our terrain was just too steep. Once, we led Daisy with the bridle to the stone wall separating the Upper and Lower pastures, jumped from the fence onto her broad back, and turned her downhill to the lake, but we found ourselves swaying queasily from side to side and that was pretty much the extent of our ride. Daisy was just too big and the path up the mountain to the creek too steep to offer much of an alternative.

One night Dad arrived home late and told Mom, who was already in bed: "There's a present for Pat in the chicken house." It was too late to explore, but early the next morning I ran over to the derelict shack, pushed open the door, and there, wobbling on its legs, was a day-old calf that Dad had acquired for five dollars. Possibly its mother had died. I was thrilled with the tiny brown-and-white Hereford, whom I named Oscar.

Dad showed me how to stick my fingers into his mouth and, when the calf sucked them, insert a bottle of warm milk. Oscar followed me around like the pet he was, rasping my arm with his tongue for the salty flavour, grazing near me as I lay daydreaming among the long grasses of the Upper Pasture. We garlanded him with flowers and entered him in the high school parade with Molly the cow. Oscar was the first of several calves that I raised to help pay for my college tuition, since the veal we didn't eat ourselves we sold to our neighbours.

We tanned the skins of our calves and used them for floor rugs, to the bewilderment of visitors: "There is Oscar, and that one is Rosco, and the pretty one is Felix, and you are about to sit on Angus in this chair." But we all clearly understood that the purpose of our calves, no matter how beloved, was to supply food, and we never shed a tear when they too went off to the butcher.

Years later, when I sold tickets to the famous Saturna Island Lamb Barbecue, I discovered that some children never made the connection between animals and what they ate on their plate until they saw the 26 lambs racked around the barbecue pits. When children returned to the ticket booth bawling their eyes out, I tactfully suggested ice cream instead, although they sometimes settled in all innocence for hot dogs.

For variety we also raised pigs in the pen behind the house. Our first pair were Clancy and Claribel, fat, happy porkers, followed the next year when Jim and I were into our jazz phase by Lee and Lena, named for saxophone player Lee Konitz and singer Lena Horne. We stored our meat in a locker in a sawdust-floored freezer in town, down by the lake. Usually I was responsible for picking up the frozen meat for dinner and one spring I discovered we had eaten all the veal, which we all preferred, and were left with 414 pounds of pork. It was years before I could face pork again, and then only in curry, in Sri Lanka.

We had chickens, which I loathed—noisy, messy, petty animals that I refused to look after—and Nicolas the Christmas turkey, whom we ate with relish for tattling on us when we snuck home after curfew, gobbling away in his pen after midnight until our irate parents woke up. Served him right, the beastly bird.

But we were almost bested by Goofus, the Goose Who Hated Women. Another reject salvaged by our father, Goofus regularly escaped from his pen until he had the run of the place—banned past the kitchen door but otherwise free to roam about assaulting anything in skirts. Since I was rarely out of my jeans, I was safe from attack. But I would watch a group of women emerge from a car, pet poodles in their arms, skirts billowing, and observe how the ladies, dogs, and skirts folded back into the automobile in the face of a full frontal attack by Goofus, wings outstretched, skittering over the ground at a ferocious speed. Oddly, his one exception was my sister Norah, who took a liking to the rebel and would slip a dog's leash over his scrawny neck and walk him down to the lake for a daily swim.

When it was Goofus' time to supply Thanksgiving dinner, he was swiftly dispatched but defiant to the end, since we couldn't figure out how to extract the goose feathers from his wiry body. Finally, following Dad's suggestion, we positioned him on top of a copper wash boiler filled with water and steamed him. For two or three days Goofus lay on his back on the wood stove, pale legs stuck in the air, his unattractive body slowly shedding feathers until he was deemed ready for the oven. I don't think we roasted him, repugnant little goose that he was. Mother probably popped him into a soup instead.

Our father regularly brought game home with him from his East Kootenay travels and our favourite was elk, although venison was a popular second choice. Later, when I lived in Yellowknife, I cooked caribou and moose, using the skills I had learned on the Blue J. The edict that we had to eat what we shot curtailed our teenage enthusiasm for popping off mud hens and squirrels with Jim's .22, since these are: (a) difficult to skin, and (b) not very tasty. Young Tom, with great élan, shot a bear that was marauding in the apple orchard one evening using Dad's old .38-.55 rifle. The bear went into the freezer.

The fact that our little brother had shot a bear bruised our egos so Jim and I set off up the mountain to find our own bear. The path led up the mountain along the creek that was our water supply to ravines and rockslides, and when we finally spotted a black bundle in a tree in a narrow cleft, we took no chances. Jim raised the rifle to his shoulder and fired. The shot jolted Jim back like a body blow. A porcupine fell out of the tree. "Damn," said Jim. Killing porcupines was illegal; they were so dumb they were protected in case a lost hunter might actually need to dispatch one for survival.

Equally dismaying was the fact that the local conservation officer, Ted Rutherglen, was visiting Dad's surgery with his torn-up cougar dogs at the time. No help there in the art of skinning a prickly porcupine, spines at full flare. Finally we turned the animal on its back and gingerly skinned it as we would a rabbit. Mother turned it into a tasty hunter's stew and later served it to an unsuspecting conservation officer on his next visit.

Dad was the only veterinarian between the Okanagan Valley and Lethbridge in Alberta, and although he was a government employee, people showed up with their sick pets or called on him for help after hours and on weekends. We turned the summer kitchen, attached to the back of the house, into a small and efficient surgery, albeit one with bags of mash and oats by the door for the livestock and the chickens. By this time I had abandoned my plans to be a cattle rancher and had settled on a career as a wildlife veterinarian so I enjoyed working with my father. I liked how he showed me what he was doing so I could learn from him; his first career, after all, was teaching.

My favourite cases were milk fevers, where a cow developed an often-fatal paralysis after giving birth. I would accompany Dad up some back road to a small farm snuggled onto one of the sunny bench lands overlooking the lake. The procedure was always the same: everyone stood around the inert cow in her stall, her head turned in to her body, a symptom of milk fever. "Too bad for the Old Girl," my father would say, shaking his head and commiserating with the despairing farmer. "It's a real shame." This meant that either the Old Girl deserved better after a lifetime of loyal milk-giving service, or she was just a young thing, an important investment with a future ahead of her.

Then we would attach a rope to her head to secure it, raise a vein in her neck, and pump in some calcium solution to revive her. Sometimes Dad was called too late and the cow would die. But often, after a wait, she would finally hump herself to her feet, staggering in her stall before walking disdainfully out of the barn, swishing her tail, to where the other cows all stood about like curious old gossips, and she would make it clear that the whole episode was a great deal of fuss about nothing. My father's fee never exceeded $15.

In the surgery we spayed dogs and neutered cats and removed cysts and performed other small animal practice procedures. Dad's normal operating table was usually a smooth plank, upended against the wall, where the animal hung upside down at an angle so that the interior organs would be easily accessible. It was usually my job to serve as his anaesthetist. My responsibilities involved padding gauze around the end of a cone shaped like a milkshake tin with the bottom cut out, pouring in some ether, and holding the cone over the snout of the animal until its paws relaxed, sedated. Dad administered Demerol to put it to sleep. During the operation I would monitor the colour of the animal's gums and eyeballs to ensure it was staying under, administering extra whiffs of ether if I detected any signs of recovery. Although I was not allowed to perform any surgery beyond cleaning and stitching wounds, Dad's boss, Dr. Gunboat Smith, permitted Mom and me to administer rabies shots if Dad was unavailable, since speed is of the essence in treatment of a domestic animal bitten by a possibly rabid wild animal. We rarely lost a patient, large or small.

When we did, there was always the pet cemetery, located below the stone wall separating the Upper and Lower pastures. Jim and I planted little wooden crosses under the apple trees with the names of the pets for the comfort of their grieving owners, who visited the graves with pet treats and toys. Unfortunately, we could not always plant Buster the Wonder Dog or Kitty below the crosses, since the ground in the orchard was stony and shallow and it was much easier to dig Buster's last resting place in the loamy soil beside the house. Although we felt pangs of guilt when owners trudged up the hill to the pet cemetery to cry beside Buster's ghost grave, only small pets were accommodated there. The pet cemetery is gone now, buried below a subdivision foundation. I wonder what ghost pets haunt the houses that replaced the cemetery.

We also practised small deceits with pet treats left by owners when they boarded their spoiled chihuahuas, treats such as jellied chicken and canned peaches and specialty cheeses. Our father was a firm believer in a balanced diet for all animals, so every animal boarding with us was served nutritious meals while we kids quaffed the specialty foods stored in the pantry. Dad was a meat-and-potatoes man himself and the only time he ever argued with Mom in front of us was when she tried to replace the lunchtime mandatory potato dish with a lettuce salad. Rabbit food, fumed my father. How was a man supposed to put in a full day's labour fuelled only by rabbit food? He drove off to town and the Hume Hotel until peace was made and twice-daily servings of potatoes were restored.

Housing the dogs and cats and the odd boarder presented a problem. The guest room was turned into a recovery room and doggy bedroom for a time; two beautiful collies and two boisterous springer spaniels, Colonel and Major, had access to the twin beds. Colonel and Major loved the Blue J, their special holiday home, and would take any opportunity to escape from the house and head up the mountain. This event would trigger a midnight scramble in the moonlight up the rock face that marked the rump of Elephant Mountain to search among the tamaracks and scree for the missing Bad Boys, who returned joyfully to their beds once they were run to earth.

With up to 30 dogs in residence at times, sleeping by the fire and peeing on the Chinese rug while cats clawed at the curtains, Mother realized that the Blue J, as Animal House, was running at capacity.

Clearly we needed a better doggy hotel. Mom hit upon the idea of using an old streetcar that was currently acting as a skaters' change room on a pond up the hill behind the town of Nelson and had suffered much damage from skates, graffiti, and at least one attempt to light a bonfire in it. It cost Mom $10 to buy the streetcar from a grateful city and another $100 to haul it across the lake on the ferry and to its position near the house below the Lower Pasture.

Supplied with a cement floor (which was easy to clean and disinfect) and with walled kennels inside and wire fences outside, the streetcar could accommodate about 10 dogs. Cats and kittens were stacked in their kennels in the front, where the streetcar operator normally sat, and in the back where the passengers climbed aboard. It was a most satisfactory solution, and close enough to my bedroom for me to throw boots, shoes, and other objects at the kennels from my dormer windows on those moonlit nights when the dogs howled. The city of Nelson has since rehabilitated Number 23, and she now runs smoothly on a track, in all her restored grandeur, from Lakeside Park to town and back. I ride her every time I visit, although I had to correct one conductor who was telling the tourists that chickens were once kept in it. Dogs and cats, yes. Chickens, never.

Money was always a problem for us. Four children within five years meant we all hit high school and university around the same time, and our letters home contained grateful thanks for small cheques and pleas for extra aid, accompanied by tales of small, proud economies we carried out. At Christmas, when my sister and I would stare pouting at yet another set of weekday panties, labelled Sunday through Saturday, or young Tom asked for a bicycle, Mom would always say, "But we gave you each other, dears." The "dog money" paid for many extras, such as my high school graduation dress, which I loathed since my mother made it out of black-and-blue striped nylon, while my classmates wore strapless pastel formals.

Mother's next idea was to sell crafts to the tourists who drove by on the highway bordering the West Arm. Dad's tours through the Kootenays, testing cattle for tuberculosis, took him to many small studios and Doukhobor homes that produced fine weavings and bowls and spoons carved from apple wood. We had nowhere to operate a craft shop, until Mother thought of buying the superstructure of the paddle wheeler *Naksookin*, tied up at the dock in Nelson, forlorn and abandoned after authorities deemed the vessel unsafe even for sea cadet use.

When we were teenagers, paddle wheelers still swanned their way gracefully up and down Kootenay Lake, sunlight glinting on the spray from the stern paddle wheel. It was a stupendous treat to be allowed to accompany Dad on the ship when he visited the small communities that peopled the lakeshore.

But relics were not yet valued, and restoration and upkeep were beyond the tax base and priorities of City Council, so Mother acquired the *Naksookin*, which was towed up the lake and beached below the house. The day I knew my mother had power was the day I watched hydro crews remove the electric lines along the highway so that the salvaged superstructure, containing the main saloon, two staterooms, and the captain's bridge with its wheel, could be swung ashore.

Although the paddle wheeler was converted into the visionary craft store, Mother was too busy with the animals to staff it, and her partner in the venture, Pat Galbraith, a housewife and neighbour, was too occupied with her young family. So the stern wheeler and the lot it stood on were sold to another friend for a ridiculously low price. "But she is such a nice lady," explained Mother when I returned, irate, from economics classes at UBC—a career in economics had now supplanted my hopes for a career in wildlife management—to learn about the steamboat sale.

She is there still, converted to an elegant summer home, in the exact spot my mother chose, her name given permanently to the bay in front of the main house, now surrounded by a subdivision. You can see her as you drive by on the highway about three miles from the bridge that replaced the ferry on the West Arm of Kootenay Lake.

As for the Blue J itself, it was up for sale, beautifully restored, when I last visited during the final summer of the twentieth century, returning for informal reunions with my high school classmates, the Class of '52. I walked up the grand staircase and through the familiar rooms and dreamed the dream of Coming Home. Maybe I'll buy it back. Who knows?

CHAPTER 6

The Class of '52

TRADE SECRET:
*Friendship is like a garden: it needs to
be cultivated with attention, watered with
regularity, and nurtured with affection.*
—Dora Sanders Carney

The idea of having a band reunion emerged when some of Nelson High School's Class of '52 were brunching on the Patons' porch during the Nelson Centennial celebrations in August 1997. Rachel and Angus had invited those of us who had turned up for the weekend or who still lived in the Kootenays to their home near Kaslo, British Columbia, and we started reminiscing about the Band and Mr. Cowan, our band teacher nearly 50 years before.

In a fluid, fast-paced world, for many of us in the Class of '52 our high school friendships have remained steadfast through the years. Nelson itself, Queen City of the Kootenays, has survived against all odds in a forgotten corner of British Columbia and our Kootenay heritage has glinted through our lives like the gold and silver ores in the granite mountains surrounding the lakeside city.

Classmates stay in touch. We were a close-knit group in our small high school, which offered a solid but bare-bones curriculum: reading, writing, arithmetic, science, home economics for the girls and industrial shop for the boys, and French taught by Miss McKay, with her distinct Scottish accent.

My siblings and I commuted from the Blue J by school bus, or by hitching rides home on the ferry if Jim "Iron Foot" Carney played soccer or Norah and I were in the school drama production of *Little Women*, where I played the role of plain Jo and Norah played pretty and talented Amy. If we were really stuck, we could always catch a lift on the tailgate of the garbage truck.

The Band was the heart of our high school experience. So it wasn't difficult to organize the Band reunion when we realized during the Centennial brunch on the Patons' porch how many of us had actually played in the Band. Jim had played trumpet. Connie Romano, Joan Stromstead, Rachel Johnson, Trudy Pentland, and I were on clarinet. Duffy Franklin and Don Laishley played trombone. Vince Borch was on French horn, and Ron Monty, Bill McIvor, and Ron Chandler on sax. Who played drums? Evie Reisterer, of course! We started making a list.

It was a perfect day. The sun glistened on the glacier across Kootenay Lake and magnified the shimmering waterfall that fell down the timbered slopes into the cleft between two mountains towering above the shoreline.

It had been a perfect weekend. I had ridden in an antique car in Nelson's Biggest Parade Ever as local girl and BC Senator, waving at the populace, which included many members of the Class of '52 cheering, gagging, and giving the Trudeau middle-finger salute as I passed by until I stuck out my tongue and waggled my fingers in my ears in a very unsenatorial manner.

We had ridden Streetcar No. 23, the very one that Mother had bought and moved across the lake to our animal farm. We had met some of the Class of '52 at Wait's News Stand (News Magazines Milkshakes) on Baker Street, where we used to congregate after school in the 1950s to order one milkshake to share and "pine floats," or water and toothpicks for the rest. At least, that is what Evie says. Evie is the nexus of the information network that keeps us in touch, reporting regularly on where we all are and who, alas, has died. Sigh! We've lost about nine of the Class so far.

Later we had all gathered for a Centennial picnic at Lakeside Park to visit and to hear Duffy and Angus play in the Nelson City Band. Duffy played trombone, just as he had in the Nelson High School Band. Angus, who was not technically a Class member but had married Rachel Johnson, who was, played tuba just as he did in the Yellowknife City Concert Band in the 1970s while Rachel and I both played clarinet, just as we had done in the Nelson High School Band. Then we were third clarinet. In Yellowknife, where the talent pool was smaller, we were upgraded to second clarinet.

While the Nelson City Band played, we took pictures of each other; Evie and Connie and Rachel and Linda Maddaford and Bev Lythgoe and Roseanne Zabawa. It is amazing how much we all look the same as we did in high school. I rarely remember any of my friends by their married names, even after forty-odd anniversaries of weddings to the same spouses.

It no longer matters what we do or have done with our lives; we either have done what we wanted to do or we haven't. We rarely discuss our children: they are either employed or not, in jail or not, famous or not. We are mainly important to each other.

As we sat on the grass, our former physics teacher, Earl Jorgensen, approached us and said that every time he saw me on television or heard me on radio discussing free trade or softwood lumber or saving lighthouses, all he could think of was how I had sung "They Can't Take That Away From Me" with the Kampus Kings, a jazz band organized by Jim and his friends, including Ron "Zoot" Chandler on tenor sax.

Mr. Jorgensen stood under the park's green canopy of trees as children splashed in the lake and families sunbathed on the beach and sang "They Can't Take That Away From Me" with his voice cracking a little on the last note.

We were Mr. Jorgensen's first class when, fresh out of UBC in the 1940s, he took the Kettle Valley railway train to his first job in this isolated former mining town, regional centre for West Kootenay. The Class of '52 had teased him mercilessly, hanging Bob Nuyens out the window and dropping huge rocks on the classroom floor; Mr. Jorgensen had ordered, "Put that down," and Jamie Tattrie did! Finally, a sorrowful Mr. Jorgensen informed us that we had convinced him that he lacked talent as a teacher and had no rapport with young people and therefore he was quitting—not just Nelson High School, but the teaching profession altogether.

We were stunned, stealing looks at each other, our heads down as we sat quietly at our desks. We knew that he and his wife Dorothy had just had a baby and times were always tough in the Kootenays. We took up a dime-and-quarter collection, bought a mug-and-spoon baby gift, and apologized. Mr. Jorgensen decided to stay.

One member of our Class, Roy Gates, went on to study advanced physics, work in the Canadian atomic energy industry, and join the prestigious Rand Corp. in the United States. We learned of his accomplishments when Roy attended our thirty-fifth reunion. The Class of '52 was always having reunions in a town where the reunion business was big and growing as mining ceased and government jobs were moved to Cranbrook and Kamloops. We had the twenty-fifth reunion in 1977, down in the old Rod and Gun Club, when we re-staged old scripts of "Teentime," the radio program that many of us had produced on the local radio station CKLN. My duties included marching into the studio and playing Beethoven's familiar "Fur Elise" on the piano when the featured Local Talent forgot to arrive on time.

We celebrated our thirty-fifth reunion in 1987 in the Eagles Hall above the drugstore where we once learned square dancing and the heel-toe polka at Junior Joymakers. At the reunion we danced the Chicken dance (I wondered what my cabinet colleagues would think if they saw me flapping my arms and wagging my bum). Joan Stromstead played the piano, as she always did, and Mike Halleran, encouraged by the applause, sang encore after encore until someone had to drag him off the stage. His sister Pat was ahead of us in high school. They were the other local Irish tribe across the lake; the Hallerans lived up Six Mile Creek with their turkeys, while Three Mile Creek flowed through the Carneys' rocky pastures.

Many of the Class members who organize these reunions stayed in Nelson and married each other, like George Trainer, who worked for the railway, and Evie Reisterer, who trained as a nurse. Evie used to send notes to George in his laundry when he was studying at the Catholic seminary. "He had to think about it," Evie said. Apparently he did. They have eight children and nineteen grandchildren and counting.

Some of us moved back after careers elsewhere, sometimes from Alberta, like the Patons and Duffy, a former RCMP officer who left the force to marry Flo, or moved back from the Coast, like music teacher Joan Stromstead and her husband Ian Horner. Ian is from nearby Rossland but can speak Nelsonspeak, which relates everyone and everything to Nelson. When I asked Ian why an electronics company had located in Nelson, he answered: "Because a Smithson married a Godfrey." Made perfect sense to me.

Others married each other and moved away but kept their home place in Nelson, like forestry executive Don Laishley, who married Mary Lou Harrison, who was a few years behind us in school. *"Another class reunion?"* says Don's secretary, organizing his schedule.

The most important guests for our Band reunion, of course, were our music teacher Don Cowan and his wife Joyce. We had also been Mr. Cowan's first class after he graduated from UBC.

Most of us had never had any music lessons before he tackled the job, using borrowed instruments in our school. I was an exception, having taken piano lessons from Mrs. Foster on her Chickering baby grand in her small apartment above the Capitol Theatre and playing in the West Kootenay music festivals that nurtured our ill-founded fantasies of becoming concert pianists.

We gathered in our Band room in the old red-brick high school, "up the hill" under the shadow of Silver King Mountain, usually after class, to practise with our assorted instruments. Our choices of instrument were dictated largely by what was available. But ah! The joys of performance! We played for school assemblies. We played in Nelson's numerous street parades, trying to avoid the old streetcar tracks and cracked pavement. We played marches and old standards—whatever sheet music Mr. Cowan could purloin.

Our greatest thrill, however, was playing out-of-town trips, billeted with local students, in exotic locales such as Fernie, Creston, Grand Forks, Salmo, Christina Lake, Nelway, and even Trail, the smelter town. We wore white shirts, peaked caps, and blue gabardine skirts or pants. The Kampus Kings were a dance band that provided music for our high school socials and occasionally at the Playmore Dance Hall near Slocan Junction, where big bands like Claude Thornhill played if their managers were desperate for a gig.

On Friday nights in our lakeside home we listened to jazz jockey Bob Smith's program "Hot Air" on CBC radio, the cool sounds of Zoot Sims and Stan Getz and Chet Baker floating on the quiet mountain air. Jim once wrote Bob Smith a fan letter. Tickled by the thought of teenagers in the far-off Kootenays tuned in to his show, Bob sometimes closed with: "God bless jazz fans everywhere, and especially the Carney twins in Nelson." Once he had jazz icon Woody Herman close the show with a tribute to the Carney twins in the Kootenays, although

85

we doubted Woody knew where the Kootenays were. Yet years later when Jim was a CBC television producer shooting a program in New York, he met Herman in a jazz club. "Carney, Carney," mused our musical hero. "Weren't you the kid in the Kootenays?"

Jim eventually produced a local jazz show on CKLN called "Jazz with Jim." When he couldn't get in from his summer mining job in Salmo, the show became "Progressions with Pat." Occasionally it became "Jazz Progressions" if we both showed up at the studio. The highlights were the interviews Jim did with touring musicians, such as Louis Armstrong as he sipped soup in the dining room of the old Hume Hotel, now the Heritage. Jim and I were often together and even then, as a teenager, I marvelled at the thoughtful way the Greatest of the Greats treated us kids—green, innocent, ignorant of the world beyond the black spruce-clad mountains cradling our narrow valley.

Sometimes the musicians invited us to Vancouver to hear their bands. Jim and I would climb on the Greyhound bus for the 12-hour trip over the Cascades to the Big Smoke, staying with our city cousins and turning up at the nightclub clutching our complimentary tickets. Despite being underage, we were never turned away. We would be seated at a ringside table, admonished not to order the ginger ale—it was too expensive for our finances—and left to enjoy the music. Sometimes musicians like Harry Carney (no relation), the celebrated sax player, came to sit out a set with us as we sipped our water.

We made that bus trip down to the coast when Duke Ellington came to town, meeting Bob Smith at his studio in the old Hotel Vancouver. We walked across the street to the Hotel Devonshire in the rain to meet the band. Stick-thin, I wore my shiny, paddy-green raincoat and hat while my equally stylish twin brother wore his baggy strides and bomber jacket. It never occurred to us to be shy.

The hotel suite door was opened by—wow!—Ol' Sweet Pea himself, Billy Strayhorn. The famous arranger of "Take the A Train" and "Lush Life" and other Ellington classics was wearing baby-blue-coloured jeans, his brown body bare from the waist up. He was so small, so cute, I just wanted to pick him up. Drummer Louis Bellson was making spaghetti in the suite's kitchen. The musicians discussed their music with us as earnestly as if we were critics for the jazz publication

Downbeat. Jim actually played his trumpet with The Duke on the same stage! He was aged 16 or 17 at the time.

This was the world Don Cowan opened to a couple of kids in the Kootenays. But we weren't the only ones enriched by our music teacher. About 48 former students answered our letters, drafted by Trudy Pentland, Bev Lythgoe, and myself. "Well, we just can't help it," we wrote. "Another reunion is in the works, this time for all Nelson High School Band members (and choir members) who were Don Cowan students and, of course, the Kampus Kings. Don and Joyce Cowan are now living in Victoria and his health is what you would expect since we were his first—and probably his worst—class as a young teacher fresh out of school. Any costs will be minimal for tea and cookies, but bring music, mementos, and memories."

On the night of Saturday, February 21, 1998, we all gathered at the home of Trudy and her husband George Friesen for a buffet supper and practice session. Unfortunately, Trudy had broken her leg at the last minute. She sat in state in her chair while the girls' choir practised "Blue Moon" under the guidance of choirmaster Len Lythgoe, Bev's older brother.

I was assigned second soprano, insisting I was an alto until someone showed me a clipping from the *Nelson Daily News* in 1949 and there, among the choir names, it said Pat Carney, second soprano. Most of us had never sung anything much in the past 50 years but it was amazing how, after about an hour of rehearsal, we all came together, feeling for the notes as we sang our parts.

We listened to a tape of Shelagh Rogers' CBC radio program that dedicated "Anniversary March" to Don and Joyce Cowan. Trudy had arranged that. Radio had played a big part in our teenage lives.

The next day we showed up at Spencer Castle, a beautifully restored Victorian residence and our reunion site. Tenor sax player Bill McIvor had hauled over a piano in his station wagon. "To think you kids are doing this," marvelled Don Cowan, who still played in the Navy Band at age 78. We kids, of course, were all in our sixties by now.

Don has the same open face and curly hair he had at age 28, when he and his 21-year-old bride Joyce arrived in Nelson 50 years earlier, staying at first in the old motel across the lake. "We were so naive that when we heard two men in the next room say they had to finish a couple of cases by morning we thought they were lawyers," he told us.

Mr. Jorgensen also attended, wearing his blue-and-white Nelson High School beanie cap. His name was on the Class of '52 mailing list and he had been invited inadvertently. "I know I'm not supposed to be here but Dorothy and I were in the neighbourhood," he confessed happily.

There were pictures, including one of Jim playing his trumpet with Duke Ellington, and snippets from the mimeographed sheets that our grad class had produced. Our school was too poor to produce a yearbook more than once every three years. Jim's tribute read: "This earnest young chemistry student was missing a compound he brewed, dropped a match in a phial, and after a while, a trumpet came out and blewed." No one claimed authorship.

There was no set program. The girls' choir arranged itself on the stairs of the Castle's living room, as elegant as any concert hall with its panelled walls and stained-glass windows, and sang "Blue Moon" from photocopies of our original song sheets.

How hard we had worked! What joy the music had brought us all! How amazed our spouses were, at least those who had not sneaked out, like George, for a cigarette on the patio! Some of the men formed a barbershop quartet and sang "When You Wore a Tulip."

"You don't know what you did for us," Ron Monty informed the Cowans. He recounted how, as a young kid, he had listened to the new music teacher play "Valse Pamela" on his saxophone at the June 1949 Nelson Junior High School graduation and thought, "I want to be a music teacher too." Ron then put his saxophone to his lips and played "Valse Pamela," a sentimental, syrupy piece full of voluptuous, fruity trills that is now out of print, but when he played it we were all enthralled. Several Band members, like Len Lythgoe and piano player Tom Pagdin, had also gone on to become music teachers.

Ron Chandler, who had lived with my family to save himself the long school bus trip from Balfour, noted: "You showed us that we could still amount to something even if we got only 52 per cent in chemistry," and then he burst into tears. The Band experience had led to his eventual career as Associate Dean of Music at the University of Toronto's Faculty of Music. Ron's graduating tribute read: "Goosey goosey gander, whither do you rush? Why, out to Balfour on a yellow bus. There I met a sax man who blew a clarinet, chasing poor fishies with a great big net."

Duffy admitted that he took Band because he needed three credits and his grad tribute explained why: "Shine on Mr. Moon up in the sky, shine bright tonight on my love and I, I sure the heck am handsome though I may not be so bright and I know I'll get some loving when I get the car tonight."

Pat Halleran had actually earned a living for a while as a torch singer in Edmonton. She sat down at the piano and belted out "Can't Help Loving That Man" while Mr. Cowan listened, eyes shining, entranced. Pat and Ron Monty recounted how they had once played a gig in New Denver in the Slocan Valley and been compensated with homemade vodka.

Rachel and I gave a dual account of our participation in the Yellowknife City Concert Band during the 1970s, when our clarinets' mouthpieces froze to our lips as we played in the Caribou Carnival parade in March while opal-coloured ice crystals fell from blue skies. We also described how we played on the back of Eddie Grueben's gravel truck in Tuktoyaktuk on the shores of the Arctic Ocean to drum up business for the concert that night in the local high school. "Jesus Christ, Superstar" was our big number, which was sure to draw gasps from audiences who had probably never seen instruments except guitars and the odd accordion.

For our finale, we sang a toast to the tune of a Class of '52 favourite, usually sung with kerchiefs over our heads, "Sun, Sun, Sunflower Seeds." It went:

We're the kids from Cowan's Band
Come to honour a man that's grand
You only taught us three short years
You were still wet behind the ears
You tried to teach us to sing a scale
And blow a horn without a "wail"
Often we were way off key
You had our parents' sympathy
Now we're old and grey and know
Just how hard you worked to show
Us to listen and appreciate
Music and rhythm we could create . . . SO . . .

Health and happiness to you
May your worries all be few
Fill your glasses everyone
And toast our Maestro Don! (Three cheers!)

I suspect the author was Evie.

Then we all went over to Macaroni's Grill for food and wine and discussed plans for the next reunion. Four days later, in Calgary, when the love of my life Paul White finally proposed after 45 years, I played "Blue Moon" on a clarinet at three o'clock in the morning. He had given me the clarinet as an engagement present.

When we were married that September, Rachel and Angus represented the Class of '52, bringing with them a round-robin letter written by Class members at a barbecue for Jamie Tattrie, who was back in town with his wife Evelyn. They also brought an Irish Blessing that our Anglican priest used to conclude our wedding ceremony:

May there always be work for your hand to do
May your purse always hold a coin or two
May the sun always shine on your windowpane
May a rainbow be certain to follow each rain
May the hand of a friend always be near you
May God fill your hearts with gladness to cheer you

Vintage Class of '52!

A year later, in 1999, some of us returned to the Kootenays for the wedding of the Patons' daughter Katherine. Since the little church couldn't hold all the guests, some of us stood outside. Then a thunderstorm knocked out the power during the reception at a local restaurant, so we had to use buckets of water to flush the toilets and the bridal toasts were delayed. The members of the Class of '52 sat at the same table and admired each other's spiffy clothes and planned another dinner at the restaurant, partly owned by '52 classmate Joy McEwan, since it could probably use the business.

One evening a group of us gathered at the Trainors' lakeside place to drink wine and trade news and meet my husband Paul. He had first seen me when I was 18 years old, working as a waitress at the Lodge on

Kootenay Bay, carefully making banana splits without the bananas. Paul was then on his way back to UBC after working in the mine at Kimberly in East Kootenay. He plays a mean trumpet—not bad credentials for a Class spouse.

As we went to bed in the cabin at the edge of the lake, near the beach chair where George likes to sit, his binoculars trained on the nudist beach at nearby Red Sands where we had held teenaged corn roasts in our bathing suits, Paul observed: "Your Class of '52 is very special. I've never seen anything like the deep bonds you have for each other after all these years."

"Hmmph," I said, busy with my thoughts. Our fiftieth anniversary is coming up in 2002 and we should start planning. Maybe a reunion in 2001 to plan for the big Five-O. What about an August corn roast on Laishley's beach? At least we won't have to steal the corn this time.

CHAPTER 7

Journalism

T R A D E   S E C R E T:
To be a good reporter,
PICK UP THE PHONE
and ask the tough questions.
Never take no for an answer.
—Newsman Paddy Sherman

My siblings and I always knew that if we couldn't get a real job, we could always write. This innocent assumption came from our mother, who wrote stories, articles, poems, and once, in her youth, an advice-to-the-lovelorn column, and whose family included reporters, authors, editors, artists, and even publishers. My father, however, believed that a real job meant being a doctor, lawyer, teacher, accountant, nurse, or some other profession that paid regularly. So, our youthful thinking went: while we were becoming doctors, lawyers, teachers, and so on, we would learn the trade and pay our way by writing.

Alas. All four of us spent much of our careers in journalism or related fields, while the goal of a Real Job faded. I was a newspaper reporter and columnist for 15 years, Jim left newspaper work for a life-long career in television and documentary filmmaking, and Norah wrote radio commercials and worked in advertising, while the areas left for the youngest, Tom, were the Canadian Press wire service and public relations.

I don't know whether the talent is in the genes, but even my son John Patrick inherited the knack from both his mother and his father, a well-respected newsman. "How do you actually write?" he asked me when he was 18 years old. We were in Kenya, where Jim was working for the United Nations, and we were watching crocodiles making their way up a muddy river in a game park.

"Think rolling and recording, like making a videotape," I said. "Where are you? What do you see? Hear?" We watched two young Kenyan girls moving through the forest, like tropical birds in their yellow kerchiefs and red skirts, making birdlike calls: "Jambo, jambo!" I continued: "What do you feel on your skin? For instance, what are those two crocodiles doing now?" JP watched the two reptiles move through the clay-coloured water, propelling themselves with their tails. "They're sculling," he said. "You've got it," I said, satisfied. He has a Real Job, as a pilot, but if he was ever laid off, thinks Mom, he can't milk cows or plant potatoes but at least he has the tools to learn the writing craft. His sister, Jane, regularly wrote for local newspapers in the clear, practical style of her father during her years as an elected regional politician.

Jim's and my first foray into journalism was through radio. When we were about 15 or 16, the announcer-manager of Nelson's local radio station CKLN failed to show up for work during the Christmas season and the owners asked Mother to fill in because of her advertising experience. This gave Jim and me the run of the station, playing records and writing commercials. My first effort was: "The north winds doth blow and we shall have snow, so order your heating oil from Blah Blah Fuel Co. now." Mother thought it was brilliant.

When, at age 17, Jim and I took the Greyhound bus to enrol at the University of British Columbia as first-year students, we joined RADSOC, the campus radio club. Years later, when I was appointed to the board of directors of Rogers Media Inc., which operates the radio, television, and publication assets of the communications giant, I proudly told Ted Rogers of my hands-on experience. He had the grace to laugh.

At UBC Jim studied music and physics before majoring in English and political science, and I discovered the fascinating world of economics, and gave up my plans to be a veterinarian like Dad.

But at UBC, the action revolved around *The Ubyssey*, the sassy, iconoclastic student paper that liked to think it was the best university paper in Canada, and it probably was. Its alumni included famed poet Earle Birney, future Prime Minister John Turner, legendary humorist Eric Nicol, Lister Sinclair and Pierre Berton, night beat columnist Jack Wasserman, Toronto news veterans Ron Haggart and Val Sears, and many others. *The Ubyssey* was published in the basement of Brock

Hall, the student union building. I can still recall the soaked-in-the-walls smell of ancient coffee, mouldy cheese sandwiches, sweaty running shoes, and the faint aftertaste of stale beer. I wanted badly to join, but I was too shy to seek acceptance from the awesome editors of this campus institution by myself.

In a typical twin transaction, Jim and I stood outside *The Ubyssey's* door, trading favours. The final agreement was that Jim would join the student paper with me if I would go downtown—the fearsome world outside the UBC stone gates—to help him choose a pair of strides, those baggy, chain-decorated pants popular in the 1950s that, when accessorized with a scalped crew cut, turned young men into premature versions of Homer Simpson of television's "The Simpsons."

We pushed open the door, and entered the rest of our lives. Like most "pubsters," our studies were secondary, although Jim's trumpet-playing with the campus jazz band commanded equal time for him. He joined the sports department, John Turner's former arena, and I joined the news staff, eventually graduating to writing a column about campus politics called the "Gripe Vine." I collected the information by playing blackjack upstairs in the Alma Mater Society offices with campus politicians Ron Bray, Ron Longstaffe, Jacques Barbeau, Bob Hutchison, and other future legal beagles.

Our *Ubyssey* colleagues included some of the most famous names in contemporary Canadian journalism. My first editor was Joe Schlesinger, the future cosmopolitan CBC foreign correspondent who had escaped from Czechoslovakia and Nazi persecution and entered UBC. I was working at the copy desk with him when the radio announced that Stalin died. "This will change our world," Joe informed me, an impressionable teenager. Joe made great cabbage rolls, eking out our student budgets. He was a kind and helpful mentor, who later worked as a celebrated journalist in both North America and Europe, including for the European edition of the *New York Herald Tribune* in Paris, before returning to Canada and the CBC. When Joe received an honorary degree from UBC in 1992, he told the students that working for *The Ubyssey* had taught him that news could be fun. Until then, he said, news to him had to be about death and disaster and the clashing of armies, the disappearance of his family during the Holocaust, and the dispirited camps of displaced persons.

The student paper, with its reports on student pranks—hoisting a VW Beetle up the university flag pole, anti-pubster engineering students chaining *Ubyssey* columnist Allan Fotheringham to Birks Clock at Georgia and Granville streets, re-enacting Lady Godiva's nude ride on horseback—showed the sunshine potential of journalism. I like to think that Schlesinger's *Ubyssey* experiences contributed to the wry humour he displays in his television reports.

Fotheringham was my second *Ubyssey* editor, a curly-haired skirt-chaser from Chilliwack High School in the Fraser Valley, whose first column for the high school paper *Tatler* was about students' complaints about the cafeteria food, and who has been dining out on scurrilous stories about Canadians and Canada ever since—for the last 25 years from the vantage point of *Maclean's* back page.

We have remained lifelong friends, although sometimes we wonder why. At UBC I was so shy that if he boarded the bus I got off at the next stop, fearful that the Great Editor might actually speak to me. He was taking religious studies and wrote many of his editorials in a biblical style that I greatly admired. Once, when he asked me to come down to complete a CBC interview plugging his new book because he had to leave the show early, he told listeners: "Pat and I have been friends so long we are stuck with each other." Then he exited, leaving the stunned CBC interviewer mute.

Other pubsters included television personality Helen Hutchinson, who defeated me to claim the Canadian Women's Press Club scholarship with a submission of poetry, an unlikely pubster talent, although I won the coveted prize the next year at age 19. The most memorable result was my expulsion from the Georgia Pub, a student hangout, when I was discovered to be underage, while my twin brother cheerfully raised his beer glass to me and remained at the table as I was hustled out.

Peter Worthington of the *Toronto Sun* was also a pubster, although I knew him better when he worked at the Vancouver *Province* writing cut lines for photographs. A pubster favourite was cute, blond Alexander (Sandy) Ross, who wore white shoes and played rude songs on his guitar. A great magazine writer and editor, he once consoled me on an unsuccessful magazine piece I had written: "Trying to change your writing style is like trying to change your soul." (Editors should take note.)

Sunny-tempered Sandy had a boundless capacity for friendship. He would vanish for years and then reappear and take over your life. Once, during a conference in Ottawa, he did just that, showing up in my MP's office and ordering my adoring staff to do his bidding, and then vanishing again. His premature death from a stroke in his mid-fifties was treated as a disaster by his family and friends.

Another *Ubyssey* editor was Peter Sypnowich, a left-leaning student who took me on my first real grown-up date—steak, salad, and red wine in a downtown restaurant, rather than the communal pubster spaghetti supper—and who was the first man to break my heart. To maximize the number of staffers who could attend a Canadian University Press conference in Edmonton, we cashed in the two allocated tickets and hitch-hiked to Nelson to pick up my family's car and continue to Edmonton. On the way back, Syp drove off the mountain road at an icy corner in the Kootenays, leaving me in hospital with a broken nose, while he took up with another pubster, Marci, whom he later married. But first he returned to Nelson and our Blue J home to explain events to our patient parents. The accident forced me to drop some university courses and I completed my third year with a minimum of credits in political science and economics. This led me to make the fateful decision to drop out of UBC and accept a job offer with the *Province*.

Jim and I were already serving as campus stringers for the paper, Jim for the sports pages and myself for the news pages. We were paid 25 cents a column inch for our efforts but we also had the opportunity of summer jobs. We were sharing a basement suite off campus and those small cheques were vital to us. At one point in our student life, Jim and I had literally one nickel between us.

As stringers, we phoned our stories in to the rewrite desk. The rewrite chief, Gordon Dickson, told me: "Speak up or shut up." I was enchanted by his direct style, and in 1956, when I turned 21, I married him. Gordon, an RCAF veteran, was 15 years my senior. Jim, working for CBC in Prince Rupert, did not attend the wedding. It was the first time we had ever been separated for any period of time.

It was a newspaper wedding, held in St. Anselm's Anglican Church on campus, which I still attend when in Vancouver. The young minister was understandably nervous, since many of the guests had spent the afternoon in the beer parlour and were obviously drunk. My father bought a pink-and-white Ford station wagon to drive the bride to the church, and subsequently drove it for 16 years. My mother, taking anti-rabies shots for an animal bite, draped her swollen belly in a blue shift and laboured out of the car.

The bride wore a $25 white cotton pique dress, all I could afford, and carried white daisies, which I loathe to this day. I was attended by my college roommate, Margie McNeill, who has tactfully forgotten this fact; my sister Norah, who ran off during the reception with the best man, Hugh Watson, with whom I shared a mutual aversion; and the groom's seven-year-old daughter Jane. I often think that I decided to marry Gordon when Jane, then aged six, walked into the *Province* city room on her first day of school. I looked at this confident little girl, with two missing front teeth, green eyes, and black, bobbed hair, and decided she needed a mother. In fact, I needed her; *she* read me *Winnie the Pooh*.

The *Province* editor, famed war correspondent Ross Munro, announced that he would bend the rule that barred married couples from working together in the newsroom, a decision he had cause to regret when a few months later Gord and best buddy Hugh Watson, loaded to the gills, made obscene phone calls to columnist Jean Howarth and threw the rewrite desk typewriters out the city room windows. I was still wearing my blue bridal negligee when I stood at the top of the stairs in our West End apartment building and watched reporter Bob Reguly, an ex-paratrooper, carry an inebriated Gordon over his shoulders up the steps. I was shocked speechless. Gord and Hugh were suspended without pay for a week.

Boys would be boys, but girls could only be girls in the newsrooms of the mid-fifties. Like most beginners, I was assigned to write obituaries, an experience I used later in life to write the obit of my close cousin Betty O'Keefe, who died of cancer, and my ex-husband Gordon, who died of an alcohol-related gastric condition. Once I mastered writing obits, my future was framed by the social pages, which were ruled by the iron-gloved and gloriously hatted editor Pat Wallace.

The only woman on city-side was Aileen Campbell, now a neighbour on Saturna Island, who sat in the newsroom lobby for days before city editor Bruce Larsen, the 29-year-old boy wonder, eventually hired her. There was also a woman sportswriter, Nancy Horsman; what was the world coming to!

When I finally argued my way into the city room and the rewrite desk, Larsen fired me because I couldn't spell. I bought a copy of a book called *Six Minutes a Day to Perfect Spelling* and won my job back. When I became Minister of International Trade in the Mulroney government in 1986, my department circulated a memo warning that Minister Carney wouldn't tolerate poor spelling and grammatical errors.

City editor Larsen wouldn't assign me to the "cop shop" or graveyard shift because I was a wife and mother. To discourage me, he sent me out to collect a picture of a four-year-old traffic victim from the grieving parents. But I had the luck to be assigned to the typewriter next to a wiry Brit reporter, Paddy Sherman, who taught me the secret of success: "Pick up the phone and ask the tough questions. Never take no for an answer."

Paddy, who refused to allow his four children to enter the newspaper business, is an accomplished alpine climber; he eventually scaled the corporate cliffs to become president of Southam Inc. and chairman of Pacific Press Ltd., which owned the *Province* and the *Vancouver Sun*. I served on his Pacific Press Ltd. board of directors until Southam Inc. closed it down.

The rewrite desk man was responsible for taking the facts, phoned in by a leg man on the scene, and transforming them into terse news style, with the age-old formula: key facts in the first paragraph, other important facts in the second, and then further details in the rest of the story, long or short.

Hmm. My first major rewrite job involved a train wreck in the Fraser Valley, causing fatalities. I wrote: *Seven people were killed today when a transcontinental train jumped the track near Boston Bar in the Fraser Valley.*

But then I thought: don't use a passive voice when an active one will serve. So I rewrote: *A transcontinental train jumped the track near Boston Bar in the Fraser Valley earlier today, killing seven people and . . .*

But how did I know for certain it had jumped the track? So I re-rewrote: *Investigators are searching for the cause of a train wreck which killed seven people near Boston Bar earlier today . . .* It took me two hours to write the story before an impatient city editor tore the copy out of my hands.

I also learned to spell people's names correctly and, when I was transferred to the composing room, to read type upside down while the newspaper was being "put to bed" or readied for printing. This talent has proven very useful, since it enables me to read briefing notes on desks of business executives and prime ministers without their being aware of it.

I learned that people freeze up when you take out a pen and a notepad, but if you put your pencil down, they will give you that sought-for quotation or information, thinking you are not recording it. The trick is to then scribble the information in your notebook while they are saying something entirely innocuous. Tape recorders are an entirely different matter, but since I usually erased when I wanted to record I left them alone. Barry Broadfoot was one of the first journalists to use the tape recorder to allow Canadians to tell their own stories in their own way, which he then edited to produce a masterful series of books on the Canadian experience during the Depression, World War II, and peacetime.

The best advice I received came from Louis Rasminsky, then Governor of the Bank of Canada. When I confessed that my tape machine didn't work and my arthritic fingers wouldn't hold a pencil, he fixed me with his urbane gaze and said: "If you ask your questions in a logical sequence and I answer them in a logical manner, you will remember the information." It worked.

It was a grand time to be a newsman. There was great competition between the two leading newspapers, the *Vancouver Sun* and the *Province*, and to a lesser extent the *News Herald*, Pierre Berton's alma mater. Former news reporters Ian Macdonald and Betty O'Keefe (no relation), in their book *The Mulligan Affair*, record that newspapers played a far bigger role in their communities than they do now. Black-and-white television was often "snowed out."

"The two big dailies ruled the roost in a rash, brash, colourful and controversial way,"[1] report Macdonald and O'Keefe, who were both on the scene. *The Mulligan Affair*, about an inquiry into alleged graft and corruption in the Vancouver police force under Police Chief Walter Mulligan in 1955, revealed Vancouver as Sin City, where bootlegging and bookmaking were rampant. The Mulligan inquiry made an ex-*Sun* reporter, Jack Webster, famous when he went on radio station CJOR every night to read, in his oatmeal accent, from his shorthand notes on the more lurid testimony, keeping his audience glued to the radio for hours on end.

Cab drivers delivered a bottle of rye for a modest markup. Gambling and hooking were ignored by police, and some policemen served as doormen for bookie joints. In defiance of anti-liquor laws, we snuck lemon gin and rye in brown bags into our favourite clubs, nightspots, and Chinese restaurants. Dal Richards and his big band ruled the roost at the top of Hotel Vancouver.

When our 7:00 a.m. shift ended at 2:00 p.m., we gathered in the Commercial Hotel pub across the street where beer was 10 cents a glass and unaccompanied men and women had to drink in separate beer parlours. There was usually crime reporter Eddie Moyer, if he hadn't gambled away all his money in the Snake Room adjacent to the city room; sports writers Nancy Horsman and Don Brown; marine editor Norman Hacking; sometimes librarian Bruce Ramsey; and rarely desk man Charlie King, whom we all knew shouldn't drink because his father was the minister at St. Paul's Anglican Church in the West End, although this constraint didn't seem to bother him when he later moved to the *Ottawa Citizen*.

The alcoholic aura that permeated the newspaper scene was something I had never experienced before. In our home, drinking was confined to the one ounce of carefully measured gin, splashed with bitters, which our father enjoyed, along with the odd beer shared with our mother. His years in China, plus old John Joseph's thirst for booze, shaped Father's attitude towards drinking. During our nickel-and-dime college years, Jim and I had no money for liquor, with the exception of the odd beer.

I was so naive that when Gordon and I attended the opening of the Polynesian restaurant Trader Vic's, I didn't realize the drinks with the pretty flowers contained alcohol. So I chose a blue drink with a floating gardenia and drank it like fruit juice. Delicious. Then I snagged another one from a passing waiter. Umm, good.

I had four gardenias pinned to my suit jacket before I headed for the washroom, feeling funny. Suddenly the room swirled. What was that? Was I pregnant? I clung to the counter. Finally I upchucked the blue drinks and swayed out into the dining room to find my husband, who unkindly informed me that I was drunk. Well, he would know. I've never drunk a floating flower concoction since.

The bane of my existence, shared by his editors, was my husband's best friend and drinking companion Hugh Watson, a cop shop and later sports writer. After his suspension with Gordon, Hugh started his own Tong War in nearby Chinatown by smashing in the windows of Chinese restaurants because of some imagined slight.

When sports editor Erwin Swangard took away his byline—the worst fate that could befall a reporter, other than the annihilation of one's precious copy by an editor—Hughie wrote a story in which the first letters of each paragraph spelled out BY HUGH WATSON.

His most delicious scam, in my mind, was his creation of a fictitious Howe Sound Basketball League, involving the tidewater communities north of Vancouver. Reports on the league's exciting games regularly appeared on the sports pages and he even asked Swangard to award the cup to the winner at the league's final banquet. Swangard, he planned, would drive to a dark, rainy Deep Cove to find no basketball league and no dinner. But someone exposed the hoax.

Hughie disliked me because I had won the heart of his drinking buddy and often beat him at blackjack, which wasn't hard, given his often-inebriated condition. Years later Jack Webster came for dinner and said he had been at a party for Hugh Watson that afternoon. "His wake, I hope," I snapped. And it was.

Gordon and I had both returned to UBC, working and studying on a full-time/part-time basis. Gordon finished his law degree after completing his pre-law requirements in one term, and I completed my economics and political science bachelor of arts program, graduating in 1960. Working and studying and raising our daughter Jane, we lived in a haze of fatigue and exam tension.

But it was also during this time that I found my own Home Place. In 1957 I had bought my first property on Saturna Island, arriving with a bunch of mostly hungover journalists who flew in via a single-engined Otter arranged by Jean Howarth. I bought the last best lot for $100 down on $980 and paid for it over nine years. My parents followed in 1961 because they couldn't agree where to be buried; my mother refused to be buried beside the Old Man (John Joseph Carney) in the Catholic cemetery near Kelowna, so they settled on Saturna because I was already there.

I asked for a transfer to the business pages, a bold move since business news was an all-male preserve, and was viewed with disdain by city-side reporters. But my newspaper career took off when a mentor, assistant publisher A.R. Williams, asked *Province* business editor Bill Ryan why I was working in the composing room considering that I had an economics degree. Bill's response was to promote me to business columnist, the first Canadian woman to write a regular business column for a metropolitan daily.

Given the number of women business writers and editors today, it is hard to imagine how novel a woman business columnist was in the 1960s. The fact is that few people knew that Pat Carney was a woman until the column was established and the editors featured my photograph at the top.

I later learned that behind the byline J.K. Edmonds in the *Financial Post* was Jean Edmonds, who became one of the first senior women bureaucrats in Ottawa, where our careers would again entwine. Several years later, when I had switched to the *Vancouver Sun*, I began a lifelong close friendship with Barbara McDougall, who wrote for the business pages before becoming a financial analyst and politician. But when I started, I was breaking new ground.

I loved the *Province*, but I ran into the invisible Glass Ceiling for women. I noticed that several bright young male reporters were obviously being groomed for editorial and management posts, while I was passed over. Finally, in 1963, I approached publisher Fred Auger to discuss my prospects. They were obviously dim. When Auger asked me why I wanted to move to management training, I looked out his office window at the small urban park below and blurted: "Because I don't want to become the Old Lady of Victory Square."

Auger looked at me kindly and said: "We all have to face the aging process, Pat." I was only 28 years old!

Toronto *Telegram* publisher John Bassett had offered me a job at twice my *Province* salary. My brother Jim had moved to CBC Toronto in 1963 and worked with Patrick Watson, Doug Leiterman, Laurier LaPierre, Beryl Fox, and other television legends on shows like *This Hour Has Seven Days*. But I was a booted-and-spurred Westerner, and moving to Toronto was not an option for my lawyer husband.

That left the *Vancouver Sun*, the larger newspaper. Although I knew that publisher Stu Keate was interested in me, I also knew that the *Sun* had a no-raiding agreement with the *Province*. To overcome this problem, I sent Keate two daily horoscopes: my Gemini one, which indicated it was time for a change, and his Libra, which suggested new challenges were on his horizon. He responded with an offer, and in 1964 I crossed the street to the Sun Tower.

The *Sun*, then as now, was famous for feuds, intrigue, infighting, and vengeful editors and reporters. Erwin Swangard had moved from the *Province* to become the managing editor. He was known in the city room, not affectionately, as The Hun. *Sun* columnist Denny Boyd tells how his four-year-old daughter asked Denny on meeting Swangard in the city room: "Is that your master?"

The Hun met me at the door of the city room and took me upstairs to a small office in the tower. "This is your desk," he said. "The Ladies' Room is around the corner. The cafeteria is upstairs. I never want to see you in any other part of the building." I sputtered about access to wire services, the business desk, and editor Bill Fletcher. But then I realized that he was trying to keep me out of the newsroom crossfire.

What I didn't realize was that after nine years of marriage, I was unexpectedly pregnant. A woman business columnist was bad enough; a pregnant WBC was reprehensible. "Pat's little dividend," teased the cop shop reporters when our son John Patrick arrived two weeks early. I was back at work within five weeks, covering the opening of a hydro dam, and never missed a deadline for the *Canadian Lumberman*, a trade magazine I freelanced for.

When both the *Province* and the *Sun* moved to new Granville Street premises built by Pacific Press, which owned both papers, the columnists were crammed into one small, windowless office at the entrance to the newsroom, sharing desks. We figured out there was no room for Paul St. Pierre, who wrote his famous Cariboo stories, so we moved his files into the elevator lobby. Paul never said a word. He took his files and his work home, an arrangement we envied. Bob Hunter, our resident hippie, didn't bother with offices.

My colleagues were among the best in the business. Each afternoon gossip columnist Jack Wasserman thumbed through the pile of possible items on his desk, phoned in or left by colleagues, and picked up the phone to check them out. When the stack shrank to only one or two usable items, he put on his trench coat and hit the nightclubs to dig up his own news.

He married Fran Gregory, a brassy blonde American singer whom he had met on his rounds. Gordon and I were invited to dinner, but the kid from the Kootenays and the American showgirl had little to discuss. Admired and respected, when Wass dropped dead in the middle of a speech, felled by a stroke, his audience thought it was part of his act.

Radio and television personality Jack Webster had left the *Sun* when I joined, but Gordon was his lawyer, and we liked Jack and his wife Margaret, tough Scots who spent years searching for their first child, who had been given up for adoption before they married. Their reunion with Joan was probably the happiest day of their lives. They were equally proud of Jack, Jenny, and Linda.

Jack was a frequent guest at our family dinner table, thrilling our children with horrific cop shop stories of murder and mayhem and challenging them to his favourite drill: "What are the four words in the English language which end in 'dous'?"[2] Professionally, he exemplified thoroughness, accuracy, and ruthless honesty, while privately he was insecure, vulnerable, and opinionated. After Margaret died, he became briefly entranced with a younger woman, but when she did not return his feelings he remained a lonely bachelor.

After our spouses died or divorced, Jack and I remained close friends, leading to much speculation about our relationship. Once, at our friend Pierrette Luca's dinner table, another guest asked Jack whether we were having an affair. "Yes," he barked. Later I admonished him. "You know that is not true," I scolded. "Gives them something to talk about," he replied.

In fact, when I was a young reporter covering the Press Gallery in Victoria, Jack took care to walk me to my hotel room door after late-night gossip and drinking sessions with politicians and reporters, then return to the party to protect my reputation, which was always under scrutiny by those uncomfortable with a woman in their world.

When Wasserman died, Denny Boyd took over his *Sun* column. Once, after I was divorced, Denny asked me out on a date and when he took me back to my door he asked when he could see me again. I silently reflected: there was the CIDA series in the Caribbean to do, a trip to Ottawa for the Budget, the tour of the northern oil fields. When I wrote, I submerged myself in my world and never came up for air until the work was finished. "In about two months," I said innocently.

"Huh?" Denny responded. He never asked me out again.

Penny Wise, aka Evelyn Caldwell, wrote the enormously popular shopping column and could mobilize thousands of people on a consumer issue. She came to work each day chanting "Only 635 (or 634, 633, etc.) more columns to write until I retire," an attitude that affected my own decision to leave journalism a few years later. I didn't want to view my own column as Penny Wise viewed hers.

When I first met Barbara McDougall, she was married to a charming, alcoholic architect while I was married to a brilliant, alcoholic lawyer, so we had that in common as well as our business writing careers. Barbara and I both swam at the YWCA, where her mile-long stint outdid my half-mile effort. Her subsequent cabinet service doubled mine, too, although we both spent about the same number of years in the House of Commons.

My longtime office roommate, Allan Fotheringham, is another friend who stayed the course. We both worried over our children. Jane had left home when Gordon and I separated in 1969, but I was still a single parent to JP, beset by nanny and money problems. At the same time, there was illness in Allan's family. The most attentive of fathers, he once confided that he didn't know how to be a parent since his father had died when he was very young, and his mother Edna had remarried when he was a teenager.

Allan and I met occasionally at a popular restaurant, the Three Greenhorns, for a lunch featuring his martinis, my scotch, and mutual gossip. We continued this chummy relationship after I left the *Sun* and was running my consulting company in Yellowknife. Sitting at our usual corner booth Allan told a dramatic story about a pending libel action. I told him a dramatic story about the loss of a major client. Allan upped the ante, saying he would probably lose his job! I played my ace; I would probably lose my company! The maitre d', hovering nearby, finally interrupted the dialogue: "You have so many problems, your lunch is on the house," he said discreetly, while Allan and I looked equally sheepish.

We shared a secretary, the energetic Ann Hartley, whom Foth called the Tel Aviv midget and whom he expected to open his mail, return his messages, and pour his coffee. I didn't expect such services. One day he gave Ann a letter from a Burnaby housewife complaining about something he wrote and said: "Tell this woman to f— off." A few days later publisher Stu Keate called Foth into his office. Waving a letter of response from the Burnaby housewife, he asked Foth why he had answered her with an obscenity. Ann had scrupulously carried out his orders! Foth says this incident taught him to read everything he signs first.

Foth badly wanted to be a newspaper editor, in the style of the much-loved Bruce Hutchison, who had defined Canada to our generation in his book, *The Unknown Country*. This passionate paean to a great nation triggered unaccustomed patriotic palpitations in our young hearts. But Allan torpedoed his editorial aspirations at the *Sun* by giving a colourful interview to *The Ubyssey* on the changes he would make to the paper when he succeeded Keate. Although I don't know what was said when he was hauled on the carpet by Keate, Foth left town shortly afterward for Toronto.

Before he left, Foth helped me with one of my first major interviews, with Canadian-born economist John Kenneth Galbraith, who was visiting UBC with his wife to speak to students. The famed Harvard professor and I had concluded a unique agreement. He would agree to taping an interview on the ferry to Victoria during the first part of the trip, which I told him was boring, if I would act as tour guide during the second part, through the picturesque Gulf Islands. Aware of my limited mechanical ability, Allan came to run the tape recorder and meet the Great Man.

Our interview revealed to me the singular advantage of the journalistic craft: it allows you to ask almost anyone almost anything almost anywhere. And a business journalist (Peter Newman knows this) can gain access denied mere pencil-pushing newsmen and -women.

The *Sun* editors gave me a great deal of freedom, as long as I didn't spend real money, and I used it to the full. My column was aimed at people who wrote me: "I don't understand the business pages, but I always read your column." I wrote about issues through the people who lived them, "guts and feathers" small loggers, fishermen, chief executives, Arctic "cat" operators.

I learned early that if I asked a businessman—businesswomen were an anomaly—how business generally was, he would cautiously recount what he had read in the morning paper. But if I asked how *his* business was doing, he would brighten up and give specific facts faster than I could scribble them down. And if I asked enough people the question, I could identify a trend.

Time magazine reported that I had a great ear for a quotation, and some became part of business lore. When I wrote the first major piece on car dealer Jimmy Pattison's triumphant takeover of Neon Products of Canada Ltd. at age 39, I asked Jimmy, whom I described as a "jumping bean of a man," why he wanted to make a million dollars. "Because that's the only way you keep the score,"[3] he replied.

When I asked forestry giant H.R. MacMillan, who laid the foundation of BC's forest economy, why he had fired so many top executives, he explained: "I never lost a man I really needed. A man must have mental furnishings." No doubt he developed his when he was hospitalized for tuberculosis before starting his lumber export business, which revolutionized the BC lumber industry, until then marketed mainly through San Francisco.

H.R. had marked me as a reporter to respect, although we later fell out when I disclosed his wife Edna's stock holdings. Invited for tea at his home after he retired, I watched enthralled as he and fellow lumber giant Aird Flavelle discussed forest opportunities in South America. As old and as valuable in their way as ancient trees, these two giants spoke with the keen passion they had shared as young timber cruisers on Vancouver Island.

It was a time when the coastal float camps were being hauled ashore and logging bunkhouses replaced with pastel-coloured "instant towns," scraped out of the bush and linked by logging roads. Laundry line by laundry line, the transient camps became coastal communities. Emotional public hearings were held throughout British Columbia on timber allocations to support pulp and lumber mills, reflecting the policy that forest resources should be used for the social and economic development of the regional communities and not just for the white smoke of a pulp mill.

I covered it all: hitching rides with the log buyers; sitting in the sun on cedar-scented log booms in some remote inlet while they negotiated deals; flying along the West Coast headland to headland, the seals and the surf below; and visiting the "back end" of logging shows, where I learned to ask the grapple operator what was happening in the woods before interviewing the office-bound corporate president.

A passionate defender of small logging operators, I won the nickname "deputy minister of forests." When John Patrick was born, corporate presidents sent roses, but nothing topped the Squamish Loggers' Association, which sent a model logging truck, loaded with logs and two dozen red roses.

Millionaire logger Gordon Gibson Sr., father of the journalist politician, asked me to edit the memoirs of his early days of logging on the Coast and in the Queen Charlottes, ripping the heartwood out of giant white spruce for World War II airplanes. After reading the manuscript I asked Gordon if a story about his sexual prowess at age 12 was true. "Hell, no," confessed Gordon. "I put that in to sell books." Not with me as editor, I retorted primly. The memoir *Bull of the Woods* sold well with the aid of a more flexible editor.

Gordon told me how once, when a storm blew up in Tahsis Inlet, he had to choose between saving his family, floating away on the tide in their float camp, or the flat raft of boomed logs. He chose the logs. "I needed the cash," he explained. He gave me a mantra to live by: "When the tide and the wind are against you, tie up to the side of the inlet and wait for slack water."

The small loggers bought their log supply through timber sales and were vulnerable to "spite bidding" by other operators, angry at losing at auction. These spite bidders bid up the price of subsequent sales and walked away, bankrupting the successful bidder, who needed the timber to hold his quota, even at an operating loss.

"Not that anyone asked me," I wrote in my column, "but why doesn't the government impose a bidding fee so that spite bidders must leave something on the table?" Gibson, by then an MLA, thought it was a grand idea and legislation imposing a bidding fee was passed. Spite bidding ceased, although some forestry executives were offended at the concept that a mere reporter—and a woman at that—could suggest how they should run their business.

My freedom also enabled me to write about British Columbia for British Columbians. While researching this book, I came across a column I wrote in 1967 about a road that the people of Bella Coola had built themselves from the coastal tidal flats where explorer Alexander Mackenzie reached the Pacific Ocean in 1793 to the tawny Chilcotin Plateau 5200 feet above.

The first man to drive a passenger car over The Road was Andy Svisdahl. He warned tourists to stay off it. Wilfrid Christanson was whistling down The Hill when he spotted a car off the road. He learned over and yelled: "Is anyone hurt? Do you need a doctor?"

"No thank you," came the reply. "I *am* the doctor."

Buster Tuck and Stan Levelton were heading for Williams Lake last fall when the engine blew half way up The Hill. They had no water and the creeks were dry so they filled the radiator with beer. It took nine bottles. Buster was relieved: "We thought we might have to use the Scotch."

"I don't know what we would talk about in Bella Coola if it wasn't for The Road," said Cliff Kopas.[4]

Once, while visiting the site of the proposed Peace River dam, my floatplane landed on the brown, current-muscled Peace River, the super-highway through the Rockies for the aboriginals and early explorers, where it merges with the Parsnip and Finlay rivers. I stood on a sandbar, breathing the spring-scented air as the cottonwood leaves spangled in the sun. When the Peace dams were built, this spot would be 400 feet under water. Did we know what we were doing? I wondered.

I filed my column from the oil fields in northern British Columbia and Alberta, where I encountered the only editorial interference from management I ever received as a journalist. At that time the *Sun* (circa 1968–69) was owned by the FP newspaper chain. Publisher Max Bell phoned to advise me that his friends in the "oil patch" didn't like my stories on the Rainbow oil and gas field in northern Alberta. I filed them anyway. Nothing more was said.

Gradually I worked my way into the Yukon, Northwest Territories, and Arctic Islands, reporting on oil and gas development and the exciting story of how Canadians were developing "made-in-Canada" approaches to cope with technical challenges and climate extremes.

Jim and I became interested in international development, which led both of us to international assignments. Jim worked as writer and co-director on the UNICEF–CBC New York Educational Television co-production "Children of the World," eventually filmed in 11 developing countries, which ran on countless TV systems around the world for almost 20 years.

Encouraged by development guru Barbara Ward, aka Lady Jackson, I examined CIDA- and World Bank-funded programs for the *Sun*, attracting the interest of former Prime Minister Lester Pearson, who had published a book, *Partners in Development*, which promoted the concept that Canada should increase its ODA, or Official Development Aid, from 0.45 to 0.7 per cent of our GNP. (In 1999–2000, our ODA was 0.28 per cent.) There was an explosion of newly sovereign countries in the 1960s and in the competitive Cold War climate development became for many people a new form of Christian evangelism.

Jim and I went to see the former Prime Minister in his unpretentious white clapboard house in Rockcliffe, hoping to interest him in a television series. He led us into a chintz-decorated living room, explaining that his wife, Maryon, had gone out for a bottle of milk, since there was a dairy strike. In our discussion he expressed reservations about Canada's inclusion of visiting hockey teams in our aid budgets. At the end of the interview, he referred to us as "universal Canadians" because of our interests, but he did not sponsor the TV series.

The *Sun* also assigned me to national economic affairs, interviewing finance ministers such as Mitchell Sharp and Walter Gordon and Edward Benson, who invariably gave me great interviews before their budget-day speeches—to the fury of my eastern-based competitors—because I had come so far to see them.

Finally, in 1968–69, the *Sun* sent me to the Press Gallery in Ottawa, where I worked with Joyce Fairbairn, now a senator and former cabinet minister, the late Marjorie Nichols, and her housemate Hugh Winsor of the *Globe and Mail*. Joyce wore miniskirts to showcase her great legs, but she was a thorough professional, serving her western-based readers before joining Pierre Trudeau's staff as a legislative assistant. Marjorie was famous for her parties, but when I stayed with her I used to date the food in her fridge.

Marjorie, a heavy smoker, died of lung cancer in 1991. Her turbaned head could be seen in the Press Gallery above the House of Commons until her last illness. Shortly before her death we visited the media "hot room" on the third floor of Centre Block, the scene of many of our journalistic triumphs more than 20 years earlier. She walked with a cane, and her large froglike eyes studied the notice board, the desk, and the pop machine that had replaced the beer machine of our era. When we left the "hot room" we both knew it was her last visit. I have never visited it since.

But I hated Ottawa and missed British Columbia and the North, which I had grown to love, and my four-year-old son was bemused by the Ottawa lifestyle, so different from the beach-boy life he enjoyed at our home at Lions Bay on Howe Sound. After a year in Ottawa, we returned home and I commuted to Ottawa to cover economic affairs for the FP chain and television shows, returning regularly to my beloved northern Canada.

One day in 1970 when I was in Ottawa, managing editor Bill Galt phoned in his trademark laconic style. "I think you should come home," he said. "Why?" I asked impatiently. It was my fifth trip east in five weeks. "Because I think the paper is going on strike," he said.

I had no idea a strike was imminent. I booked my return flight. It was a long and bitter strike. With a nanny and mortgage to support, I filed in a frenzy of freelancing, for the *Toronto Star*, the *New York Times*, the *Times of London*, on my two years of Arctic adventuring.

Driving my 1968 Valiant downtown, I listened to Peggy Lee on the radio singing "Gotta Travel On." Why not? The Carney compass heading was due north.

CHAPTER 8

Gemini North

TRADE SECRET:
*To run a successful business
you need three elements:
win the contract, do the work, and get paid.*
—Businesswoman Pat Carney

Most journalists remain journalists, or move into a related field such as public relations. Instead, I wrote myself into a new world. Like Alice in *Through the Looking Glass*, I walked through the mirror and found my professional passion, politics, and the rest of my life. And like Alice, I discovered that what I had seen in the looking glass seemed much the same, but once I had crossed into Looking Glass House everything looked quite different.

When my home paper, the *Vancouver Sun*, went on strike, I returned to northern Canada to freelance for other newspapers and magazines. Sometimes Jim joined me as a photographer, and we produced a couple of stories for *Maclean's*. One was on the evolution of self-government in the northern territories; that story led to my business career.

Another story recorded the experiences of six young northern entrepreneurs in Yukon and NWT. We forecast that two would make $1 million, two would go broke, and two would quit. One of the six was mining engineer and surveyor Paul White, a UBC graduate who was running an aero-survey company out of Whitehorse, whom I had first met when I was waiting tables at age 18. Forty-five years later, after a long friendship and love affair and a longer period of Not Speaking, I would marry him.

Neither story would have happened had I not walked through the looking glass to become a social activist rather than an economic commentator.

The story on self-government led oil and gas executive Robin Abercrombie to my Lions Bay creek-side patio in 1970 to offer me a consulting contract with Alberta Gas Trunk Line Co. Ltd., led by Bob Blair, who later headed energy giant Nova Corp. AGTL was exploring the possibility of building a natural gas pipeline down the Mackenzie Valley, and Bob wanted me to research the regulatory rules and regulations of the fledgling territorial government relating to resource development. I knew R.J. from my reporting on the oil patch in Alberta. He offered to pay me double my journalist salary for a few days' work a month. It was no contest.

At first, the consulting work was to be a short-term job until the newspaper strike was over and I returned to my business column. But I liked the work, which involved travelling in the North and meeting northerners. When R.J. mentioned that AGTL was restricted to Alberta operations by its corporate articles and was looking for a company incorporated in the NWT to carry out pipeline-related business, I volunteered: "Well, my twin brother Jim and I have a NWT company."

It was true. One night, over several scotches in the Gatineau cabin I had rented for JP and myself when I served in the parliamentary Press Gallery, Jim and I had decided to form our own company. The company would manage both his film work for the National Film Board of Canada in Montreal, where he was living, and my freelance work.

Since we were twins, we called it Gemini Productions. Since much of our work was in the NWT, we incorporated the company as a territorial one. Our northern operations were called Gemini North to distinguish them from our work in southern Canada.

We agreed on several sentimental and wholly impractical provisions, such as establishing our corporate year-end on our birthday, May 26, since we figured we wouldn't likely forget the date. Later it took our lawyer Terry Wardrup some effort—a goddamn omelette, he said—and cost us some healthy tax dollars to unscramble our creation and incorporate it in a more standardized form.

But it met AGTL's requirements, and Jim and I flew to Calgary to meet with Blair, an ardent Canadian nationalist who was determined to build a strong Canadian company to compete with the multinationals, which he did. Years later, as Energy Minister, I rejected Bob's request for several hundred million dollars of federal subsidies, which were inconsistent with our Conservative energy policies. That was ironic, since our corporate relations were amiable during the 11 years we worked together.

I cashed in my *Sun* pension plan, withdrew the $2300 accumulated over 15 years of employment in the newspaper business, and flew to Yellowknife to set up shop. Jim and I opened a post office box and a bank account. We rented office space in the newly constructed Gallery Building, over the bar. I found an apartment, which my son and I would share with employees to cut costs.

We hired Gina Blondin, a beautiful and brilliant Dene, as secretary/ receptionist. Her cousin Ethel Blondin later became an MP and junior minister in Jean Chrétien's government. Paul White sent over a former employee, Tim Brock, from Whitehorse to act as interim general manager and expediter.

I offered a partnership to a young economist, Frank Basham, who had worked for the territorial government before returning to Alberta to complete his master's degree in economics. Frank and his wife Brenda joined us in Yellowknife. A "hard numbers" econometrician, Frankly Bashful, as we called him, was a good balance for my economic expertise, which was more involved with social impact than with employment multipliers.

When Gina told me a bush pilot from Gateway Aviation had dropped off a job application, I was impatient. Dalliances with pilots, which comprised much of my social life, were one thing; why would we hire a bush pilot? However, when I finally interviewed Dominique Prinet, who came to Canada from Paris, I found he had an MBA degree plus a master's degree in electrical engineering from McGill and UBC, and an airline transport pilot licence. As a bonus, his blonde, blue-eyed wife Dominique was a linguist who spoke three or four languages. They had met when she was working as a waitress in a Great Bear Lake fish camp.

Big Dom became our third partner with Little Dom working as his research assistant. The two were a real money machine, churning out transportation and technical reports for Gemini. The addition of anthropologist Phillip Thomas completed our core professional staff, although others joined Gemini North from time to time, including my brother Tom and engineer Terry Smyth, as our client list expanded. We were in business.

We also made a point of training native research assistants for field work and report writing. One such assistant was Philippe Mercredi, a long-haired, pot-smoking hippie photographer whose work I sold to *Time* magazine. He told me later that our help changed his life.

Did I know what I was doing? Well, of course! Hadn't I been a nationally known business columnist for 10 years? Hadn't I interviewed almost every senior corporate executive in Canada on how they resolved corporate problems, correcting their mistakes in my column? Didn't I know everything there was to know about business after writing about it for years? Business, as reflected in the looking glass, appeared to be very simple.

NWT Commissioner Stuart Hodgson thought otherwise. He called in two of his friends, pilot Daryle Brown, who arrived at Stu's office in his mukluks, and lawyer David Searle, who appeared in a suit. Stu told them: "Pat here is starting a business. She doesn't know beans about it and her brother Jim knows less. It's your job to keep her out of trouble."

David Searle helped by negotiating a start-up contract with AGTL whereby the company paid a lump sum upfront at the beginning of the month and we invoiced them at month's end, resolving our cash-flow problems. Daryle helped by showing me, by example, never to pay money for business services without negotiating them first. Their advice was Hodgson's major contribution to our new territorial company since we did very little work for the territorial government over the next 11 years.

I knew I had made the transition from journalist to businesswoman when I met equipment operator Kenn Borek in Inuvik, where he was en route to develop exploration sites on Axel Heiberg Island in the High Arctic, my favourite northern place. Knowing how much I loved the region, he coaxed me over Black Velvet drinks to go along for the ride in his aircraft. But because it would mean the loss of "billing days," I refused with real regret.

While my partners focused on producing the work, I was responsible for running the company, identifying business opportunities, writing reports, and negotiating contracts. In practice, however, all three of us did the field research and everything else required to survive. The lessons I learned running my business influenced my attitude toward politics and government. The most important lesson was ensuring that our operating expenditures never exceeded our operating revenues. In 11 years of operation, Gemini North never borrowed money beyond operating lines of credit. I also learned to hire people who generated income for the company and fire those who didn't cover their costs. I learned the basics of any business: win the contract, do the work, and get paid. During our time in operation, we had only two uncollected receivables, and one involved another consultant.

But first I had to decide how to establish our billing rates. They had to be competitive, but like most northern businesses our operating costs in Yellowknife were one-third higher than our southern competitors. And we had to generate business. Our start-up contract with AGTL was just that—a start.

Finally, a geologist on a plane to Whitehorse told me the magic formula. "You have to bill your payroll plus 150 per cent to cover your costs," he said bluntly. "But that's too much," I objected naively. "No, it's not," he said. "You must cover your rent, phone, utilities, accounting and legal fees, business taxes, equipment, stationery, and other office costs.

"Your real payroll costs are wages plus another 25 per cent to cover vacations, sick leave, and other benefits. You will have travel costs, and you need to spend one-third of your time, which you can't bill, out developing new business. During that time you must still pay all your costs although you only recover the revenue from the contracts you win, and you won't win them all."

His advice proved to be accurate. I learned to cut our overhead, yelling at my staff for making long distance phone calls: "If you can't bill that call, hang up." I developed the important ability to develop a work plan and cost a contract accurately, so that we did not have to pay cost overruns out of our own corporate resources. I also learned how to negotiate, which later became crucial to my work as Energy and Trade Minister.

I learned that the best contracts were the shortest ones. At the peak of Gemini North's work with the pipeline consortium Arctic Gas, we negotiated a lengthy and detailed contract, and I found myself spending much of my time arguing administrative details, like whether we billed subconsultants at cost or with a 30 per cent markup. Since as a principal partner I was responsible for earning a major share of our revenues, time spent on administration cost us money.

In contrast, after years of working with Foothills Pipeline Co., our contract was only four paragraphs long. The first identified the parties to the contract: Foothills and Gemini North. The third set out the billing rates. The fourth and final paragraph set out the time period covered by the contract. The second, and crucial, paragraph stated simply: "Gemini North undertakes to carry out whatever project Foothills chooses to assign and Gemini North chooses to do."

My partners and I agreed on basic principles before hand, which I learned was essential to running a profitable company. Did we want to earn modest salaries and benefits and live within our corporate revenues, or did we want to pay ourselves what we thought we really deserved, financed by bank overdrafts? Many companies that chose the latter course went bankrupt, particularly in the precarious northern economy.

Did we want to leave the profits in the company and buy real estate or make other investments, or withdraw the profits and pursue our own interests? My partners and I decided to divide up the annual profits on an informal basis, topping up pension plans, paying all expenses and taxes, and depositing three months' payroll in the bank before dividing the rest among ourselves on a predetermined basis.

This approach carried us through some lean times, but it called for corporate discipline. Once I coveted a Ted Harrison painting in a Whitehorse gallery window, admiring its rosy skies and purple moons and parka-clad people. It was before Harrison became well known and the painting cost only a few hundred dollars, a fraction of its value today. But I couldn't buy the painting and still cover next month's expenses so I passed up the opportunity, even though I knew I would live to regret it.

Still, we had fun. Sometimes on a clear, sunny day when the lakes were navy blue and the air was tanged with the smell of spruce, I or one of my partners, stupefied by statistics, would bang on the wall and sing out "Director's meeting." Then Big Dominique would phone down to a float-plane charter operator in Old Town, and we would all pile into the aircraft with a bottle of wine and a picnic lunch, and fly off to one of the islands on an isolated lake. Once ashore, the floatplane tethered to a stump, we ate and snoozed in the sun.

We also had J.R. Armstrong, our protection from Revenue Canada, when we wanted to treat ourselves to dinner when working overtime.

Frank Basham invented J.R., whom he decided was an oilman from Inuvik, when Frank needed to account for an unaccountable expense. J.R. had a billing code for development costs. It was only when, reviewing the expenses, I wondered whether J.R.'s development costs would result in a firm project that I was informed of his real nature, and then I used J.R. too. Good old J.R. bought us a lot of pizza on cold northern nights when we wanted a break from working late.

As the only economic consultants based in Yellowknife at the time, we carried out a wide range of projects, including native training programs, transportation studies, social impact analysis, a polar ice project, and a potential granite quarry designed to employ natives. We would hire additional expertise where needed and act as project managers.

One of my favourite projects was the development of labour pools in the settlements to ensure that native northerners were available for wage employment while others were hunting or trapping and cutting firewood. I was given the idea by an Inuit called Pudluk in Resolute, who explained that a northerner who didn't show up for work because he was hunting might be considered an unreliable employee by a southern-based oil company. But, he pointed out, if another took his place, traditional activities could be carried out in a normal and prideful manner.

We expedited planeloads of energy and public utility executives from Calgary to Prudhoe Bay in Alaska in a chartered F-27 to look at a pipeline development that allowed caribou to graze undisturbed, and to other areas where development was banned because of calving conflicts. Either Gina or I accompanied each tour.

When flights were weathered in at Inuvik we learned the corporate pecking order; presidents might share rooms with vice-presidents, but not with mere staffers. We dissuaded the desk clerk in Inuvik from making naughty suggestions to our clients with her wake-up calls, which she loved to practise on bashful Frank Basham.

We warned visitors that the endless summer nights might keep them awake and drinking, and cautioned them to turn in at their normal bedtime. Unfortunately, that advice didn't deter a respected Bank of Canada economist who partied all night and missed the flight to the Delta exploration camps the next day, but wrote a fine report on his return to Ottawa.

No Gemini North charter ever carried booze of any kind into the Mackenzie settlements, although we sometimes packed in fresh fruit and veggies. Once I beat *Edmonton Journal* reporter Stephen Hume in a game of blackjack, where the prize was a seat out of Fort McPherson on the local bootlegger's chartered floatplane. Hume had to wait another few days for the regular "sked" flight.

Based on these experiences, I formulated Carney's First Law of Northern Development: "In the North, nothing ever happens the way it is planned, but something else happens instead." Carney's Second Law was "Don't be first, be second," since we sometimes pioneered a field and then watched subsequent work go to southern-based consultants who could undercut our higher northern costs.

A highlight of Gemini North's professional work was the production of a six-volume, 2200-page report on the social and economic impact of a proposed Arctic gas pipeline in northern Canada. It took four years to produce and over that period the pipeline sponsors—and thus our clients—changed from AGTL to various consortia, which finally merged into the multi-company-backed Canadian Arctic Gas Pipeline Limited.

The northern pipeline concept was based on the premise that Canada's accessible oil and gas reserves were declining, particularly in the West, threatening the country's energy security and leaving eastern Canadians exposed to the price and supply vagaries of imported oil. Although Canada already imported offshore oil, by the mid-1970s the country had become a net importer of crude oil and our own domestic production was forecast to decline sharply.

While oil accounted for about 50 per cent of Canada's energy needs, natural gas supplied 25 per cent of the market. By 1972 the National Energy Board reported that Canada's current supplies of natural gas were insufficient to meet expanding Canadian demand plus our commitments to our US customers, whose payments helped offset the cost of importing oil to eastern Canada. Energy shortages, inflation, balance of payments problems, a declining dollar, and thus a lower standard of living for Canadians were among the alarming prospects.

To avoid these problems the oil and gas industry turned to frontier reserves in the North, where the Geological Survey of Canada estimated that potential gas reserves in the Yukon and NWT were about 100 trillion cubic feet—more than the estimated untapped gas resources of the four western provinces.

In the late 1960s, the Americans found oil at Prudhoe Bay in Alaska and built a pipeline across the state to Valdez, where the crude oil was tankered to southern US markets. On the Canadian side, the 16-member Arctic Gas consortium applied for permission to build a 48-inch pipeline to transport natural gas (a spinoff from crude oil production) from Prudhoe Bay in Alaska and from the Mackenzie Delta in the Northwest Territories for Canadian and US markets.

The primary purpose of Gemini North's socioeconomic impact study was "to show that the proposed natural gas pipeline will affect many people, Dene, Inuit and Others, in the North. Some of these effects may be adverse and some may be beneficial. Our assignment is to identify those effects, whether they be beneficial or adverse."[1]

And we did, identifying problems associated with development such as alcohol abuse, crimes of violence, child abuse, health problems, racial tensions, and other social impacts, as well as job opportunities, increased incomes, and other benefits. No other study, before or since, has ever catalogued the range of factors and impacts generated by such large-scale development in the western Arctic.

Much of the material we collected ourselves on the ground, travelling down the Mackenzie Valley to visit the settlements, usually in the fall and winter, when the summertime academics, who came each year like blackflies and mosquitoes, had returned south. We slept in the nursing stations, the hostels, private homes, and once in the sawmill bunks at Arctic Red River where notices of receivership decorated the cook shack wall, dragging our sleeping bags and wearing our green Gemini North parkas.

We collected much of our information from the people themselves in workshops and community visits, developing at their kitchen tables population statistics supplied by the settlement manager, band chief, and local priests from band lists or whatever material was available. We returned the information to each settlement in the form of "age/sex" charts, showing how their population was aging or how young people dominated their community.

We learned to put maps on the floor or the ground rather than posting them on the wall, to glean information from hunters and trappers about where the animals and the traplines were. We always used interpreters so that the elders were informed in their own language, be it Gwich'in, Hare, Dogrib, Chipewyan, or Inuvialuktun.

We learned that each community was different, and none was uniform. Most had Dene, Métis, and white residents, while others, like Aklavik and Inuvik, had Dene, Inuit, and Others. We dedicated our report to "northerners: Indian, Inuit and Others who helped us turn figures into facts."[2]

But first, we had to explain what a natural gas pipeline was. Commissioner Hodgson told us after a tour of the Mackenzie Valley: "They don't know what natural gas is. They think it is gasoline and the pipeline will break and a fire will burn up the country." This was alarming, so we asked the pipeline engineers to build a model of an above-ground, bermed pipeline so it didn't melt the permafrost, with a small gas plant. The model was attached to a gas hot plate.

We usually organized each workshop in a circle, so it would be less intimidating, particularly for the old women, their hair covered by their blue kerchiefs. I would explain that you couldn't see natural gas, but you could smell it. I would show how natural gas was pumped up from the ground, put through the pipeline into the scrubbing plant where it was cleaned, and finally pumped through to the stove to make tea. At this point, I struck a match, placed it near the hot plate, and produced a ring of fire for the tea kettle. "Aiyee," nodded the old women in their blue kerchiefs; they understood gas-fired Coleman-type stoves. After this demonstration we asked them about their community and began our discussions, which took place over several seasons.

Our approach worked well until we reached Old Crow, a singularly beautiful village located above the Arctic Circle on the Porcupine River in Yukon. Old Crow was connected by language, family ties, and custom with Fort MacPherson on the NWT side of the mountain passes. One of the few communities that still relied heavily on traditional hunting and trapping activities, Old Crow was key to the Yukon route. It was also heavily dependent for heating on firewood, and since wood supplies adjacent to the community were being cut down, natural gas might be useful.

I set up the natural gas pipeline model before the assembled villagers who were seated expectantly around it. We had visited Old Crow several times and knew many people in the audience, including Chief Charlie Able. I showed them the gas pump, the pipeline, the scrubbing plant. But something must have jiggled loose when we transported the model through the mountains in our Twin Otter, because when I put the match to the gas-ring cookstove, the whole model blew up in flames.

"AIYEE!" screamed the audience, aghast. Old Crow voted against the natural gas pipeline. I knew when to cut our losses; we packed the model onto the plane and left.

But even with the model, information tours, programs that trained native northerners for pipeline jobs, and trips down south to visit operating pipelines, there was dissension among both native and non-native northerners, as noted in our report.

> At Old Crow, we walked through the fireweed and long grass to see one active trapper's sled dogs, staked out on their chains, and then went back to his log cabin for tea.
>
> His gracious sister told us about the trapping grounds. "Old Crow flats, it is so beautiful," she said. "In June, there are birds and beavers and grizzly bears and little cranberries, so sweet, and wild rhubarb, just like lettuce."
>
> But that night another resident dismissed Old Crow flats as a "stinking swamp." He wants the pipeline. He stood under the midnight sun and begged us to find a job for his 16-year-old son. He offered to pay us any money he had. Embarrassed, we swatted the mosquitoes and stirred the dust with our feet. There is only confusion.[3]

Although our report noted that the Mackenzie and Yukon had been under development impact ever since the early explorers, fur traders, and missionaries came north, our study showed that drinking, alcohol abuse, crimes of violence, and other social problems parallelled development. When the Mackenzie Highway finally reached the isolated settlement of Fort Simpson, the resulting social upheaval was like "taking a plate and turning it upside down," noted one native resident, Ted Trindell.

Alcohol abuse was one visible problem. In the early 1970s, alcoholism accounted for 40 to 50 per cent of deaths in the Northwest Territories. Such deaths, according to the Northern Health Service, stemmed from injuries, accidents, and violence, afflicting not only the drinker but also the family in the form of wife-beating and child neglect.

An Inuvik high school student told us:

When this keeps up, the family is broken in their hearts; their money suffers, and when they have no money, they can't buy food or proper clothes; their health weakens so sickness sneaks into the household and that sickness prevents them from going to school; their education fails.[4]

Although alcohol consumption, alcohol abuse, and related problems were present in predominantly white communities as well as predominantly native ones, our evidence showed that such problems tended to be higher in communities where development took place. However, the purchase of booze requires cash, and cash from welfare cheques, hunting, and trapping activities was just as likely to be spent on alcohol as were "development dollars." And if there was little cash, there were other alternatives:

There are many ways to get drunk in the study region . . . If you can't afford hard liquor, you can brew your own, using malt or just about anything else at hand; the cook in a government-financed institution was fermenting fruit cocktail during one research visit.

If booze is out of your price range then you can drink or sniff hair spray, deodorant, after shave lotion (often used as a chaser for wine), nail polish remover, mouthwash—apparently you can get a nice rush out of that—and that old standby, vanilla extract. . . . Some people even prefer these substitutes to the real thing.[5]

Health, education, welfare cheques, unemployment, poor housing, racial tension—our report presented volumes of data: stats, graphs, charts, and interviews. On racial tension we summarized:

Racism has a lot to do with plumbing. If you are a native living in a house without running water and your white neighbour has a fully equipped bathroom and a kitchen sink with taps, you may have two reactions. You may feel apathetic and inferior; you do not expect running water. Or you may be angry. Generally there is racial tension between the white who has, and the native who hasn't.

Racism also has a lot to do with paying. If you are a non-subsidized northerner, struggling to make a living in a high-cost, highly taxed economy and your neighbour is a native in a subsidized house you may have two reactions. You may dismiss your native neighbour as a no good, lazy, useless scoundrel, or you may be angry. In both cases, there is racial tension between those who pay and those who don't.[6]

The influx of whites into the region increased feelings of inferiority and resentment among native northerners faced with complex housing regulations that favoured the "outsiders." One Fort Norman native told us: "Look around here—the whites have better surroundings and we live in a goddamned ditch down here. Who the hell do they think they are and what the hell do they think we are?"

Many young native northerners recounted their frustrations with feeling caught between two cultures, unwilling to choose bush life with hunting and trapping as a full-time occupation but unable to find full-time wage employment and skills training, which would allow them to combine the best of both worlds.

While they wanted to preserve their culture, they never expressed the desire to have their children raised only in the old ways. As one native northerner explained: "He wants his daughter to be Indian. That is why he gave her an Indian name. But when asked what he wants for his daughter, G said: 'School, clothes, the best of everything.'"

And native land claims were a recognized priority issue after 1973, when Mr. Justice William Morrow of the Supreme Court of the Northwest Territories ruled that 16 Indian band chiefs, representing 7000 Treaty Indians, had the right to file a claim to 400 000 square miles of land including the Mackenzie River Valley and the proposed pipeline route.

Given all these unresolved conflicts, Commissioner Tom Berger, who held hearings on the terms and conditions that should be attached to the proposed pipeline, finally recommended a 10-year moratorium on any Mackenzie Valley development, which the federal government adopted. More than 20 years later, early in 2000, after land claims in the area had been clarified, the chiefs and other aboriginal leaders met in tiny Fort Liard in the Northwest Territories and passed a resolution agreeing in principle to "build a business partnership to maximize ownership and benefits of a Mackenzie Valley pipeline."[7] Senator Nick Sibbeston, a northern native from Fort Simpson, informed the Senate that the resolution marks a new era of hope and a willingness to participate as partners, not bystanders, in northern development projects.

Ironically, Gemini North's even-handed and ground-breaking report outlining both the costs and the benefits of the pipeline was received with lukewarm enthusiasm by the applicant Arctic Gas and openly criticized as the work of a "bunch of journalists" by southern academic Robert Page in his book *Northern Development: The Canadian Dilemma*. In the 1990s historian Tammy Nemeth, who wrote her master's thesis based partly on my energy policy, asked Page how he had concluded that Gemini North was composed strictly of journalists.

> He became quite flustered and very defensive and said, "Well Pat Carney was in charge and she was a journalist." I replied that you were not a journalist at the time and had a Bachelor's degree in economics and were taking a Master's in regional planning and that your group of consultants was composed of anthropologists, economists, engineers, etc.
>
> He sputtered and asked where I obtained the information. I told him it was in the appendix of the submission. Then he had the temerity to suggest the list was somehow falsified.[8]

In response, I wrote to the egg-spattered academic, his shoddy research efforts exposed, asking why he would make such a false and defamatory statement. Page never answered my letter.

His attitude was typical of southern academics who mined native lore in the sunny summer months but left the north at the first sign of frost, while we lived in Yellowknife and worked in the Mackenzie Valley until the temperatures hit minus 50 degrees Fahrenheit, when the single-engine charter aircraft rarely flew.

Gemini North's study was considered by other academics to be a solid piece of work and useful as a base line study of the region. Twenty-six years later, in February 2000, I searched the UBC Library for a copy of the report, but it was still in use, signed out by another faculty member.

Arctic Gas' application to build a pipeline failed, partly because of the consortium's failure to acknowledge the adverse social impact as well as the economic impact. But Gemini North was unaffected. We had already been signed up again by Arctic Gas' competitor Foothills, whose corporate roots were in AGTL, to examine a Yukon pipeline route.

We loved life in Yellowknife. In 1970, it was a small town of around 8000 people on the shores of Great Slave Lake, awkwardly changing from an easygoing gold mining town to a grimmer, greyer government centre as the capital of the Northwest Territories. Lawyer Brian Purdy explained how a southern Canadian made the transition when we met at the post office, a major social centre.

"At first you're exhilarated by the sense of space, the clear air, the sense of freedom, and the camaraderie of northerners," he said. "Then, when you realize how isolated you are, how far from everything and everyone, you become very depressed. Eventually, you realize that you can make a good life here and achieve a balance of sorts." Brian later returned to the South.

Yellowknife's greatest asset was not its gold deposits but its community spirit. It was small enough that when you called Four Four, the cab company, you gave your name and not your street number, and the community was safe enough that you could leave your doors unlocked. Social life was communal; we Anglicans went to the United Church caribou dinners, and when the United Church burned down, the congregation worshipped in the Anglican church.

In summer we held all-night barbecues since it never got dark, sitting in our lawn chairs wrapped in blankets against the mosquitoes and blackflies, drinking beer and telling stories. In winter, we cross-country skied on the small lakes, or on the short ski hill on the road to Giant Mine. Sometimes Gina and I skied on our lunch break just to get out into the few hours of winter sunlight.

The entire business and government community turned out to the dinners held by the city or chamber of commerce, as well as receptions for visiting delegations or dignitaries, including the Royal Family. A memorable dinner in the Yellowknife Inn was organized for a Russian delegation that made endless vodka toasts to international cooperation.

At one point I realized that only three people in the banquet room were still sober: Commissioner Stu Hodgson, who arranged to have water substituted for spirits; Barbara Ootes, the wife of Stu's assistant Jake, who didn't drink; and me, who had a cold and couldn't drink.

The evening went downhill from there; the Canadian general stationed in Yellowknife made highly inappropriate remarks about the Cold War and his wife was found necking in the coat closet with an assistant deputy minister from Ottawa. Both the general and the ADM went on to distinguished Ottawa careers.

Some of us formed the Yellowknife City Concert Band and played at concerts, at the airport to welcome back the baseball team, and in nearby native settlements. We played in the hockey arena and in parades on the flatbed of a truck, our mouthpieces and reeds freezing to our lips, our fingers clumsy with cold. Everybody played in the Band—the mayor, the nun, the milkman, the bank manager, the accountant and his wife, while our kids played in the school gym that served as our rehearsal hall.

After three years of communal living in an apartment, sharing space with employees until they found accommodation, I decided I could now afford to build a house. My first step was to buy a lot in Old Town, a fist-like point of land that intruded into Great Slave Lake and housed a cheerful clutter of floatplane bases, expediters, wholesale and outfitter stores, and the local newspaper office.

My lot was below the bush pilot's monument, on the waterfront just where the Wardair floatplanes moved onto "the step" before taking off with a whoosh of spray. After signing the cheque, I went down to view my new home, a log cabin on the property. I found that the cabin had been skidded off the property and onto the lot across the road. Well, maybe it wasn't a cabin—more like a shack. But it had definitely been moved.

My next step was to call in the drilling company so I could sink piles to bedrock and build a new home. Since I had bought the lot in winter, however, I had neglected to notice that under the snow was very deep permafrost. So when the driller had not found bedrock after drilling 100 feet down at $120 a foot, I called it quits and sold the lot to the owner of a mobile home. Today, homes worth hundreds of thousands of dollars have taken Old Town "upscale."

My next building lot was sheer granite in the upscale Matonabee area fronting on Frame Lake near my office. Frame Lake, like many northern ponds, was so shallow that when our bookkeeper's sailboat capsized, the mast stuck in the mud lake bottom. After negotiating a mortgage with my friend and fellow Band member Angus Paton, whose wife Rachel was my friend from high school in the Kootenays, I contracted with an Edmonton-based building company and awaited our new home.

On my first visit to the building site I discovered that the builder had poured the foundation two feet too wide for the house. You can use it as a planter, he suggested. On my second visit to the site, I noticed that the foundation error meant I couldn't drive into the carport under the kitchen. We compromised on a cement pad in front of the house and turned the carport into a dog run for our Samoyed, Iliga, which meant friend in the Inuit language.

On my third visit, I noticed that instead of building the house as designed, with stucco on the first floor and siding on the top, the contractor had covered the whole building in siding. Not what I had planned, but then I prefer wood. On my fourth visit, I found that the eight-foot balcony outside the living-room patio door had been reduced to four feet, to supply the building material needed to connect the front door to the carport, which we couldn't use anyway.

Time to see my lawyer, Murray Sigler, who advised me that both parties to this dispute were his clients—not an unusual situation in the North—and the builder was a more valuable account than Gemini North. So I spent my birthday drinking champagne on the shrunken balcony with a pilot friend, locked out of my house until I paid the extra money needed to connect the front-door walkway to the cement car pad.

When we finally moved in, the plumbing froze, leaving me without water in my brand-new kitchen. For six months, from November to May, when the banker, builder, city inspector, and plumber jack-hammered the cement floor of the carport to reveal the broken plumbing connection, our only running water was in the bathroom—at least when that wasn't frozen too.

We coped, washing dishes in the bathtub all winter, since the kitchen sink was frozen, and cooking one-pot meals to reduce dishwashing. This did not impress some of our guests, including novelist Mordecai Richler on his first visit north. As I hung up his parka, he asked me without preamble: "Why do the men in Calgary wear high heels and funny hats?" I realized he was referring to Calgarians' penchant for cowboy boots and cowboy hats.

Mordecai said my one-pot caribou stew lacked fat, and when he left he asked me if there was a bar service on the plane from Yellowknife to Frobisher Bay in the eastern Arctic. When I said no dice, he shrugged that the Inuit had no music, nor musical ability, and then he left. He

Foochow Road in the International Settlement, Shanghai, China, before the Japanese invasion, 1937.

Author on the Bund in Shanghai, China, with the new cityscape of Pudong across the Huangpo River, November 1998.

Grandmother Bridget Casey on the Home Place, Okanagan Valley, British Columbia.

Grandfather John Joseph Carney and his horse, Billy, Okanagan Valley, British Columbia.

John James Carney, MM, in uniform of the 72nd Battalion (Infantry), Seaforth Highlanders of Canada, 1916.

Father Jim Carney and Mother Dora Sanders on their wedding day at the British Consulate, Shanghai, China, March 10, 1934.

The Twins, Pat and Jim, at age 5 in Victoria, British Columbia.

The Carney children, Pat, Tom, Norah, and Jim, on the Home Place, Okanagan Valley, British Columbia, circa 1945.

Wheelhouse and salon of SS *Nasookin*, and Streetcar No. 23 on the Blue J, Kootenay Lake, British Columbia, circa 1959.

Gordon Sedawie

Twin brother Jim Carney and his trumpet, circa 1957.

Daughter Jane Dickson and her first husband Tiffy Reid on their wedding day, 1966. Tiffy later died in a marine accident.

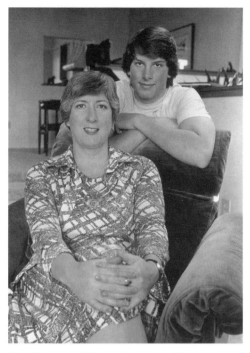

Chris Schramek

Pat Carney, MP, at home in Vancouver, British Columbia, with her son, John Patrick Dickson, age 15, in 1980.

Pat Carney and husband, Paul S. White, Saturna Island, British Columbia, 1998.

Eric Cable, The Province

Girl reporter Pat Carney covering the circus, circa 1956.

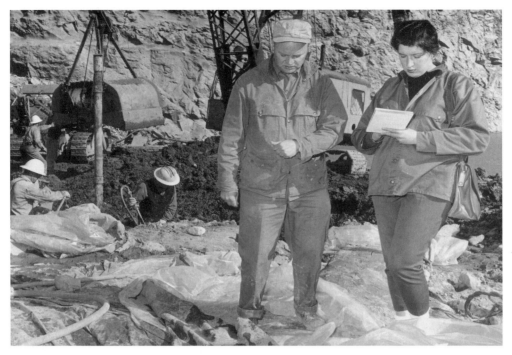

Business columnist Pat Carney on the job at the Peace River dam site, British Columbia, circa 1960s.

On Arctic assignment, business columnist Pat Carney in Tuktoyaktuk, Northwest Territories, 1968.

Jim Carney

Business columnist Pat Carney at work.

Pat Carney, President of Gemini North, economic consulting company, circa 1979.

managed to write a bestseller, *The Incomparable Atuk*, based partly on that trip when he returned south.

Other friends utilized our home's "open door" policy, particularly native friends from the Mackenzie Valley settlements, since we often bunked down in their homes when working on our projects. Once my son JP came into my bedroom and said, "Mom, there's a strange man in our bathroom." And there was, a guest of a Dene friend of mine from Inuvik who was fast asleep in the guest room.

We splashed our way along the ice-slushed shoreline of Great Slave Lake at breakup to fish for delicious, white-fleshed pickerel. Knowing I liked northern fish, a native friend from the nearby Indian village once brought me a tub of whitefish at 3:00 a.m., receiving a sleepy thanks from me. On my thirty-ninth birthday we liberated a barbecue from the golf course and cooked 88 caribou steaks during the all-night party. We definitely had fun.

But when our work shifted to Yukon from the Northwest Territories, I looked at my image in the looking glass and decided that after four years of residence the time had come to return to southern Canada as our base. Yukon was hard to access from Yellowknife.

The Prinets, who were expecting their first child, had already left for Montreal and a vice-presidential position at Nordair for Big Dom. The Bashams were also pregnant and Brenda was anxious to be nearer their families.

As an added incentive, our accountant Grant Hinchey had informed us that we were now in a financial position to send a staffer back to school for educational upgrading. "We're not sending a staffer; we're sending me back to school," I told him, and I enrolled in UBC's School of Community and Regional Planning for my master's degree.

On the day in August 1974 when we left our beautiful home overlooking Frame Lake with its ducks and muskrats, after three winters and four summers living in Yellowknife, my son and I felt we had torn our hearts in two.

While I have never lived in the North again, JP's first job as a pilot, after completing his UBC degree in physics, was flying a single-engine Lance aircraft, based at the tiny native settlement of Fort Providence where the Mackenzie River starts its journey down north to the Arctic coast. He lived in a trailer on the small airstrip located four miles from the settlement, his only companion a weasel called Ernest who ate cheese crumbs off the kitchen table.

When my nephew Joe and I flew north to visit him on Boxing Day 1989, JP met us at Hay River airstrip while Joe shivered in the unfamiliar cold. After kicking the aircraft tires, which had frozen in a square shape to the tarmac, JP flew us across the ice-white lake to the settlement. While the boys stayed in the trailer, I booked into the Snowshoe Inn downtown.

Not much had changed from the night 10 years earlier, when I had heard the click-tap-click-tap of high heels in the hotel corridor followed by a knock on the helicopter pilot's door. The chopper pilot was swinging freight across the Mackenzie, a speedway of ice chunks hurtling downriver after breakup. "Who's there?" called the pilot. "Miss America," came the reply.

Yellowknife has a special place in our family. When JP and I cross the 60th parallel separating the NWT and Yukon from southern Canada, we both confess to feeling a sense of being back in our Home Place, and we are not alone.

In 1985, returning to Yellowknife for Homecoming to mark the city's fiftieth birthday, I ran into actor Margot Kidder in the Edmonton Airport ladies' washroom. She was washing her hair in the small sink, a feat I greatly admired since I have never been able to master it. Born in Yellowknife, Kidder was also returning for Homecoming. She asked me to sign her into the airport lounge, which I was glad to do, because she told me her wallet, with her NWT birth certificate, had been stolen in Washington, DC.

"Someone in DC is running around with a birth certificate marked Indian, Inuit, and Other," Margot joked. We talked all the way to the territorial capital, where she rode a float in the parade and I watched from the hotel window with my buddies. We never met again, but if we did, our affection for Yellowknife would be our common bond.

I continued to work on economic development projects in northern Canada. But one day, I awoke in my sleeping bag in my bunk bed at Jumbo's, the trailer-style motel in Fort Chipewyan in northern Alberta, where we were trying to develop a granite quarry utilizing the community's native workforce and a deposit of beautiful pink granite. I gazed at the dust on the toilet paper, the empty beer bottles left on the floor by the previous guest, the holes in the window screen where the flies clustered, and wondered what I was doing with my life.

Fort Chipewyan was one of my favourite communities, a serene outpost on the route that explorer Simon Fraser took to the Coast, with a mixed population of treaty Indians, Métis, whites, and a Chinese family who ran the cafe and skewed the community demographics. But it was clear to me that if the granite quarry were never developed, life would go on regardless.

I had reached the burnout point experienced by every community development worker when she asks herself: "What am I accomplishing here? Am I doing more harm than good? Maybe there is more to life than Jumbo's?" And apparently there was.

Following Carney's Law that in the North nothing ever happens the way it is planned but something else happens instead, BC Deputy Education Minister Dr. Walter Hardwick called to offer Gemini North a new project.

"I'm aware of what you are trying to do, using communication systems to train northern natives in their communities, rather than bring them south," he said. Too often native kids, homesick for their own communities, failed to complete their education when they were sent "outside," and we had experimented with video and other communication systems.

"I want you to head up a Distance Education Planning Group here in BC to see how we can transmit education to people living in their home communities without bringing them down to a bricks-and-mortar college." I was intrigued with the new challenge that once again broke new ground, at least in the BC postsecondary system.

Our project group was an oddly assorted lot of brilliant educators, off-the-wall misfits with new ideas, and professionals such as ex-CBC producer Gene Lawrence, who headed the television production unit at the BC Institute of Technology. We had never heard of Canada's experimental communications satellite Hermes, but within three months we had produced 64 hours of interactive television programming, in colour, using the Hermes satellite to experiment with tele-education and tele-medicine with people living in BC communities up to 750 miles away.

We ran arthritis clinics, tele-education seminars for doctors, simulation programs for fire fighters in the field, computer instruction classes, linking community colleges across the province with UBC in the Lower Mainland, and other experiments. We learned as much from our mistakes as we did from our successes.

One of our more valuable lessons was learning never to use one technology if another one would do the job more economically and efficiently. For instance, when we lost the video component of our satellite feed on our arthritis clinics, we learned that the audio link by itself was sufficient since people don't need to have pictures of swollen joints to discuss pain relief.

I went to NASA-sponsored conferences to meet with other satellite communications experimenters. It was one of the most exciting and satisfying experiences of my career.

In the fall of 1999, as Senator Pat, I attended a dinner hosted by newly appointed Governor General Adrienne Clarkson for Canada's lieutenant-governors and commissioners serving each province and territory. In the throng of people gathered among the totems inside the Royal British Columbia Museum, I met Max House, Lieutenant-Governor of Newfoundland.

"Max!" I cried. "Do you remember Barnaby?"

"Of course I remember Barnaby," exclaimed Max, who was also one of the Hermes satellite communications experimenters and a specialist in tele-medicine. Barnaby was a northern native who had been examined live on camera for possible ulcers in the tiny nursing station of Moose Factory. Yet his doctors were hundreds of miles away in southern Canada.

There was Barnaby in his short hospital gown, glugging down some white stuff. Then we watched as the white stuff toured his digestive system on camera. "Turn a bit to the right, Barnaby, and drink some more," said one of the distance doctors. Barnaby obliged. Glug-glug-glug.

The medical team decided Barnaby did not have ulcers. Max and I, standing amid the throng of dignitaries, agreed this was one of the highlights of our professional lives.

After that experiment, Gemini North was retained by CEO Ray Peters to transform television station BCTV into Canada's first "super-station," working with the station's engineers to deliver BCTV's signal to communities within its footprint, without microwave towers and other ground-based systems. Veteran journalist Jack Webster signed up to transfer his popular radio talk show to television and cleaned up in the ratings.

One day, Yukon businessman Rolf Hougen called from the airport in Whitehorse. "Do you think we could develop a satellite-based television service to serve northern Canada?" he asked. I replied: "I don't know, but let's find out."

Hougen, who owned the department store in Whitehorse, sent down an Arrow shirt box full of clippings, notes, and correspondence with satellite pioneer Ted Turner, visionary founder of CNN. Out of that Arrow shirt box, millions of dollars later, came television communications giant Cancom, which became the first and only company in the world to create and manage a national television service delivered entirely by satellite. Later it merged with Star Alliance.

Gemini North retained Cantel Engineering Ltd. (now known as Teleconsult after Ted Rogers bought the Cantel name) to carry out the engineering, while Gemini staff identified the markets. We found that Canadians with limited television service were not all in the North, but also in southern communities across Canada, such as Cranbrook and Brampton.

After several experimental failures, financed mainly by Rolf Hougen, Gemini North and Cantel successfully designed the package of satellite signals and markets that could deliver the television service to underserved Canadians efficiently and economically. Nine years later, Cancom achieved the profit goals forecast by Gemini-Cantel, and broadcasting executive Douglas Holtby told me that Cancom's market penetration was only five per cent short of our market forecast.

It was a unique contribution to a major Canadian achievement, which encompassed huge efforts by broadcasters like Hougen, Ray Peters, and others. At least Gemini North didn't have the task of raising the millions of dollars required to build the service!

After Gemini found the mix of satellites and markets that worked, and after Hougen had paired up with Ray Peters and other top Canadian television companies, we helped prepare Cancom's successful application to the CRTC for the necessary broadcasting licence.

The licence was awarded on April 14, 1981, but by then I was a Member of Parliament, and in a possible conflict of interest since parliamentarians cannot do business with government. Nor could I effectively run a consulting company based in Vancouver while I was serving as an MP in Ottawa.

In 1981, after 11 exciting years as economic consultants, we gave up the Cancom contract, turned our other projects and staff over to our associated companies, and put Gemini North on hold with a mixture of apprehension, regret, and exhilaration. We were committed to a new adventure. Shades of Bridget Casey!

CHAPTER 9

The North Pole

TRADE SECRET:
*Know your own limits and
those of your equipment,
and never exceed either.*
—Arctic pilot Weldy Phipps

In the dying December days of 1999, we were finishing up the year's work in our Senate office in Ottawa when the fax machine spat out an invitation from Heritage Minister Sheila Copps' office inviting me to a reception to meet Denise Martin, "the first Canadian woman to reach the North Pole."

"But she wasn't the first woman to reach the Pole!" I exclaimed. God, can't these Ottawa bureaucrats ever get things right? "Weldy Phipps' wife Fran was."

I should know. The first woman at the North Pole was supposed to be me, in a publicity stunt for Northwest Territories tourism in 1971.

Instead, legendary Arctic pilot Weldy Phipps, who was scheduled to fly the 1971 expedition to the Pole, said to his blonde wife Fran: "Why should Pat be the first woman at the North Pole when you're living here?"

"Here" was their orange trailer camp and Quonset hut beside the airstrip at Resolute on Cornwallis Island in the High Arctic, where Weldy ran his charter operation Atlas Aviation, flying in Arctic darkness and daylight. Also in residence were some of the Phipps' eight children, other pilots and flight engineers, and a huge Newfoundland dog, Brandy, who shed hair over the furniture and bunk beds. "Don't eat the sticky buns," their camp cook warned me once.

Fran agreed with Weldy. Why Pat Carney? So they climbed into Weldy's famous Twin Otter *Whisky Whisky Papa* (its call letters were CF-WWP for Welland W. Phipps) and climbed down at the North

Pole, where Weldy set up a radio beacon and Fran poured tea. It was April 4, 1971, sunny, and 25 degrees below zero Fahrenheit.

The Minister's office was apologetic when I called to set the record straight. "The invitation is supposed to read the first Canadian woman *to ski* to the North Pole," said a spokesperson distractedly. It was late Friday afternoon; what was she supposed to do? "Invite Fran to the reception," I suggested.

Fran couldn't make it, but I went to congratulate Denise on her awesome achievement. At age 33 she had the trim, taut look of a super-athlete. In 1997 Denise had guided the first all-women's North Pole Expedition, which conducted a relay-style race to the Pole. We spoke of pressure ridges and "leads" of open water in the ice and cold that seared your lungs. "Congratulations, but don't do it again," I chided. Denise smiled. "That's what my mother says," she replied.

I wondered what Denise would tell a future daughter setting off on a similar adventure. When we do these things, in our twenties and thirties, they seem perfectly natural achievements. Alas, the years make us more cautious. I sat in my dark December office and thought back to a sunny April in the Arctic, where ice crystals sparkled down from the white sky, and my craziest Arctic adventure.

In terms of frustration, disappointment, near-mutiny, and a sense of high adventure, our 1971 Canadian expedition to the North Pole was your average Arctic expedition.

For class, it couldn't touch the one headed by Italian millionaire Guido Monzini, who was also heading for the Pole that April by retracing American Robert Peary's 1909 route, accompanied by 330 sled dogs, 23 Inuit, and a sledgeful of champagne and caviar.

For achievement, it was upstaged when Fran Phipps climbed down from *Whisky Whisky Papa*, the alcoholic Twin Otter, to become the first woman to reach the North Pole before the Canadian expedition even left Alert, our jumping-off point on the tip of Ellesmere Island. This made us realize how Capt. R.F. Scott must have felt when he arrived at the South Pole on January 17, 1912, and found Roald Amundsen's flag, which had been placed there on December 14, 1911.

Ever since 1607, when an obsessed Henry Hudson forced his crew within 575 miles of the Pole, people have died (as he did), suffered, lied, and fought to get there. The quest for the Pole, described by author Farley Mowat in his 1967 book, *The Polar Passion*, is the serial story of repeated acts of self-torture driven by self-interest, overwhelming ambition, or blatant chauvinism.

In point of fact, my attempt to be the First Woman at the Top of the World had been set up with my friend and *New York Times* reporter Ed Cowan. "If you can put through a radio-telephone patch from the Pole, I promise to buy you life's biggest, coldest martini," he wrote me in a letter.

"How tall are you? What will you be wearing? Why do you want to go?"[1]

It wasn't my idea, actually. The publicity stunt was the creation of NWT Commissioner Stu Hodgson, part of his dream of expanding tourism in the Arctic, and his concept of parking a Canadian woman at the Pole, albeit at the taxpayer's expense, was designed for media attention. No self-respecting Inuit would have bothered.

The stated objective was to launch Weldy Phipps' inaugural tourist service in his ski-equipped Twin Otter from Resolute Bay to a staging base at Lake Hazen on Ellesmere Island and then to the North Pole. By this time I was running Gemini North in Yellowknife, and Atlas Aviation was a client.

I first met Weldy in 1968 in the Arctic Circle Bar in Resolute, when I was reporting on Arctic oil and gas exploration and he was counting polar bears. In the bar that night, Weldy and I traced the polar explorers through the Arctic. Over drinks we sledged with William Edward Parry, who was hauled by his sailors in 1828 to within 450 miles of the Pole. Over more drinks we debated the fate of Franklin in the ice trap off King William's Island in 1845.

Once, in the Queen Elizabeth Islands, Weldy and two geologists had found a cairn left by British explorer Sir Francis McClintock in 1859. From the cached documents they located one of his abandoned carts and toasted the famous explorer with his own booze.

My favourite explorer was Fridtjof Nansen, a Norwegian scientist and explorer who rammed his ship, the *Fram*, into the polar ice north of Siberia in 1893 and drifted within 243 miles of the Pole cap. The drift over the top of the world was planned to take four years. But bored after two years, Nansen left the ship in the ice under the command of Otto Sverdrup and skied and sledged home. It took him 15 months. He dedicated his journal to his wife, Liv, "who christened the Ship and had the courage to wait."[2]

We drank a toast to Nansen.

After I moved to Yellowknife to establish Gemini North, Weldy phoned me. "I need the name of a doctor," he said gruffly. "I know a good doctor," I said, thinking of our family doctor. "I don't want a good doctor," grumped Weldy. "I want to pass my medical for my pilot's licence renewal."

In 1962, Weldy had pioneered Arctic flying and modern northern exploration by inventing balloon tires for his Piper Cub, a little two-seater aircraft with hotrod engines that could land on snow, ice, slush, mud, sand, or moss, the fat, low-pressure tires acting almost like snow-shoes. They became known as "tundra tires" and opened up the North to "offstrip" flying.

Weldy's world was the starkly beautiful islands and icescapes of Ellesmere Island, with its muskox herds; Axel Heiberg, with its chocolate-coloured mountains; and Ellef Ringnes and Amund Ringnes islands, named like others to honour the Norwegian brewmasters who financed the Norwegian polar expeditions. The Arctic deserts of Melville and Prince Patrick and Devon islands as far east as Greenland were within his range; the Queen Elizabeth Islands, the Sverdrup Islands, and the Parry Islands were all familiar to him.

Weldy became famous for his Arctic flying exploits, rescuing stranded adventurers, supplying food and supplies to isolated camps and scientific expeditions, making emergency medi-vacs to transport sick and injured people to hospital. Once he flew a doctor into Grise Fjord on Ellesmere Island, the most northerly Arctic Inuit community, to deal with a whooping-cough epidemic 250 miles north of Resolute. He landed his plane on the sea ice below the high cliffs in the November dark, and kept the plane warm and the engines running while the doctor treated the sick.

He was also the first pilot to routinely land and take off during the dark months, when there is no sun, from early November to the beginning of February. Arctic pilots, including my son, JP, tell me that flying is best in these months, when the air is too cold to hold moisture and visibility is clear. Ice fog and "white-outs" with blowing snow and near-zero visibility arrive with the sun.

Flying in the dark, without a spark of light, over the frozen empty spaces for hundreds of miles is a lonely experience and I once asked Weldy how he managed to fly for years without losing a single passenger. His reply became my personal mantra: "Know your own limits and those of your equipment, and never exceed either."

Our North Pole expedition was headed by Commissioner Hodgson and his wife Pearl, who had specific instructions not to step off the Twin Otter onto the ice before I did, and included his great friend Air Marshall Hugh Campbell, a member of the NWT Council, and the late Ed Ogle of *Time* magazine. Also on board at the Commissioner's ingenuous invitation was a California film crew who planned to plant the American flag and a letter from then California Governor Ronald Reagan at the Pole, thus threatening to create an international incident over ownership of the territory around the Pole.

The Canadians informed the American crew that they must plant their flag within the Alaska sector, even though the United States has been slow to embrace the theory that polar countries have the rights to the longitudinal pie slice between their Arctic coasts and the imaginary point at the North Pole. Only Canada and Russia have endorsed the sector theory, since they have the most to gain.

At the start of our expedition in Yellowknife, nobody knew where Weldy was. He was supposed to be caching fuel in the vicinity of the Pole. When our advance party, which included my brother Jim, stopped at Eureka, the weather station on the west coast of Ellesmere Island, on April 4, 1971, they found Weldy was touching down at the Pole with Fran. Her greetings crackled through the radio shack. A plaintive message was telexed over from Isaachsen, another isolated Arctic weather station on Ellef Ringnes Island: "How about dropping a woman off here?"

I was curling my hair in the Officers' Mess in the Canadian Armed Forces camp at Alert, on the tip of Ellesmere Island about 500 miles south of the North Pole, when I heard the news. Everyone watched me cautiously, waiting for my Irish-tempered reaction. But I laughed. Good for Fran! If I were her, I would have done the same. But the Commissioner was determined to press on, despite Fran's scoop. Like others before and after us, we wanted to reach the Pole.

To reach the North Pole, first fly to the Canadian Forces station at Alert on Ellesmere Island. Those struggling over the ice with sled dogs or skis usually push on to Ward Hunt Island just beyond the airstrip. Then fly a heading of 036 grid to T-3, an ice island that in 1971 was drifting 230 miles offshore and trapped in the polar pack. Alter course to 089 grid and continue for 290 nautical miles.

At the millennium there might be a dozen Twin Otters dispersed around the Canadian shores of the polar basin, but there were none when we took off from Alert in 1971. There were no radio aids. The compass was useless, skewed by its proximity to the magnetic North Pole southwest of us off Ellef Ringnes Island.

When Weldy rejoined us, we flew north from Alert in two Atlas Aviation Twin Otters piloted by Jack Austin and Dick de Blicquy and crammed with a cairn, champagne, box lunches, emergency radios, sleeping bags, and two 45-gallon drums of fuel. The plywood floor of *Whisky Whisky Papa* was slivered with ice that chilled my sealskin-booted toes.

We flew in tandem over the beaded, fractured ice. If we went down, we would roll up like a ball, said Austin. Weldy, looking like a grizzled Arctic muskox, worked at his charts on an upended fuel drum at the rear of the plane, taking sun shots and checking wind drift. Austin, looking like a bearded Arctic seal, never took his eyes off the control panel, holding the Otter level and on course so that Weldy could take his readings. We flew at an altitude of 10 000 feet at 140 knots.

What do you do en route to the Pole? The Commissioner read *Where Eagles Dare*; on its back cover Richard Burton promised it was the Best Adventure Story I've Ever Read. Jim slept like an Inuit, head turned into his parka hood. I thumbed through an article entitled "The Glamourless Polar Regions," which stated that the North Pole trip is a routine, boring flight.

I moved up front to the co-pilot's seat to chat through the headsets with Austin and to examine the endless ice below us, glistening wetly in the sun, studded by rubbled rounds of blue ice. The Inuit have many different words to describe different ice conditions but this is what you need to know about ice: blue ice is ancient polar ice that has never thawed. It is so hard that should you crash, it would pound you like an iron fist. Smooth, white ice is young ice, sometimes one year old, often land-fast ice. Flying over the Arctic, you can tell where the rivers run into the sea by the colour and texture of the ice. Black ice is bad ice, rotting ice. You never land on black ice without fear of sinking.

I became entranced with the High Arctic and its island archipelago as a journalist, hitchhiking by air through the Arctic islands covering the development of Canada's oil and gas resources. I was particularly fascinated by the Norwegians, men like Nansen and Otto Sverdrup, called the King of Arctic navigators.

Arctic exploration was the nineteenth century's space-age equivalent, the last frontier for global exploration by young adventuresome and scientific minds seeking new worlds to conquer. The Vikings were the first European Arctic explorers to penetrate the secrets of the ice. The Norwegians believed there was an open polar sea behind the enormous masses of ice that blocked their path, if only the polar sea could be reached.

After completing his first voyage, Sverdrup and the *Fram* returned to explore the Canadian Arctic islands in 1898 to 1902, naming features like Butterporridge Point, Bay of Woe, and Norwegian Bay, claiming the region for King Oscar of Norway. Although the islands discovered by the British had been turned over to Canada in 1880, no Canadian had ventured north of the entrance to Davis Strait off the coast of Labrador.

Canada was embarrassed and Norway indifferent. In 1929 Sverdrup invoiced Prime Minister Mackenzie King for $67 000 to cover the costs of his High Arctic explorations in return for relinquishing Norwegian rights to his islands. After interminable delays, his invoice was eventually paid in 1930, only 15 days before his death, and Canada gained its Arctic island heritage.

The Norwegians' view of the Arctic was of an uninhabited pristine wilderness. The opening chapter of Nansen's journal starts: "Unseen and untrodden under their spotless mantle of ice the rigid polar regions slept the profound sleep of death from the earliest dawn of time. Wrapped in his white shroud, the mighty giant stretched his clammy ice-limbs abroad, and dreamed his age long dreams. Ages passed—deep was the silence."[3]

But 75 years later there were Inuit communities in the High Arctic, at Grise Fjord and Resolute, and the sound of drilling rigs and seismic exploration rang through the chilled air. Weldy and his big-wheeled Alcoholic Otter covered distances in hours that had taken the *Fram* years. Gazing out the cockpit window, I marvelled at the Norwegians' accomplishments.

"Look at that. T-3, the island, right where it's supposed to be," said pilot Jack Austin, with quiet satisfaction. He had been navigating by dead reckoning. Awed, I looked out the cockpit window. In the middle of all the rubbled ice, tinted blue-green at the base of the ridges, was a pure white sheet of smooth, slick ice, glinting like a skating rink, which had broken free from the Ellesmere ice shelf, floating like an ice island in the polar ocean. We landed and taxied up to a collection of scattered trailers that housed the US Naval Arctic Research Station. We tumbled out of the Twin Otter and headed for the cook shack, which sported a large sign promising the Finest Food North of North America. It was 25 degrees below zero Fahrenheit and the ice cracked under our feet like frozen bullets.

Drop-in visitors were rare at T-3, and the crew gave us coffee and warm greetings. The Commissioner presented T-3 manager Bill Beck with both the Canadian and Territorial flags, since T-3 had drifted in the polar ice cap, like Nansen's ship the *Fram*, and was now in the Canadian sector. Like Nansen, we pressed north, our aircraft taking off on skis.

Ninety miles from the Pole, the ice-crystal fog misting the polar pack grew thicker. Silver leads of open water snaked through the pressure ridges. "How do you know when you've reached the Pole?" I asked Weldy. This was long before the era of satellite communications and GPS navigation systems that you can carry in your pocket. He grunted: "You shoot to within one minute of latitude. Then count sixty and land."

Our program called for us to "arrive North Pole 1200 hrs. CST, erect cairn, emplace flag, lunch."[4] But the ice fog misted the ice below. Weldy needed enough light to cast shadows on the ice surface so that he could measure the height of the hummocks to ensure a safe landing. This time, he didn't get it.

If I couldn't sit up front in the co-pilot's seat, I usually managed to sit on the right-hand seat behind the cockpit where, peering through the cockpit door, I could read the aircraft's control panel, alarming both myself and the pilots. Down, down, down circled the Twin Otter until the altimeter read 500 feet. Then, to my relief, the needle climbed up, up, up. Jack Austin was aborting our attempt to touch down at the Pole.

There was a moment of gloom and then we all agreed that T-3 was where the action was. When we returned to the ice island, three flags were flying above the cookhouse—the Canadian, the Territorial, and a spanking new Stars and Stripes.

On T-3 there is a sense of continents spinning away to the South. The ice island is approximately five miles long, two miles wide, and 150 feet thick. Riding above the polar pack on top of the Arctic Ocean, it plies an oval course across the top of North America at an average speed of roughly two miles a day.

The year before our expedition, during an argument fuelled by home brew, a man was murdered on T-3. The United States, arguing that T-3 is a ship, claimed jurisdiction for the murder trial. But Weldy, an elected member of the NWT Territorial Council, pointed out that T-3 was drifting into his High Arctic constituency.

The night of our failed expedition we hauled our cold sleeping bags out of the Alcoholic Otter and its twin and slept on the floor of the US Navy cook shack. The next day we returned to the Canadian Forces base at Alert. The Commissioner called the expeditionary party together and asked for suggestions. "I suggest we join Monzini," said Weldy, referring to the Italian who was sledding across the polar pack with caviar and champagne.

But some of the party had jobs and families and second thoughts. In the end, half of us were sent south to civilization on a Learjet. The rest of us, including Jim and me, committed to stay until the weather cleared. We jumped into a Bombardier, a tracked vehicle with skis for moving over frozen ground, and trucked down to the airstrip to see the group depart.

The pilots of the Lear jet knelt on the wings, covering the jet intakes with their bodies to protect them from blowing gravel kicked up by a Hercules aircraft on take-off. We waved the group off, feeling separation pangs. I thought of Otto Sverdrup, who waved off Nansen as he headed over the ice on skis and sleds, and then returned to the frozen *Fram* for his one o'clock dinner.

The fire-engine-red camp of Alert glistened in the sun on the snowy plateau about a mile away. On the way back to the camp, the Bombardier's gas line froze and the vehicle stopped. I jumped down to walk back to camp. "Hey, don't do that," said the driver sharply. "You don't have your wind pants on." He told us that recently a man, too casual about the cold, had walked to the end of the 5000-foot strip to check the radio beacon. Suddenly a wind came up. In the Arctic, a temperature of minus 20 degrees Fahrenheit and a wind speed of 20 miles an hour produces a wind chill of 53 degrees below zero Fahrenheit. Temperatures of minus 30 and a 40-mile-per-hour wind will create a wind chill of 100 degrees below zero. By the time the man had returned to camp he was frostbitten from the waist down.

We waited for the weather to improve, swapping yarns over coffee. Weldy had landed at the Pole six times. The first time was with Ralph Plaisted, the American who in 1968 made the first successful surface crossing of the polar cap on snowmobiles, despite a horrendous lack of direction. Weldy dropped instructions from *Whisky Whisky Papa* by canister: "Follow the lead for 10 miles and then turn 45 degrees north. And I mean *NORTH*."

People have parachuted near the Pole and swum under it in frog suits and tried to sail over it in a balloon, which unfortunately broke in two. There was the British couple who tried to ski to the Pole and were rescued by Weldy 51 days after they set out.

There was the British schoolteacher whose team's strategy was to travel light through the offshore rubble of ice, relying on Weldy to drop supplies in the smoother ice beyond. The evening of the day the party left, Weldy headed the Alcoholic Otter down the airstrip, preparing to take off and drop supplies. Halfway down he met a member of the expedition walking back. The party was barely a mile offshore. "For God's sake, drop the sleeping bags," gasped the man.

There was the Italian Monzini out there on the ice, with his dogs and dentist and shears for cutting off frozen toes. He had landed earlier on the Alert airstrip in his Hercules, the airborne Arctic camel, which returned to Denmark for 20 000 pounds of pemmican for the dogs. Jack Austin sampled some down on the strip.

Weldy was navigating our voyage to the North Pole with a cracked and strapless watch, so Jack Austin and I snowmobiled to the canteen to buy a new one. The measure of homesickness in Alert could be read in the canteen card display: "To My Darling Daughter. To Mother. To My Wife."

One Timex watch was priced at $7.85, the other at $13.00. The purchase of this critical navigation aid—Nansen became lost when he let his chronometer run down—must be financed from our beer money. Jack bought the cheaper watch, grudgingly exchanging it for the other when we realized the cheap model lacked a second hand.

Every morning Weldy would bring coffee to the ladies' quarters in the Officers' Mess, where his wife Fran and I were staying, and tell us the weather was lousy and we had no fuel. So every day we sat in the mess—dubbed the ladies' lounge—while the Commissioner bargained and bartered for fuel and we "waited for weather," as northerners say.

Waiting in the Arctic is an art. Usually you play cribbage or visit. During the long, light days we did both. I learned that Fran Phipps was not your average housewife. She had a warm, lilting voice, honey-coloured hair, and a trim figure, despite bearing eight children then aged twenty-three to three years. Six lived at Resolute in the Atlas Aviation trailer complex, where for years Fran cooked for the crew and monitored the radio and taught the kids not to eat the coloured snow outside.

Frances Cool was a 19-year-old Ottawa typist, crazy over airplanes, when she met Welland Wilfrid Phipps, her flying instructor. She married him a year later and never finished her pilot's licence course. "Not when I had myself a pilot," she said. In the early years of their marriage Weldy was away about half the year, so Fran moved the family north to Resolute. She liked the Arctic. "Weldy and I are very adventurous. We do a lot of things on the spur of the moment and it has worked out well."

Weldy sat in the mess in his duffles, the knee-high woollen liners of his boots, recounting how he was once fined $50 and costs for eating an ice-cream cone in the bar at Churchill. A former prisoner of war during World War II, barnstormer, and parachute jumper, Weldy had spent 20 years in the North when we met.

Jack Austin was a master at waiting during his 20 years in the North. When he retired from the RCMP air division, the people of Pond Inlet on Baffin Island in the eastern Arctic gave him a trophy for spending more time in Pond waiting for weather than any other Twin Otter pilot. Once he was forced down on the sea ice off Baffin Island for 11 days. He and his Inuit passengers played cribbage. Now he smoked a pipe in the Alert "ladies' lounge" and told the California film crew that a policeman's job is to help people. "Not in California," said the cameramen.

The white veil of weather lifted and lowered. The Hercs droned overhead. The *New York Times* wired a request for my vivid, personal account of our dramatic adventure. I barely looked up from my crib board.

The average tour of duty for the 200 Canadian Forces personnel at Alert was six months. One day a young man stomped into the mess hall and shouted: "Who's got 108 days left?" His messmates yelled back: "*Nobody's* got 108 days left."

"I do," said the young man sadly.

By early April the sun spins around the horizon 24 hours a day. Governed by the tilt of the earth's axis, it never climbs more than a few degrees above the horizon. Day and night are irrelevant in a white world that shifts from pale sunlight to misty white-out. Nor does your watch help. At the North Pole, where latitudes converge, technically time does not exist. It is zero-zero-zulu all the time.

We came from a world where day dawns and night darkens, where the sun arcs across the sky. We were suspended, lost, in this new one. We ate breakfast when we expected lunch. We slept when we were tired and got up when we awoke. In time, we became euphoric; beyond keeping warm and being agreeable, nothing mattered. It was an Arctic high. It takes a while to wear off when you return south.

Every evening the Commissioner and Air Marshall Hugh Campbell marched down to Crystal City, the local nickname for the Ministry of Transport weather station, to check the weather. I followed with six husky dogs snapping at my sealskin kamiks. We gathered in the radio room to check the telex and try to reach T-3, 200 miles and six time zones away, through the static.

Every evening the telex chattered: "NO NEW INFO FROM ICE ISLANDS THEREFORE PROBABLY XTNSV LYRS ICE XTAL CLD WITH SNOW FOG AND STRATUS REDUCING VSBY AT POLE SURFACE CONDNS 05x lic BS WIND 33320 GRID LITTLE IMPRUMNT LIKELY FOR SATURDAY." Rough translation: Conditions awful. Ceiling 500 feet, obscured, visibility one mile, ice crystals and blowing snow.

"I don't believe it," the Commissioner roared with each poor weather report. "How do they know what the weather is like at the Pole? If I followed that kind of advice, I'd still be in Yellowknife. Worse still, I'd still be in Ottawa." Weldy greeted the news by showing off his trick of drinking scotch while standing on his head.

One day we flew to Greenland. We followed fjords tongued with great glaciers and flew over the battered wooden huts of Fort Conger, the winter camp of the 1881 Greely expedition to the Pole: the few survivors ate the corpses of their companions. Once Weldy marked out an airstrip with the skulls of the muskox they had shot.

Then we flew across the heaving ice of Hall Basin to the shores of Greenland's Polaris Bay, named by the American polar explorer Charles Francis Hall after his ship *Polaris*, which had set a new record sailing to latitude 82 degrees, 11 minutes north, 100 years earlier. Hall then turned back to the bay that he had called "Thank God Harbour," where he died suddenly after drinking a cup of coffee, claiming his crew members had poisoned him. Weldy searched the bay's shoreline for a place to land.

It was a shining day. A skeleton moon rode in the pale sky and the white sun poured light over the ice. We landed on smooth sea ice some distance from shore and picked our way single-file through the giant green icebergs to land. We walked up the frozen, flinty beach to the 1871 grave of the explorer. Three years before our visit, Hall's ice-preserved body had been exhumed and examined, revealing the presence of large quantities of arsenic. But the cause of his death remains a mystery.

It was all still there: the grave, cookstoves, cannonballs, shovels, and other odds and ends, mute testimony to mutiny and murder and for some escape over drifting ice pans when the *Polaris* became beset in ice near Baffin Bay on its return journey. Nineteen crew members were forced to winter on the ice when the floe they stood on drifted away from their ship. They were kept alive by the native survival techniques of two Inuit assistants.

Cold burned our flesh. Lichen flamed on the shale slabs of the gravestones. We were haunted by the sense of recent ghosts. There was no trace of the expedition that had exhumed Hall. The Commissioner stuffed the pockets of his parka with cannonballs. "We can't take those, we're in a foreign country," we protested.

Finally, the Commish took a cannonball to present to the Governor of Greenland. The rest of us took pictures before walking back over the sea ice to the aircraft and the warmth of the Alert ladies' lounge, and the cook shack known as the "Igloo Gardens."

On our last attempt, Jack Austin was filing his flight plan over the radio when I hauled myself into the cockpit of the Alcoholic Otter and asked what the weather was like at the Pole. "How the hell do I know?"

grumped Austin. "We're going to go and find out." He flicked on his radio again. "It's Atlas and it's red," he intoned. I realized that detail might help anyone who came looking for us if we crashed. "Roger roger," said Alert radio. "Who cares about the goddamn weather?" said the Commissioner from his seat in the aircraft. "Sit down and relax. Not a thing you can do about it."

After take-off we flew past the marshmallow mountains of Ellesmere, starkly shadowed across the worried ice. The only radio signal we could pick up was from a Russian ice island on the other side of the Pole. Every few minutes Jack Austin would radio: "T-3 this is *Whisky Whisky Papa*. If you read, Bill, please turn on your beacon." Victor Bravo, Victor Bravo beamed the Russian station. There was only shouting static from T-3.

I thought that zeroing in on one lonely ice island amid a sea of pack ice below, using dead-reckoning navigation, was not particularly appealing. But then the alternative of landing on the pack ice was not attractive, either. "There it is," said Jack, beginning his descent to T-3, right there under our aircraft's nose.

There are six time zones between Alert, on Atlantic time, and T-3, on Alaskan time, and we always arrived during their sleep shift. It was now 6:30 a.m. Alaska time. Base manager Bill Beck woke up Inuit assistant Charlie Brower and told him: "Quick. There's a plane running round loose up there." When we trailed into the Finest Food North of North America, the Commissioner informed the American base manager that nine of us were prepared to camp on his cookhouse floor until the weather cleared.

This suggestion was coolly received by the base manager. He and the Commissioner disappeared into the radio shack to debate the issue. The weather was hazing quickly. Bone-weary and feeling mutinous, we were beginning to sympathize with Hall's crew, who had resented being pushed farther north.

The Commissioner stomped back into the cookhouse. Clearly his sought-after approval to billet on the cook shack floor was not forthcoming. "I wouldn't drink the coffee, Mr. Hall," grinned *Time* magazine correspondent Ed Ogle. The rest of us tried to look mutinous. It wasn't hard. We had spent seven days attempting to reach the Pole.

In the end, we simply turned back, like so many Arctic expeditions. We heard the Air Marshal tell the Commissioner we were at the point of no return and it was time to pack it in. Dispirited and disappointed, we trooped back one last time to *Whisky Whisky Papa* and flew back in deteriorating weather to Alert.

The Learjet was already on the strip and we piled in. Flying at 40 000 feet, we could see the top of the world curve away below us, as a globe should, the Arctic islands floating like jigsaw-puzzle pieces in the ice and open water.

After T-3, Alert looked like an outpost of civilization, Resolute looked like a town, and Yellowknife, with its single 11-storey apartment building, looked as urban as Toronto. When we landed at Edmonton in spring weather, about a hundred-degree change from T-3, we piled into the Edmonton Inn and slept like survivors from the *Voyage of the Damned*.

My hero Nansen had reached 86 degrees, 13 minutes, and 6 seconds of latitude. For us it was 85 degrees, 21 minutes north, the latitude of T-3. It took him 15 months on the ice and us a few hours by air. Denise Martin and her companion Matty McNair, who did reach the Pole, spent 81 days on the Arctic ice covering 500 miles.

As for the Italian Monzini, with caviar and champagne, we circled his camp on the way back and left him out there on the ice. He was rescued before he reached the Pole, stranded by melting ice and open leads.

More than 100 years after Nansen's journey, his ice-limbed giant is part of the Inuit territory of Nunavut. The drilling crews have left, beaten by the costs of developing the oil and gas resources. Gemini North was once asked by a client to study the feasibility of moving natural gas south by using a pipeline over the ice. I called it Project Nansen. At the time the feasibility was zero; the ice ridges were too high and shifting.

Tourists visit the North Pole in Twin Otters to have their pictures taken and their wallets emptied. Weldy did establish a tourist camp on Lake Hazen, Ellesmere Island, but it later burned down.

Weldy collected the range of aviation honours, including his appointment to the Aviation Hall of Fame in 1973. He was made a Companion of the Order of Canada in 1976. He and Fran left the North in 1972 for Prince Edward Island and a two-year cruise through the Caribbean and the Bahamas, encountering little ice fog on their journey. Weldy died on October 29, 1996, aged 74, a true Canadian hero.

Our fascination with polar exploration continues on foot, by balloon, by sled, and on skis. In addition to Denise and her 1997 ski expedition, in 1995 Canadian Arctic explorer Richard Weber and his Russian teammate Mikhail Malakhov became the first people to ski to the Pole and back again, covering 950 miles in 121 days using muscle power alone; no sled dogs, snowmobiles, or supply drops.[5] Nansen would have been proud. Weber counts 10 trips to the Pole among his 35 Arctic expeditions and is planning others, including an attempt to prove that American Robert Peary never reached the Pole in 1909.

And 20 years after our aborted polar expedition, my son JP was flying a group of Young Presidents to the North Pole on a red-and-white Kenn Borek Aviation Twin Otter, a corporate successor to Atlas Aviation, at $11 000 a pop. Thumbing his radio switch on the yoke, or controls, he told the other pilot: "My mom did this once."

"Did she make it?" asked the other pilot. "Nope," said JP. "That makes you one up on her, eh?" said his companion. They landed on skis, jumped out of the Twin Otter onto the pack ice in the brilliant sunshine, and had their picture taken with their freezing, ice-whiskered passengers. I have it on my desk.

CHAPTER 10

Macho Men

TRADE SECRET:
You are not a real man unless you've lost
$100 000 mining for gold in the Klondike.
—Yukon saying quoted by Paul S. White

I n the summer of 1999, Paul White and I flew up to Yukon to visit
my daughter Jane and her husband, Malcolm Duncan, who had
left the crisis-plagued BC fishing industry to open an ice-cream
and candy store in Dawson City, centre of the 1898 Klondike
Gold Rush. Surveying the other passengers on the Boeing 737 to
Whitehorse, I wondered where all the macho men had gone.

When I first went north as a business columnist for the *Vancouver
Sun* 30 years earlier, my fellow passengers were largely mining engineers, truck drivers, drillers, cat operators, pilots—muscled men in
plaid shirts and heavy pants and big boots who dug wealth out of the
ground in isolated camps scattered north and south of the Arctic
Circle. My *Oxford Dictionary* defines macho as "manly, virile." They
were that.

The passengers on our 1999 flight, however, were mostly shod in
hiking boots, wearing fleece vests or jackets and jeans, with video
cameras bulging out of backpacks, secured with water bottles and
sleeping bags. Many were trim and fit but hardly a muscle could be
flexed among them.

Two of the few macho men on board were geologists John Brock
and Wayne Roberts. John played a significant role in the exploration
phase of Anvil Mines, once the largest lead-zinc-silver producer found
in Yukon, which pumped money into the territorial economy and created the town of Faro, home to 1200 people before the mine shut

down in 1998. Despite an anti-mining political environment, John and Wayne are still prospecting.

Paul White is definitely a macho man. He surveyed the Anvil property and later ran the largest placer gold-mining operation in Yukon in 1990 at Indian River. He outran a moose, both ploughing through snowdrifts, when he was 47 years old. He hangs a sign from the mothballed Faro Hotel in his study: "Welcome weary travelers. Sled dogs outside please."

Faro wasn't yet born when I walked the Anvil property back in the late 1960s, when it was only a flagged potential mine.

In the summer of 1968 I flew to the Dawson airstrip and leaned against a dust-spattered, mosquito-pocked Fargo pickup, waiting for my twin Jim, who was filming in Yukon. I never drove into town, but I could see the coils of mined river gravel writhing in the streambeds, evidence of placer mining in the past.

Jim rolled up in the local mining recorder's car, late as usual. We heaved our camera, tape recorders, and gear into the DC-3, seats stripped out to make room for freight, and headed over the mountains to Inuvik in the Mackenzie Delta. On board we spread out our maps. Do we go to the Arctic Islands from Inuvik? Or do we go to Coppermine on the central Arctic coast? Or should we head upriver to Yellowknife? Since there were no scheduled flights where we were going, it depended on what aircraft we could hitch a ride on.

We were there to record the intense interest in oil and gas and mining exploration, which had fired the North, sparked by new mineral discoveries and the creation of Panarctic Oil Ltd., an innovative consortium formed by the Canadian government, mining giant Cominco, and a handful of independent Canadian companies. Panarctic's mission was to find oil in the islands of the Arctic Ocean to rival the sheikdoms of the Middle East, which had a stranglehold on crude supplies to eastern Canada and the United States.

Then, the sense of high adventure associated with High Arctic exploration had attracted hundreds of macho men to the North.

Now, macho men are definitely an out-of-date concept. The new male role model in the year 2000 is the bespectacled Internet geek, or the e-commerce merchant, or the day-trader speculator. In the first month of the new millennium two New York psychologists released a survey showing that young men were falling prey to a form of male bulimia with their obsessive desire to make money on the stock market and Internet.

Blaming the financial media for the "devastating disorder," Drs. Eric Smith and Adam Cohen of New York University announced that our brightest young men "are squandering their enormous potential for growth and personal happiness on a meaningless obsession with dot-coms, bandwidth, relative net worth, and the fleeting indices of success, such as stock overvaluation . . . they binge and purge, or rather purge then binge."[1]

I'll take a macho man over a bulimic one any time. Men like "catskinner" (caterpillar driver) Leo Vanderleest, whom Jim and I met on Melville Island in the High Arctic about 1500 miles north of Edmonton on that trip in 1968. Leo "walked" his D-8 caterpillar tractor nearly 200 miles through the freezing, wind-slammed Arctic spring, pulling a cat camp behind him.

The cat camp, to house an oil-exploration crew, consisted of an eight-man sleeper, a cookhouse, a wash car, and a utility trailer. The cook, two catskinners, and a mechanic travelled with him. It took them three weeks, travelling on sea ice and frozen land, ahead of the summer melt, using Leo's watch for a compass. I wrote in the *Vancouver Sun*:

> Melville Island is a frozen desert at the top of the world, a land mass of sandstone and shale sediments dumped off the Arctic coast of Canada by the northern rivers and emerging from the polar sea in response to grim geological forces. Its arid wastes support little animal life and no permanent human population.
>
> Leo, of course, hasn't the faintest idea he should be a Canadian legend. He is a big, good-humoured catskinner, ear-flapped and parka'd against the snow flurries of an Arctic August. When I met him, he had just walked his cat another ninety miles, travelling alone, day and night, with some food, fuel, and a tent. "Nothing out there but mud and musk-ox horns," he complained.[2]

Jim and I had hitched a ride to Drake Point on Melville, rolling out our sleeping bags next to the generator in the spare utility shack. Everything had been airlifted in and living quarters were sparse. The crew in camp hung blankets from their bunks for privacy. Craving a shower, I figured I could sneak one after crew change. Wrong. A young "juggie," or seismic crewman, walked into the washroom and found a naked woman in the shower. "Holy fuck," he exclaimed. Later, in the cook shack, he apologized for his language.

Drake Point camp is fourteen orange trailers and four tents, a small spark of life in a lunar landscape. Low hills slant away, and a sterile lake glimmers through the mist. An Arctic tern circles over the plywood privy, and a grey Arctic fox steals bread from the garbage pile.

Behind the camp stand the Bell 204 choppers and a Hiller F-1100, twentieth-century equivalents of the nineteenth-century British explorer sledges. A ghost of a sun shines through the snow flurries, and the ground is frozen hard. I walk down to the wind-stirred lake, picking up a tern feather, a small yellow poppy, purple saxifrage. The land is terrifying in its barrenness.

Only Canadians give it manageable dimensions.

The most macho of the oil and gas executives was the late Charles Hetherington, president of Panarctic Oil Ltd., and the visionary who drove the search for oil in the High Arctic in order to protect Canada's energy supplies, at least until alternative energy sources could be developed.

As Energy Minister, in 1985 I signed the first production certificate for High Arctic oil in the recreation room of the Panarctic camp at Bent Horn, Cameron Island, in the presence of Richard Nerysoo, then Leader of the Government of the NWT, who presented me with a necklace with three whale images to commemorate the event.

Then the first crude oil ever tankered out of the Arctic left Bent Horn, headed through the ice-choked channels to a refinery in Montreal.

Other macho men on Melville were helicopter pilots like Jim Ritson, who transported equipment and crew out to plot the shot lines and to shoot seismic, mapping the underground structures that may— or may not—be oil-bearing. I flew out with him on one trip.

We fly over the snow-filled wadis of this northern desert. The black tracks of the Nodwell drilling unit wander off through the eroding sand and the sun throws cones of light on the pack ice piled up against the shore. When the sun shines, the land softens, like worn brown velvet. Then you can sense the yellow poppies in the lichen, and where the ice has torn free from the shore, the open water turns cobalt blue. But the mists close, the colour fades, and the land resumes its harshness.

We come up over the hill on line 37 where the drillers are working. The helidrills are designed to be moved by choppers, which can carry 4000 pounds under Arctic conditions. A driller climbs up on the tower of the helidrill and holds up a ring for the chopper to snag on to. In cold weather his wrists freeze.

Jim jockeys his chopper over the tower, picks it up and flies it, swinging, a mile up to the red and blue flag of a shot point. Then Jim flies up the line, dropping powder off at the shot points near a huge salt dome, which has barreled up through the earth's surface like a bullet. If there is oil on Melville, it may be trapped against the impervious plug of the salt dome.

It is a grey, blowing world. "And it is the middle of Goddamn August," says Jim as he spins up and around to 1500 feet while he serves as radio relay between Drake Point and Sherard Bay. Then down, and back to packing drills.

On another journalistic assignment, I flew on a Hercules north into daylight from the midnight-black of Edmonton. Tired, I crawled into a trailer in the belly of the aircraft and slept on a pile of mattresses.

The Hercs are the airborne camels of the Arctic desert. You see them, great lumbering beasts squatting on the strip of some nomadic camp, their tail-wing the height of a five-storey building, their low-slung underbellies jammed with pipe, drilling mud, fuel bladders, helicopters, tractors, trailer units.

Below us, the Arctic Islands lie in landfast ice like smooth, albino seals. Ravines run black lines over their bare white backs, and the shadow lines of their clamshell cliffs angle into the mist.

The Herc will be the first to land at the new airstrip scraped out of the sand at Rea Point on Melville. We descend to look for the strip. The compass swings uselessly this close to the magnetic north pole. We pick up a caterpillar trail in the snow and follow it to the airstrip. The met man is the cook.

"What's the weather like down there?" asks the pilot. "Not good," glooms the cook. The Herc circles the camp. "Can you see the utility shack from the cook shack?" asks the pilot. The utility shack is bright orange. "Yeah," says the cook. We brace ourselves. The Herc lands with a jolt, thudding down the strip. Cans, cameras, equipment clatter from the shelves. "You've got to be ding-a-ling to fly in this country," says the young flight engineer.

Freddy Carmichael is definitely not ding-a-ling—definitely a macho man. He was running his own air charter service out of Inuvik when I first met him, and was famous for his dogged and often successful searches for missing pilots, downed in the Mackenzie Delta. His ancestry is classic Mackenzie Delta: Inuit, Dene, and Other. His dream of training other aboriginal kids as pilots sustained his career.

Many macho pilots died on the job—too many to even think about. Not, however, Daryle Brown, the meanest man who ever flew. That's why, whenever we had a choice, we flew with him anywhere in the Northwest Territories. He was too mean to die young.

A former gyppo logger from Kingcome Inlet on the BC coast, young Daryle saw a floatplane land by the camp. "I'm going to get me one of them things," he said, and headed north. When I met him he was chief pilot for Wardair's Yellowknife operation. He and his then wife Joyce and their two kids, Vicki and Barry, were good friends of ours.

Daryle didn't just buckle up his seat belt; he strapped his plane on. His checklist was "Noise, gas, no red lights, and we warm her up on the climb." He headed for the nearest bar at touchdown. "It's getting at 'er time pretty damn quick," he'd say. "Eight hours from bottle to throttle and if you can't hack her, drink lots."

He'd stagger out of his iron cot in some Arctic transient centre where our party was communally bunked with our sleeping bags and groceries, and stare out the window, hoping for the respite of bad weather. "Cheez," he'd say. "The whole damn world is clear."

"Airplane for sale or rent, seats to let, 50 cents," he often sang, as we flew over country where the altitudes were given tentatively as 3000 feet, plus or minus, and the maps warned "No relief data" and "Unnamed point," and we could tell the ice ended because of the dark water sky.

Once I flew with Daryle over open water, scummed with ice-sheets, somewhere north of Southampton Island and the Bay of God's Mercy in Hudson Bay. It was near sunset and the open leads shone like silver in the shadowed ice.

I am sitting in the co-pilot's seat, admiring the view, when I realize that Daryle has not taken his eyes off the instrument panel. He sits there, his wolf parka thrown over his shoulders, his hands clutching the controls, headset on the back of his rumpled head, smoking his cigarette down to the butt, his stubby eyelashes flickering back and forth over the dials. I also realize we have been out of radio contact for some time. We should be spotting land, but there is nothing down there but ice and thirty-seven degrees below zero weather.

"Where are we?" I ask. "Dunno," says Daryle morosely. "Are we lost?" I ask timidly. "S'pose," he glooms. We drive on in dead silence. "The trouble with this kind of flying is you have to luck out all the time," Daryle says unexpectedly. "Like in the barrens, if there is no beacon, you just pick out a heading and go.

"Sometimes you get the feeling that you should crank her around again another ten degrees. Everybody does it different. And sometimes you get the feeling that this is not the day. Someone looks at the weather and says, 'It looks good to me.' And you say, 'Well, she don't look good to me,' and half an hour later you're fogged in."

He cranks the Twin Otter around to watch the sunset. Pilots who watch sunsets can't be all bad.

On that trip to the Belcher Islands our aircraft touched down on wheels in two feet of snow and lurched to a stop, stuck, although the local Bay man had told us on the radio the ice was suitable for landing. Our party and the local Inuit carved an airstrip, 20 feet wide and 500 feet long, out of the snow before sunset the next day. We fashioned a scraper out of old fencing pulled by a Ski-Doo, sawing the snow into blocks, and manually chucking it onto one side of the strip. The snow blocks were piled five feet high.

I've done ten years of bush flying and the strip looked pretty narrow to me. The book says the Twin Otter needs 1,200 feet. "There is all kinds of room," said Daryle. "I just wheel down and roar at her." He backed the Twin Otter to the end of the strip. He put on the brakes and revved the engines up to full take off power. Then he let the brakes go, and we catapulted down our hand-made strip.

We were off. Then, inexplicably, the Otter started dropping again. I watched the ice come up and knew with dreadful calm that we were going in, when Daryle leveled that plane out twenty feet off the ice, wiggling his wings to thank the Inuit who stood astounded, shovels in their hands, and we zoomed off for getting at 'er time in Great Whale River. It was March 17, St. Patrick's Day.

Daryle eventually hung up his headsets and headed back to the Coast, buying a charter boat. He was once seen towing a single-engine Beaver aircraft behind his charter boat across the Gulf of Georgia. He was last seen living on board, tied up to a marina at Sidney, British Columbia.

Daryle's great buddy and mentor was another macho man, Stu Hodgson. The ex-labour lawyer was appointed Commissioner of the Northwest Territories, charged with establishing self-government there in 1967, by moving the nucleus of a territorial civil service from Ottawa to Yellowknife, the gold-mining town on the shores of Great Slave Lake, which was chosen as the territorial capital. No doubt the people, many of them Inuit, who established the new government of Nunavut in Frobisher's former field camp at Iqaluit in 1999 were also macho men and women.

Stuart M. Hodgson, commissioner of the Northwest Territories, czar of Rupert's Land, chief executive officer of an area eight times the size of France, with the powers of a premier and a lieutenant governor, stood in his mukluks, white sleeves rolled up to his elbow, washing dishes 200 miles north of the Arctic Circle.

"They'll all know where we are tonight," he said, swirling a mop, and placing a cup on the drain board. "Spence Bay, Tuktoyaktuk, Coppermine. They'll know we didn't make it to Resolute, and they'll know we're going tomorrow. It's the moccasin telegraph. Everybody knows everyone else, even though they've never met, and what everybody else is up to."

That's still true of the North. In 1997, 25 years later, I flew to Yellowknife with my future daughter-in-law, Anna Greive, a beautiful blonde German girl whom my son John had met when both were working in the Maldives in the Indian Ocean—John as a Twin Otter pilot, Anna as a tour director.

We were en route to Inuvik, where I was invited by the Government of the NWT to participate in a workshop on Protected Areas strategies. I was chair of the Standing Senate Committee on Energy, the Environment and Natural Resources, and we had issued a report on Protected Areas, a subject of intense interest to me. I took Anna to the Mackenzie Bar in the Yellowknife Inn for a familiarization drink. A woman at the next table said, "Pat Carney!" When I admitted it, she leaned over to our table and said: "Do you know that Willy Adams' first wife died in Rankin last night?"

"No," I breathed. Willy, now a senator, had been a territorial councillor when I lived in Yellowknife. "Yesssss," whispered the woman, who said she was an Inuit interpreter. We had never seen each other in our lives, but she knew I would want to know.

Not all the macho men were pilots or oil and gas employees. Some were miners who tramped the tundra looking for mineral wealth. "That's what you get for going to school," pilot Daryle Brown would say, dumping a geologist off in the middle of the barrens. Some, like Charles Fipke and Stewart Blusson, who found the diamond deposits near Yellowknife, were successful. Most were not. But they kept on following their dreams; men like independent prospector Ozzie Sopracolle.

Ozzie has 1000 claim tags among his gear, and nine men out in his camp waiting to stake them. He's been sending his men out on floatplane, two and three at a time, not telling them where they are going until they are airborne. "Where are we going?" they ask. "Oh, up north," says Ozzie. "They know I'm up to something, but they don't know what or where," he confides to me.

"Of course, interest isn't fading in Coppermine," protests the mining recorder in Yellowknife. "Why, just the other day a prospector walked in here and asked for 1000 tags."

I'd love to be in Yellowknife when they find out Ozzie hasn't been working in Coppermine. He's staking those thousand claims in the islands off Bathurst Inlet.

Other macho men were community leaders like Lucassie Kittosuk, and federal development officer Ernest Seiber, in the Belcher Islands. Refusing a $15 000 government grant to launch a co-op because they would have to repay it, Kittosuk and his council used Seiber's $1000 community development fund to help expand a thriving carving industry, using Belcher soapstone; Belcher birds are collectors' items.

> The Belcher Islands are a jumble of snow-scraped rock, stained with dog urine, and littered with oil cans, dumped into the bottom of Hudson Bay by some volcanic accident, 85 miles off the coast of Arctic Quebec. There is no relief from nothingness, and the wind, and the cold.
>
> In a tent house buried to the rafters with snow, two boys carve by the pale flame of a Coleman stove. They have no money to buy fuel. Yet the Inuit on these unlovely islands are groping towards economic self-sufficiency . . . Essentially they are doing it themselves.

I admired these people for their independence, spirit of adventure, commitment to Canada and to the North. Men like John Dennison, who built the ice road from Yellowknife to Coppermine in the dead of winter. Men like young Mel Dienes, who flew into an Arctic island in mid-February, when the sunlight increased by 15 minutes each day, to build the gravel airstrips for the exploration crews.

To talk to them on the job, I hitched rides through the Arctic for two years, visiting camps, sleeping on the floor of an office trailer, carrying my Elizabeth Arden makeup case, and also my sleeping bag, mosquito bar, hiking boots, so that if the plane went down somewhere the pilot wouldn't have to worry about me. After all, the pilots weren't about to give me theirs.

On one assignment I hitched from Halifax to Resolute on Cornwallis Island to see the American oil tanker challenge Canada's sovereignty over the Northwest Passage by flying no flags. I flew to Prince Patrick Island, where the cook had made cream puffs because he had heard I was in the neighbourhood.

I visited Rea Point on Melville and flew out with the drilling crew, who slid their dinner trays down the aisle of the aircraft when they were through with them. I helped the exasperated flight attendants collect them. Money couldn't buy the experience, and I loved every minute of it.

While some critics assailed the impact of development on the environment, most of the operations I observed in my travels operated under increasingly strict government land-use regulations on pollution and destruction of the environment.

They say oil exploration crews are tearing up the North; some certainly have in the past. Oil crews have dug the big blades of their tractor bulldozers into the moss, trenching the tundra. They have filled lakes with empty red fuel drums, and littered campsites with garbage, and ploughed up fish streams. And their presence raises the fear of tundra fires that burn the lichen needed by the reindeer herds. Ottawa has made it clear all this must change.

So we set out one day, flying down the east channel of the Mackenzie River, 20 feet off the surface of the ice road winding through the river willows. Blond, 28-year-old pilot Herbie Bachor was born in a trapper's cabin in the bush south of Aklavik. He went to Vancouver once; couldn't stand the place.

The Beaver airplane's instrument panel showed we were flying below sea level. "Higher, please Herbie," I said, scrutinizing an abandoned exploration campsite on the riverbank. It was whistle clean. Herbie pulled the Beaver fifty feet off the ground, up the side of a ridge, so I could see where tractors had winched the camp up the hill. The tracks were barely visible in the moss-tufted snow.

"Higher, Herbie," I pleaded, just as we roared over the ridge, and there were the barrens, a white explosion of space. On the horizon, Reindeer P 60's oilrig stood against the pale grey sky. Herbie landed his Beaver on the jade-green ice-strip, and we tumbled into the cold. I never saw a rig so clean.

Waste was burned, and trash trucked back to town on the ice road. No engine oil stained the snow. The catch basin for the drilling mud had been formed by banking snow rather than drilling a hole in the ground. Shoes, or metal discs, were placed under the corners of the tractor blades to keep them off the ground.

"No one is pretending that oil exploration will leave the landscape untouched," said federal land use official Wilf Taylor. "If an oil company is doing something wrong, we jump on him with both feet. If it's doing okay, we leave it alone."[3]

While some critics objected to the impact on native culture, I remembered how Ellen Norris, a native living in Inuvik, explained to me that she preferred to have her children in the hospital rather than the muskrat camp out in the Mackenzie Delta. And I thought of the children I had met.

Two little Inuit boys play in the sea misted grasses of Coppermine on the Arctic Ocean, beside a pile of caribou skins. "What are you playing?" I asked Stanley, aged 10. "Cowboys and Indians." "What are you going to be when you grow up?" "A pilot," says Stanley. "A helicopter pilot," adds Michael.

Now, of course, many native children have the opportunity to be part of both worlds, by learning and preserving their culture, and acquiring the knowledge and skills required to operate in the twenty-first century. One who did that is engineer Frank Hansen, an Inuit businessman who operated Imperial Oil Ltd.'s bulk fuel station in Inuvik.

When I returned to Inuvik with Anna in 1997, Frank offered to drive us down the ice road on the Mackenzie River to a rig that was drilling on the tundra, which was due to complete any day. We drove onto the frozen river in his pickup and onto the ice highway, carved out on the east channel, and headed north towards Tuk.

It was March, my favourite month in the Arctic. The white sun blazed the surface of the ice, and black spruce lined the frozen river, outlined against a blue sky so bright you couldn't look at it too long. Anna sat in the back of the pickup with another Imperial Oil man, her blue eyes shining out of the fur-fringed hood of her red parka.

The ice road wound down the wide channel, following the curve of the river itself, and I saw something I had never seen before in all my Arctic travels—a mirage dancing in the sunshine on the ice road ahead of us. "Looks like tidal falls to me," I said, reflecting my West Coast culture. "Looks like a flock of geese to me," said Frank, reflecting his northern heritage.

We drove up the bank of the river and there was the tundra, covered with snow in colours ranging from grey to mauve to pale pink. There was the drilling rig, standing alone, the small camp unit for the drillers nearby. We got out of the truck and toured the rig, which was draped with protective material so it looked like it was wearing skirts against the wind-chilled climate. At the end of the tour we enjoyed coffee and conversation in the cook shack; it was too cold to talk outside.

When we returned to the pickup, we found the doors of the truck were locked. "Who did that?" said Frank, rattling the truck door. It was 30 degrees below zero and we were 50 miles from Inuvik, with little chance of hitching a ride on the ice road. Frank went back to the cook shack, found a coat hanger, and fiddled with the pickup's door lock until it opened, while we stood around the truck shivering, cold seeping through our boots from the frozen ground.

That's a macho man.

When I returned to Yukon with Paul in August 1999, there were few trucks on the 500-mile stretch of road between the airport at Whitehorse and Dawson City. The silt-green Yukon River flowed grandly north between the dun-coloured Ogilvie Mountains that separate the Yukon from the Northwest Territories. The soil edging the highway's crumbling shoulders was iced with white volcanic ash, stifling tree growth in the vast Yukon river valley, scarred by the dark tree sticks and black, silky ash of old fire burns. Magpies, with their distinctive black-and-white markings, darted into the bush. The sky was an arc of clear, cloudless blue.

The small airstrip at Dawson, where I had first entered the Yukon and Northwest Territories 31 years earlier, hadn't changed much; still quiet, small planes tethered to the grass, windsock streaming in the wind, lumpy-looking hill at the end of the strip. As we approached Dawson City the fading flags of fireweed, symbol of Yukon, signalled the approach of autumn in August; so did the fog in the valleys in the early morning.

Gold fever built Dawson City, then and now. It was a small trading post located on a ledge of silt where the Klondike and Yukon rivers merge below the timbered hill known as the Dome, until George Carmack, Skookum Jim, and Tagish Charlie, following the advice of prospector Bob Henderson, found gold in the gravel of Rabbit Creek, and staked the first four claims on August 17, 1896.

Within days the creek, renamed Bonanza by Carmack, and its southeast fork Eldorado Creek, had been staked out by gold hunters. When the first gold shipments reached San Francisco and Seattle in

1897, the Klondike Gold Rush, the largest in history, fired the imagination of a western world experiencing hard economic times.

It is hard today to imagine the impact of the gold fever. Some estimates suggest more than 100 000 people set out for the Klondike and about 30 000 "cheechakos," or outsiders, actually arrived. Many climbed the steep snow steps cut into the mountainous Chilcoot and White Pass trails, hauling their mandatory ton of supplies. Then, after surviving the Yukon winter until the ice freed the lakes and rivers, they floated their supplies on hand-built rafts and boats more than 500 miles down the snags and sandbars of the Yukon River to Dawson City where poverty, disease, and death awaited many of them.

By May 1898, the North West Mounted Police checkpoint at Tagish Point recorded 4735 boats carrying 28 000 people en route to the gold fields. In 1898, the Yukon Field Force marched 500 miles to the Pelly River in Yukon from Glenora, British Columbia, to reinforce the presence of the red-coated North West Mounted Police, securing Canada's sovereignty over Yukon from the rapacious Americans in Alaska.

At the height of the Gold Rush in 1898–99, Dawson City's population had soared to between 20 000 and 30 000, living in log cabins and tents, the largest Canadian community west of Winnipeg. Vancouver and Seattle—whose mayor headed for the Klondike—doubled in size, and the provincial capitals of Victoria and Edmonton tripled.

By the turn of the century the gold fever had broken as big corporations bought out the independent miners and built the huge dredges that, floating in ponds of their own making, dug the streambeds down to bedrock, sluicing the gold-bearing gravel to recover the gold and leaving snakes of gravel in their wake. Dredge No. 4, restored as a historic site near Dawson, is two-thirds the size of a football field, and eight storeys high. Built in 1912, it worked Bonanza and other creeks from 1913 to 1960, when it ceased operations.

About $500 million worth of gold was recovered from the gold fields before the rich deposits ran out and the big corporations left in the 1960s. Since then, independents have returned to mine the tailings, recovering particles of gold left by the big mining companies and looking for the next motherlode. They have been joined by a growing invasion of tourists who are willing to pay good money for the privilege of panning for gold and reliving the Klondike experience.

Dawson City, which had dwindled to a village of less than 1000 by the 1940s and lost its status as territorial capital to Whitehorse in 1953, has experienced a rejuvenation as a carefully restored historic heritage site, where the very air enhances the spell of lost hopes and future dreams. I count myself among the losers, refusing the offer of a lot in Dawson City at a cost of $25 back in the sixties.

My son-in-law, Malcolm Duncan, is a macho man himself, even though he traded his back-breaking work harvesting prawns and fishing for salmon in all weather from Alaska south to the Fraser River, to make waffle cones and fudge above the Klondike Cream and Candy store on Front Street in Dawson City, where Jane deals with the customers, mainly tourists, in the shop below and the gift shop next door.

It is, in a way, a new form of mining, or trolling for cash, but Malcolm dreams of his own placer gold operation, a dream still shared by many for whom, in the words of poet Robert Service in his poem "In the Spell of the Yukon":

There's gold, and it's haunting and haunting
It's luring me on as of old:
Yet it isn't the gold that I'm wanting
So much as just finding the gold.[4]

Panning for gold is in Malcolm's blood. For the last 10 years, his mother Cledia, now in her mid-eighties, has been gold-panning in the Yukon and British Columbia's Cariboo country with her family. A friend blades a section of streambed with his cat, uncovering fresh gravel. Then Cledia and her younger sister Nina haul their lawn chairs and gold pans into a stream eddy. There they sit in their chairs in the water all day, gabbing, garbed in boots and mosquito hats, moving their gold pans through the current, shaking the gold to the bottom of the pan. Back at the motor home Cledia proudly shows me a small bottle containing the results of 10 years of effort—less than one ounce of pure gold!

Gold mining as an independent placer miner is a good way to drop $100 000 or so just for openers, Paul tells Malcolm. But he agrees to drive out to the gold fields the next day.

It is a cool, sunny day. The air has the clarity of crystal. Jane and I travel in the motorhome, the men in the truck. I don't know where we are heading at first when we turn off the highway at Hunker Creek, driving past Last Chance Creek and up a winding dirt road, occasionally surprised by the odd pickup truck headed for town. We pass the occasional D-8 cat, camp trailers, piles of gravel in the creek beds, skeletons of old camps. Muddy water in the creek means someone is sluicing upstream, Paul explains.

At the summit we climb out of the motor home to inspect the log bones of Hunker House, an old hostel or roadhouse that serviced thousands of miners who worked in the gold fields. The view is spectacular. We look back at the Dawson Valley to the north. Old fire burns, the colour of the plant Indian paint brush, rust-fringed with brown, paint the cheeks of the mountains. Far in the distance we can see where Indian River, glinting in the sun, winds out of the mountains and through the valley below us on its way to converge with the Yukon River.

Paul and Malcolm take the pickup down the road edging Dominion Creek to look at a gold claim Malcolm is interested in, gleaned from morning coffee conversations in Dawson cafes. When they return, we take the turnoff down into the valley, travelling miles on dirt roads.

At Quartz Creek, Paul points out the camp of Stuart Schmidt, a fourth-generation gold miner who was raised in the gold fields and runs several mining operations in these creeks and valleys. Schmidt is a macho man. His great-grandfather was in the 1849 California Gold Rush, and his grandfather was among those men who climbed the Chilcoot Pass in 1898. Schmidt learned the business from his father. He and his wife Nancy Schreiber operate the Gold Claim in Dawson City, where visitors can buy raw gold, local art, and fossilized mammoth ivory, buried during the last ice age and recovered from the gold fields. Used for carving jewelry, the ivory is legal in Dawson City.

Down in the valley where Quartz Creek merges with Indian River, we eventually arrive at the site of an abandoned dredge, noted on the gold fields map as Number 7, sitting on its haunches in its pond of gravel like a giant grey mammoth itself, its arm-like appendages sticking into the air, a fossil from the Gold Rush days. We park in the shade of an old fuel tank, part of Paul's former placer operation, and barbecue steaks on the tailgate of the pickup. I walk over to observe the heaving humps of gravel in the river, where rivulets of water force their way through the ruined riverbed.

After searching in vain for the grave of a miner in the bushes, we gingerly drive across a planked bridge at the dredge, following the road for about a mile to Paul's old camp to the right of the road, on a small hill sloping down to Indian River. His former truck is parked, abandoned, across the road.

During the early 1990s, Paul explains, he had 20 men working 12-hour days in two shifts. There were other operators on the Indian River, and up to 10 "cats" or caterpillar tractors working the river gravel, digging down to the bedrock, dumping the gravel into sluice boxes to recover the gold. At night their lights looked like a small town in the black valley. Although the technology is more efficient now, the concept of sluicing the gravel to recover the gold remains the same as in Gold Rush days.

Although we find the camp buildings in good shape, vandals have knocked the glass out of the trailer windows. A good clean-up, paint job, and some glass would make the camp useable again. I examine the "board bed" where my husband once slept in his sleeping bag, exhausted, grimy, after working the claim, and driving back to Dawson for men, parts, and supplies. Paul pulls a notice off the wall; it says: "Paul S. White is a notary public."

I open the door of the "rec room," a separate building outside the cook shack where the men played pool and watched TV when they came off shift. The cook shack itself is in good repair, with its communal tables and big industrial stove. A sign hung on the back of the door identifies the company that bought the operation from Paul in the mid-1990s. In the bush outside there is a separate sauna building, near the Gold Room, where the crew once cleaned the gold recovered from the gravel, melted it down, and cast it into bullion. Beyond and below the Indian River gleams, its gravel back broken by the mining, machines, and muscle power.

I am overcome with emotion. What brutal effort, what dreams, what blind drive pushed them past exhaustion to find the gold? All that physical burnout for this ecological ruin? The worn-out machines? The worn-down men? The women left God knows where? I find my breathing becoming more shallow as I recreate the effort in my mind.

We kick around the camp debris in silence, then leave the campsite, driving back up the Bonanza turn-off, up over hills and small stream valleys. On the way we drop in for coffee at Bob Cattermole's camp, now Last Chance Creek Bed and Breakfast, where tourists spend $50 a night to live in camp, sleep in bunk beds, and pan for gold in water buckets of gold-flecked gravel. I knew Bob when he was a log broker on the West Coast, before he too caught gold fever.

We stop at the Discovery claim on Bonanza Creek, small, swift, and much sluiced, walking through the river willow to the site of Low's Fraction, where a chain-man staked a few feet left over from the claim staking, panned $500 000 worth of gold, and blew it all. We drive past Eldorado Creek, where 10 000 people lived at Grand Forks, eventually mining the very land the town stood on. We stop at a huge hole in the ground, where Malcolm's friends are using machines to remove the overburden to reach the pay zone underneath; I can see the dark streak above the bedrock.

It is late at night and the cats are still working in the white northern evening as we drive the 50 miles or so back to Dawson City. It has been a strange, serene day, echoing with the silent screech of machines, and sluices, and the voices of macho men over the past 100 years. I brush away the skeins of ghosts veiling the scraggy black spruce trees and small scrub willows, and think instead of supper, and maybe some modest action at Diamond Tooth Gertie's Gambling Hall.

Several months later, Stuart Schmidt calls Paul at our Saturna Island home. Paul has just returned from Siberia, examining gold properties near the city of Magadan close to the Arctic Circle. Stuart is on his way to Brazil. The talk is of gold, and gold prices, and development costs, and mining matters. The macho men are still around, but exploring new visions and vistas. Yukon's gold fields didn't necessarily make them rich, but gave them something else instead.

It's the great, big, broad land 'way up yonder,
It's the forests where silence has lease;
It's the beauty that thrills me with wonder,
It's the stillness that fills me with peace.[5]

Very macho, indeed.

CHAPTER 11

The Candidate

T R A D E   S E C R E T :
If you want people to vote for you, shake their hand,
look them in the eye, and ask them for their vote.
Often they will give you it.
—Pat Carney, MP

I was wearing my green Gemini North fur-trimmed parka when, in early 1978, I swung into the Foothills Pipeline Co. Ltd.'s office in the Lynn Building on Steel Street in Whitehorse and picked up the pink telephone callback slip with the name and number of an executive member of the Progressive Conservative riding association in Vancouver Centre. My company was the socioeconomic consultant to Foothills, which was proposing a natural gas pipeline from Alaska through the Yukon to southern Canada and the United States, and I had been performing a right-of-way "reccy," or reconnaissance, to identify potential problems along the proposed route.

I looked at the slip and debated whether to return the call. A few days earlier Tony Saunders, a top Tory and Joe Clark organizer, had visited my Vancouver office to suggest I should run as a Progressive Conservative candidate, possibly in Vancouver Centre, the big urban riding that covers everything shown on a picture postcard—the downtown business core, Chinatown, the densely built West End, modern False Creek, trendy Kitsilano—even Stanley Park.

"Why me?" I had asked, expecting to be flattered, told I was brilliant, a modern Joan of Arc saving the country from the socialist hordes. But that came later. "Name recognition," said Tony frankly. "You've been a well-known journalist and people recognize your name."

"But I've worked mostly in northern Canada for the last eight years, running an economic consulting company," I replied. "I know a lot about

169

the boondocks, but nothing about Vancouver Centre or any urban riding for that matter, outside of Yellowknife and Whitehorse and maybe Inuvik." Saturna Island, where I had my summer cottage, had only 284 permanent residents at the time.

"Doesn't matter," said Tony. "The Liberals have Iona Campagnolo. The NDP has Pauline Jewett. We want you."

I wasn't sure I was a Conservative. As a business columnist I had been scrupulously neutral. Journalists in my family were supposed to be "political eunuchs," according to my Uncle Wilfrid, himself a former reporter for the *Toronto Star* and *Financial Post*. We were raised with old-school journalistic values.

So when someone from the PMO had phoned to ask me in 1974 to serve as a western member of the prestigious Economic Council of Canada, I blurted: "But I'm not a Liberal." "Doesn't matter, as long as you're not a member of another party," the caller said frankly. Which I wasn't.

But if I was anything, I was probably a Conservative, given my parents' politics. For all the years he was a civil servant working for the BC provincial government and later the feds as a veterinarian, my father was close-mouthed about his political preferences, although as a small child I gleaned the impression that Mr. Mackenzie King was not a nice man. But once he retired, my parents revealed themselves to be True Blue Conservatives, posting lawn signs and canvassing for the Conservative MP in their riding of Vancouver Quadra, where they had moved after Dad retired. They adored John Diefenbaker (Mother had known his wife Olive) and flew the Red Ensign on the wall of their bedroom when the Liberals adopted the red-and-white Maple Leaf. "A Band-Aid," my father snorted.

If genes had anything to do with it, I was a Conservative. Besides, I was a businesswoman, drowning in red tape and forms and regulations and taxes, paying a high marginal rate of personal income tax. So I was definitely a Conservative. But not a prospective candidate. Newspaper editor and former Conservative researcher Geoff Molyneux explained why. "A true politician will travel hundreds of miles with a raging cold in order to address six people in a freezing hall and I don't see you doing that," he said frankly. "You aren't committed enough to The Cause."

When the PC riding association called to set up an appointment to meet me, I already knew I wasn't going to run. I had written down my reasons in my field journal explaining my feelings for the North. "Yukoners are great collectors," I wrote.

At Mile Post 594,[1] on the Alaska Highway at Iron Creek Lodge, Peggy Kerik has collected 706 spoons. At Mile Post 635, the town of Watson Lake collects signs from other places, modestly labelled as "The Famous Watson Lake Sign Posts" and prominently displayed at the entrance to town.

At Teslin, Mile Post 735, the local improvement district manager Bonner Colley has collected enough native and northern relics to fill a small museum. Sam Magee's lounge in Whitehorse at Mile Post 918 has autographed dollar bills nailed to the wall, while the Mogensons at Pine Valley Lodge, MP 1154, are collecting enough business cards to paper their cafe. Farwest Texaco at Beaver Creek near the Alaska border, MP 1202, has somehow persuaded 500 truckers to give up their caps. Yukoner Drew Dunn collects T-shirts with signs like "Vasectomy Means Never Having To Say You're Sorry"; and "Some Do, Some Don't, Some Will, Some Won't, I Might."

Peggy and her husband Steve, who was out doing some work for the Department of Public Works, have operated the lodge for 20 years and she told me, as she dragged on her boots to go gas up a big truck, that she was plumb tired of serving the public. The tiredness shows on the signs on the wall. Beside her framed spoon collection she has posted a handwritten sign that answers the most asked questions. No, there are only four duplicates; Yes, she polishes them once a year; Yes, she belongs to a spoon collectors' club. Beneath the clock on the wall there is a cranky sign, "Yes, this is OUR time," noting the difference between Yukon time and the rest of Canada.

Two truckers come in for coffee on their way to Sulphur Creek near Dawson City. They are hauling a drag line for placer mining, and we discuss the relative price of gas along the Highway, where you have to double the posted price shown on the gas meters because they don't show prices over a dollar. The waitress brings out a bottle of Hootch, the Yukon rum, and we agree it should be used to water the flowers because, if you drink it, you might break out in an alcohol rash, and the truckers quietly tell me how Peggy and Steve lost their two sons in a Christmas season fire years ago.

When Peggy came in she told the truckers to be sure to look up Bill Gibson who was now living in Sulphur Creek, and when we left I had learned in the course of a tea-break Peggy and Steve's past life and present ambitions and had glimpsed their greatest tragedy. When Peggy sang out "Goodbye, Pat," as if she would know me for the rest of my life, I knew she probably would and that wherever we met in Whitehorse or along the highway we would pick up our conversation where we left off.

I remembered Irene Mahoney in Teslin, who had seen me once on television for five minutes two years ago, so that when I walked into her tiny office she said "Hi, Pat." We discussed the problems of a community with only 19 private taxpayers and about living in Atlin when there were only four pay cheques, one for the DPW man, one for the mining recorder, one for the airplane expediter, and the fourth we couldn't remember; maybe a Forest Service employee.

Irene reported that Paul White and the Liberal from Ross River had been in town earlier that week, and we discussed all the familiar people whom I had met before and will meet later, but all of whom know each other. I had already talked to Paul on the phone, trading itineraries about who was going when to Dawson City. I knew where Paul was standing to use the phone in the cabin in Ross River and I could see, in my mind's eye, the slant of the snow-covered ridge through the windows behind him and the antique placer mining tools nailed to the log walls and the Franklin stove from Dawson City, as shiny as it was in Klondike days.

I remembered dozing in that room after flying in from Whitehorse over the Pelly Valley, listening to Paul on that phone at midnight comforting a helicopter pilot who was en route to Whitehorse from a mining camp where a pickup truck had backed into his chopper with alarming results.

I wondered if there were a handful of people in Vancouver Centre who could appreciate my concern for the chopper pilot's dilemma or who would understand pilot Bob Ambrose who, when I asked him how a pickup truck could back into the helicopter, replied that it was perfectly clear that the truck had *attacked* the chopper. The same thing had happened to him, he explained, but it was a rented truck and Avis never did figure out what happened.

Bob Ambrose and I are good friends although I hadn't actually met him until a few months earlier. For years I heard through mutual friends what Bob Ambrose thought and what he was doing and for years he heard the same things about me. So when we actually did meet, drinking tequila with his wife Mary Lou at their Ross River home with showers and running water, it was almost incidental.

Back in Watson Lake Motel Cafe Edith Bohmer introduced me to a handsome young Tahltan Indian, Gordon Franke, and his wife from Telegraph Creek. Gordon said he knew me from my newspaper days when I wrote about my northern travels for the *Vancouver Sun*. Later we flew south on the same Canadian Pacific jet and he told me that he used to fly the Beech aircraft out of Cambridge Bay for Gateway Aviation.

Well. Of course, I know Cambridge Bay and Gateway Aviation and that particular Beech aircraft, whose gyroscope had a peculiar way of regressing, that later crashed and killed two Inuit and a Yellowknife nurse who was a friend of ours. We discussed pilots and aircraft and the general superiority of Tahltans to the rest of the world to the amusement of Gordon's white wife. I learned how Gordon had spent a year in Mexico passing himself off as a Mexican, learning his Spanish in the marketplace and how once he left Cam Bay on a dark, polar December morning and arrived in Hawaii that night, and he jumped, clothes and all, into the hotel pool to see if the warm tropical water was real.

Before we parted, I had accepted an invitation to travel down the Stikine River the next summer with a couple I had never met until 2 p.m. that day. Gordon and I already knew that we would not likely agree on native politics, although we would quite likely agree on the general superiority of Tahltans, but we would forgive each other these small transgressions for the shared joy of exploring the Stikine.

Back in Watson Lake, hotel owner and Liberal Archie Lang would probably discuss Pat Carney's campaign strategy over drinks in the bar, with some interested Liberal who may pass it on to my potential Liberal opponent in Vancouver Centre for all I know or care. What is important is that when I go back to Watson Lake, Archie will know most things that have happened to me and I will know most things that have happened to him.

And that is the central issue. I can describe the voters of Vancouver Centre by their age, sex, voting habits, ethnic backgrounds, religious affiliation, the number of telephones, non-family households and single parent families. But I do not know their past hopes and present ambitions and not much of their personal tragedies, and when we pass on the street we don't smile and say, "What's new in Beaver Creek?" and "Did you hear how the pickup truck attacked the helicopter?"

At some time in our life we have to recognize who we are and while I may not be a northerner I recognize that is where my heart is and where my friends are and that is where I mostly contribute. And that is why I don't feel I can run in Vancouver Centre. I have a date to go flying over the Kluane ice fields with ice pilot Andy Williams on the first clear day there is not too much wind, and I should go back to Carcross with Edith Bohmer and visit her aged aunt who still runs her own trap lines. Then there is the trip down the Stikine in June or July with the Frankes and then of course there is tequila and gossip in Ross River and driving down the Haines Highway to go crabbing on the Alaskan coast. The North is where I have to be.[2]

But life is a crapshoot. The pipeline through the Yukon was shelved. I argued hotly with Paul White about politics and other things, such as our shared future, and never returned to Ross River. Mary Lou and Bob Ambrose eventually broke up. Nor did I fly over the Kluane ice fields with ice pilot Andy Williams or travel down the Stikine with the Frankes, although when I returned with Paul White to see Archie Lang and his wife Karen 20 years later, that part was true: we did know what had happened to each other.

Instead, I woke up one day and wondered *If*. *If* I could actually win a nomination to run as a candidate in an election. *If* I could win an election. Would anyone vote for me? Would people actually walk into a polling booth, read the list of candidates, and carefully, with the stubby pencil tied to the polling station, mark an X beside my name? If they did, what would happen? What great adventure, or calamity (Paul White's view, based on a stint as a ministerial aide to Jean Chrétien when he was Minister of Indian and Northern Affairs), or unknown future would unfold? Could the shoals and currents of politics be as exciting as the canyons of the Stikine River or the Kluane ice fields?

I decided to throw the dice and see what came up.

It is one of the marvels of democracy that almost anyone can run for Member of Parliament. Anyone with $1000 and 100 signatures can file her nomination papers; when I ran in 1979, it was only $200 and 25 signatures. Nor need it be expensive; the main costs are for pamphlets, letterheads, posters, and buttons, which are typically covered by supporters. And if you don't have such support anyway, why run? I know a woman candidate who charged her whole campaign on her Visa card and spent years paying it off. Yet former NDP Member of Parliament Lynn Hunter said her total costs for a successful nomination were $1500. My first contested nomination, which attracted several candidates, cost $8000, none of which I paid, nor did I know who among my supporters did.

Normally, the successful candidate is the person who signs up the most members at $10 a head for adults and $5 for youth and delivers them to the nomination hall in sufficient strength to win a clear majority. There are rare exceptions. Prime Minister Jean Chrétien handpicked a Canadian-Chinese woman, Sophie Leung, to run in an ethnic Vancouver riding even though she had been defeated in other nomination attempts. Despite considerable controversy, she won the seat. In other cases, a party leader has refused to sign a candidate's nomination papers on the grounds that he or she did not meet the political party's standards.

But generally, federal office in Canada must be one of the most accessible political positions in western democracies. To become a candidate, you must be an eligible voter, that is, any Canadian citizen age 18 or older. The only restriction is that you must be someone who has not lost her right to vote by having been found guilty of committing an offence that bears the penalty of losing your right to vote.

Edmonton publisher Mel Hurtig and I once speculated that it was theoretically possible to take over every riding in the country. Later, he helped form the National Party, which fizzled out, and he is still attempting to do just that with his campaign to encourage poor Canadians to enter federal politics in order to focus attention on their plight.

It helps, but is not mandatory, to be a member of the political party. Two of my longtime associates, public relations experts Diana Lam and Ray McAllister, revealed that they were card-carrying Conservatives and they hustled me off to sign up. McAllister made another revelation: Vancouver Centre has a large homosexual population, and "we"— he stressed the word—believed that Carney would make a good candidate. I had no idea Ray was gay, but he proved to be instrumental in showing me a different society, with its fears and defiant demands for equality. When Vancouver Centre later became the first riding to win substantial core funding from our Conservative government for

AIDS Vancouver, which was and continues to be one of the leading AIDS organizations in Canada, Ray's trust in me was confirmed.

In retrospect, my candidacy contravened almost every guideline in the *1999 PC Handbook* for candidates. It cautions: "Be ready to give answers to questions like":

> Why do you want to run? *Because the Tories say I am an economic Joan of Arc who owes it to her country.*
>
> What experience do you have? *None, in either politics or in being burned at the stake.*
>
> What are your main policy concerns? *What policies?*
>
> What qualities do you have that make you a good candidate? *According to the backroom boys, I am a woman candidate with a high recognition factor.*
>
> What kind of time commitment will you make? *What time commitment is required?*
>
> How will you raise the money for a campaign? *Hmm. Good question.*[3]

One day the telephone rang in my Gemini North consulting office in Vancouver. "My name is Jim Macaulay and you don't know me," said the caller. "I am John Fraser's campaign chairman. We know you don't know the first thing about winning a nomination and John would like to send in our team to help you."

I had known John Fraser, MP for Vancouver South, for years since we shared similar environmental concerns, and I was touched by his thoughtfulness. "Thank you, but the party people told me that if I ran they would supply all the resources and money required," I said naively. "You'll find they have few resources and less money," Jim said, grimly and accurately. We arranged to meet. In short order Tory veteran Margaret Maxwell set up shop in our offices and briskly started organizing the files. Diana Lam sent over red-haired, blue-eyed Janice Whitters to organize me. Thirtyish Janice informed me that she was willing to work six hours a day, four days a week, for two weeks; she stayed 22 years and counting, the one constant in my political career.

My political learning curve had started with my entry into a world of turf wars, grandiose commitments, empty promises, and false loyalties. There are many good things about politics; it is just hard to recall them.

The Liberal tide had turned after years in power, and the Trudeau era appeared to be ending. In 1978 the Conservative candidacy in Vancouver Centre, which was traditionally a cabinet seat, was a coveted prize. Several people competed for the nomination, including constitutional lawyer Ted McWhinney, who lived in the riding. At the time I lived in the adjacent riding of Vancouver Quadra. Ted lost the Conservative nomination and subsequently ran successfully for the Liberals in Quadra. He is such a courtly gentleman that no Conservative opponent dared to call him a political turncoat in campaign jousts.

My main opponent for the nomination was former Conservative MP Douglas Jung, the first Canadian-Chinese MP, who had served under Conservative Prime Minister John Diefenbaker and had the added advantage of potential ethnic support since Chinatown was then in the riding. Doug had a distinguished service record. In World War II he was part of a small unit of about a dozen Canadian Chinese who were intensively trained in commando-type tactics and designated for highly dangerous missions throughout Southeast Asia. Doug risked his life for Canada at a time when Canadian Chinese weren't even allowed to vote.

I watched the old pro work the crowd when Margaret Maxwell hustled me off to a meeting at the Primrose Club, a Conservative institution associated with former British Prime Minister and Queen Victoria confidante Benjamin Disraeli. The meeting took place in the UBC Graduate Student Centre. The prime force in the Primrose Club was tiny Queen Sinclair, with snapping dark eyes and a stiletto tongue.

Margaret Maxwell gripped me firmly by the elbow and guided me through the rouged and powdered and tinted ladies: "I want you to meet Mrs. Ball, a tireless worker." Exchanging my cold coffee cup for a fresh one, Queen Sinclair announced that Pat Carney would now speak. Panic attack. Clutching my cup, I stammered that I was very pleased to be there and that I was a UBC graduate and I hoped they would support me, and sat down.

Then Doug Jung said he was pleased to "renew" his acquaintance with so many "old friends." He gave a gracious tribute to former Conservative External Affairs Minister Howard Green, a BC icon, and said how great it had been to serve with him in the House of Commons. He mentioned that Howard Green was seconding his nomination. He posed with a group of pretty young girls—a thorn among the prim-roses—and left to great applause. I met a woman in the cloakroom who accosted me with the announcement: "Bilingualism today, French tomorrow." I escaped, alarmed and amused.

The nomination meeting was held in Kitsilano High School Auditorium in the spring. It was jammed, since our membership had doubled from about 400 to 800 as our supporters signed up new members. Since Centre was considered a bellwether riding, political operatives from the other parties lounged against the back wall of the auditorium.

I was locked in a room by my campaign manager Gary Anderson to admire my makeup in the mirror and rehearse my speech while in the hall people marched around with balloons, bashing each other with poster poles and hurtling partisan accusations of ballot-box stuffing.

"I hope you liked the band," I said when I finally took the stage, referring to the straw-hatted musicians who, between speeches, had gamely played "When the Saints Go Marching In." I told the requisite joke, about the fisherman who gave away his bagpipes to a child on the fish dock at Prince Rupert because he hated the child's mother. I gave a shrewd economic analysis of the consequences of a Liberal re-election, correctly forecasting double-digit inflation; after all, it was my experience as a businesswoman and business journalist that had attracted the Tories' interest in my candidacy.

"I am seeking the Conservative nomination in Vancouver Centre tonight because one symptom of the Liberal distemper is the economic mismanagement of this country," I said, trashing the Liberal deficit, wasteful government spending, excessive regulations, and an inflated bureaucracy. I believed every word of it. I always wrote my own political speeches.

"The temper of the times is conservative," I concluded. "Increasingly people are seeking conservative values, linking compassion for the less fortunate with a sense of personal responsibility, encouraging restraint in spending and satisfaction in productive endeavours.

"Is anyone prepared to tell me that a Conservative government that seeks to incorporate these values will be a government without the support of the people?" I believed it then and I believe it now.

With a blast of trumpets and a barrage of balloons, I won. It was my first and last contested nomination.

But the air slowly ebbed out of the campaign balloons. Prime Minister Trudeau was in no hurry to call an election as long as the polls indicated that he couldn't win. As a high-profile political candidate I found my consulting clients unwilling to commit to the long-term contracts Gemini North needed to meet the payroll and pay the rent. To my shock, I learned that a government contract had been cancelled at the insistence of a Liberal senator on the grounds I had run against the government: it is the Liberal Way, one Liberal explained. In spring 1979, a year after my nomination, I reluctantly withdrew on the grounds I couldn't afford to stay the political course.

However, within days Pierre Trudeau dropped the writ for an election on May 22, 1979, and under pressure from the riding executive I flip-flopped back into the race since there wasn't time to find an alternative candidate, as we weakly explained to the media. Not a great way to start a political career.

Canadian federal campaigns are fought on the backs and feet of volunteer workers. Unlike American campaigns, where candidates can and do spend millions, Canadian campaign expenditures after the writ is dropped are tightly controlled by law and limited to $1 per person for the first 15 000 voters, $.50 per person for the next 10 000 voters, and $.25 per person for over 25 000 voters.[4] In my campaigns the limit worked out to little more than a postage stamp per capita, enough for posters, pamphlets, balloons, and the all-important campaign button. In Centre we also found the funds for snazzy white windjackets for winter campaigns to protect canvassers from traffic in the rain-darkened streets. Volunteers canvass each household to identify the Conservative vote, the undecided, and the committed opposition so that on Voting Day the campaign team can Get Out the Vote, calling people and transporting them if necessary to the polling station. We also signed up the PCs' first known transvestite member, an enthusiastic canvasser.

The candidate is usually on the doorstep too, and usually on the run. I tell my UBC planning students that the best way to learn about a community is to work on a political campaign; it is one of the last legal ways you can encourage people to open their doors and talk to you. In Centre I learned where the latchkey children lived, left alone when their parents were working; how barking dogs indicate an empty house; and why seniors are barricaded behind their doors, afraid to open them to strangers. I discovered horrible housing conditions, housewives drunk at 10:00 a.m., and skid-row deadbeats. I learned not to ask whether the wife or husband was available when canvassing gay households. And after some scary incidents, we ensured that our pretty young women canvassers worked in pairs.

Campaigning in swing ridings like Vancouver Centre, where the vote can go either way, is best described as body snatching. From early morning bus-stopping to suppertime canvassing to evening all-candidates meetings (in one campaign we did 28 all-candidates free-for-alls, including media shows). In campaigning, the object is to ask people for their vote.

I am by nature shy and reticent. When my first campaign manager Gary Anderson informed me that I had to walk up to a stranger, grab his or her hand, and say, "I need your vote," I was alarmed. When Conservative MP David Crombie and his campaign manager Barbara McDougall told me I had to accost people in shopping malls with pamphlets and hand them out in front of liquor stores, I was horrified. Who, me? My first paying job as a teenager in Nelson had been to stand on a street corner and hand out bread slices, a task I failed at.

Finally the party sent Flora MacDonald to teach me campaign techniques. Flora was a veteran campaigner who had started with the Conservatives as a secretary in the party offices. Dragging me out from behind a lamppost, where I was hiding, she propelled me firmly into a Robson Street grocery story. "Good morning," she beamed at the three Chinese looking out from behind the melon display. "I want you to meet your Conservative candidate in Vancouver Centre." They beamed back. Everybody knew Flora.

A couple of blocks later I thought: I *can* do this. Flora went back to her Kingston riding. Buoyed by her merciless cheerfulness, my campaign team and I headed that evening to the corner of Robson and Thurlow, one of the busiest street corners in Canada, when people throng the sidewalks after work, headed for their apartments in the West End.

For my first attempt, I chose an elderly lady with curly grey hair who was crossing the street. When she reached the curb, I stuck out my hand and said bravely: "I'm Pat Carney, your Conservative candidate in Vancouver Centre, and I need your vote." The benign-looking senior cradled her hand to her body and snapped viciously, "I would rather my hand withered and dropped off before shaking hands with a Conservative," and walked away. Stunned, I put my shunned hand back in my pocket, chilled to the core.

But after that difficult beginning we had fun. We flew barrage balloons marked CARNEY over the beaches and barnstormed the bridges and gathered for beer at a Kitsilano pub—looking for voters, of course. I told a fascinated Christina McCall, co-author of the Trudeau biography *True Grit*, that I wanted to be the Minister of Myths and Magic to enchant Canadians with a sense of our mischievous national spirit. We had Conservative leader Joe Clark searching through the gardens of Kitsilano for the infamous and invasive Gypsy Moth.

I knew it was important to have a political philosophy. Tory friends had confided that they hadn't voted for Flora MacDonald when she ran for Conservative leader in 1976, not because she was a woman, but because she lacked a philosophy. A union leader in Prince Rupert told me that although he liked me, he would vote for a dead fish if it was NDP because of the party's philosophy. My own daughter told a French reporter I would make a fine MP, but when asked if she would vote for me, she replied, shocked: "No way. I'm NDP."

So I set off in search of a Little Blue Book with the aid of Ottawa historian Allister Sweeney, who collected Tory speeches and utterances. MP Jean Pigott discussed honesty and thrift and peace in the family. Fine by me. MP John Fraser spoke of love of country and Queen and the land until his wife Cate took him home. Leader Joe Clark ruminated that Canada was a community of communities. MP David Crombie was given to quoting Tory icon D'Arcy McGee, but I reminded him that D'Arcy was shot on Ottawa's Sparks Street in 1868.

Policy pundit Bill Neville was seated on a twin bed in a hotel room typing the Tory women's policy on a typewriter balanced on his knees when I finally tracked him down. He was unimpressed with my search for a Little Blue Book. "Haven't you seen the polls?" he asked. "Didn't you receive the policy papers? Aren't you aware of the party's views on energy and budget cuts?"

I had no problem with any of this but in the end, resting from campaigning, I sat on my Saturna Island dock and painted my toenails and read Alice Munro and sailed and drank wine and hunted for oysters on the shore rocks and kept to my fiscal conservatism. Allister, twirling through the maypoles of his mind, decided I was a Zen Tory.

We held illegal parades ("Of course we have a licence, Pat") and found a white convertible that we converted into the sign-draped Patmobile. I swam each day at the YWCA to keep in shape. When I broke my toe leaping over a bench in the dressing room, the Patmobile drove me up to see my doctor in the Fairmont Building on busy Broadway. While I was in the doctor's office a huge naked man ran through the doors of the building and jumped into the backseat of the Patmobile, draped with "Vote for Pat" signage. My crew didn't know what to do. A crowd gathered, fascinated. "His face was not the first thing you saw," admitted volunteer driver Lex Poulus. Finally, a medical team arrived and took the man away. It made a great story for the canvassers who gathered at the Bimini Pub.

Our volunteers included the experienced men and women who worked the phones in the campaign office, young people looking for excitement—many romances start during campaigns—and kids, like 12-year-old Tim Crowhurst and teenager Mark von Schellwitz and others who went on to careers in politics, serving in MP and ministerial offices in Ottawa. They served their apprenticeship at the bus stops and in the community centres of the riding, learning how democracy works.

We had the advantage of being the underdog. No one took us seriously, considering that Liberal candidate Art Phillips had been a popular former mayor of Vancouver and the NDP candidate Ron Johnson had run several times and had strong union support. But while the cameras were panning smooth shots of Phillips' handsome profile and his talented wife Carole Taylor, a successful television personality, we were knocking on doors and shaking hands at bus stops.

And on Election Night, when he announced that Joe Clark's Conservatives had won a minority government and that Pat Carney had won Vancouver Centre for the Conservatives by two votes, the CBC announcer couldn't keep the surprise out of his voice. The Returning Officer ordered a recount, and the next day I left for China with my cousin Betty O'Keefe to collect information and pictures for my mother's memoir of Shanghai.

I was so green at politics I had no idea I would be so exhausted. In Beijing I phoned *Globe and Mail* correspondent John Fraser to find out the results of the recount. After much rustling of wire copy John announced that I had lost the recount by 95 votes. Somehow, in the vastness of China my loss didn't seem to matter. But it mobilized my campaigners. Ninety-five votes equals one West End apartment block, they told me. If only we had made one more canvass, a few more phone calls. One elderly man phoned to say he and his wife accounted for the two votes; they had motored over from Bowen Island in their boat. Those two votes became a mantra for our tired troops.

Janice Whitters and I were secretly relieved. We had done our duty. Gemini North was involved in some exciting satellite communication projects, project-managing tele-education experiments, creating a superstation with BCTV television station, doing the initial studies that laid the foundation for Cancom. Our reaction to the narrow win and subsequent loss was "Whew!" My family was also pleased.

But nine months later Joe Clark's fledgling government fell with the defeat of Finance Minister John Crosbie's disastrous budget, which included a gas tax of 18 cents a gallon. We gathered in Tory Lyall Knott's West End apartment to watch the replay on television. My son JP, then age 14, who had campaigned with enthusiasm, showed up with a Canadian flag. Pressure was applied. Phones rang. Promises were made: "If you run again I'll come out for your nomination speech," pleaded Joe Clark, who never did, sending an exhausted and angry John Fraser in his place. I gave in and agreed to run again.

This time the campaign had an edge to it. Art Phillips, who had won the seat and was the MP, was chippy and confident; in elections, the incumbents hold the advantage. But my team remembered that two-vote edge in the first campaign and worked furiously to identify the necessary votes. The media took us more seriously.

And I was a better campaigner. Street soliciting was a big issue in this campaign and on the corner outside our Thurlow Street campaign office, a blonde prostitute conducted her own campaign with a button proclaiming PCs SUCK pinned to her wine-red dress. Finally I went up to her and held out my hand. "I'm Pat Carney and I am the Conservative candidate in this riding and I need your vote," I said firmly, looking directly into her eyes; eye contact is important. I also invited her into the campaign headquarters for coffee. For the rest of the campaign she regularly came for coffee, holding forth on the trials of her trade, winning the fascinated attention of my uptown campaign workers.

I never knew how she voted, but on February 18, 1980, we won the riding. Carole Taylor cried when she and Art Phillips came to the Hyatt Regency election-night headquarters to concede defeat. It was a blow for Art at the time, since Pierre Trudeau defeated Joe Clark, and Art lost his chance to sit in a Liberal cabinet. Later he told me it was the best career move that ever happened to him, freeing him to develop his investment business and live the life of the laid-back Lotus Eaters with his wife and family.

I knew the feeling. In a piece written for the *Vancouver Sun*, I described what it felt like: "The morning after, you wonder why you ever thought you wanted to be a Member of Parliament for Vancouver Centre," I wrote. "The night before was victory time with champagne and cheers and hugs from your campaign workers. Now as you walk your little white Westie along Kitsilano Beach you note the pale spring flowers and the ice cream mountains and the slow sea mists and wonder what you've done with your life."[5]

But it was too late to change my mind. In a generous gift of time, my friend Rae Parker offered to move into my home during the week to house-mother my son. Janice Whitters decided to move to Ottawa with me since, she said, "it is easier for me to learn The Hill than for someone else to learn to work with you." We set up the constituency office, with one table, a chair, and half a dozen constituency files handed over by the crushed Liberals. Two of my volunteers, Susan Knott and Kathy Sanderson, staffed the office until Tory Senator Jack Marshall phoned me from Newfoundland to tell me his former constituency secretary Marjorie Lewis was in Vancouver and available and she was the best constituency person he had ever had in his years as an MP.

We were on our way.

CHAPTER 12

Blue Star

T R A D E   S E C R E T:
*As an elected politician, trust your instincts,
your gut reactions. They are what got you elected.*
—Former Conservative MP Jean Pigott

I was waiting at a bus stop in my Vancouver Centre riding one sunny day, admiring False Creek with its sailboats and seagulls and Granville Island ferries, when a young man came bounding up. "Thank you so much for helping to bring my fiancée to Canada from the Philippines," he said. "She's here now and we're very grateful."

"I'll tell Marjorie Lewis, my constituency assistant, since she did most of the work," I told him. "But why don't you bring your fiancée to our Neighbourhood Night at False Creek Community Hall and introduce her to our Canadian parliamentary system?"

When the couple showed up that night, I cheerfully introduced them to the hundred-odd constituents gathered in the hall. When I finished, a woman stood up and asked: "Why are we letting all these foreigners into the country?" That question brought a young woman wearing a beret to her feet. "Why don't old rednecks like you stay home?" she said. "This man has a perfect right to bring his future wife here." That started it. Within minutes, the audience was volleying views back and forth while I sat back and listened, and the young couple looked frightened. At the end, the majority welcomed the young Filipina woman to her new home. Another Neighbourhood Night was under way, democracy unfolding as it should.

Neighbourhood Nights were my way as an MP of dealing with Vancouver Centre's large and diverse population in the heart of the city. Greeks, Chinese, Poles, Germans, and French Canadians augmented the mix of British, American, Scandinavian, and native Canadians. Rich and poor, conservatives and socialists, young and old, were clustered in distinct neighbourhoods within the bigger city. A planner by training, I knew that the traditional Town Hall kind of MP "accountability" session would never work in Vancouver Centre. So we evolved the concept of informal "circles" of meetings throughout the year, in the West End, False Creek, Fairview, Kitsilano, South Granville, West Point Grey, Oak Street. We met in schools, church halls, local legion halls, community centres, and cultural centres. Our volunteers dropped pamphlets on neighbourhood doorsteps or in mailboxes and tacked up posters in community laundromats and bulletin boards, using English or French or Chinese or Greek depending on the constituents' needs.

I loved my riding. Each neighbourhood had different issues and voters raised their concerns at Neighbourhood Nights.

At Kitsilano House, the issues raised were bank profits, mortgage rates, housing, seniors' problems, the budget, foreign affairs, fisheries, and problems experienced by Greek immigrants who spoke little English. At the Chinese Cultural Centre, the state of the economy, immigration policies, and family reunification were discussed. At the West End Community Centre, people argued about street soliciting, gay and lesbian rights, battered women, tax revolt, dog bylaws, metric, foreign landlords, rent increases, seniors' health, and private ownership of handguns. At the False Creek Community Centre, a spiffy development, people debated abortion, the Vancouver Symphony, and bicycles on the seawall. At Carnegie Centre, the downtown eastside, residents were concerned about drug overdoses, infected needles, poor housing, and lack of services.

I had worked in native settlements where people tied messages to the branches of trees on trails separating the community. Vancouver Centre was simply a larger settlement inhabited by several tribes.

At most meetings, I sat on a stool, semicircled by the audience, and gave a brief account of what I had been doing in Ottawa and the riding as their MP. Then the audience took over with questions. Staff and volunteers took notes, and if I didn't know the answer we included it in the next printed householder or *Report from Parliament*. Volunteer translators and interpreters were always present. People with personal requests gave their addresses to our ever-willing volunteers who made the coffee, and stacked the chairs, and paid the rent out of our volunteer contributions to the Vancouver Centre PC Riding Association.

If a social historian ever wanted to explore the temper of the times in the 1980s, the notes and reports from Neighbourhood Nights record it; so do the constituency logs where Marjorie Lewis and Freda Betker noted every call and caller. I read every letter from a constituent and reviewed every answer, mounted in large felt Green Books that I lugged into the House of Commons or home to read after work. They are stacked in boxes in the National Archives.

Life as the MP for Vancouver Centre was never boring. I could have spent all my time in the riding. But an MP is a parliamentarian and Parliament was my workplace.

When I was first elected in February 1980, Janice Whitters and I flew first class to Ottawa at Gemini North's expense. Born in British Columbia, Janice had never been east of Manitoba and I wanted her to enjoy the experience. I have spent more than 30 years flying to Ottawa and have never liked it. But when Janice peered excitedly out the window at the city below as we approached the airport, we both had gold dust on our shoulders. We were the anointed ones. The voters had entered the polling booths and marked their ballot for CARNEY. Not all the voters, but enough to win the seat by a margin of about 1500 votes. Not bad for a swing riding.

With her usual calm competence, Janice set about organizing our two offices on the first floor of the Confederation Building and hiring Carole Chenevert, an experienced Hill worker, as office staff. Our offices were narrow and cramped but Bill Kempling, the Whip, informed us that it had the bonus of an en suite toilet. We were impressed with our importance.

But we soon tired of pulling on our boots and trudging up the hill through the snow to the Centre Block or waiting for the little green bus that transported MPs and staff around the parliamentary compound. So when I discovered an empty office in the West Block, we swung into action. Carole whipped the name Pat Carney MP into the nameplate above the door and sent over two cardboard boxes emblazoned with the name CARNEY to take possession of the empty room. Janice had the phones changed and called the movers. When we were safely ensconced, Janice told the Whip. He was enraged, writing us that just because women MPs were paid the same as men, we did not enjoy special privileges.

My colleagues were also displeased with our office-raiding tactics. Parliamentary offices were assigned on the basis of seniority and West Block, with its tunnel to the House of Commons in the Centre Block, rated high on the list. Perrin Beatty, first elected in 1972, met me in the elevator and asked what I was doing in the West Block. I told him our offices were there. "But I'm not in the West Block and I am a PC," he exploded. "So am I," I replied, innocent of the fact that he meant he was a former cabinet minister and privy councillor in Joe Clark's government, not that we were Progressive Conservatives. In time, I became just as jealous of my prerogatives, insisting that PC be listed after my name as a member of the Queen's Privy Council.

I had quickly learned that Ottawa operates on seniority and I raced to be sworn in as an MP and to receive my MP pin from the Clerk of the Commons ahead of other new MPs, since the date of "pinning" established one's seniority in the caucus and protocol list. Tales were told of the rivalry between two senior MPs who had signed up within hours of each other, but the first one "pinned" had the advantage.

But I was the only new Conservative elected in the 1980 election, defeating the last surviving Liberal MP west of the Lakehead. Two senior Alberta MPs, Doug Neil and Gordon Towers, invited me to their offices for drinks. "You are our Blue Star," said Doug Neil gruffly, referring to the traditionally Tory blue colour used in our campaigns and party literature. Blue Star. I wondered how Flora MacDonald would feel about that.

I heard the first of many caucus addresses by the Party Leader, in this case Joe Clark. I have served under five party leaders, and the first post-election caucus address is always the same:

En anglais et en francais: Congratulations on our victory. You may all think you got here on your own brilliance, but let me tell you that the real reason that you're here is because of My Leadership. It is My Leadership that will lead us to victory (keep us in government) in the next election. Look around you. The only friends you have are the people in this room. No one else. Don't trust your staff. They are sleeping with the NDP and spilling all your secrets to the enemy. Don't trust the media. They are out to get us at every opportunity. God did not ordain that you have to speak into every microphone stuck into your face. Don't worry about the other parties. Under My Leadership if we stick together we will Sweep The Polls.

But despite the novelty and the undeniable thrill, I was grappling with some personal demons. I did not want to be in Ottawa, which I viewed as a snow-spattered, red-brick railway town, nor did I really want to be an MP. My personal and family life was in tatters. I worried about my 15-year-old son, JP, left in the care of family and friends in Vancouver. Every weekend I flew home to teenage traumas, veterinary emergencies, past-due bills, and errands, and when I returned to Ottawa, I had to deal with constituents who didn't realize that when they phoned at midnight it was 3:00 a.m. Eastern Standard Time. My time. Suffering chronic jet lag and sleep loss, a western MP's normal state is deep fatigue, in my case accentuated by back problems that had hospitalized me shortly after the 1980 campaign.

It did not help that my Ottawa digs were a sublet apartment that was dowdy compared to my Kitsilano ocean-view townhouse. My salary had dropped from a stable self-employed $85 000 a year plus to around $30 000, but I was supporting two homes, and the MP expense allowance did not cover the costs. I burned with homesickness and deep-seated resentment. When I had asked my campaign manager, lawyer Lyall Knott why didn't he run for office, he replied: "I can't afford it." Why did he think I could?

To make matters worse, I didn't understand the system, despite my years in the Ottawa Press Gallery. "One's first reaction as a new MP is the overwhelming triviality of it all," I wrote in the *Vancouver Sun*.

The days are crammed with committee meetings, caucus, constituents, question period. Signing the correspondence paper-clipped into your huge green book as you sit out your duty time in the House, you wonder just what you've accomplished at the end of a fourteen-hour day.

The constitutional debate may split the country forever, but what is really bothering you is your pool key. In six weeks you have never been able to gain access to the swimming pool in your apartment building.

The first time you don't have the right key. The second time the pool is closed for renovation. The third time you have the pool key but not the key to the pool corridor, and the supervisor tells you that the man with the key lives in the next building.

It is 10 o'clock at night and raining. You are standing there in your skimpy bathing suit. You are not going to the next apartment building to look for the man with the pool corridor key. Instead, you inform your staff, you are going into exile until somebody can find a way to get you into the swimming pool.[1]

I found myself called back at night to vote for legislation I didn't understand. I was anxious to be assigned a critic's role such as Communications so that I could maintain my hard-won expertise in the rapidly developing area of satellite communications. I had won an award for Innovation in Education from the BC Institute of Technology for my project management of the Satellite Tele-Education Program (STEP), and I needed to maintain my professional skills in case I lost my seat in the next election. Instead, Joe Clark assigned Communications to a more senior MP and I was allocated dreary roles such as Secretary of State. I wrote Joe a series of angry letters, reminding him of his promise that if I ran I would be able to hone my competitive edge in my satellite communication career. My final letter simply stated: "Well?"

The worst blow was my discovery that despite many promises, I could not use my MP travel allowance to bring JP to Ottawa to be with me. Instead, in the middle-aged WASP world of the House of Commons in the 1980s, an all-party members' services committee decreed that single-parent MPs were not entitled to a family travel benefit allocated to married MPs. Travel allowances were restricted to spouses only.

But I was a single parent, separated from my teenager by a continent. I couldn't possibly afford to fly JP back and forth between Vancouver and Ottawa. The only government travel available to us was a seat on a military aircraft, but children under 16 had to be accompanied by a parent, not a possibility for a single mom or dad if they were in Ottawa and the child was in the riding. MPs and their families were entitled to rail passes, without provision for food or accommodation, which was useful for MPs in central Canada but useless for MPs from eastern or western Canada.

The classic dilemma for the western MP is the decision whether to move the family to Ottawa, away from their roots, or leave them in the riding with friends and family. As a single-parent family, we had chosen the latter. What was I to do? Something very rash. I announced that as an MP I opposed any measures that discriminated against any Canadians or restricted their ability to participate in the democratic process. For that reason, I said I would not take my seat in the House of Commons until the members' committee reconsidered the implications of their decision to refuse single parents the use of the travel allowance for their children. I would continue with my normal duties in my constituency and on the House of Commons committees, but my empty seat would remind Canadians that a Parliament that discriminates against certain groups in society cannot effectively represent that society.

Although it all sounded very principled, it struck a public cord of resentment against a Parliament with few women and almost no native or minority-group MPs. The street reaction in Vancouver Centre and my mail was strongly supportive.

But I gradually became aware that I had stupidly placed myself out on a very precarious limb. I was the only mother elected west of the Lakehead; my caucus colleagues were largely indifferent, spiced with malice. Serves that Pinko NDP Red Tory, probably lesbian, right. The handful of other women MPs did not share my single-parent problem. The male-dominated members' committee appeared to be in no hurry to review the issue. Days passed, and my seat remained empty. I began to worry that I might have to resign, since my constituents were entitled to representation in the House of Commons itself.

Finally, I wrote to Jeanne Sauvé, the first woman Speaker. A parliamentary break intervened and there was no answer from her. Then she asked me to come to tea in her speaker's suite behind the House of Commons Chambers. We knew each other, since she had once been a journalist, and in 1972 she had been among the first three women MPs ever elected from Quebec. She was married to Maurice Sauvé, a former Liberal cabinet minister who, she explained, looked after their son Jean-François when she was in Ottawa. Their family home in Montreal was about an hour away. So while she did not share my problems of distance and single parenthood, she understood them.

As we drank our tea, we discussed how hard family life was on politicians, both male and female—the long hours, the constituency demands, the separation from families, the high divorce and marriage breakdown rate among MPs left on their own, tired and vulnerable in Ottawa. She told me she planned on announcing, as Speaker, that MP travel allowances, while not increased, could be used by "designated next of kin," which included children, parents, dependent relatives, and other family members. JP could come to Ottawa with his mother.

Politicians sometimes forget that all things political are local; constituents care about the issues that affect them personally. About one-quarter of Vancouver Centre households were headed by single parents, and the fact that their MP had defended their status was something they related to with warmth. Years later, people on the street or on the ferries approached me to congratulate me on one of two issues—my fight for equal status for single parents, and my vote against a government bill dealing with abortion. Only my continuing fight for more recognition for British Columbia has received more comment. The big achievements of negotiating energy accords or carrying the file on the Canada-US Free Trade Agreement may be more historic, but for my constituents, home and hearth issues counted more.

I had learned this lesson from my former *Vancouver Sun* colleague and friend Paul St. Pierre, the famous playwright and Chilcotin storyteller who was elected a Liberal MP for Coast-Chilcotin during Pierre Trudeau's first government. When I told him my daughter Jane had mentioned that the fishermen in her Pender Harbour neighbourhood, part of Paul's riding, were complaining that they rarely saw him, he responded: "Well, they should realize that when I'm attending the United Nations Law of the Sea conferences in New York, I'm working on their behalf." Unfortunately, they didn't. Paul was defeated in the next election. Jane went on to become a popular local politician, winning huge majorities and her final election by acclamation, by supporting issues such as the local garbage dump.

Other winners from the Speaker's ruling were MPs themselves, who could now take family members to Ottawa for parliamentary functions or simply for company. NDP Ian Waddell, a bachelor, swore his Scottish mother gave me her vote in return for her seat on the plane. MP wives could send an older child to be with Dad while they stayed home with the younger children. MPs from all parties told me that my fight and the Speaker's ruling had improved the quality of their family lives enormously.

The only person not impressed was my own son, who was passionately attached to his West Coast roots and rarely went to Ottawa. When Ottawans asked him if he enjoyed skiing at the local Camp Fortune ski hill in the Gatineau, JP answered: "Why would I? We ski Whistler." My twin Jim and I had owned a small condo at the famous skiing resort, and JP had learned to whiz down the bunny hill as a four-year-old. I sympathized with him. I went to the Capital's mid-February "Winterlude" events, standing on the ice as the cold seeped through my boots, watching a hockey game, chewing away at Beaver Tails, a flat doughnut-like delicacy, and tried to view Ottawa winters as an experience. When we lived in the Northwest Territories we learned that cold could kill you; in Ottawa we learned winters could bore you to death.

In the House of Commons, I was already learning, as BC's first Premier and MP Amor De Cosmos did before me, how little British Columbia counted in Ottawa. In 1871 De Cosmos led the movement to bring the Crown colony of British Columbia into Confederation. But in 1879, as an MP, he was so fed up with the Liberal government's failure to honour its commitment to build a railway across the continent linking British Columbia to central Canada that he introduced a bill in the Commons "for the peaceful separation of British Columbia." No one seconded it and the motion failed.

On May 15, 1980, in one of my first questions in Question Period, I raised the issue of equity in allocating federal economic support programs between the provinces with the likeable Jean-Luc Pepin, then Minister of Transport. Considering the $200-million loan given by the feds to Chrysler Canada and other programs, I asked: "How can the Minister justify the government's failure to accede to a request by Premier Bennett of BC that the feds provide 50 per cent of the $215 million required to build the rail line that would enable coal from northeast BC to be shipped to Japan?" When Jean-Luc smiled a negative response, I retorted: "The Premier of BC has made it very clear that he considers that the federal government is not in the habit of funding anything west of the Lakehead."

A few minutes later I was on my feet again raising a question of privilege with the Speaker. "During the course of my question, I repeated the remarks of the Premier of BC which expressed his frustration in dealing with the federal government on any cost-sharing arrangement," I told the House. "While I was asking the question I heard the Prime Minister [Trudeau] say, and I am supported by my colleagues, 'She talks just like Lévesque, always being gypped by Ottawa.' Madam Speaker, as a western MP I find the Prime Minister's remarks unacceptable . . . since it impugns motives to me." I asked the Speaker to direct the Prime Minister to withdraw his remark.

Prime Minister Trudeau did not rebuke me, a green and junior MP, for my attack. But to his discredit, he invoked an argument that enrages many westerners when they raise grievances with the feds: "I cannot recall her exact remarks but I did hear her say words to the effect that the federal government spent no money west of the Ontario-Manitoba border. That is the kind of remark which I said is exactly the kind of remark Mr. Lévesque makes when he says no money is spent by the federal government in Quebec. If the Honourable Lady[2] did not say that or words to that effect I will withdraw my remarks." We both agreed to check the "blues," or transcripts, of Question Period, and the matter was dropped.

I returned to the theme of western alienation in my maiden speech on October 23, 1980. It was an exciting time in Canadian history, since we were debating the repatriation of Canada's Constitution from Britain, and the adoption of a Charter of Rights. The House of Commons rang with the Canada debates, passionate speeches for and against the proposed changes, and when I rose to give my speech it was under the guillotine of "closure," or a move by the government to force an end to the debate.

It is customary in a maiden speech to praise one's constituents and constituency as the best in Canada. I did that and then launched my attack:

> Vancouver Centre is the very heart of Vancouver. Our riding is often termed "Lotus Land" in honour of our lifestyle. In China, where I was born, I remember the lotus as eternally serene, warmed by the sun and blessed by the rain—like our riding—rising out of the muddied waters. Mr. Speaker, at the moment we in Lotus Land are finding that the waters are very muddied indeed. We have a Liberal government that is proposing

to diminish the power of the provinces and increase the powers of the federal government in the national interest.

But this government cannot represent the national interest, Mr. Speaker. It has no elected representatives west of the Red River Valley.

The core of my argument was that the proposed amending formula as outlined in the Liberal motion would establish second-class status for British Columbia and favour the central provinces of Ontario and Quebec, since any changes in the Constitution under the proposed amending formula would require the approval of 80 per cent of the population. In addition, any change must be approved by a province with 25 per cent of the population of Canada as a whole.

"That means that Quebec and Ontario can always veto a change in the rules. But BC will never have equal rights, nor will any western province, nor will the Atlantic provinces. The right to set the terms of Confederation will lie forever more with central Canada and central Canada only."

Then I added a view that still holds:

Our problem here, Mr. Speaker, is that there are two prevailing views of national interest. In the West we have historically viewed our country as a nation from sea to sea to northern sea. But Honourable Members across the floor of this House have consistently defined the country in terms of their own self-interest.

They have defined Canada as being the equivalent of central Canada. We, in the West, have never accepted this limited role of Canada. Our concept encompasses the West and the North and the Atlantic provinces. And only when the interest of the regions can be satisfied can we honestly say in this House that we have met the test of the national interest.

Some Honourable Members: Hear, hear!

My speech made the CBC national news. During my political career it has developed into my "regional rant" or political mantra. But in the end the Liberal government changed the amending formula, adopting in its place the clause that any changes to the Constitution must be approved by seven provinces containing at least 50 per cent of the Canadian population. This compromise retains powers for central

Canada while appearing to be more equitable, but it has effectively created a constitutional gridlock. Over the years I have been part of several parliamentary initiatives to create more flexibility for constitutional change, but so far success has always eluded us.

I was still coming to grips with my rashness in uprooting my son and myself from the freewheeling, independent life we had lived and loved. About this time I received my one and only letter from my former love, Yukon mining engineer Paul White, who wrote sourly from the Vancouver Club that from what he could see from my television appearances, clearly under the stresses and excesses of my new life, my "centre of gravity had shifted." It was true I had gained weight, eating caucus doughnuts and committee-room sandwiches and airline meals.

On November 18, 1981, 18 months after arriving in Ottawa as a new MP, I wrote in my diary:

> By now I am over most of my resentment at being elected and forced to
> uproot in an election most of us did not want and which was simply the
> product of incompetence, over my anger at finding myself in the 1952
> chauvinistic atmosphere that prevails on The Hill, over my frustration at
> the loss of my professional skills—or at least the opportunity to use
> them—and finally settled in our elegant little Ottawa condo at #22
> Bruyere Street, where I am writing this at 6:45 a.m. while JP sleeps
> below and the grandfather clock ticks away.

In the House of Commons, MPs seemed to spend more time at war games than at work. My "black book"—my sporadic political journal—records one such antic, dealing with a major constituency problem, street soliciting by prostitutes in Vancouver's West End, which was under siege by pimps, prostitutes, heavy traffic by "johns" or customers cruising the streets in their cars, and drug transactions in public parking lots and street corners.

I had mounted a major campaign to encourage the Liberal government to introduce legislation making it illegal for prostitutes to solicit clients in public places.[3] But when the Liberals finally moved to introduce a bill to refer the issue to committee, the NDP refused to give it the necessary all-party consent without debate. One reason may have been NDP Svend Robinson's rumoured ambitions to run against me in Vancouver Centre. Svend, who was the first MP to come out of the closet as a homosexual, may have felt that his Burnaby constituents would be less sympathetic to his sexual preferences than Centre, with its large gay population. In my experience, gay Canadians, like their "straight" fellow citizens, vote on issues that concern them, issues such as housing and jobs and taxes, and not on the basis of their sexual preference. In any event, the reference on soliciting did not pass. Legislation was finally passed by the Mulroney government in December 1985.

My black-book notes record the political volleys that followed:

> More war games on soliciting. I had prepared a S.O.43 [a Standing Order 43, or statement by an MP during Question Period] on the reference . . . but [Liberal MP] Jim Petersen signalled me to meet him behind the Speaker's Chair and told me Svend was going to introduce it [the reference] on Motions. Jim said he wanted me to do it and gave me his copy of the reference. Much scurrying around. Jim came across [the floor of the House] and sat in my seatmate Toronto MP John Bosley's seat and wrote a notice to the Speaker asking her to recognize me first, which she did. The NDP vetoed it. I phoned a furious Vancouver Mayor, Mike Harcourt, and Vancouver Centre MLA, Gary Lauk, who said that if Svend was run over by a truck not to call them . . . JP still not speaking to me.

It seemed that I couldn't win, either at home or at work. But gradually I learned the parliamentary ropes, including the basic rules of lobbying for change. When Lloyd Axworthy, then Minister Responsible for the Status of Women, tried to mothball a conference on Women and the Constitution, 1200 women descended on Parliament Hill on the weekend of February 14 and 15, 1981, many wearing butterflies, the symbol chosen for the conference.

Led by editor and feminist Doris Anderson, who had succeeded my aunt Byrne as editor of *Chatelaine*, and MP Flora MacDonald, we proposed changes to the Charter of Rights to ensure that equality for women was enshrined in the Constitution. Under pressure from Flora during the following Monday's Question Period, Prime Minister Trudeau indicated he would be willing to consider amendments to the

Charter. The concession breathed fresh air into the stifling, chauvinistic atmosphere of the male-dominated Commons.

A few weeks later I received Joe Clark's endorsement to be our "critic for the Status of Men" to protect the male minority from discrimination from the female majority. Among my lighthearted suggestions was the establishment of an Advisory Council on the Status of Men, similar to the agency set up for women. I learned politics can be fun.

I met a commitment made to my gay constituents to introduce a private member's bill, C-242, to prohibit discrimination on the grounds of sexual orientation as recommended by the Canadian Human Rights Commission. After talking to my Vancouver Centre gay voters, I had been moved by their terror of reprisals from landlords and employers if their homosexuality was revealed. One young man, working as a professional in a small interior town, told me of his daily and humiliating fear of being "outed." I took my cue from a compassionate David Crombie, MP for Rosedale and a former mayor of Toronto. "All they want, Pat, is to be treated like anyone else," he explained. Despite the defiantly in-your-face gay balls, gay parades, drag dressing, and sequins-and-feather demonstrations by some gay activists in Vancouver Centre, I found his assessment to be accurate. Although the bill was "talked out" and defeated, it was the first time any MP had introduced such a bill in Parliament, and many of my voters—both straight and gay—wrote to support me for a move that, at the time, broke new ground.

My skills improved in Question Period, where I sat in the second-row benches behind star coaches like Don Mazankowski, MP for Vegreville, and Jim McGrath, MP for St. John's East. Once Maz was driving through his Vegreville riding when he heard me on the radio nailing Finance Minister Allan MacEachen to the wall; he was so delighted that back in Ottawa he jumped out of his car and kissed me full on the lips.

But it was my work as deputy finance critic skewering MacEachen's budget in November 1981 that finally won my Tory colleagues' respect. Tory finance critic Mike Wilson had assigned me the task of organizing our response to the Liberal budget, which was tabled November 12. The following day my seatmate, John Bosley, took me aside to tell me that the Toronto Stock Exchange had plunged and real estate and oil were "falling off the board." As a former business journalist I was intrigued, and I hit the phones to business contacts across the country.

For a novice MP, leading off Question Period for the opposition parties is a thrill as well as a responsibility, and I had the enormous fun of asking the government at the beginning of the next Question Period: "Since the budget was introduced last Thursday night, construction has stopped on 3200 rental units worth half a billion dollars, from St. John's, Newfoundland, to Vancouver, throwing 3400 people out of work. When the Minister of Finance brought in his restrictive budget, was the government aware that these projects would halt, that these jobs would be lost, and that an entire industry would be wiped out?"[4]

Inexcusably, MacEachen was not in the House and his deputy, Pierre Bussieres, caught off guard, mumbled an incoherent reply. This allowed me to turn the knife further, telling the startled House that the Minister of State for Finance "has managed to enunciate what economists call the enema theory of fighting inflation by flushing out the economy."

Some Honourable Members: Hear, hear!

Buried in the fine print of the budget papers was a measure that eliminated the ability of developers to deduct for tax purposes certain "soft costs" associated with construction of rental units, effective on budget day. The government seemed unaware of the negative impact on the economy and the enormous loss of jobs that would result from this unexpected move on projects already costed and under construction or on the drawing boards. Instead, the Finance Minister treated the business press to an elaborate lunch.

On November 17, I said:

Yesterday, while the minister was hosting his luncheon featuring scallops, filet mignon and endive salad, thousands of Canadians were laid off construction sites and thousands more will be without homes because of changes in the budget that affect the deductibility of soft costs. By polling developers across the country we have identified 13 000 rental units which have been cancelled or are in limbo since the minister brought down his budget. About 8000 of those rental units are in Vancouver where 1200 people have been sent home from work sites.

Since the government is blowing away more than $1 billion worth of new construction in return for only $30 million of new revenue in the next four years, will the minister at least postpone the date on which the new measures take effect, from November 12 to January 1, 1982, to allow those projects which are now under construction to go ahead?[5]

Veteran Liberal warrior and Deputy Prime Minister MacEachen was forced to retract or, in parliamentary language, "clarify" his measure, saying that he was "pleased to answer her today in a positive way" and that soft costs and other costs incurred on building already under way would continue to be deductible, along with certain interest expenses.

In the end, the Finance Minister retreated on more than two dozen budget measures, destroying the budget's credibility and creating a suspicion that the Laird of Cape Breton's taste for high living had damaged his reputation.

"I am slowly becoming a heroine as it dawns on everyone that I discovered a major flaw in the budget," I wrote in my black book. "Mike Valpy of the *Globe and Mail* lunched me to find out how I discovered something the *Globe's Report on Business* and finance officials didn't. I told him a good business writer checks out why the stock market drops."

In time, I was appointed Parliament's first woman finance critic when Mike Wilson and John Crosbie took time off to contest the leadership of the Conservative Party.

Parliamentary respect crosses the floor. A few days after my speech about MacEachen's budget, the *Globe and Mail* reported on the front page that the Vancouver Museum had bid for and won Captain Vancouver's chronometer and that three-quarters of it would be paid for by federal funding thanks to Vancouver Centre MP Pat Carney. I knew nothing about it. Back in my office I asked, "What genius is responsible for this?" Janice Whitters put up her hand. When the museum phoned our office for help, she had called the ministerial office of Francis Fox, Secretary of State of Canada and Minister of Communications. Then I recalled how Francis had stopped me in the lobby of the Confederation Building and told me his office was going to pay for Captain Vancouver's chronometer. I looked at him blankly. "Your staff asked for it," he said. I looked even blanker. Finally, I came to my senses. "Thank you. Great staff work," I said.

I also learned how to work the media—my former profession—from a political perspective, a complete reversal of my role as a former member of the Parliamentary Press Gallery. My best shot was aimed at then Solicitor General Robert Kaplan, whom I continually nagged to introduce legislation to ban street soliciting for the purposes of prostitution, the political preoccupation of my West End voters. After successfully fending off my verbal attacks during Question Period, Kaplan entered the Centre Block elevator with me. As the doors closed he said, "At least soliciting is good for the chip wagons in the Market," referring to the french-fry and poutine vendors in Ottawa's Lower Town. "Why?" I asked ingenuously. "Because everyone knows that after you've had sex you're hungry," he replied. I couldn't believe my luck. In my office I went straight to the phones and dialled the popular and influential CBC radio show "As It Happens." "Do you know what the Solicitor General just told me?" I said to an astonished Michael Enright, host of the show. "He says street soliciting is good for the chip wagon vendors because everyone knows that you're hungry after having sex!"

Poor loose-lipped Kaplan. The media splashed the story. The cartoons were great. And the experience taught me never, ever, to say anything anywhere in public that I wouldn't want to read on the front pages of the local newspaper.

In early 1983, I was given a big break. At the suggestion of West Vancouver Tory MP Ron Huntington, my name was put forward as a co-chair of the elections committee of the 1983 Conservative leadership review of incumbent Joe Clark's performance. Many in the party never forgave Joe for the political gaffe with the budget that had brought down his government. The victorious Trudeau Liberals used their new majority to introduce hated measures such as the National Energy Program, which taxed oil wealth away from the western producing provinces and distributed it to central Canadian consumers. In the 1981 leadership review, a third of the Conservative Party voted for a leadership convention. With only 66.1 per cent of the vote against a convention, which compromised his leadership, Joe had drawn a wobbly line in the political sands. If he did not do better in the 1983 leadership review, he told the party, he would resign as leader.

Ron Huntington was anti-Clark. He may have thought showcasing the Tories' western female MP and Blue Star would put a fresh face on the party, but he was also aware that as a rookie MP I was not a member of any of the warring party cliques and owed allegiance only to my enthusiastic campaign workers, who had elected a Conservative against a Liberal tide. With my co-chair, the charming Jean Guilbault, we conducted the leadership review vote at the Conservative general meeting in Winnipeg on January 31, 1983, aided by Carman Joynt of the accounting firm of Touche, Ross and Co. Carman, a kinsman of the famous Canadian poet Bliss Carman, is the only chartered accountant I've ever met with a mischievous sense of humour. It helped cut the tension during the three-day event, celebrated by midnight fire alarms that drove the convention hotel guests into the snowy night, relentless upbeat audiovisual presentations, pushing and shoving among belligerent, liquor-fuelled delegates, and the sight of Clark loyalist Flora MacDonald dancing a jig.

But even Carman's humour failed him as he, Jean, and I peered at the paper recording the result of the vote. The question: Do you wish to have a leadership convention? The answer: YES–795; NO–1607. Carman Joynt swiftly calculated the percentage. We were stunned by the result: 66.7 per cent, a fraction above the 1981 level of 66.1 per cent set by Joe as his benchmark. All the work, the drama, the high hopes were for nothing. The party had not moved away from its doubts about Joe. He was dead in the water, torpedoed by his own ambition.

As Carman left to give the results in a sealed envelope to Clark, his wife Maureen McTeer, political strategist Lowell Murray, and other aides waiting tensely in a nearby office, Jean and I brushed by the reporters, who were thrusting their cameras and tape recorders at us like lances, and prepared to announce the result to the delegates gathered in the Winnipeg Convention Centre. Joe took the stage with a grim-faced Maureen and made a dual announcement: he was both resigning the leadership and planning to run again for the leadership of the Progressive Conservative Party. The other leading contenders were John Crosbie, the failed Tory Finance Minister; Mike Wilson, the earnest MP with the Bay Street smarts from Toronto; and labour lawyer Brian Mulroney, a party activist in Quebec since the days of Prime Minister John Diefenbaker.

The action then moved to the Ottawa Civic Centre on June 11, 1983. The team of Jean, Pat, and Carman was back in action, setting out the guidelines and setting up the machinery for the leadership vote. Books have been written on this dramatic and historic event, which led to the election of Brian Mulroney, who changed the economic foundation of Canada during his two terms as Prime Minister. But in reality, our team was too busy checking delegate lists for phony names and trying to referee the unruly participants, particularly John Crosbie's rough-and-ready Newfoundlanders and Brian Mulroney's Quebec ruffians, each trying to gain some advantage in the rules, to pay much attention to many of the unsavoury aspects of attempted delegate stacking, arm twisting, kneecapping, lying, and outright cheating carried out by the various protagonists.

I took time out from scrutinizing scrutineers to vote in all four ballots. My first vote went to Mike Wilson since I feared only his mother, wife, and campaign workers would vote for him and I didn't want him to be too morose. His first ballot vote was 144. On the next two ballots I voted for Joe and Crosbie respectively, so I could claim impartiality, but on the final ballot I voted for Brian Mulroney. Why? Probably for the same reason other delegates did. The mood was for change, with Conservatives running ahead of the governing Liberals. A decent and likeable man, Joe had blown his chance. Although I did not know Mulroney, he had called me, his voice as glossy as an oil slick, to say he understood that as election chair I could not choose sides. I knew he was the choice of the right-wing elements of the Tories, including those in my own riding association, while I was a left-of-centre Red Tory.

But as the son of an electrician with small-town roots, Brian filled the yearning by the Tory "outsiders" like myself to grasp the brass ring of power, to displace the well-trousered, pinstriped suits of Toronto, a clan so foreign to me I viewed them as aliens from another planet. While Conservative supporters traditionally come from families with middle and high incomes, many have small-town roots and values. Socially remote from the glitzy centre, regionally based, many of us felt that the bilingual ex-truck driver and Laval law graduate would recognize *our* Canada, the immense nation beyond Ontario's cottage country and Quebec's Eastern Townships, and that he offered Canadians a more encompassing view of our country than Joe could. To westerners, he represented the possibility of a more egalitarian Canada, where a Canadian could make his or her way up from the mill floor of a forest town to the smoked-glass skyscrapers and mahogany-panelled offices of corporate and political power.

Many of us wouldn't recognize a pair of Gucci shoes or purse if we wore them, but we understood the Conservative mantra of individual self-reliance, social responsibility to others, and duty to one's country, and Mulroney adroitly appropriated the mantle of the Boy from Baie Comeau. And that is why so many Conservatives later felt Mulroney betrayed them. While never a Bay Street man like Mike Wilson, his extravagant lifestyle and deviance from right-wing dogma bewildered many of his western MPs who thought he was one of them. They fumed silently in the caucus when he supported (to my delight) measures to protect homosexual and other minority-group rights: "A gay man or woman is someone's child, someone's brother or sister," he once told the silent group of mostly middle-aged men.

They burned with resentment when he openly wooed Tory MPs from Quebec but scorned the western MPs' warnings of the Reform wave that eventually swept each one into oblivion and beached the Conservative Party on the electoral rocks of humiliating defeat. And although he liked to quote his maxim "Ya dance with the lady that brung ya," he left right-wingers and western MPs feeling like wallflowers at the dance.

But all that was yet to come. When he walked into the Conservative caucus room for the first time as leader he looked around the Railway Committee Room and said disarmingly: "So this is what caucus looks like." By acknowledging his New Boy status among the elected MPs, the party's front-line troops, he won their grudging respect. His immediate offer to embrace his opponents and their staffs, giving them important shadow cabinet and party positions, healed many wounds ulcerating on the Tory body politic.

Mulroney rewarded me by giving me my dream job, the shadow cabinet position of energy critic, charged with developing a new energy policy to replace the Liberals' loathed National Energy Program that had seared federal-provincial relations between Ottawa and oil- and gas-producing Alberta, and with potential oil and gas producer Newfoundland and Labrador.

And I paid him back. A few months later, Brian and I flew to St. John's, the capital of Newfoundland, to sign the Principles of the Atlantic Accord with Premier Brian Peckford under which we would develop the Atlantic province's offshore resources when we were in government. As an MP, I had successfully negotiated the Accord with Newfoundland's Energy Minister Bill Marshall, who had failed to reach any agreement with Liberal Energy Minister Jean Chrétien in a sulphurous and acrimonious dispute.

It was an historic and unprecedented action. It was also unabashedly cheeky, since Brian was still Leader of the Official Opposition and I was a mere MP when we signed the document to cheers and a flourish of pens. But the Conservatives were running ahead of the governing Liberals as a federal election loomed. Out of power for most of the century, we had to do more than promise change. We had to prove that we could deliver it.

Joe Clark had shown that the Conservatives could win an election. But Brian Mulroney would show we could govern Canada. The Atlantic Accord was proof.

CHAPTER 13

Minister of the Crown

T R A D E   S E C R E T :
*In any negotiation, focus on what people really want,
not necessarily on what they are asking for.
Identify what both sides need in order to reach an agreement.
And when you achieve it, CLOSE THE DEAL.*
—Energy Minister Pat Carney

A few days after the September 4, 1984, election sweeping the Conservatives to power, I was back on Saturna Island, making blackberry jam, when the telephone rang. Damn! The jam was almost at full rolling boil, the most crucial stage. I turned down the heat and picked up the phone.

It was Dr. Fred Doucet, the newly elected Prime Minister Brian Mulroney's officious-sounding aide. "The Prime Minister would like to see you tomorrow at 11 a.m. in the Chateau Laurier," he said importantly.

Not for the first time and certainly not for the last, I bit my tongue at the infuriating stupidity some Canadians reveal about our country. It's enough to burn your jam. "Freddy," I said tightly. "I am on an island off the West Coast of the continent. I cannot possibly be in Ottawa by 11 a.m. tomorrow."

"What about 5:30 p.m.?" Freddy asked. I calculated time zones, airplane schedules, and transport times and agreed. After I hung up I called an air charter service and ordered a floatplane to take me back to the mainland. No sense in pushing my luck.

I knew that the meeting with the Prime Minister would probably involve my expected appointment to his cabinet, since Vancouver Centre was traditionally a cabinet seat. I also knew what post I would likely be given—Minister of Energy, Mines and Resources (EMR). The media were suggesting that Energy would go to Harvie Andre, the hard-edged Calgary MP, but Harvie was too close to the oil patch for political comfort.

For the previous year, when Mulroney had moved me from finance critic to energy critic in his shadow cabinet, I had exhaustively prepared our Conservative energy policy, which would replace the much-hated National Energy Program, imposed by the imperious Liberals on the western producing provinces and despised by westerners as "an arrogant brain-dead act of mayhem"[1] since it stole oil wealth from the West and distributed it to central and eastern Canada.

In unprecedented detail, I had organized task forces and study groups, visited energy projects, met with industry officials, produced policy papers and discussion points, and steered the complex policy through the shoals of the Conservative caucus. I was ready for the job.

It would be years before I learned how my efforts as Energy Minister were undercut by Alberta, the province with the most to gain from our Conservative policies, and by the very federal bureaucrats who were sworn to implement them. They were clearly distracted by the presence of a woman in such a high-profile and technical role; they were quick to perceive me as ineffective and indecisive, as I implemented the most ruthless overhaul of energy policy in Canadian history with the unprecedented assistance of large and small oil and gas producers themselves.

But all that was to come.

My new eminence required new offices, looted from the vanquished Grits. Janice Whitters and I visited 580 Booth Street, home of the Department of Energy, Mines and Resources. I was pleased that capable Quebec MP Robert Layton had been appointed Minister of State for Mines. As we mounted the steps, EMR information officer Ann Jamieson sang out: "Good morning, Minister." I looked around to see whom she meant.

Later my new chief of staff, Harry Near, who was setting up my office, informed me that I should fire Ann. "Why?" I asked. "Because she's a Grit," snapped Harry, who had worked for Joe Clark's Energy Minster Ray Hnatyshyn, and presumably had experience in these matters. "Besides, Erik Nielsen [Deputy Prime Minister] would approve. It shows you are taking charge of your department."

Well, in *that* case. Poor Ann. I learned that the 140 members of her department gave her 140 roses when she left. I never knew why Near chose Ann for the hatchet job. I was relieved when I heard she had landed another government job. After that I never fired any other staff on political grounds, nor did I ever ask any of my employees what their politics were. Our office served all constituents, all Canadians, not just Conservatives. Not every politician, particularly Liberals, shared my view.

Still! Some 140 people in the information department! That's what we had been elected to cut! And cut we did. By the time I left the department nearly two years later, EMR staffing was sharply reduced, as many bright bureaucrats switched to the deregulated private sector, and the departmental budget had been reduced by billions of dollars.

When Janice and I arrived at the twenty-first floor of the Booth Building we found the strangest scene. Most of the furniture had vanished. No desk, no sofa, no TV set. Just a chair and a coat rack. When I asked my deputy minister, Paul Tellier, where the ministerial furniture had gone, he pursed his lips primly and said he didn't know. Later we figured it out. Ministerial furniture allowances were richer than MP furniture allowances, so possibly the departing Minister, Gerry Regan, had taken the furniture with him.

The bureaucracy we inherited had a casual attitude about expenditures. Touring the ministerial office, I noticed a small windowless room, about the size of an apartment storage closet. I mentioned I would like a cot installed so I could periodically rest my bad back. A few days later my administrator, Irene Lister, who had served in my MP's office, told me grimly that she had something to show me and opened the door of the closet.

It was crammed with the most luxurious bedroom furniture I had ever seen. A cherry-wood bed, the most expensive sheets, a chest, a beautiful cheval mirror. We were appalled that a ministerial request could result in such extravagance. "Send it all back," I instructed Irene. She did, relieved that I had not yet caught the ministerial disease of self-indulgence. After that, I rested on the office sofa or the cot in the ladies' lounge.

But some Conservative ministers learned to play the game. Our ministerial coffee cups and informal china were charged to our ministerial expense accounts, and became ministers' personal property. Naively, we ordered our ministerial china from Woolworth's and when we left the department we donated it to a young couple who were setting up house.

But my successor at EMR, Marcel Masse, reportedly amassed a collection of fine china and crystal and other knick-knacks while occupying the grey, bureaucratic offices at EMR. Under the rules, he could take them with him when he moved to another portfolio.

At Booth Street, my job was to address the grievances of western producers by replacing the National Energy Program (NEP) without alienating consumers in Ontario and Quebec, who had been its biggest beneficiaries. And I had to do it quickly, before "bureaucratic paralysis" set in. The new Conservative cabinet was steeped in the belief that the bureaucrats who had created the policies would block our attempt to change them. Our fears had some foundation.

Traditionally during the period from the dropping of the writ to election day, bureaucrats in each department prepare different briefing books containing the bureaucratic version of each political party's policies on the issues within that department's mandate. When the new government is elected, every new minister receives a briefing book outlining his or her party's policies, and how they mesh with the department's ongoing programs. The other briefing books are presumably destroyed.

For departments like Foreign Affairs and International Trade, briefing books can be extremely valuable because, in truth, Canada's foreign policy doesn't change much from one government to another. While different governments may have different initiatives—such as acid rain for the Conservatives and land mines for the Liberals—Canada's day-to-day foreign and trade policies continue on an even course. A famous example is Jean Chrétien's post-election conversion to free trade, after promising to tear up the Free Trade Agreement during the election campaign.

But in the case of Energy, the bureaucrats didn't have access to details of our Conservative policy, which had been produced with direct input from the energy industry and approved by our caucus while we were in Opposition.

So when Deputy Minister Paul Tellier and his officials handed me the briefing book they had prepared, I flipped through it, handed it back, and said: "Thanks, but this time we are going to brief *you*."

Tellier accepted our briefing with subdued grace, but heatedly opposed my next request. The atmosphere was poisonous between Ottawa bureaucrats involved in the NEP and their provincial counterparts, as well as with the energy industry, I explained. Therefore I wanted the deputy to switch teams.

In short, I suggested that the officials who had worked on the scorched-earth western energy negotiations under the Liberals should be assigned to the Atlantic offshore file. Conversely, the bureaucrats who had been involved in acrimonious Atlantic negotiations should be sent off to deal with western concerns.

Tellier stridently objected. Sitting on the couch in my Hill office, once occupied by former Energy Minister Jean Chrétien, he argued that such a public reassignment would hurt the careers of the officials involved. But I was adamant. I would meet my provincial counterparts with new faces at the table. Tellier finally conceded, without grace, but his action probably saved his job. Our 1983 Conservative caucus report, written while we were in opposition, concluded that as a matter of principle the deputy minister and all major authors of the NEP should be replaced in both EMR and Finance.

Two candidates proposed to replace Tellier were Bob Johnston, then our Canadian Consul General in New York, and Bob Richardson, then the head of the Foreign Investment Review Board, which our government had promised to reform and replace to increase investment and create new jobs. Both men later served with me in International Trade.

Tellier did not have to honour my request to switch teams. The deputy minister, not the minister, is responsible for staffing. The fact that he switched won my confidence and helped secure his role as my deputy minister until the Conservative energy policy was in place. In fact, some senior officials stayed in place of necessity, but some new faces helped improve the negotiating atmosphere.

A few days after this confrontation, the Prime Minister called me in Calgary during my meeting with the Canadian Petroleum Association (CPA) and informed me that he wanted to replace Tellier as deputy minister of EMR because of his association with the NEP. I replied that it was, of course, the Prime Minister's choice but Tellier's replacement at this time could delay negotiations while a new deputy was brought on stream. The PM asked whether I was comfortable with

Tellier as my deputy and I said cautiously that so far I was. Nothing more was said on the matter. Essentially Mulroney wanted to do what I had asked Tellier to do—change the players on the team. Consistency is not an attribute of politics.

In fact, Tellier and I worked together so well that when the negotiations were finished and the Conservative energy policy largely in place, Prime Minister Mulroney chose the tough-talking francophone for his own deputy as Clerk of the Privy Council!

The energy conflict touched the very core of Canada's Confederation, which is the relationship between the federal government and the provinces. Under Canada's Constitution each level of government exercises specific powers. Other levels of government cannot usurp these powers without agreement.

The heart of the energy conflict lay in the differing views of the producing provinces and the federal Liberals over the ownership and management of Canada's energy resources. This debate reached a flash point during the period in the 1970s and 1980s when volatility in world markets, sky-rocketing oil prices, and uncertainties of world oil supplies were perceived as a threat to Canadian consumers.

Brrr, shivered the politicians, chilled by the thought of angry Canadians living in a cold climate and relying on an extensive network of energy-consuming trains, planes, trucks, and automobiles to link the country together.

The federal position was stated by Prime Minister Trudeau in 1975. "We do not think it equitable or fair that surplus profits return solely to the provinces producing oil," he told the House of Commons. "In the government's opinion, the whole country should take benefit from any windfall profits."[2]

In vain, opponents argued that the federal position did not apply to other provincially owned resources, such as forestry, hydro power, and mineral production. In vain they argued that the heavy-handed approach to the "have" energy provinces (in the West, the Atlantic, and possibly the North) reflected the elemental fear that Canada would always be run for the benefit of the "have not" energy provinces, specifically Ontario and Quebec.

East-West tensions ran high. While eastern media complained about the "blue-eyed Arabs" of Alberta and other western provinces, western bumper stickers angrily proclaimed: "Let the eastern bastards freeze in the dark." On the Atlantic coast, the federal Liberals insisted that the offshore oil and gas resources of Newfoundland and the Maritime provinces belonged to the federal government, not the provinces, who insisted on their right to their resources. A decision of the Supreme Court of Canada upheld Ottawa's position on the issue of federal ownership of the offshore resources.

In the West, the energy-producing provinces had their own agendas. Alberta Premier Peter Lougheed was committed to using energy revenues to diversify his province's oil-dependent economy, and he fought Ottawa's attempts to dip into provincial resource revenues. British Columbia and Saskatchewan each had their own energy priorities aimed at flexing the muscles of their economies, decreasing their "colonial" status in a Confederation dominated by central Canada.

But the Liberals saw the world differently. The Trudeau government stopped short of nationalizing the Canadian oil and gas industry, but in the budget tabled on October 28, 1980, Finance Minister Allan MacEachen announced the National Energy Program developed by then Energy Minister Marc Lalonde, which shackled the development of the West to the imperialist priorities of Quebec and Ontario.

Volumes have been written about the NEP, but essentially it confiscated the profits of provincially owned energy resources by increasing Ottawa's share of oil and gas revenues at the expense of the producing provinces. It then used these confiscated profits to subsidize petroleum prices to Canadians generally.

The NEP also diverted exploration and development away from provincial lands to federally owned lands, through heavily taxpayer-subsidized programs that were intended to favour Canadian companies operating in frontier areas such as northern Canada. The biggest beneficiary was the state-owned Petro-Canada headed by ex-Ottawa bureaucrat Bill Hopper, who ran an extravagant operation from the Red Tower in the heart of Calgary, commuting weekly from his Ottawa home in a company jet.

While one aim of the NEP was to increase "Canadian content" among private-sector energy companies at the expense of the multinationals, the effects of the NEP, tilted heavily to the interests of the state-owned Petrocan, were harsh on smaller Canadian companies that saw their drilling and exploration opportunities in the provinces diminish. The big bucks required to move into the frontier lands of the Arctic or the Atlantic offshore were beyond their financial resources.

The NEP also sought to increase the use of alternative energy resources, providing consumers with incentives to convert automobiles from gasoline to propane or natural gas, and to subsidize the conversion of oil-based heating systems to propane, natural gas, or electricity. While laudable in concept, it was extravagant in its execution. "You sent me the $800 for the furnace," stated one letter in my ministerial in-basket after I became Energy Minister. "Now please send me the money for the chimney."

As a newly elected MP from the West, full of dreams about the West's place in Confederation, the brutal unfairness of the NEP was like a slug in my gut. I reflected the burning resentment of many westerners, fuelled by the fact that an energy minister and prime minister from Quebec were stealing the resource revenues—owned by the western provinces under our Constitution, and which we needed to finance our own development—in the interest of national "fairness" but essentially for the benefit of Ontario and Quebec consumers.

Our Conservative energy policy was developed while we were in opposition with the unprecedented consultation and co-operation of the western-based oil and gas producers, who agreed to my request to form task forces to identify the key problems and suggest workable solutions to the Conservative government-in-waiting.

The idea for industry task forces was proposed by my legislative assistant Brenda Brown, who volunteered the fact that Ontario Premier Bill Davis had used the concept to tap the expertise of private industry that was unavailable in the public bureaucracy. My initial reaction was negative. "That's a kite that won't fly," I informed her. My concern was that an industry-based approach could spark an energy war between consumers and producers in the politically volatile atmosphere.

But when I presented Brenda's idea to the Canadian Petroleum Association (CPA), representing Big Oil, and to the Independent Petroleum Association of Canada (IPAC), the two leading industry associations responded with a full-force effort that involved 250 to 300 people. Under energy executive Arnie Neilsen, some 30 people were seconded to work full-time for about three months on what then CPA president Ian Smyth called "the single most important consultative effort in the industry's history."[3] Alberta's Energy Minister John Zaozirny was also available to meet with the Conservative MP energy critic, another rare vote of confidence.

I was going directly to the grassroots to find out what people thought worked and didn't work, a technique that had worked well for me in journalism and economic research. "I'm trying to wrap my mind around an extraordinarily complex [energy] policy and find out what's in the minds of the players," I told the *Globe and Mail*.[4]

Sorting through the industry's suggestions, my small staff and I drew on the political advice of our Conservative caucus, which reflected the concerns of both eastern consumers and western producers, to develop a national policy that would harness energy as an engine of growth for a moribund Canadian economy.

Other members of the shadow cabinet were also working on their policy agendas in preparation for taking office. Brian Mulroney did not want to repeat Joe Clark's failure to effectively govern in 1979, when his government was defeated over a fumbled non-confidence vote on John Crosbie's budget.

National reconciliation, improved relations between the federal and provincial governments, and the use of energy resources as an engine of growth for all Canadians were dominant themes in the 1984 election and were clearly endorsed by Canadians through the Conservatives' decisive election win.

When Allan Gotlieb was Canadian Ambassador in Washington, he told me few ministers ever have the chance to reverse national policies. Instead their mandate is merely to tinker at the edges. But as an innocent abroad in the world of politics, it never occurred to me that I couldn't do my job. Once again, as I did so often in my life, I was fighting on new battlefields without the shield of experience.

A few days after I was sworn in, I took my coat off the rack in the empty offices, picked up my briefcase, and hit the road. First stop was the linchpin of Confederation, Ontario, the biggest winner from the Liberals' NEP since consumers' energy costs were in fact subsidized by westerners who received below-market prices for their oil and gas.

I met with Ontario Energy Minister Phillip Andrews and his officials on October 1, 1984. The complexities of Confederation are revealed in notes of the meeting. The Ontario minister said Ontario had no objection to world prices for oil (which would benefit the western provinces). His quid pro quo was lower prices for natural gas (which would cost the western provinces). He indicated that Ontario wanted equal treatment with Quebec. We announced a task force to review our energy-conservation agreements to end duplication.

The next day, October 2, I met with Saskatchewan's stoic Energy Minister Paul Schoenals. His concern was that our western agreement might be based more on Alberta's needs and desires, and would not reflect Saskatchewan's heavy dependence on heavy oil, which was less profitable. Going to world oil prices, the goal sought by Alberta, would hurt Saskatchewan's heavy oil producers and the provincial treasury.

The same day I flew to Calgary to meet with Alberta's affable Energy Minister John Zaozirny, whose boss, Premier Lougheed, set Alberta's policy, which was to move to world prices for oil by December 1, only two months away. My goal, keeping Ontario's concerns in mind, was to ask Alberta to forego a scheduled increase in natural gas prices to which the province was entitled under its agreement with the Liberals.

Next was two days of meetings with industry associations, which essentially pressed for deregulation of oil, since prices would be higher, but not for natural gas (as sought by Ontario) since gas prices would drop. I also met with Bill Hopper, head honcho of Petro-Canada, who was asked to put his ambitious expansion plans on hold pending further review by the new government, which was also discussing possible candidates for his job, although this was not mentioned.

By October 5, I was in Victoria to meet with BC Energy Minister Steve Rogers, an Air Canada pilot on political leave, who told me how he sunbathed on the nose of his DC-9 during his turnaround trips to the Caribbean. Always my favourite provincial counterpart, Steve returned to flying for Air Canada when he left politics after serving as Speaker of the BC Legislature.

Rogers stressed the need for an active role for British Columbia and supported the idea of flexible border prices, sought by Alberta producers, but he wanted the issue postponed until after the current round of negotiations, a non-starter with Alberta. I told him candidly that I could not support the BC government's terms for a Vancouver Island natural gas pipeline that would sell natural gas below cost and require financial assistance from Ottawa.

The western energy ministers and I agreed to meet again at the end of October to try to mesh these conflicting agendas into a coherent agreement that would be acceptable to the consuming provinces of Ontario and Quebec. I had already received a letter from Nova Scotia Energy Minister Joel Matheson complaining that our energy policy would divert oil and gas exploration to western Canada and away from the Maritimes. And Quebec wanted assurance that it would get a deal at least as good as Ontario's.

The only province that appeared happy with our agenda was Newfoundland and Labrador, with whom, as Conservative energy critic, I had negotiated an Agreement in Principle with Energy Minister William Marshall. The Agreement in Principle was signed by Brian Mulroney as Leader of the Opposition and by then Premier Brian Peckford to great acclaim on June 14, 1984, three months before the general election won by the Tories. This historic accomplishment is evidence of what can be achieved before politicians are captured by their bureaucrats and ensnared in the emasculating jaws of the "machinery of government" that often grinds such initiatives to dust.

As an MP and Tory energy critic I had met with Bill Marshall, a gentle man of keen intellect, after the Supreme Court had ruled that the offshore oil and gas resources belonged to the federal government, not to Canada's tenth province, which had been a full Dominion when it joined Canada in 1949.

We were eating lunch in the provincial dining room of the Confederation Building in St. John's, Newfoundland. Marshall and I were alone except for my legislative assistant Brenda Brown, who tells me she does not remember the conversation because she was wholly absorbed with the fact that the waiter's fly was open as he served us.

Marshall described his difficulties with then Energy Minister Jean Chrétien, who brought nothing in his pockets because he didn't understand the issue and couldn't take a technical briefing and thus had robbed Newfoundland and Labrador of the cod and the oil and natural gas resources, which were the dowry the province brought to Confederation.

I had heard quite a bit about the cod and the oil and gas and the dowry before I interrupted Marshall, asking: "What if we treated the oil and natural gas as if they were on land?"

Bill Marshall's eyes lit up. "You mean like Alberta?" he queried. Alberta, we all knew, was rich because of its oil and natural gas. "Sure," I answered, thinking it through. "Forget about ownership. It's the royalty revenues and job spin-offs that count. So what if we treated the offshore energy resources as if they were based on land?" We developed the idea all afternoon, took it to our bosses, and the Atlantic Accord was born.

Basically, the Accord called for joint management of the offshore, with the province netting the greater share of royalty revenues if, in fact, the offshore was developed. This was the basis that allowed Hibernia and other offshore energy to be brought on stream and was later extended to Nova Scotia. It is probably Marshall's and my greatest independent contribution as politicians to Canada's economic development.

As Energy Minister, I met with Marshall and his Newfoundlanders on November 22, 1984, the day after Nova Scotia Minister of Mines and Energy Joel Matheson and I had signed the $200-million Canada-Nova Scotia Development Agreement that approved the initial offshore Nova Scotia energy projects, and three weeks after the western energy ministers and I had reached an interim pricing agreement in Vancouver on October 29, barely a month after my appointment as Conservative Energy Minister.

In fact, by November, I had already presented a report to cabinet on our discussions, meeting regularly with Prime Minister Mulroney, without officials, to discuss negotiating positions, and making decisions with little or no cabinet input beyond that of Finance Minister Mike Wilson, who controlled the energy taxing powers.

With the Prime Minister's backing, I bypassed the normal cabinet process of committees and discussion and consensus. He told my cabinet colleagues that while the process was unorthodox, our energy decision-making was going ahead full steam, thus discouraging their interference or comments. He justified the procedural shortcuts by saying our caucus had already approved our energy policy while we were in opposition. I didn't realize how rare this was until later in our mandate, when the bureaucracy slowed us. In fact, we completed our energy agenda in a matter of months with the enthusiastic effort of my deputy minister Paul Tellier and our able team of officials.

My black book records my emotions on February 7, 1985: "I am suffering from a euphoric hangover. Yesterday, Bill Marshall and I initialed the Atlantic Accord, in a day which went from looming failure at worst to success at [last] with some breathtaking moments in between and today I am tired, wiped, drained, depleted and happy."

Marshall and I closed our deal after we asked our officials and aides to leave us alone in the room. By now trusted friends, we quietly reviewed what we could agree on, leaving disputed items to the last and finally dealing with them. I called the Prime Minister to confirm our agreement and Marshall called Premier Peckford. "How did you do that?" my chief of staff Harry Near marvelled. But Marshall and I had already agreed on the principles in our earlier negotiations when I was a mere MP and Tory energy critic; without the distraction of other agendas pushed by aides and officials, we were able to close our deal.

My black book continues with the account of Mulroney and Peckford's signing of the Accord:

The PM and I have just flown into St. John's in a Challenger, near midnight, from Ottawa. Lots of snow on the ground. The PM has flu-grey shadows under his eyes and is wearing a handsome Finnish forest green suede suit . . .

The PM, looking tired, says: "I guess everybody is thrilled to be going to St. John's on a Sunday night." He and I sit in parallel chairs and talk about selling energy when Accords[5] are through.

He has been on the phone to Lougheed, Buchanan, Peckford[6] and says: "I have a lot of compliments for you." He is aware of the probability that J. Crosbie and McGrath [Jim McGrath, another Newfoundland Tory MP] will take all the credit. We read our briefing books and then had supper . . . the PM started telling stories.

We talked about who was doing well and who wasn't. I learned that the PM watched the replay of Question Period, which we called the Late Show, each night and critiqued our performances.

We discussed how people in politics get beyond their capacity—Joe Clark, he said, would have been a good minister of DINA [Indian and

Northern Affairs] or national director of the Party. He talked about how sick the 1976 convention was . . . it is wonderful to have the PM's unfettered attention for two and a half hours!

We joked about the *Montreal Gazette* story that Ottawa was boring because the Tories weren't partying—they were working too hard. "If that is the worst thing they can say about us," said the PM, "we're doing okay."

On February 11, I recorded in my black book:

An emotional day. A cold, grey, snowy one, low cloud lidding the spectacular harbour of St. John's. The day we signed the Atlantic Accord, old men kissed me and young men, in school jackets, asked me to autograph their copies. A day Premier Peckford said—he is planning an election—[was] the most important in Nfld's history. But arguably the most important since the Island joined Confederation . . .

We had a briefing breakfast with the PM and our Newfie caucus (a dour lot). Jim McGrath still black about being left out of cabinet.[7] Senator Doody asked me how/when we are going to set up the (joint management) agency "since Christ is not available."

Then the PM, Premier, myself, Marshall, J. Crosbie [signing as the Attorney General of Canada, who told us he had to be there and who could blame him?] entered the Hotel Newfoundland board room to cheers and applause. The entire national media had managed to materialize on the island.

I could see Paul Tellier, Len Good, Cy Aubrey of the joint negotiating team. There was a table with gold pens all marked with our name—Hon. Pat Carney—Offshore Accord–Feb. 11, 1985—and a podium. The PM led—me second—Bill Marshall—John Crosbie and Premier Peckford.

I talked about how all Canadians in all the regions could identify the national interest; I wrote it myself and it was pretty good. The PM said how eight months ago he made a promise and he kept it. Bill Marshall said I was sensitive and decisive—I got a big hand—and that the Accord had turned "the PM" into "our PM" and the "shrug into a hug."

Crosbie was Crosbie, funny, moving, outrageous—"It's a man, it's a plane, it's super Carney." Brian Peckford summed up the Accord in a way— "the rights to 700,000 square miles"—that made the PM visibly nervous (what had Pat done?) and sounded, as I said to him, like a giveaway by us.

But there was no doubt Newfoundland felt it had won what it wanted—equality!

To my exasperation, John Crosbie, political minister for Newfoundland and Labrador, managed to block my face with his outstretched hand when the formal photos were taken!

By March 28, five months after we sat down at the table, the western energy ministers and I signed the Western Accord, replacing federal government intervention in energy with market pricing and a promise to phase out a much-loathed natural gas revenue tax. On October 30, after a busy summer of negotiations, I announced the Frontier Policy governing oil and gas exploration on federal lands in northern Canada. The next day, October 31, the end of the gas pricing year, I announced the complicated and technical Agreement on Natural Gas Markets and Prices, which deregulated natural gas prices to the benefit of consumers, particularly in Ontario and Quebec. I delivered both policies in the House of Commons, my favourite venue for policy announcements, much preferred to press conferences.

And I was named "Oilman of the Year" by the respected industry publication *Oilweek*, despite the fact that I was banned from the men-only Petroleum Club, which did not permit women members. Instead, I invited industry executives to meet me at *my* club, the YWCA.

Not everyone was pleased with my efforts, however. One Toronto consumer wrote: "Miss Carney, Why are you giving everything to the Western Provinces? We will have to pay for years for your mistake. In giving the Western Provinces what they want you have screwed the tax payer."[8]

No other Mulroney cabinet minister had accomplished so much in so short a time. Since I also maintained my home in Vancouver during this marathon of effort, and worked hard in the riding on constituency concerns, I was happy but exhausted.

Thus it was a shock to learn in 1999 that bureaucrats in both Ottawa and Alberta had demeaned my efforts during this period. A document dated October 26, 1984, found in the Alberta Provincial Archives by history student Tammy Nemeth, written by a provincial bureaucrat and summarizing "observations received from a senior federal bureaucrat concerning the status of federal/provincial negotiations,"[9] was extremely unflattering.

Reviewing a meeting between Finance Minister Michael Wilson and myself, it depicts me as an overwrought and uninformed minister. It quotes Wilson telling me to "stop shooting volleys into the night. You are in no position to negotiate when you have no officials you trust, and, as a result, no reliable facts and figures."[10]

This meeting took place on the eve of my successful negotiations in Vancouver with the western energy ministers on interim pricing!

The essence of the dispute between Wilson and myself reflected the different mandates and responsibilities of cabinet ministers. The Energy Minister might set energy policy, but the Finance Minister controlled energy taxes. Noting, correctly, that Finance would have major input into energy policy in the Mulroney government and that "Pat Carney is trying her damnedest to be a good friend to western Canada," the vitriolic document described my various "inadequacies," such as having no credible staff, being disorganized, mercurial, and lacking personal credibility, "especially when she is under any amount of pressure."[11]

The document concluded that it would be in Alberta's best interest to encourage Mulroney to support Carney "and allow her to handle energy issues . . . her intentions are good and if she was put in a position where she could develop some credibility with the Prime Minister and her cabinet colleagues, she affords us the best avenue for achieving some of our objectives."[12]

"This document had a significant effect on Alberta's officials," writes Nemeth. "After 26 October 1984 their tone, when discussing Carney and the federal EMR officials in internal memoranda, was decidedly more disparaging. It is ironic that the provincial officials believed the negative comments that were conveyed by one of the very bureaucrats hated by the province and they affected future discussions."[13]

In another memorandum, written by Alberta's Deputy Energy Minister Barry Mellon on November 27, 1984, it was reported that "Federal EMR is in a state of suspended animation, with little or no communication between Ms. Carney and her senior officials." Mellon's assessment added:

In this context, Ms. Carney is at a distinct disadvantage in dealing with Mr. Wilson on major energy issues.

She appears to be inadequately or poorly briefed, with no obvious game plan or strategy to follow up on the federal government's pre-election commitments. Mr. Wilson, in contrast, is well briefed by his officials and, moreover, seems to have the authority to hold back or veto any decisions or proposals put forward by EMR.[14]

Mellon's memo reinforced my view of him as a man with a chip-on-the-shoulder attitude that served neither his minister, John Zaozirny, nor his premier, Peter Lougheed, both of whom supported the main goals of our Conservative energy policy.

Nemeth concludes in her thesis: "There is considerable evidence that the comprehensive study undertaken by Pat Carney as Opposition energy critic was translated into the government's energy policy. Therefore, the claims that there was no strategy and no game plan in EMR are patently false. How did officials at both the federal and provincial levels develop such misleading impressions?"[15]

Nemeth notes that the first unsigned statement had two names handwritten in the margin of the first page. The first name was federal bureaucrat George Tough, who had been an assistant deputy minister of energy under NEP mastermind Marc Lalonde, and on the Conservative government's hit list. When I was Energy Minister he was ADM of the Economic Programs and Government Finance branch of the Department of Finance. The second name was Alberta bureaucrat Myron K. Kanik, who worked closely with Tough in the 1981 energy negotiations under the Liberal government.

Mellon believed that the NEP authors still in place in Finance were indeed trying to sabotage the Conservative government's policy and negotiations. He reported:

> ... the resistance to recent provincial proposals on energy issues
> obviously is coming from federal finance officials, who very clearly have
> the final say [at the bureaucratic level] on fiscal matters. These are the
> same people [Mickey Cohen and George Tough] who helped plan and
> implement the NEP ... Moreover, the finance officials involved in
> energy policy review normally deal with EMR's energy policy group
> headed by Dr. Len Good, who in the past has been as negative on
> proposed changes to policy as are his finance counterparts.[16]

Nemeth concludes:

> If the Alberta officials believed that Energy was disorganized and that the
> control over energy policy was in the hands of Finance, then it would be
> more likely to work with Finance officials.
>
> Many of the Finance officials were the ones who had created the NEP,
> thus by shifting the focus away from the EMR officials to the Finance
> officials there would be more of an opportunity for the bureaucrats to
> maintain aspects of the NEP that would otherwise be discarded by Carney.[17]

Hindsight shows that this conclusion could easily be the case, since
the stance taken by Michael Wilson and his officials did, in fact, undermine the effects of the Conservative energy policy. It imposed great
hardship on the West, its oil and gas producers, and its people when
Finance failed to remove an odious and discriminatory tax after oil
prices plunged in 1986, throwing thousands of westerners out of work.

Again burning resentment fed the simmering emotion of western
alienation but this time it was worse, because Prime Minister
Mulroney himself had promised to remove the unfair tax, the
Petroleum and Gas Revenue Tax (PGRT). Among the most despised
features of the Liberals' NEP, the PGRT imposed a tax on oil and gas
revenues, not profits, plus a resource royalty, normally the prerogative
of the provinces, which own provincial resources under our
Constitution. The fact that the feds were helping themselves to
resource revenues in addition to normal corporate taxes was particularly galling, since Ottawa did not tamper with provincial resource revenues in other provinces.

Canadian corporations are normally taxed on their net profits, after
operating expenses, amortization, and other charges are deducted. But
the PGRT was not income tax-deductible. This federal tax on "gross"
revenues rather than "net" revenues after expenses discriminated
against companies operating in the western oil and gas fields.

And to really rub it in, the cheques sent by the western producers to
the feds were used to finance exploration elsewhere in the country and
to subsidize all Canadian consumers, thus cheating the western
provinces of the competitive advantages of lower energy prices that
could boost their struggling economies.

The Conservative energy policy called for the removal of federal taxes on oil and gas revenues, replacing them with taxes on profits, but when the chips were down Mike Wilson and his finance officials didn't want to give up the money, which amounted to about $2 billion annually to the federal treasury.

Since the NEP was a massive tinker tax toy, collecting streams of revenues from the western oil and gas producers and pouring the cash into massive frontier expenditures and consumer subsidies, we in EMR knew that any changes to the fiscal regime would have to be phased in.

Wilson and his NEP-influenced officials insisted that changes in energy taxes must be fiscally neutral, but in fact some of the fiscal "packages" that crossed my desk even suggested continuing the punishing and discriminatory PGRT after the NEP expenditure commitments had been paid for.

The western provinces, whose treasuries were being raided by Ottawa, were wary of the government's intentions. They were aware that Ottawa's energy policy under the Liberals reflected central Canadian fears that manufacturing and other industries would move west to benefit from lower energy costs, weakening the traditional domination of Confederation by Ontario and Quebec.

BC's Stephen Rogers was blunt. He wrote me after the October meeting:

> I believe that your government is in danger of being mesmerized by the deficit and, therefore, might be largely restricted in taking some of the essential fiscal moves related to energy. For the energy sector to be stimulated, it will need some very clear signals from the federal government that taxation and fiscal regimes are going to be different. Pat, don't let the accountants take over and remember where you said you were headed, and the reasons why.[18]

Saskatchewan's Paul Schoenhals was more formal but no less explicit. After months of haggling with Finance officials, he wrote me on March 20, 1985:

> By any other name, the PGRT is a federal royalty on a provincially owned resource, and no other industry in Canada is subject to such a discriminatory levy.

During the 1984 federal election campaign Mr. Mulroney promised to eliminate the PGRT and to tax Western Canada-based oil and gas industry on the basis of profits, like any other industry in Canada. The federal counter offer on fiscal issues, submitted to our deputies on March 6, simply proposes to replace the existing PGRT with a modified version, no matter what it is called.[19]

While the Western Accord partially addressed these concerns by calling for a phased-out tax, none of us contemplated that world oil prices would plummet and that the rich stream of oil revenues would dry up into a rivulet. Nor did we anticipate that Ottawa would continue its revenue tax, while the suddenly cash-poor industry reduced their payrolls, service sectors, suppliers, and drilling programs, all jobs held largely by western Canadians.

Calgary-based *Oilweek* quoted an industry spokesman that no one east of Manitoba really cared what was happening in the West. "There are 20 000 people out of work in Alberta in the last four months. If it were anywhere else in this country, it would be a national disaster. And we are estimating that it could be 50 000 by the end of summer. That obviously leads to deep social unrest."[20]

The industry that fought price controls did not ask for price supports to bolster its cash flows, but it did expect Ottawa to accelerate the phase-out of the PGRT. Wilson, however, didn't budge. "At its worst, industry downsizing wiped out 85 000 jobs," recalls Ian Smyth, "and nobody in Ottawa appeared to give a damn."

Distraught, I wrote the Prime Minister stating that failure to remove the PGRT, as promised, would cost us dearly in political support in the West, an important Conservative base facing massive job losses, bankruptcies, and social upheaval. Alberta caucus members were facing concern and disbelief from their brutally hammered constituents about our failure to keep our promise. Failure to act could undermine Canadian energy self-sufficiency, since many western producers were not viable at the lower prices, I wrote the Prime Minister. If Canada's dependence on imported oil to serve eastern Canada increased, eastern Canadians might push to limit western exports to the United States, fuelling new energy wars.

Mulroney's reply, clearly drafted by bureaucrats, suggested that my view provided a valuable background for further discussion and that we needed to develop a better understanding of the regional impacts of energy.

I was stunned. This attitude was so shockingly insensitive that I could only conclude the PM never received my letter. I wrote him back that the regional impacts of retaining the PGRT would tar us with the Liberal NEP brush. We did not need to develop a better understanding of people thrown out of work, I added acidly.

My frustration was enhanced by the knowledge that if these terrible layoffs were occurring in Hamilton, Montreal, Sydney, or Moncton, my colleagues at the cabinet table would pay attention. But as they shuffled their cabinet documents and discussed beet sugar and cod and steel prices and Quebec separatists, I felt in my soul they were smugly satisfied that those cowboy yahoos from the west were taking it on the chin.

The attitude of the Prime Minister and the Cabinet changed my view of this Confederation called Canada forever. But Energy was no longer my responsibility. In the 1986 summer cabinet shuffle, I was given a new challenge: Minister for International Trade.

CHAPTER 14

Free Trade

TRADE SECRET:
In trade negotiations, always be prepared to walk away.
That way you don't leave anything on the table.
—Simon Reisman, FTA Chief Negotiator

Prime Minister Brian Mulroney, wearing his trademark sweater, was sitting behind his desk in the small green study off the entrance hall at 24 Sussex when I was ushered in for my second cabinet assignment in June 1986. He was in his Irish Boy-O mood. "How would you like to be Transport Minister?" he asked. "It's usually a western appointment."[1]

I was taken aback. Transport was then the largest ministry in the federal cabinet, a big promotion from Energy, Mines and Resources.

"What about Maz?" I responded. Don Mazankowski loved being Transport Minister—planes falling out of the sky, railway trains colliding. But the image in my mind was of endless railcars of prairie wheat. "Don't worry about Maz,"[2] said the Prime Minister, looking surprised.

I walked to the window, looked at the line of cabinet limos, their occupants waiting for their futures, and then said the unthinkable, the unforgivable: "I don't want to be Transport Minister." The PM, who had been leaning back in his chair, now sat up. "What *do* you want to be?" he asked. "I want to be Minister of International Trade," I said. For someone from British Columbia, where every ship at every coastal port is headed for foreign markets and where most railcars loaded with lumber are headed for the Atlantic Seaboard, Trade was more interesting than Transport.

"Why not? You can sell anything," admitted the PM, clearly reflecting on my performance as Energy Minister. Later, when he informed the media, "I've handed Carney the ball; just watch her run with it," I was appalled. His exuberant challenge meant the media would make sure I fumbled it; as a former reporter I was constantly under their suspicious scrutiny.

My letter of mandate from the Prime Minister for the International Trade Ministry upgraded the role of Trade in view of the upcoming Free Trade Agreement negotiations. The mandate stated that Joe Clark, Secretary of State for External Affairs, and I would form a new "senior partnership" in which Clark would have full responsibility for foreign affairs and I would have a leading role in all trade matters.

I was also assigned the chair of the Priorities and Planning Subcommittee on Trade, taking over from Joe, who was named vice-chair. The subcommittee was the principal forum for forging a consensus within the cabinet on the complex issues involved in the negotiations. My mandate letter said I was to give strong, clear direction to the negotiating team. Henceforth Simon Reisman, the chief negotiator, was to report to the sub-committee through me.

Until then I had paid only polite attention to the free trade debate in cabinet. The PM had told us that he had been persuaded that the Macdonald Commission's report on Canada's future, which supported free trade, was the only solution to the quagmire of Canada's high unemployment, stagnant growth rates, high government debt, and low productivity. Trade Minister Jim Kelleher was a likeable but cautious colleague whose cabinet presentations enervated rather than energized discussion.

We were surprised when, without discussion, Brian Mulroney said he had engaged Simon Reisman as chief negotiator because of his experience in negotiating the US-Canada auto pact in 1965. Besides his reputation as a pugnacious cabinet scold, he was known to us as a "Town" Liberal, one of the handful of past or present civil servants inalterably allied with Liberal administrations. Other candidates, such as the personable and engaging Jake Warren, a former federal trade official, seemed more obvious choices.

Reisman also disliked working with women. In fact, the PM had admonished him about his exclusively male negotiating team. Mulroney was a slow convert to gender equity, but once hooked no prime minister before or since has been more diligent in its application. So I was not surprised at our first lunch in the Pearson Building when Reisman jabbed the air between us with his jaw and said: "You may be the Minister, but I am not your deputy. I do not report to you."

Since I had run my own consulting company in northern Canada, often working for macho male energy clients, and since I had been Canada's first female business columnist for a metropolitan paper, I was used to this attitude. But it was true that Reisman, who had refused to report to the "fancy pants" Foreign Service crowd in External Affairs, had established his own Trade Negotiations Office (TNO) in a separate and lavishly outfitted office in downtown Ottawa. My deputy minister Gerry Shannon confessed to me that relations between the TNO and External were strained.

"Well, Simon, I am the Minister with the free trade mandate, so let's just get on with it," I responded. Thus started the most difficult period of my cabinet experience. I had been handed the ball, but it had been hijacked by a renegade bureaucrat who had no intention of handing it back to any cabinet minister.

But at the end of the day, to use a Trade phrase, it was cabinet ministers—Finance Minister Michael Wilson and me as Trade Minister—quarterbacked by the Prime Minister's chief of staff Derek Burney (one of the External fancy pants) who kept the free trade ball in play.

The conflict centred on Reisman's reluctance to divulge the status of the negotiations either to me or to cabinet. His reports were sweeping generalizations: the Americans were engaged on a number of issues; progress was being made over a broad front; many technical issues were being discussed. But he was vague about the details. Only later did I realize he told us so little because he had very little to tell.

At First Ministers' meetings with the premiers, Reisman and his deputy Gordon Ritchie were long on the Canadian negotiating positions but short on the American offers. The premiers had valid concerns, since many of the issues affected by free trade involved provincial jurisdictions; the federal government needed provincial agreement to make any deal work.

These meetings were held in the Langevin Block, initially without note takers or translators. I was the only outsider present. I started taking notes after one premier made a particularly outrageous claim to a prime ministerial promise that in fact had never been made. The PM's eyelashes fluttered, a sure sign of concern, and I reached for my pencil.

The meetings were always chaired by Mulroney. I sat at his right, and Reisman and Ritchie at his left. Ontario's David Peterson sat beside me, his cigarettes tucked into his briefcase on the table; across from him was Quebec's Robert Bourassa. The western and maritime premiers ranged around the end of the table. At the last meeting, New Brunswick's Richard Hatfield asked us all to sign a book—we knew then that he was facing electoral defeat.

The premiers outlined their shopping lists, from beer pricing to duty remissions to agriculture. At one meeting Peterson laid down his pen and told Bourassa, the main advocate of free trade, that he honoured Bourassa's views but didn't feel right about the whole concept: "It's a philosophical issue with me." The two premiers then engaged in a civil and courteous debate from their provincial perspectives— Ontario, heavily dependent on existing trade with the United States, and Quebec, with its hope of greater economic independence through expanded markets.

In concept, free trade between Canada and the United States was simple. We were already each other's best customers. Under free trade both countries would agree to phase out all tariffs on each other's goods and some services over a 10-year period. This would allow Canadians access to the huge US market and enable the United States to be more competitive in Canada. For the United States the benefits were less apparent; still, a free trade agreement between the world's two greatest trading partners would signal US commitment to gaining access for its citizens to world markets elsewhere. The only items exempted were our ability to protect Canadian culture, our politically sensitive agricultural-management systems (read Quebec and Ontario dairy producers), and our social programs (read Medicare). These were, we told the Americans, off the table.

I took to the road to sell free trade. As I toured the country, I found marked differences in people's attitudes to free trade. The maritime provinces, with their easy access to New England, were more open to the idea. Ontario, which already shipped 95 per cent of its exports to the United States (mainly automobiles), was a harder sell. The prairies, where the nearest US city might be several hundred miles away, seemed up for the challenge. BC's views were mixed, but some people recognized that free trade with the US might open other markets. "If I could sell my frozen omelets in the US," a Surrey businessman asked me, "could I sell them in Hong Kong, too?" The answer was an enthusiastic: "You could try."

But I found that few people understood what free trade really involved. Our standard line that free trade would open up the US market to Canadian products by reducing tariff barriers brought yawns and blank stares. So I sent my staff out shopping across the border in Buffalo for a shopping bag of goodies. At a breakfast meeting in Halifax, I tested my new sales pitch.

Pulling out a woman's purse, I said: "This purse costs $x dollars purchased in the United States. But you have to pay a 25 per cent duty at the Canadian border. With free trade, there will be no duties, and the purse will be cheaper." Aahh, said the audience. I repeated my pitch with a girl's jean skirt, a baby outfit, and finally, to oohs and aahs, a teddy bear, giving the US price as well as the tariff payable at the border. "But you won't have to smuggle the stuff across the border, as you do now," I told my audience who cast guilty glances at each other, "because with free trade these products can be made in Canada and sold here and in the United States." Aahhh, breathed the audience members.

My final pitch was to display some fish-stick packaging, which I had removed from a fish company's office display in Halifax. As I held it up, I told my engaged audience: "Fish sticks are a simple product, made here in Canada and sold in the United States. Fancier product lines, which employ more people, are kept out of the US market by high tariff barriers. But with free trade,"—here I whipped out a shrimp and scallop package—"the tariff barriers will be eliminated and we can make higher value products in Canada, which sell for higher prices and create more jobs!"

No polls were taken, but it was clear that my shopping bag spiel (ideal for TV) conveyed the message more clearly than any expensive brochure could.

But, in reality, there were deep divisions and stresses. How did we define culture, anyway? Whose jobs would be lost and which industries wiped out? What about our traditional commitment to regional development? What about water exports? In the Trade Executive Committee of cabinet, which I chaired, we wrestled with problems of quality control and lower US standards in certain areas, such as fish inspection.

And how would we settle disputes between us? Early in my mandate we were involved in a bruising trade war with the United States over Canadian softwood lumber exports. Although Canada pursued the issue using the established quasi-judicial process in place, at the end of the day, a key US official bluntly informed his Canadian counterpart in private that no matter how substantive our case, we would lose it. This secret conversation occurred the day after four provincial ministers and I travelled to Washington and were promised a fair hearing.

On one Washington trip, US Commerce Secretary Malcolm Baldridge coolly told me that Canada would lose key softwood lumber markets in the US regardless of trade rules because the US southern lumber producers were in hock to their southern bankers. In the corner of Baldridge's vast panelled office was a highly polished saddle; months later he died, pierced by his saddle horn, when his horse rolled on him. I was sailing with my twin in the American San Juan Islands near Saturna when I first learned of his death. We sailed home in time to pick up the telephone message that a Challenger aircraft would take me to Washington for the funeral service. Nancy Reagan, wife of the President, and Barbara Bush, wife of the Vice-President, both wore black and white, clearly coordinated even in grief.

Among other areas of cabinet concern were labour adjustment policies. Finance Minister Wilson insisted, reasonably, that anyone who lost a job would blame it on free trade; he was adamant that he did not want to book billions of adjustment dollars into his budget, which was still in deficit.

John Crosbie and I were equally adamant that the public would be reluctant to support free trade without an income "safety net." It was a cabinet standoff; at the end of the day Mike won his fiscal point, and no funds were forthcoming, but John and I had correctly identified a critical political problem that would develop when the free trade debate went public.

Our caucus was also unnerved by the general lack of information. West Kootenay MP Bob Brisco reported a scare campaign that under free trade the United States would drain the Kootenay Lake system and take control of the hydro power generated in British Columbia. A major political problem in British Columbia was that free trade reinforced the concept that the United States simply wanted access to our resources for processing south of the border.

My predecessor Kelleher had organized Canadian industries into 15 sectoral groups—the largest participatory effort by government until that time—to advise us how and when they wanted tariffs phased out. This was an excruciating task, since those industries that faced a high tariff barrier into the US markets wanted quick access and those that had been protected by high Canadian tariffs wanted to slow down the exposure to American competition. I was amazed at the number of pet-food manufacturers who wrote to us.

My cabinet colleagues also wanted to know how their own departments and responsibilities would be affected. My job was to take the negotiating mandates for each sector (transport, communications, and so on) to cabinet for approval. While often general and open-ended, the mandate discussion allowed my colleagues to express their frustration about the lack of information.

What powers were being traded away? How would Canadian sovereignty be compromised? What exactly was on Canada's table, anyway? To our mutual frustration, I had very little information to provide.

Joe Clark was supportive. In a handwritten note he wrote: "Don't let our colleagues get depressed about the prospects of an agreement. Some of the Cabinet has always been reluctant to pursue this agreement. They will seek an opportunity to bail out. Your message should continue to be that this is going to be very tough, but very much worth pursuing."

As political minister for British Columbia I was often on the West Coast. On one trip I read a detailed newspaper report on negotiations that had never reached the cabinet table. The paper quoted a "Canadian senior official." My chief of staff Perry Miele called to say that Reisman had admitted giving the information to the reporter. Furious, I tried all morning to contact Reisman. Perry finally dragged Simon's secretary out of her hairdresser's to locate him. When I reached him, I said: "Simon, you are a hard man to find." I reminded him that the PM had said budget secrecy applied to the FTA, that Reisman had discussed classified cabinet material in the article, and that we had agreed we would not comment on media speculation.

"You have violated your oath of secrecy," I said, my scrawling notes of the conversation reflecting my fury. I reminded him that at the PM's direction, I hadn't yet taken some of the issues such as agriculture and immigration to cabinet, and my cabinet colleagues would be deeply concerned to read about their issues in the media. In reply, Simon accused me of being "uptight" and "hysterical."

"Here is the situation," he added. "This man was trying to reach me to write an article and I tried to straighten him out on a number of things. There is not a single thing in that article which has not been discussed with the provinces in detail." Since that was probably true, it was no comfort to me. Our cabinet appeared to be the last to be informed of our own intentions.

Reisman said Joe Clark had told him he should be talking up free trade to the press and added: "When you took over, we had a good discussion of this in a meeting in your office." I countered: "I never told you to discuss cabinet documents or to do what you're doing!"

Simon then went into his mantra: "I am telling you that I am not your deputy minister. You are in no position to give me direction . . . If you want a peaceful discussion with me on damage control, face to face, come to Ottawa; I'm willing to listen. If you want to get into a pissing contest with me, you will lose. Don't give into the mode of giving me direction." Then he hung up.

At this point I was, if not hysterical, at least in a flaming Irish temper. I called Paul Tellier, then Clerk of the Privy Council, telling him an oath of secrecy had been broken: "As a cabinet minister, I am asking you to look into it."

I wrote to Reisman: "I wish to establish, as a matter of record, that the information flow from you as negotiator to me as Minister has been insufficient and in my view imperils cabinet acceptance of any agreement which you might negotiate with the US."

Reisman was equally dismissive of the private sector. When a respected banking expert, William Macness, sent requested information to the TNO, Reisman replied: "This is a free country and you are entitled to any views you wish. If you have any notion that they are helpful or that I find them useful, I wish to disabuse you of any such notion."[3]

Sleepless with anxiety, I also wrote the Prime Minister a careful letter outlining my concern that Reisman was undermining our democratic cabinet process. Mulroney called me to his office and told me bluntly that my cabinet colleagues were criticizing my performance. I blew up, suggesting that he order his negotiators to be accountable to ministers, as my letter of mandate stated.

At one point, as I headed out the door, he pulled me back in to continue the hot-tempered exchange. The faces of his two top officials waiting in the anteroom—Chief of Staff Derek Burney and Clerk of the Privy Council Paul Tellier—were ashen. When I returned to my office I wrote to the Prime Minister suggesting that his allegations were so disturbing that we should mutually examine whether there was any point in my continuing to play a role in his government. The fact was, I wrote, that neither I nor my cabinet colleagues were adequately informed about the free trade initiative, and the credibility of the government was at stake.

My letter was returned in the person of Derek Burney himself; there would be no record of it in the Prime Minister's files. But Mulroney had the disarming ability to pull no punches and hold no grudges after such brawls. "It's a good thing we're Irish," he would tell me after we had both cooled down.

But once he explained to Burney and me, alone with him in his corner office, why he gave Reisman such rope, ignoring our Canadian traditions of ministerial accountability and the cabinet process. "If we fail to get an agreement," he confided, "I don't want Simon saying we didn't give him the whole nine yards." That was Simon's favourite expression.

I thought it a high price to pay for undermining cabinet confidence and the democratic process in an historic undertaking that we knew would change the face of Canada. And an unnecessary one, since Reisman dropped the ball himself. On September 23, 1987, Canada's chief negotiator walked out of the free trade talks, suspending negotiations.

We already knew the negotiations were at risk. At one meeting Reisman told us: "The ship is still afloat but [it is] taking water still. It is a question of whether we can get to port." He outlined stalemates on subsidies, intellectual property, government procurement, services, and so on. There were indications of backsliding by the Americans on key issues such as agriculture, sugar, and other major trade irritants, plus the issues of dumping, countervail, and other trade "remedies."

Reisman said he didn't know whether the Americans had given up and were spinning out the last days or whether they wanted negotiations to go to the wire "and to shake all the fruit off the tree, including some of the leaves." He added that we might be unable to complete the agreement at the negotiating table. Political efforts might be needed involving the PM and President Reagan.

On a crucial issue, the dismantling of unfair US trade laws, the Americans wouldn't move until we were prepared to limit our subsidies paid to specific industries. And we would need mandates on investment, alcohol, everything. US Secretary of the Treasury, Jim Baker, believed that the key Canadian proposals only brought us up to the US position and therefore the US shouldn't have to pay for them by negotiating on other items.

This worried me since the cabinet was still not clear on what we had actually negotiated. On September 21, two days before Simon walked out of the negotiations, I wrote in my black book:

> Met 2–6 pm Sunday in Langevin [Block] with Derek [Burney], Joe [Clark], [Mike] Wilson, [Gerry] Shannon and [Gordon] Ritchie, at my request, supported by Wilson, in order to learn something—anything—about the Canadian proposal on subsidies. At the start of the meeting we learned— Joe and I—for the first time that Mike Wilson had gone to Washington with Derek Burney to see Jim Baker on FTA.
>
> What a bombshell! First, it was my file, and I was not even informed! Second, Joe naturally feels that he is in charge of our bilateral relations, not Mike, and Joe is suspicious of the Wilson-Baker relationship. Joe thinks Mike kowtows to Baker and I have seen Mike revert to a schoolboy in knee pants in Baker's presence in Paris.
>
> Finally, we had agreed in cabinet committee last week (Maz in the chair) that we would send political message only—Derek to Howard Baker [a White House official]—and that there would be NO ministerial intervention at this stage. One can only conclude that the PM did not want Joe and I to know; this news will only confirm media's views that the PM will do anything to get a deal.
>
> I can only conclude—as Ritchie sits there with a thick binder of text that no minister has ever set eyes on—that the reason that details of this deal are being kept from me is because they realize I would never approve it. And the details I heard yesterday—US will get access to our logs—our limited ability to give assistance to industry—the pain US is planning to inflict on our food processors—confirms my view that the US is using

the FTA to enshrine in a treaty all the worst aspects of their proposed legislation, as they did in the Dennison letter on lumber.

M [Marjorie] Nichols told me Saturday that the NDP is saying they could get a deal with the US—they would simply shut down defense! But the problem it creates for me is that Joe will withdraw even further—he left before the end of the meeting—from the FTA (keeping to his agenda) and I will be, as I have been, alone in my battle against SR; I have fought for the involvement of Ministers for a full year.

Not one person in the town has assisted me—not Maz, not the PM, not Joe, not Tellier, not Derek. Ironically, last night at Barbara McDougall's dinner, Charlie MacMillan [one of the PMO advisors] confirmed that I am being set up as the fall guy.

The problem was that the US side was not unified and was splintered into about 10 fiefdoms. Canadian Ambassador Allan Gotlieb had already briefed us that under the Reagan administration Congress was, in fact, government by lobby groups; consensus about major issues such as free trade was almost impossible. He reported that one powerful US finance committee member had said he wouldn't vote for an agreement because he was angered by paying three dollars for an Ontario fishing licence.

The Americans wanted an agreement on financial services and investment. ("If we don't talk about investment, we have nothing to talk about," Jim Baker informed me at the Organization for Economic Co-operation and Development (OECD) meeting in Paris in May 1987.) Reisman said he had shown the proposed investment chapter to the Americans and the Americans were "not displeased." Some cabinet ministers were uneasy, stating that they themselves had not decided how far we should go. Investment was our ace card because it was a top priority for the Americans, and the negotiators seemed to be playing it prematurely.[4]

At one cabinet briefing, I wrote a note to Derek Burney saying we might get an agreement too good to reject but not good enough to accept. Burney wrote back: "Your question is key. We may get a deal, but is it the one we can sell?" The Prime Minster was adamant; no deal could be sold or signed unless it contained a method of settling trade disputes in a fair and transparent manner. But the negotiations were stalled.

At a tense meeting of ministers huddled in the cabinet room on September 22, the day before Reisman walked out of the negotiations, ministers reviewed the Canadian and US positions on the key issues of investment and subsidies. Deputy negotiator Gordon Ritchie informed us that the pieces of paper were "not converging." On the deal-making of a dispute settlement mechanism, there was no common ground, since both parties would have to agree to be bound by the process, a principle that the United States was unwilling to accept. Burney suggested that the negotiators stick to our "yellow light/red light" strategy, which called for us to proceed with caution and then walk, if necessary, to administer an "electric shock." The basis of withdrawal would be to have Simon table Canada's fundamental position and then hand it over to the political leadership.

Administering a shock assumes that the Americans are shockable, the Prime Minister observed dryly, and the events of the last two days were not promising. Barring a miracle, he said, the free trade initiative had collapsed.

A damage-control strategy was swiftly sketched out. The full Cabinet, the provinces, and the key advisory groups were to be briefed. So were key newspapers—the *Globe and Mail*, *The New York Times*, the *Washington Post*. The paper trail would indicate that the Americans had negotiated in bad faith.

The Prime Minister correctly warned that as soon as the trade talks failed, the opposition would shift their attack to the competence of the government. I was so engrossed in the issues I didn't realize that I was, in fact, to be the sacrificial lamb. My black-book entry for September 23 notes:

Yesterday, [Tuesday] a bitter day. 8 a.m. meeting—Joe flew back from New York, Ritchie flew back from Washington—indicated that negotiators [were] "two ships that pass in the night." (That was clear to me from dealing with USTR and Commerce—I cut my teeth as Trade Minister on the dispute over softwood.)

We decided to stick to yellow light/red light scenario, then into P&P [Planning and Priorities meeting] where the PM made some bizarre statement about how the opposition would go after Carney for her resignation, and that he wanted us all to be cool, relaxed, calm—he told me I was too tense—sitting there for two hours, tense, etc.

That rocked me and I went back to my office in tears. Derek Burney phoned; JW [Janice Whitters] took the call, saying I was going home. "She is really upset, isn't she?" said Derek. "Yes," said Janice. Derek said he spoke to the PM after; the PM didn't mean to suggest that it would all fall on my shoulders, he would take some of the blame, etc., e.g. he apologized.

I went home, had two scotches, and went to bed. JW checked on me at 5 p.m. I had soup and Wasa bread and was in bed by 11 p.m. Today's paper quoted Peterson as saying I was irrelevant to the trade talks—the legacy of Wilson's bizarre trip to Washington—his discussions with Baker were counterproductive.

In the aftermath of the Free Trade Agreement I also discovered that Wilson's trip led to rumours of a secret deal with Jim Baker on financial services and on the exchange rate for the Canadian dollar, which plagued us in selling the deal. But on his return from Washington on September 23, with television news channels reporting the walkout, Reisman had no deal to sell. At a late-night meeting in the Langevin Block with the core group, which included Mulroney, cabinet ministers Lowell Murray, Mike Wilson, and me, as well as Tellier, Burney, and Gotlieb, Reisman looked shrivelled, his eyes like dried raisins. He couldn't engage the Americans on the key issues, he told us. The proposals the Americans had put forward on regional development and cultural issues were unacceptable to the Canadian government.

With the clock running out on Congressional approval to fast-track the negotiations by midnight on Saturday, October 3,[5] it was up to the ministers to fire the salvos that would get the Americans' attention, focusing on their loss of face internationally if they couldn't get a free trade agreement with their best friends and largest trading partners. Wilson, Carney, and Burney, as the PM's Chief of Staff, were dispatched by Challenger Jet to Washington accompanied by our officials.

We met American Treasury Secretary James Baker and my counterpart US Trade Representative Clayton Yeutter in a Treasury Building conference room located near Baker's office. Burney, as the PM's representative, faced off against Baker, with the rest of us arranged around the oval table. It was a short agenda. Did the Americans want a Free Trade Agreement or not? If so, did the Americans have the political will—and the political ability—to conclude negotiations?

Baker, along with then Vice-President George Bush, his friend, were lean, well-connected Texans who bestrode their world like political giants at home and economic Goliaths abroad. I had had my own reality check with another of the breed, Commerce Secretary Malcolm Baldridge. But Baker, mindful of the rich rewards available to the United States through the pending reform of the world trading system, which would open up new markets, and the need to show good faith in negotiations with Canada, made the necessary commitments.

The Canadian team flew back to Canada and reported to the Prime Minister in his study at 24 Sussex. As we reviewed the day, tense and exhausted but totally focused, Mulroney's teenage son came into the room wearing a plaid nightshirt and unaffectedly kissed his father goodnight and received a hug in exchange. For Mulroney, being Dad was always more important than being Prime Minister.

On October 2, we returned to Washington for the final negotiating session, again in the Treasury Building. This time we split into three teams: Carney on trade, Wilson on financial services, and Burney on the PM's priority, dispute settlement. We met periodically to review our progress and sign off on each other's commitments, often with minimal information. I have a collection of notes from that table, one from me to Wilson warning him we would be hit by a US trade action on wine the following Monday, assuming the FTA failed, and his reply that we were running out of time.

If free trade was a Leap of Faith as Mulroney called it, our three-circle negotiating process was an Act of Trust between us. Periodically we reported our progress to Mulroney, while our ministerial colleagues waited in the cabinet room in Ottawa.

Our American counterparts didn't bother to call Reagan. Baker said the President was watching a movie. The Prime Minister said later he didn't call the President because he too knew Reagan was watching a movie.

Once, when we were alone in his office during a meal break, munching on take-out fried chicken, a puzzled Baker asked me why dispute settlement was so important to Mulroney. "Because there is no point in having a trade agreement without a fair and workable method of settling disputes, given our trade-war experiences with your country," I told him. This seemed to satisfy Baker.

After one break in the negotiations, I found that among my own papers I had inadvertently scooped up the American document outlining the US bottom line on a number of contentious issues. Delightedly I showed it to Reisman and asked him if it was useful. Simon hesitated, said, "Not particularly," and walked away.

But at the trade negotiating table Reisman and I for once were in perfect harmony. Most mundane issues had been settled at the bureaucratic level under the capable nitpicking of deputy negotiator Gordon Ritchie, who was never at a loss for picayune details, although sometimes he made them up, he once confessed. Only issues in dispute were kicked upstairs to ministers.

Reisman sat at my left, with US Chief Negotiator Peter Murphy sprawled in his chair across from us. Gaunt, gangly, doomed to die later of a brain tumour, Murphy was a former textile negotiator, one of the American jackbooters who stuffed textile quotas down the throats of poor developing nations. Finesse was not part of his makeup.

At the end of the table, our bureaucrats would start each round by outlining trade items and the issues in dispute, usually how fast tariff walls would be lowered. The trick was to attain balance—an American undertaking to match every Canadian commitment.

Simon would cock his head: "Do you have an interest in subway parts, Minister?" he would ask. "No, Simon, there is nothing in it for us," I would reply. Forget Bombardier and those thousands of jobs in Quebec; Reisman and I gambled on the fact that we knew our economy better than the Americans did, except for the obvious. Reisman's "Are you warm to automotives, Minister?" drew a lukewarm acknowledgment from me.

We were guided by the advice of each industry group on their preferred time frame for tariff reductions. Briefed by our officials, only once were we surprised and that was on Murphy's specialty, textiles. He proposed a restriction that we knew would shock the Canadian industry. It was taken off the table months ago, said Reisman. But at the end of the day it was the deal-breaker for a demoralized Murphy and we paid it to the justified concern of the Canadian industry; in fact, in retaliation, Canadian manufacturers overcame the barrier and outperformed their expectations.

Between sessions, Reisman and I walked the hallowed halls of Treasury arm in arm while he recounted his negotiating experiences in the GATT and elsewhere, and while I told him of my entrepreneurial experiences in northern Canada. He admired that; someone had always paid his overhead, he said.

When we met for the last time on the last day in the Treasury anteroom overlooking the White House, it was 15 minutes to midnight. We thought we had the deal. Then the Americans rushed in, shoulder to shoulder, and announced that there would be no deal without concessions on culture.

Wilson and I were poker-faced. This time we had the cards. We could not deal on culture, we informed Baker and Yeutter, because we had no mandate from cabinet to negotiate it. For this round the Americans had to fold their hand and accede to the agreement on the table. It was 11:50 p.m. when we sent the Agreement in Principle to the Congressional clerk and 1:00 a.m. before we left the Treasury Building.

We adjourned to the Canadian embassy, where Sondra Gotlieb poured drinks and served sandwiches in her bathrobe, while the dog ate off our plates and peed on the corner of the fireplace in the living room. Tipsily, we phoned Allan Fotheringham's answering service to say: "Have I ever been wrong? You have! Minister Carney and Mrs. Gotlieb." Foth had predicted we would fail.

We left the ambassadorial residence at 2:45 a.m. I was up at dawn to do a live interview with Pamela Wallin, revealing the details of our fried-chicken take-out dinner in Jim Baker's office at Treasury, so tired and hung over that my eyes teared. Wilson and Burney were furious. Even though I reported our "three-ring circus" in an even-handed style, they clearly felt upstaged.

The next day, my notes read:

Brisk, crisp day. Blue sky, sunny. I am sitting in USTR waiting to read text. Simon's wife Connie has just given SR hell for not phoning last night . . . "Aw, honey," SR is saying. "I wish you wouldn't say that . . . don't be that way . . . it's unfair . . . A real battle zone," he says, hanging up. "You see how unreasonable women are?"

My black book continues:

JW [Janice Whitters] told me that Friday on the way in from the airport
SR [stopped the cavalcade] and peed in the bushes. His new saying is:
"He's so mean he'd sell his asshole and shit through his ribs" . . . SR and
I have just been called down to meet with CY [Clayton Yeutter, my
counterpart] and troops to review wine—issue is whether wine stores in
BC should be grandfathered. . . . only one I know of is in Van Centre.[6]

    SR and I play good cop/bad cop. SR says issue is insulting, diddlyshit,
clerk's stuff, shameful to bring it to ministers etc. and I pick up to
negotiate deal we had previously agreed to (BC boutique for US and
January 1 markup for them). We walked over to the Mayflower for lunch
in the fall sunshine, comparing negotiating techniques. SR says always
be prepared to walk away, that way you don't leave anything on the table.
Jake Warren says SR, always wants a deal so puts too much on the table.
I say my four rules are first, find something you agree on . . .[7]

My notes end: "Time to read the text before signing the Agreement."
    On October 4, when we signed the document, the Elements of the
Free Trade Agreement, I complained to Reisman that although I was
Trade Minister, Mike Wilson's signature as Finance Minister was
above mine. "Don't complain, Minister," said Reisman. "I was the chief
negotiator, and my name comes last."
    The agreement still had to be fleshed out into detailed text by offi-
cials. At 2:45 p.m. on December 10, 1987, my deputy minister, Gerry
Shannon, sent me a note from the Prime Minister's Office. "Minister—
we now have an agreement. The Prime Minister has been informed."
    The next day, after tabling the completed text in the House of
Commons, the PM phoned me in my fourth-floor Centre Block office.
"It's a great day, a historic day," he said. "One of the greatest days in
Canadian history." I looked out my window at the pewter-grey skies
above the snow-banked Ottawa River. I thought of the small manufacturing plants scattered throughout Ontario and Quebec, too small to
compete, of people too old to retrain, of opportunities now lost for a
future largely undefined. I realized in the silence of his office, on this
great day, he was alone. No bands played, no hero's welcome awaited.
"Yes, Prime Minister," I said.

But the technical review by bureaucrats still lay ahead. "The Devil is in the details," said Gordon Ritchie, who could identify with both elements. My first battle was over West Coast fishing. The agreement worked out with the Americans accommodated concerns of the Atlantic fishery, but ignored the equally valid—and different—concerns of BC's fishery. At a special meeting attended by Maz, Wilson, and Burney, my concerns were treated with indifference, to the detriment of our fishermen. "Surely you can deal with it," said Mike, as if inequitable treatment for British Columbia was of little or no importance. Once again, Ottawa shrugged at the world beyond the Lakehead.

I was also very tired. My black book is littered with unsent letters and notes: "To Staff: you are a wonderful staff, but I am taking my life back. I might even enjoy it—and so will you!"

One journal entry written in Vancouver is headed:

Long Day! Swam in Pan Pacific pool for one half-hour. Warm sunny morning (8:30–9.00) and could hear the ships and floatplanes. There are worse ways to start the day. Then

　　—talked to [Health Minister Jake] Epp re. getting $150,000 for AIDS;

　　—talked to Premier [Vander] Zalm and then Burney about Moresby [park in Queen Charlotte Islands, or Haida Gwaii] BC's position has validity in regard to loss of logging shutting down Queen Charlottes until park phases in;

　　—saw Dr. Perlman, who says I need time off;

　　—took five and one half-hour flight to Ottawa arriving 10:40 p.m., then 11 p.m. meeting on autos with TNO [Trade Negotiation Office], 12 a.m. [midnight] meeting with Wilson, Michel Cote [Minister of Regional and Industrial Expansion], 1 a.m. vote on capital punishment (I voted against)— then home for six hours sleep before cabinet at 9:30 a.m. Later tomorrow, I will take the 6:30 p.m. [flight] back to Vancouver—for a working stretch of 30 hours out of 36 hours!

At times I was so crippled with arthritis I could hardly walk. I was also heavily involved in Multilateral Trade Negotiations (MTN) taking place in Geneva, which were aimed at expanding global trade in goods and services in markets where Canadian export interests were crucial.

The following March, when I was in bed with flu at home in Vancouver, Mulroney called me to see how I was. When I returned to Ottawa he called on March 24 to say he wanted to see me at 24 Sussex at 10:00 a.m. the next day. I wore my blue suit. We met in his den off the front hall and moved into the silent, formal living room. I heard a child—Nicholas?—crying upstairs.

We discussed the morning's polls—the NDP were 20 points ahead in British Columbia. The Prime Minister said I would win my riding in a walk, but he was worried about my health. The free trade negotiations were over and the new phase would move to the House of Commons, where the legislative process would take place. The battle in the House would be fierce.

He was going to make some changes to the cabinet; he tapped the breast pocket of his shirt, as if he had a list—and he was going to change Trade. I had two choices: I could accept another senior post (unspecified) and remain as a P&P cabinet minister, or if I had the desire to leave politics, this was the time to do so. I could have anything I wanted—an ambassadorship or lieutenant governorship. But he had to know today because he was on his way to see Maz and he had the list in his pocket.

My journal shows I was feeling vulnerable and defensive, but in retrospect I realize that Mulroney had no choice. I was worn down and ill. Deputy Prime Minister Don Mazankowski had surveyed ministers to see who would run again: I had replied, honestly, that I couldn't make that commitment since an election was possibly a year away.

What was a prudent prime minister, with an election to win, to do?

But Mulroney was wearing what I called his CF-18 face, a shiny, bravado look. The breast-pocket tapping reminded me of a childhood episode, when a Singer sewing-machine salesman spread five one-dollar bills in front of my cash-strapped mother. Then Mulroney looked at his watch, preparing to leave.

Serenely—don't get mad, Joe Clark had cautioned me when I told him about the meeting—I replied that I planned to run again, but with my back problems I couldn't commit to run. I had been hospitalized a week after my first election. However, changing me from Trade would hurt me. It would be viewed as a demotion.

Nonsense, what he had in mind was not a demotion, replied the PM. I had a good public image. I had an image in Ottawa of fighting with my bureaucrats—the reason was that I was a woman—but that was okay, I was a minister; I could do what I wanted. But out in the country people thought I was honest, that I had integrity; his mother liked me.

I replied, again serenely, my arm resting on the back of the chair, supporting my head, that my problem was *not* that I was a woman, but that *he* had taken away my authority. If Simon didn't have to take direction, others didn't either. He said he never interfered with a minister except in the national interest—trade, tax reform, official languages, film policy.

I was amazed that it did not occur to him that moving me from Trade would allow the opposition to attack the Free Trade Agreement. We ended the meeting without any commitment from me and without resolution.

He did not announce any cabinet change that day as he told me he would. But thinking it was my last day as International Trade Minister, I went to Willson House to chair an MTN discussion with Mike Wilson, Sylvia Ostry, our ambassador to the MTN in Geneva, and American economic guru Paul Volker. "Did great job," I wrote myself.

Back at my Hill office I cleaned up my correspondence, writing my last letter to my US counterpart, Clayton Yeutter. In my green correspondence folder was a letter from a 109-year-old: "Dear Lady of the Realm. Thank you for all you do for your country." Great timing!

Wondering when a cabinet shuffle would take place, my executive assistant Martin Green and I boarded the government plane and whistle-stopped through southern Ontario on a free trade speaking tour to rally the Conservative troops. When we returned to Ottawa I was summoned to the Prime Minister's bare, plainly furnished office in the Langevin Block, scene of so many FTA dramas. "I'm moving you to Treasury Board," he said without his normal folksy preliminaries. "It's the second most senior economic ministry in the cabinet, next to Finance."

He was right; it was not a demotion. Treasury Board, which manages the government's spending and staffing, is one of the most powerful central agencies in the federal system and the only ministry established under the Canadian constitution. All other departments are "ad hoc," established according to the needs and temper of the times. I would enjoy Treasury Board.

But first I had some unfinished business to attend to.

With his task mainly accomplished, Simon Reisman found himself largely ignored by the Town and reverted to his mischievous ways. While I was still at International Trade, Sylvia Ostry brought me a letter Reisman had written to GATT negotiators in Geneva, advising them that he was in charge of the MTN, undercutting her authority. The PM decreed that Sylvia was our MTN negotiator and Simon's job was to sell the FTA in the country.

Still, I was surprised to learn that when Simon's contract was up, there were no plans to honour this exasperating man for his contribution to his country. Although I had moved on to Treasury Board, I told Simon the Government of Canada was going to host him a dinner and he could invite anyone he wished. He chose ministers, his TNO staff, and the FTA media stalwarts, Hy Solomen, Chris Waddell, Debbie McGregor, Mike Duffy, and Pamela Wallin.

The dinner was held in the ninth-floor banquet room of the Pearson Building, headquarters of External Affairs. My assistant Mijanou Serre dug the silver plate out of External's cupboards and decorated the room with large photo blowups of Simon. The tasselled menu featured $12 cigars and a dessert called "Belle Patricia." "It's like royalty," said Simon, awed. "It *is* royalty," I told him.

It was a wonderful evening. Maz, Mike, and Burney attended. After the brandy was poured, Simon and I did our good-cop/bad-cop routine, based on our experiences at the negotiating table in Washington. I recounted how assistant negotiator Alan Nymark and I had negotiated the wine-store item because I had one in my constituency of Vancouver Centre.

I presented framed cartoons from 1876 and 1880 editions of the *Canadian Illustrated News*, featuring earlier free trade debates, giving one called "Retaliation" to Simon, "Duty to One's Country" to Ritchie, and a Gilbert and Sullivan HMS *Pinafore* cartoon for an absent John Crosbie, my successor, as "our star performer."

Simon suggested that we go into business together "post politics" and that I could have top billing.[8] "I'll tell you the problem we had," he impulsively told our fascinated guests. "Do you really want to get into that, Simon?" I cautioned, but he plunged ahead. The Prime Minister gave him *carte blanche*, he said. "That's French. I know what it means.

I'm from Montreal." But then the PM said he gave Pat Carney the ball as Minister of International Trade and, "watch her run with it." Simon added: "It took a couple of weeks to straighten that out."

Was all that pain and anguish, then, a matter of male ego? Will we ever find out? As we broke up at 11:30 p.m., Simon confided he was taping his memoirs for the National Archives. "I'll be kind," he told me, his eyes misting. The pissing match was over.

For now.

CHAPTER 15

Cabinet

TRADE SECRET:
When you climb a snowbank, don't be diverted by rabbit tracks.
—Rt. Hon. Brian Mulroney, Privy Council

The Mulroney inner Cabinet is meeting at Meech Lake, in the conference room on the second floor of Willson House in the Gatineau Hills located about 30 minutes from Ottawa. In fact, it is the Priorities and Planning (P&P) Committee of Cabinet, comprising the dozen-plus people who run the government of Canada during the Mulroney era.[1]

P&P normally meets at least once a week at 9:30 a.m. on Tuesdays, around an oval table in the panelled Cabinet Room at 320-S in Centre Block, under the benign gaze of Sir John A. Macdonald, Canada's first prime minister. Closed drapes on the windows screen cabinet discussions from possible espionage tactics originating in the US Embassy across Wellington Street. When we were novice ministers, Gordon Osbaldeston, retiring Clerk of the Privy Council, wrote in briefing notes marked "For Ministers' Eyes Only" that Cabinet and P&P Committee meetings were to commence *precisely* at the time they were scheduled and that ministers should be present prior to that time.

The Prime Minister put it more bluntly: P&P attendance was an absolute requirement unless you were "dying or dead." He added: "This is the most exclusive club in town, so be here." The fact that some ministers might be at the other end of the country on official business was never an excuse.

The full Cabinet meets only once or twice a month. But when the Prime Minister wants the full attention of his cabinet ministers, without parliamentary distractions, we meet at Meech Lake, amid the granite rocks and spruce forests of the Canadian Shield. The men wear sports shirts or sweaters, depending on the season, and the women wear slacks. The media clusters on the porch steps of Willson House, where RCMP cars are parked in the driveway.

The low-ceilinged conference room would look at home in a Canadian Legion hall. The Prime Minister is sitting at the middle of one side of the rectangular table. His back is to the window overlooking Meech Lake, the name given to his doomed constitutional initiative to win Quebec's acceptance of the Canadian Constitution Act of 1982, by amending it to reflect Quebec's concerns that it be recognized as a "distinct society" and devolving specific powers to all provinces.

Prime Minister Mulroney and the 10 provincial premiers signed the historic agreement on constitutional amendments on April 30, 1987. None of us at this cabinet table could have anticipated that Meech would fail when two provinces, Manitoba and Newfoundland, refused to ratify it in 1990.

I am seated across from the Prime Minister.[2] When he became Tory leader in 1983, my initial reaction to the "Sunshine Boy from Baie Comeau" was the mild cynicism many westerners feel toward easterners, especially those from Quebec. "When he wrote me in 1980 to congratulate me on my Maiden Speech in the House of Commons, I thought: Pushy," I informed my constituents in one of my candid newsletters.[3] "When he wrote my son to congratulate him on his high school graduation, I thought: Well. When he sent me a handwritten note saying that my energy policy presentation was superb, I thought: Maybe. When he wrote me that the Atlantic Offshore Accord was a tribute to my skills, my talents for conciliation and tough negotiation, I thought: Wow!"

Fourteen years later, after he publicly denied that I had not been invited initially to his self-serving "FTA @ 10" conference in Montreal on June 4–5, 1999, in my role as the International Trade Minister who went to Washington to help negotiate and sign the original Free Trade Agreement, even though I protested to him on the telephone, I have a clearer sense of his "Blarney con Carney."

But while I'm a member of his Cabinet, Mulroney and I have an easy relationship. Although I am always respectful, I am never afraid to speak my mind. We are very attuned to each other by our Irish heritage and temperament. We could read each other's faces. "Look at Pat, she's in great pain today," he would say at a cabinet meeting. No one else at the cabinet table would be aware that I was suffering an arthritis flare. When we had a verbal flare, he would say: "It's a good thing we're Irish."

Seated on my right is Finance Minister Mike Wilson, who is resplendent in a pink shirt and grey-and-pink argyle sweater. There are no formal place cards; Mike and I sit together because our cabinet roles—International Trade and Finance—are closely linked.

Mike has a trick few people notice. If a colleague sends him a note, and Mike reads it and sends it back, this means he has rejected it. If he tucks it under his cabinet papers, this means he will follow it up. Mike also has the worst temper in Ottawa. He first admitted this when we met in his MP's office in the Confederation Building. In fact, his sister had advised him not to go into politics, he said, because of his terrible temper. What? Mild Mike Wilson, with the Clark Kent eye-glasses? Yes. Once, as Energy Minister, I affably agreed to a request by a provincial energy minister who was facing an election to announce a project we had already announced at least twice. Shortly afterwards, Mike phoned me at my home in Vancouver, so angry and hostile that my executive assistant Pierre Alvarez held my hand to keep me from dissolving in shock.

But Mike Wilson also taught me an important lesson: never mouse-trap a colleague at the cabinet table on a controversial issue. Always raise the issue first in private, even if you disagree. And make sure your allies are on side before the meeting even starts.

Wilson's relationship with the Prime Minister is more enigmatic: Bay Street versus Baie Comeau. Once my colleagues and I watched, discomforted, as Mulroney taunted Wilson, jeering at him for the fail-ure of an unpopular budget provision on pension reform. "But the PM was briefed on the budget. Didn't he know about the proposal?" I asked my deputy minister, who was present at the budget briefing. The offi-cial hesitated. "The PM knew about it," he replied. Eventually Mike Wilson backed off under pressure.

Next to Mike sits Flora MacDonald, Minister of Communications and the doyenne of Tory women MPs. Red-haired and well tailored, Flora was defeated in her 1976 bid for Conservative leader by Joe

Clark, who appointed her the only female foreign affairs minister in the world in his short-lived 1979 government.

Her abrasive relationship with her deputy minister Allan Gotlieb is reflected in her published account of the ways bureaucrats betray their ministers: by limiting options presented for ministerial decisions; by failing to inform; and by giving breathless briefings at the door of the cabinet room when it is too late to learn the file.[4]

Totally committed to her work, Flora pays a price in terms of her personal life, as do many politicians. Her speaking schedule is so heavy that sometimes she asks an aide to do her hand laundry and repack her suitcase. Normally sharp-faced and sombre, Flora can convulse listeners with her pointed political stories. Campaigning in 1961 for Conservative MP Margaret May Macdonald, widow of the sitting MP, Flora sometimes gave speeches for shy Margaret since, she told me, nobody in the PEI audience knew the difference.

But Flora's feminist role diminishes her male colleagues' view of her considerable competence. In the Mulroney Cabinet she would attempt—and fail—to ensure that Canadian film audiences had access to Canadian films in the face of heavy American opposition; Canada's Flora versus America's Jack Valenti.

Beyond Flora sits Perrin Beatty, Minister of National Defence. The former boy parliamentarian, who was first elected at age 22, also served in Joe Clark's short-lived cabinet. "Perfect Perrin," we called him unkindly, mainly because he was the perceived pet of veteran Yukon MP and Deputy Leader Erik Nielsen, who gave him the highest rating, second only to Alberta's Don Mazankowski, in Erik's published assessment of his fellow Tories.[5] While this was hardly Perrin's fault, his "I-am-perfect-and-you're-not" attitude, including his quickness in criticizing his colleagues, rankled some of his colleagues at the cabinet table, including me.

Farther down the table sits Barbara McDougall, Minister for Employment and Immigration. As mentioned, I first knew Barbara in the 1960s when we were both business writers at the *Vancouver Sun*. A Conservative and campaign manager for former Toronto mayor David Crombie when he ran for MP in Rosedale, she was involved in politics long before I was recruited. She and David bought me drinks in the bar of the Hotel Vancouver and urged me to run in Vancouver Centre.

"Why don't *you* run?" I asked her testily. "I can't afford it yet," she said pragmatically, "but I've already chosen my riding."

Barbara was not the Conservative Party's choice when she sought the nomination in Toronto's St. Paul's—the macho Conservative Backroom Boys preferred a local athlete—and I met her once at a local cafe when she was knocking on doors for support.

It was raining, and she looked like a woebegone wet seal, hair plastered to her neck and face. Since she was a successful investment analyst, I wondered why she was motivated to brave the lions in the political arena. Possibly because the belly-bulging, pinstripe-suited lions of the PC Party in Metro Toronto had become politically de-clawed and thought of her as a pussycat. They were wrong, and she won her nomination and two subsequent elections, in 1984 and 1988, withdrawing from politics when the same suits decided Kim Campbell was a more trendy choice for Conservative leader in 1993. Wrong again.

At the end of the table to my right is Lowell Murray, the Leader of the Government in the Senate. Famed for his alleged strategy skills, he is the minister responsible for the Meech Lake Accord. Like all major cabinet decisions, there is surprisingly little discussion of the actual details of Meech at the cabinet table; instead, they have been dealt with in Murray's committee. The P&P discussion on Meech is mainly political. When we review the subcommittee's report, I tune out Lowell's laborious and egregious language and note that the seven main provisions[6] of Meech would apply to all provinces and would work well for British Columbia. I sign on with little debate.

Fumbling through his papers and seated next to Lowell is former House Leader, Minister of Justice and Attorney General Ray Hnatyshyn from Saskatchewan. He tells us terrifying tales of his Cossack ancestors and is proud of his Ukrainian background. Ray's father was a senator and his mother is in Nairobi, attending a women's political conference, celebrating her seventy-fifth birthday at my brother Jim's home. Ray's disarming manner defuses his enemies and hides the pain he endures from his arthritic hips. That manner will also win him a term as a popular governor general, when he unlocks Rideau Hall's locked iron gates, bolted by his predecessor Jeanne Sauvé, so that the public can enter the park-like grounds.

Next to Ray is Minister of National Revenue Elmer MacKay, the quintessential Nova Scotia politician, who gave up his traditionally Tory seat so that newly elected Tory leader Brian Mulroney could run and win in a by-election to lead his party from the Opposition benches of the House of Commons.

When Elmer returned to the House in the 1984 election, he used his cabinet position to hustle funds for his province. Among my papers is a handwritten note from Elmer obviously written during a briefing dealing with new funds for Nova Scotia. "Pat: Don't look so nonplussed. You *know* Nova Scotia gets very little!"[7]

Once, lobbying me for funds under the Canada-Nova Scotia Energy Agreement, Elmer brought out a map showing the Patricia Carney Highway to the natural gas fields. When I pointed out that the gas fields are, first, offshore and, second, in the other direction, he said he expected me to build that highway, too. A decade later, his MP son Peter serves as Tory House leader in the Second Coming of Joe Clark.

At the other end of the table, on my left, is Quebec minister Robert de Cotret, who earned his reputation—and a Senate seat—as a brilliant economist who gave up both when he ran and lost under Joe Clark. As President of Treasury Board, which manages the government's spending, he knows how the system works and where the political slush funds are.

When I was Energy Minister, I learned that the Quebec ministers administered a multimillion-dollar money pot called the Laprade fund to finance energy projects, but I could never find out what projects were funded, or why. I later learned it was a long-established floating slush fund that had begun during a previous administration.

Later, when I became President of the Treasury Board, I was told that for architectural and construction projects there was one system for the Ontario side of the Ottawa River and another for the Quebec side. On the Ontario side, the contract is given to an architectural firm, and this firm then awards all of the subcontracts. On the Quebec side, the contract is given to an architectural firm and the minister then awards all subcontracts. My deputy minister, Gerard Veilleux, told me that only five or six people in Ottawa know this system and how it works. Presumably Robert is one of them.

At de Cotret's left sits Lucien Bouchard, Mulroney's Laval classmate and personal Quebec recruit, who parachuted into the inner

Cabinet before he was even an MP. A brooding presence at the cabinet table, where he is resented by some of his colleagues, he is an effective Minister of the Environment, introducing the innovative and Canada-wide Green Plan. I first met Bouchard in the gilded offices of the Canadian embassy in Paris, where he served as our ambassador. He was excited about the forthcoming visit of French president Mitterand to Canada. "It is an historic meeting," Bouchard told me, engaging me with his enthusiasm. "It is the first time that the president of France [will] go farther than Ottawa. He will go to Toronto, the West."[8]

With typical ambassadorial zeal, Bouchard said the opportunities in France were huge: "The barrier is the minds of Canadian investors." I found it hard to equate this man, an eloquent Canadian visionary intent on defending Canada's interests abroad, with the volcanic separatist who had threatened Canada's existence after leaving the Cabinet over his perceived betrayal by Mulroney at the time of the Meech Lake constitutional accord.

Absent from the table is the "other" Bouchard, Benoit, Secretary of State, who spoke little English when first elected as MP from Roberval, Quebec, but quickly became fluent, to the shame of us tongue-tied anglophone ministers. He eventually served as ambassador to Paris, as did his more famous namesake.

Beside Bouchard is Manitoba's Jake Epp, the earnest and even-tempered Minister of National Health and Welfare, who was often my seatmate when Cabinet met at 320-S in Centre Block. A compassionate man, he has the painful assignment of informing his cabinet colleagues that thousands of Canadians are unaware that they are doomed to illness and death because they received tainted blood from the Canadian Red Cross.

When Jake Epp becomes aware of the problem, it is too late to correct it. We all look at our cabinet documents in silence, overwhelmed by emotions too powerful to face, and move on to the next item on the agenda.

At the end of the table lounges Minister of Energy, Mines and Resources Marcel Masse, who occasionally uses government aircraft as flying limousines. As Energy Minister I sometimes used the Petro-Canada plane to travel to Inuvik or Bent Horn in the High Arctic, and to visit North Sea offshore oil rigs in Norway, but his use of it earned it the moniker Air Masse when he succeeded me as Energy Minister. When he was Minister of Communications, Masse, a charmer, dropped into a fundraiser my innovative campaign team had staged in the Vancouver Art Gallery and told the assembled volunteers that he had made 38 trips to Vancouver since he became minister. He neglected to say that these trips were often en route to Whistler's ski runs.

On Mulroney's side of the table sits Indian and Northern Affairs Minister David Crombie, the longtime "tiny perfect mayor" of Toronto, who left politics after the first Mulroney mandate. A sweet man, who was helpful in advising me on how to deal with the complex riding of Vancouver Centre, David is not above exhibiting a touch of uncharacteristic pomposity. After a few years in Cabinet he returned to his beloved Toronto.

Don Mazankowski sits to the Prime Minister's right, as befits the Deputy Prime Minister, who often played chief executive officer to Mulroney's chairman of the board role. I first saw the young MP from Vegreville, Alberta, home of the painted Ukrainian Easter Egg, when he sat in the House of Commons under the leadership of the jowled, finger-shaking Chief, John Diefenbaker.

Maz's charm lies in his ability to carry out difficult and often dirty jobs without alienating the people affected. But you never know what Maz is really thinking, or where his loyalties lie, beyond his commitment to the leader—any leader—and to Alberta. He gives people the impression that he is secretly on their side of any dispute.

Maz replaced veteran Yukon MP Erik Nielsen, who acquired the nickname "Velcro Lips" for his sleepy-lidded silence on almost every issue—that is, until he wrote an autobiography scathing in its criticism of his boss, Brian. This was after Erik had gone on to his just reward: a well-paid patronage post with car and driver. Mulroney was taken aback by Erik's written disapproval of him: "He doesn't have a single good thing to say about me,"[9] Brian told me, phoning from the Prime Minister's Harrington Lake summer residence to Jean and Arthur Pigott's farm, where Barbara and I were visiting, a year after I left the House of Commons. "You could have knocked me over with a feather. If I was unkind I could understand, but his final words to me was [sic], 'In 30 years in public life no one has ever treated me as generously as you and Mila have.'"

PC candidate Pat Carney and PC leader Joe Clark, 1979.

Colin Price, The Province

MP-elect Pat Carney on election night in the riding of Vancouver Centre, February 18, 1980, with exuberant campaign manager Lyall Knott and campaign workers.

Gerry Penny

Kent Kallberg

Long-time associate and parliamentary assistant Janice Whitters, who has served with the author through her political career.

Minister Pat Carney with her young constituents celebrating Canada Day, 1987, at Canada Place in her riding of Vancouver Centre.

街坊之夜
NEIGHBOURHOOD NIGHT

本人身爲雲哥華中區國會議員誠意邀請閣下蒞臨
AS YOUR MEMBER OF PARLIAMENT FOR VANCOUVER CENTRE, I WOULD

參加非官方的晚會，互相討論及關心於閣下有關的各
LIKE TO HAVE YOU JOIN ME FOR AN INFORMAL EVENING TO DISCUSS ANY

種問題，商討閣下爲雲哥華中區選民的有關事務。
THOUGHTS AND CONCERNS YOU, AS A VANCOUVER CENTRE CONSTITUENT, MAY
HAVE.

日期：一九八二年五月廿五日(星期二)
DATE: TUESDAY, 25 MAY 1982
時間：下午七時半至九時半
TIME: 7:30 P.M. TO 9:30 P.M.
地點：片打東街五十號 中華文化中心
PLACE: THE CHINESE CULTURAL CENTRE 50 EAST PENDER STREET
VANCOUVER, B.C.

敬請光臨　指示一切
I LOOK FORWARD TO SEEING YOU.

Neighbourhood Night poster, 25 May, 1982.

Question Period performance by Energy Minister Pat Carney entertains Prime Minister Brian Mulroney and her Conservative colleagues, circa 1984.

Kent Kallberg

Chinese Vice-Premier Li Peng and Energy Minister Pat Carney, circa 1985, at UBC Faculty Club.

Philip Hersee, Expo 86 Photographer

International Trade Minister Pat Carney and Princess Margaret at State Dinner, Expo 86, Vancouver, British Columbia.

International Trade Minister Pat Carney and Prime Minister Margaret Thatcher at Expo 86, Vancouver, British Columbia.

Allan Fotheringham, Jack Webster, and Pat Carney, circa 1987–88.

Political cartoon, 1987.

Ministers Pat Carney and Barbara McDougall at Progressive Conservative Party function, circa 1987–88.

Prime Minister Brian Mulroney, Free Trade Chief Negotiator Simon Reisman, and International Trade Minister Pat Carney, 1988.

First Ministers' meeting brings Prime Minister's quip: "It's a good thing we're Irish." Circa 1986.

Mulroney was worried about my reaction to Erik's negative report card on me. "I can tell you that your performance was absolutely outstanding. That's what I tell everyone. And it is 10 times harder for a woman. Look, let's not be diverted by rabbit tracks. We are entering the sixth year of a Conservative government—the longest since John A. Macdonald."

On the Prime Minister's left sits former Prime Minister Joe Clark, who opposed Mulroney for the leadership and withdrew into his role as Secretary of State for External Affairs, serving with caution and commitment, particularly on Commonwealth issues. During the second Mulroney mandate, he emerged as sponsor of the ill-conceived Charlottetown Accord on the Constitution. Like the majority of British Columbians in all 32 ridings, I voted against Charlottetown.

I recall my conversation with the PM en route to St. John's in the government Challenger, when he cited Joe as an example of a minister who had risen above his competence level. If it galls Joe to see Mulroney move in on his files, make decisions, and take the credit, Joe rarely reveals it. Although, when discussing my own possible post-cabinet appointment, Joe curtly admitted that he was "informed but not consulted" on many key ambassadorial appointments.

Joe's biggest problem is his tendency to procrastinate. He often fails to make necessary decisions on time and sometimes refuses to make any decision at all. After regaining the position of Tory leader in 1998, when popular Jean Charest returned to Quebec to head the provincial Liberal Party, Joe's failure to consult with his caucus before taking positions on issues triggered the departure of scarce Tory MPs.

At the end of the table sits another former Tory leadership candidate, John Crosbie, an immodest man of modest achievements, whose folksy public *persona* masks an insatiable ego that drove him to claim credit for other people's work, including the development of Newfoundland's offshore oil and gas resources,[10] and negotiating the Canada-US Free Trade Agreement, which he admitted in the House of Commons he hadn't even read. As political minister for Newfoundland and Labrador, Crosbie regularly reports that scientific studies show the Atlantic cod are disappearing and that fishing quotas should be cut, adding that he won't be the minister who tells his fishermen to stop fishing because of some soft-headed scientists. Unfortunately, he will be.

As the political minister for British Columbia, in charge of the regional ministers' office, my job is to coordinate our federal initiatives with provincial priorities and wishlists and to get along with provincial and regional politicians. I am also responsible for politics and patronage appointments in British Columbia except for those involving potential judges. These are discreetly left to Speaker John Fraser and the justice minister. Because a minister relies on her appointees to ensure that her policies are carried out, I enjoy the politics and support the patronage appointments if the candidate is qualified. But too often I am battling with candidates whose only qualifications are their Conservative Party membership cards.

I am also the only P&P minister from British Columbia. This is a major disadvantage, mainly because I have no back-up, no one to murmur "She's right" or "That's true." My political soulmate John Fraser used to serve on Priorities and Planning with me, but a year after his appointment as Fisheries Minister, he was gone. Unfortunately, he became a victim of the "tainted tuna" scandal in September 1985, as reported by the sensationalist CBC television program "The Fifth Estate." The plot line was simple: Canadian fisheries inspectors rejected case lots of canned tuna from the StarKist plant in New Brunswick. The company appealed, querying the inspectors' assessment of product quality. Minister Fraser, reminded by Conservative premier Richard Hatfield that 400 jobs were at stake in a poor province, ordered an independent review by the New Brunswick Research and Productivity Council that, in the end, repudiated most of the fisheries inspectors' findings. Fraser ordered the canned tuna released.

"Fifth Estate" reporter Eric Malling, a personal friend of mine, went on air stating the canned tuna was "tainted and unfit for human consumption"—something no fisheries inspector had ever stated publicly. But it was meat and potatoes for the Opposition parties in the House of Commons, who taunted the "tainted tuna" minister to resign. Ironically, Fraser did not resign over the tuna issue, but rather because he unwittingly contradicted Prime Minister Mulroney on television over who ordered the tuna off the shelves—the PM or the minister. When he was called to 24 Sussex to meet with Mulroney, the letter of resignation was awaiting his signature.

Years later Fraser was philosophical about the loss of his cabinet power and privileges. "I never whined, and I never complained,"[11] Fraser said, always the good soldier. "Someone had to back down, and it wasn't going to be the Prime Minister." Fraser returned to public prominence as Speaker of the Commons, serving with even-handed distinction.

The chief public servants sit at flanking tables, sufficiently distant to give Cabinet a sense of intimacy, but close enough to record the all-important "record of decisions," which concludes the Cabinet's collective decision for immediate action and future history books. Privy Council Office official Harry Swain has warned me to read each and every record of decision affecting my portfolio because it is not unknown for the recorder to "spin" the decision to the bureaucracy's liking rather than to ministerial direction. Unfortunately, I don't have time to do as he advises.

Paul Tellier, Clerk of the Privy Council and the most powerful bureaucrat in Ottawa, sits at a table behind Lucien Bouchard. He's wearing a sport shirt and sweater, and is possibly unaware that Mulroney wanted to fire him for his role in the infamous Liberal National Energy Program. Eventually the PM elevated Tellier to be his own deputy minister after we successfully implemented our energy accords early in our mandate.

Before he left Energy, Tellier bequeathed to me the Tak Tanabe collage that hung in his office—on loan from the Art Bank and that I coveted—and a piece of advice. "The Town"—the Ottawa power bureaucracy—had decided that I was not a "team player," he confided to me over lunch. In return, I protested they didn't want women on their team, which he denied.

At another table sits the Prime Minister's Chief of Staff, Derek Burney. Burney is an example of my trade secret: "Don't be first; be second." When I was given International Trade, Joe Clark took me aside and suggested that I ask the PM to assign me Burney, a former Ambassador to Korea, as my deputy minister. Well! I already had a former External Affairs bureaucrat as a deputy minister, thank you very much. I wasn't yet ready for another. So when Mike Wilson pulled me aside and suggested Gerry Shannon as a hard numbers Finance official with a Trade background I opted for Shannon.

The Prime Minister later chose Burney as his own emissary to pilot the FTA negotiations through the shoals of Washington politics. After the negotiation of the Free Trade Agreement, Burney served as Canadian Ambassador in Washington. Although some of us felt Burney had "gone native,"[12] there is no doubt his career was better served as chief of staff to the Prime Minister than in International Trade. Burney cut Mulroney off from his buddies, reorganized his staff, and isolated him from his Cabinet. I came to view Burney as a former geisha turned bureaucratic bully. Cindy Boucher, our communications aide, recounted how she attended a top-level meeting in the PMO on my behalf. When she told the group gathered around the oval conference table in the Langevin Building that she was there to represent International Trade Minister Pat Carney, bureaucratic Burney replied: "That's your problem."

Beside him is the current Deputy Minister of Finance, lawyer Stanley Hart, a friend of the Prime Minister. Although academics claim that Canadian prime ministers are the "political equivalent of the Sun King,"[13] Mulroney always complains that his actual powers are compromised by the need to balance regions and gender in his cabinet selections, or Canadian Bar Association views on potential judges, and similar constraints on the heads of Crown corporations. But Mulroney exercises the right to appoint deputy ministers, the governor general, and lieutenant governors, although the latter, he told me, weren't very important, forgetting that he had once offered me the BC position. His ministers have little say in the appointment of their deputies, unless sparks from personality clashes threaten the government's agenda.

The agenda for P&P Cabinet meetings opens with an informal political discussion. The PM begins by outlining his activities and views on current issues. Wrapping his hands around his coffee mug, his nicotine gum in an ashtray, Mulroney recounts how President Reagan confided to him that acid rain comes from trees and how the Romanian delegation tore the telephones out of the elegant guesthouse at 7 Rideau Gate because they thought the phones were bugged. He tells us that Premier Vander Zalm of British Columbia thinks that the ancient spruce forests in Haida Gwaii, or the Queen Charlotte Islands, should be cut down rather than converted to a park, because some of these trees are 1000 years old and will start rotting fairly soon.

Mulroney dismisses the Reform Party threat that worries the Alberta caucus: "Don't be diverted by rabbit tracks," he says. We will all win our seats in the next election if we sing from the same song sheet. He complains about certain media coverage (although publicly he says he doesn't read the papers). No one has a better grasp of caucus concerns—he told us once that the only thing he fears is the caucus—and he reports on MPs' birthdays, family deaths, and marital pressures.

The PM speaks affectionately of his own family, reporting his children's achievements and repeating Mila's insights, which are spiced with common sense. He discusses the party's election readiness, complaining that Ontario's fabled Big Blue Machine doesn't exist in reality. One party official, named to the Senate, isn't pulling his weight because he thinks he is a real senator.

The PM has a wonderful sense of the ridiculous. On one occasion, when I was recounting people's problems with the metric system and how a group of us once stood around The Bay's fabric table, trying to estimate the fabric we needed, he leaned back in his chair and said: "Why didn't you call *me*?" His written language was different: after our first Christmas in power he read us his New Year's thoughts and I reflected in amazement how stilted his writing was compared to his silver tongue.

After Mulroney opens the discussion, we go around the table. Today I start, outlining political issues in British Columbia, which include funding for the Vancouver Island natural gas pipeline, immigration issues, the demands of the Social Credit provincial government, and the state of the party and the Opposition (mainly the NDP). At the end I add that, based on the number of people who approached me on the street, at my Neighbourhood Nights, at the jazz festival, at upcountry events, British Columbians don't like the idea of nuclear-powered submarines currently under discussion.

Immediately the Minister of Defence objects. Polling shows British Columbians *love* nuclear-powered submarines, he says. The PM adds that polling shows coastal British Columbians love nuclear-powered submarines more than anyone in Canada except Nova Scotians. I shrug. In my experience, a good MP knows the issues at least three months ahead of the polls. Not my issue, I say. But it is for many British Columbians.

We move around the table, listening to each minister's assessment of the state of the nation. An Ontario minister gives her report and adds that her constituents don't think much of nuclear-powered submarines either. The PM signals the clerk to arrange lunch in the attic for him and the Defence Minister. Months later, after more polling, nuclear-powered subs are dropped from the government's agenda.

We address agenda items on emerging government plans and policies. First is the proposed privatization of Montreal-based Air Canada, which would help level the playing field with western-based Canadian Airlines International. I don't want to influence anyone's views, says the PM, but you do remember that in the last campaign I said Air Canada is not for sale? Much work has been done on this file. I look with suspicion at my Quebec colleagues. They keep their eyes on their briefing books. The Deputy Prime Minister, an Albertan, avoids my glare entirely. Air Canada is eventually privatized, but not today.

We discuss other issues, but we all know that the PM has a briefing book, prepared by the Clerk of the Privy Council, sitting on the polished table. It will say that on this issue Minister Carney will propose such and such, supported by Minister Clark. Minister Wilson has some reservations and Minister de Cotret objects. We suggest that you deny or defer this issue. The Clerk's information comes from his network and from the meeting he holds with all deputy ministers the day before P&P to identify problems and propose acceptable compromises. A minister can rarely overrule the PM's preordained briefing book unless the PM himself agrees with his minister. I once overruled it when I arrived at the meeting, fresh from a tour of North Sea oil rigs, loaded with posters and oil samples and sheer enthusiasm, and talked my reluctant colleagues into agreeing to put more money into the development of the Hibernia offshore development, which at that stage was little more than a dream.

After a discussion of House Business and Economic Matters, we move on to committee reports, which are appended to the P&P "cab docs," along with the communication plan. The three main committees are Economic and Regional Development, Social Development, and Treasury Board. There, proposed legislation and policies are scrutinized, attacked, defended, and eventually rejected or accepted by committee members drawn from the full Cabinet.

Except for Treasury Board, any cabinet member can attend a committee meeting if his or her interests are at stake. Ad hoc lobbies are formed to support the sugar beet subsidy, important to the prairies, or the steel plant and coal mining subsidies, important to the maritimes, or cultural initiatives. Treasury Board, the only cabinet committee enshrined under the Constitution, does not permit "cabinet drop-ins." Its committee members are normally drawn from ministries that are not Big Spenders.

All programs that involve government expenditures end up at Treasury Board for approval.

Over time, I served as President of Treasury Board, vice-chair of the Cabinet Committee on Economic and Regional Development (CCERD), and member of the Foreign and Defence Policy Committee and of Security and Intelligence, which rarely met and had less to report, although we were once shown how the Russians had bugged the computers in the US embassy in Moscow and warned that spooks and spies were monitoring our activities.

The appended committee reports, dealing with the nuts and bolts of government, are adopted without comment. Our P&P agenda finishes with a review of pending appointments. As we review the list, we can blackball any name we wish, without debate or explanation. While we might be asked privately for our reasons (she's a Liberal, he's a drunk, he's notoriously incompetent), normally we are not.

Cabinet adjourns around noon. As we pick up our cab docs or call out to a colleague, I reflect on the fact that all the major decisions I have been involved in have rarely been made at Cabinet. Sometimes changes are made if a concern is raised, but these cases are exceptions. Decisions are typically reached in private with the PM, or in private meetings with cabinet colleagues, or in committee. An example is the decision over the CF-18, a decision that, in my view, changed Canadian history by hardening western alienation, breathing life into the Reform movement, and bringing on the slow death of the Progressive Conservative Party.

The CF-18 was a state-of-the-art, frontline fighter produced by McDonnell Douglas Corporation in the United States. When Canada bought 138 CF-18 fighter aircraft in 1980, the terms of the contract stipulated that when all aircraft were delivered, engineering support would revert to the Canadian Forces, a boost to Canada's aerospace industry. On July 24, 1984, Supply and Services Canada issued a letter of interest to all major Canadian aircraft companies soliciting bids for the lucrative contract. Three consortia emerged—IMP Group of Halifax, Canadair Ltd. of Montreal, and Bristol Aerospace of Winnipeg. An interdepartmental evaluation team reported that both Bristol Aerospace and Canadair bids were compliant and technically acceptable. The evaluation team recommended that the Bristol Aerospace group be selected, "based on having presented the most favourable price and technical proposal."[14] The results of this evaluation were forwarded to the Minister of Supply and Services, Monique Vézina of Quebec. The following account is based on my notes.

> We knew that the CF-18 decision was pending, but like all other major Cabinet decisions it was never discussed in Cabinet, nor in the Economic Committee of Cabinet.[15] One morning we were all summoned to a full Cabinet meeting. [Bill] McKnight [Minister Responsible for Western Diversification], and I sat at the end of the table near the double door entrance to the Cabinet room. [Treasury Board President] Robert de Cotret sat across from MBM [the Prime Minister], under the portrait of Sir John A.
>
> The PM explained that the meeting had been called to consider the special item of the CF-18. The PM had a look that I always thought of afterwards as his "CF-18" look—greasy skin, sleazy manner, as if a faint shine of perspiration had broken out on his skin.
>
> He said Treasury Board had met earlier that morning and had made the decision. He laid great emphasis on the fact that TB had *made* the decision; we were there simply to listen to it. McKnight and I muttered to each other why the hell did "they" [meaning PMO, etc.] bother calling Cabinet anyway.
>
> Robert pulled out a typewritten statement and started reading the formal ministerial announcement awarding the contract to Quebec. I wondered cynically how they could make a decision at an 8 a.m. TB meeting and have the statement prepared in time for the Cabinet meeting; subsequently I learned that the TB ministers had been similarly "informed" and had not in fact made the decision. De Cotret is probably one of the few ministers who actually knew how it was handled. I never felt there was any point in discussing it with him.

When de Cotret had finished reading the prepared statement, the PM said that there were packages prepared for us, particularly political ministers like myself. We were to phone our respective premiers and advise them of the decision. He made some comments stating that this was a difficult situation for Manitoba ministers like Epp and Charlie Mayer [Minister of State (Canadian Wheat Board)], but it was a decision taken in the national interest (sweat shining on his brow).

Joe Clark, sitting on his left, leaned across the table, his left arm jabbing in that curious way of his, finger poking the air in front of him, and said: "*Whatever you say, don't say it was in the national interest.*" We were all hushed: Joe rarely said anything that publicly contradicted his successor, and there was untypical force in his voice.

There followed an incident that first raised in my mind a choke of doubt about the PM, about his fundamental bedrock ethics, which I had never previously entertained. Yes, he might be shallow; of course he was political, maybe he did want everyone to like him. But these are not fundamental flaws.

I went up to him to receive my instructions on dealing with "the Zalm." I can recall it clearly. I came up to them as they turned to leave the table, the PM on my left, halfway to his feet, and Maz on my right, still sitting in his chair. "Tell Vander Zalm he will get his ice-breaker," the PM told me, referring to the BC premier's push to get an ice-breaker built in BC. "When?" I asked, ever the practical politician. "By Christmas," said Maz. I shrugged, collected my handy printed material and went back to my office.

I had trouble reaching the premier, who was taking a few days off. I was not unduly upset that he was unavailable, because I was worried that he would announce the ice-breaker at the first opportunity and deny the feds the chance to orchestrate the announcement for our own advantage. I reported my failure to Jamie Burns, an aide in Maz's office. It would not have occurred to me to deliberately disobey the PM. My notes continue:

A few weeks later I mentioned at the Cabinet table the PM's offer of the ice-breaker-before-Christmas deal to BC. The words were barely out of my mouth when the PM, rising to a crouch in his seat, pointed a pencil at me sitting across from him and said: "I said no such thing! Retract your statement immediately."

Stunned, I looked at Maz; surely he could not deny the incident to which he had been a party? But Maz merely glowered, saying nothing. "Retract your statement," said the PM in a state of high excitement, glancing at Jake Epp sitting beside me and at the astonished Privy Council Office secretaries scribbling in their notebooks behind me. "There are note-takers in the room!" said the PM. "What will Jake Epp think if you make a statement like that?"

It was all too clear what Epp would think. Still, in cold shock, I stammered something which was not a retraction—I could not do that—but which skirted the ice-breaker issue, and the PM relaxed and resumed his seat. I turned to Jake and whispered: "He did say that." Jake smiled. "I know," he said. After Cabinet I tackled Maz, reminding him of my conversation with Jamie Burns, who confirmed it. Maz cocked his head and looked sheepish. "Well, it's past history now," he said, and walked away.

We never discussed the issue again. The ice-breaker was later cancelled, showing how tenuous such "deals" are in reality. But for me an important gut-deep issue had been learned. When the chips are down, the PM will abandon you to save his own skin. He is a person with a very selective memory. Never ever let yourself get into a situation where you need him to back you up, because he will collapse on you, cave in, vanish, just when you need him.[16]

That is exactly what happened during the Free Trade Negotiations with the United States.

At the end of his first mandate, Brian Mulroney gave each of his ministers a bound document, with our names inscribed in gold on the cover, titled "Achievements of the Government of Canada, September 1984–November 1988." Searching through the document, I cannot find any reference to the CF-18 contract under the section on Supply and Services. Maybe it is buried elsewhere.

CHAPTER 16

Political Life

I n the game of government, Canadians like to have one team on the ice and at least one other on the bench, ready to take over the play. And when the electorate decides to Throw The Bums Out, the transfer of power between political parties can be as exhilarating as winning hockey's Stanley Cup.

The Conservative win in 1984 was described by *Time* magazine as "a landslide of Rocky Mountain proportions."[1] The Tories' tide took 211 of 282 seats, including my re-election in Vancouver Centre, more than double the number of seats won in 1980. Our party won a plurality of popular votes in all 10 provinces, the first time in 20 years that the governing party had such national backing.

Prime Minister-elect Brian Mulroney, a smiling Mila at his side, told 3000 cheering supporters in the indoor hockey rink in Baie Comeau, Quebec: "Canada has responded to a call to national unity."[2] The 16-year Liberal reign, interrupted by the nine-month Joe Clark regime, collapsed like a punctured campaign balloon. Ecstatic Tories poured into Ottawa in a daze of delight to celebrate victory and the Conservatives' return to power in a power-mad town. Among them were newly elected MPs, their families, their campaign teams, friends, and relatives. Several years later my former cabinet colleague Ray Hnatyshyn told me he didn't know how many relatives he had until he was appointed Governor General. That was the scene in Ottawa in the fall of 1984.

Conservatives filled the hotels, the National Arts Centre, the Hall of Honour in Centre Block on Parliament Hill. The buzz was about potential cabinet postings, likely winners and losers, possible patronage appointments. It slowly dawned on me, a second-term MP, how vindictive some of my fellow Tories were about their 16 years in the political wasteland, how angry they were at Joe Clark for squandering power, how much they thirsted for revenge against the Grits who had hogged the power, pomp, and patronage.

Even worse were the Trendy Tories, generally young lawyers and professionals, who nimbly jumped aboard the Tory roller coaster as it picked up electoral speed, abandoning the Tories for other parties just as swiftly when the ride ended in 1993.

Our Conservative caucus colleagues had campaigned as a close-knit, stouthearted army intent on victory. I experienced a pang of compassion when we gathered in the lobby of Parliament's Centre Block before boarding the buses to Rideau Hall for the Cabinet's swearing-in ceremony. Prime Minister Mulroney had sworn his future Cabinet to secrecy in order to stump the media, and we didn't know who was in or out until we separated for the buses—the new cabinet members in one bus, the rest of the caucus in other buses.

Good! Newly elected MP Barbara McDougall was in Cabinet! Even though she was staying at my place, we hadn't confided our cabinet appointments to each other, so strong was Mulroney's hold on us. But as I boarded the bus, I caught the wistful gaze of Alberta MP Jim Hawkes, one of many re-elected Conservative MPs who felt he had earned his seat at the cabinet table, as opposed to the novices who took their places by reason of region or gender or political favours. BC's Benno Friesen was another capable soldier of sound judgment and solid performance who watched others less qualified take a seat at the cabinet table.

At Rideau Hall, we were sworn in as cabinet ministers, placing our hands on the Bible for the Oath of Allegiance, promising to "keep close and secret" Privy Council matters and to be "vigilant, diligent, and circumspect" in dealing with the "Queen's Majesty" affairs.[3] We had our photographs taken and basked in the adoration and admiration of our friends, shrugging off the palpable envy of some of our colleagues.

None of my family ever made it to any of my three cabinet swearing-in ceremonies. My twin brother Jim was working for the United

Nations in Africa, my son was in school, and my daughter was raising two children in a BC coastal village. Their real worlds took priority over my pomp and circumstance.

When we had settled into our new offices and our new sense of importance, we suffered through a blizzard of memos, notes, briefing papers, and instructions emanating from the bureaucrats in the Privy Council Office (PCO) and the politicos of the Prime Minister's Office (PMO). We were to carry our cabinet documents in zippered folders and secure them in a locked cabinet when not using them. There was no need to spill them on the marbled floors of Parliament for the media and the Opposition to find, decreed the Prime Minister.

The flaw in this arrangement surfaced when the RCMP informed me that one of my drivers was reading my cabinet documents in the car between meetings. When asked why, the driver said he found them fascinating. He also removed from my felt Green Books letters that he thought might upset me. That would certainly lighten Pat's correspondence, Joe Clark observed dryly. The driver was later fired.

Photocopying cab docs was illegal, and the originals were not to leave Ottawa, a rule more honoured in the breach than the observance. Our staff and our governor-in-council appointments must have security clearances. We would always have access to cab docs for the period we were ministers.

It was improper for a cabinet minister to write to a regulatory board, but we could write to the minister responsible. We were not to assume responsibility for the actions of a Crown corporation. Instead we should write: "I am informed that . . ." Similarly, deputy ministers often wrote marching orders to their ministers that started with the phrase: "You may wish to consider . . ."

We must inform the Prime Minister's office 72 hours in advance of any public statements and also call the Deputy PM. Travel schedules were to be filed with the PMO. A private railcar was available—I never used it—but staff and guests without a pass required a coach-class ticket!

We were to assume that our telephones could be easily bugged: "If it can be listened to, it probably is," one briefing warned. Mulroney was particularly leery of car and cell phones. Whenever a cabinet minister phoned him, the Prime Minister invariably asked: "Where are you?" If the minister was phoning from her car, Mulroney would order her to hang up and call from a secure phone. A secure phone system travelled with the Cabinet for meetings out of Ottawa.

Many of these instructions were impossible or ineffective; the driver who read my mail passed a security clearance. A "48-hour rule" for placing items on the cabinet agenda quickly faded. The Prime Minister helped curb an irritating practice when he announced that we should ignore staffers who called with the message, "the Prime Minister asked me to call you . . ." If he wanted to speak to us he'd call himself, he said. And he did. My son JP became accustomed to saying: "The Prime Minister is on the line for you, Mom." In Vancouver, I usually took the calls at my kitchen table.

Once we had staffed our offices and met with our officials we faced our next challenge, the Opening of Parliament and Question Period. This was an ordeal for me because in Opposition I had a reputation for hard-hitting questions. I expected to receive a few hardballs in exchange.

As a woman, a westerner, and a Blue Star Tory, I was seated behind the Prime Minister in the House of Commons, so that I could gain television exposure when the cameras were focused on the PM. Each desk had a glass of water, filled by the House of Commons pages. Each minister was given a long black folder containing possible questions and answers relating to his or her department. I studied mine and placed it on my Commons desk, next to my glass of water.

Unfortunately, when the Prime Minister stood up to great applause to answer his historic first question, I inadvertently pushed my black folder forward, upsetting my glass of water. The water pitched right into his prime ministerial seat. The glass itself rolled down the aisle between the rows of Commons seats and came to a stop on the carpet in full view of the cameras.

What to do? The Prime Minister sat down. He visibly wiggled in front of me, as the water seeped through the seat of his pants. He rose for the next question, jabbing the air with his finger. I took the opportunity to bend down into the aisle, hair falling forward, to retrieve the glass, which lay just beyond reach. When the PM sat down, I sat up. I tried again on the next question, falling into the aisle like a domino when he stood up to answer. Bemused Canadians watched this performance on national television. I watched the replay that night, mortified.

I never did pick up the glass, kicking it viciously under the seat when Question Period was over. The Prime Minister never said a word to me about the matter, although he must have wondered why his pants were wet!

Question Period briefing was a crucial part of our schedule. Unlike our stint on the Opposition benches, when we fought to get on Question Period to help establish our public reputations, as cabinet ministers we were happy to stay demurely in our seats and out of trouble. An exception was John Crosbie, who gloried in insults, taunts, and jokes. He was at his best jousting with his fellow Newfoundlander George Baker. But his tongue got away from him when he called Ontario MP Sheila Copps "Baby."

Some ministers were QP hogs. The day after the Free Trade Agreement was signed in Washington, the PM stood at the door of his corner office and said to Finance Minister Mike Wilson and me: "Okay, Mike, you take investment questions, Pat will take trade, and I'll take dispute settlement." But once the cameras were on him, Mike wouldn't sit down, standing to answer all questions, to the media's amusement and comment.

Normally we answered questions relating only to our own ministerial mandates, but sometimes we acted for ministerial colleagues. Since I knew my files, I normally gave as good as I got in QP, but once as Trade Minister I managed a Gilbert & Sullivan–style performance as Acting Minister for External Affairs when Joe Clark was ill in hospital. The issue concerned some hostile shoving and pushing taking place between two Latin American countries. Now, no minister can know everything, and Joe and I agreed that in order to build ongoing relationships with our foreign counterparts, I would focus on Asia, my major interest and area of expertise, while he would deal with South and Central America, areas that interested him. To me, these Americas were simply somewhere south.

So when I was asked what action Canada was taking, I stated confidently, on the basis of my briefing, that Canada viewed the situation with grave concern and we had instructed our Ambassador to so inform the delinquent country's Foreign Affairs Minister. In the diplomatic dance, an ambassadorial visit is a major performance, and the Opposition External Affairs critics sat up in their green-backed chairs.

After I sat down, however, an envelope appeared on my desk, sent by the External Affairs grey eminence monitoring QP from the lobby, with a note stating that actually, Minister, we hadn't sent the Ambassador, but merely dispatched a Diplomatic Note, a much less ominous response.

I then scribbled a request to Speaker John Fraser that I be recognized because I had unfortunately misled the House, a serious parliamentary sin. When he recognized me, I announced my new information with suitable humility to a surprised House. The Opposition critics settled back in their chairs, relieved. Another international incident averted!

However, I had barely regained my seat when *another* apologetic note appeared from behind the lobby curtain saying, sorry, Minister, we haven't dispatched the Diplomatic Note at this point. Furious, I marched up the aisle of the Chamber to the telephones in the lobby and called Cy Taylor, the deputy minister, who admitted that despite the information given me by his own department, Canada was planning *no* diplomatic action at this time. Picturing an alarmed Joe Clark rising from his hospital bed to rescue Canada from armed conflict with a banana republic, I marched back down the aisle and, again, informed a bemused House of Commons of my inadvertent error. The next day Joe Clark resumed his place in Question Period.

When the Prime Minister was out of the country, senior ministers served as Acting Prime Minister for short periods. When it was my turn, I savoured my power. It took only three ministers to sign an order in council, authorizing a cabinet decision or creating a new law. What could I do? Send out the Army? Grant a National Holiday? Change my deputy minister?

It was the Prime Minister's prerogative to name our deputies, which made some cabinet ministers feel vulnerable. In the early days of Mulroney's administration, rightly or wrongly, we were deeply suspicious of some of our civil servants.

When I attended my first briefing as Energy Minister with my deputy Paul Tellier in the sparsely furnished ministerial offices at Booth Street, the first item on the agenda was to increase the Petroleum Compensation Charge that was paid by most users of petroleum products under the Liberals' NEP. It was running a deficit of nearly $1 billion.

As Tellier and his officials sat nervously in their seats, I gingerly scanned my first beige-coloured cabinet document and calculated that the proposed increase amounted to around 18 cents a gallon, or the same amount that John Crosbie intended to implement as Finance Minister in the Clark government, which was subsequently defeated on Crosbie's budget. Eeek. I dropped the offending document as if it were poison. Did these evil bureaucrats think Mulroney's ministers were that stupid? A startled Tellier told me that the similarity of the figures was a coincidence. But I knew the PM would never buy this spin, and the figures were altered.

Tellier and I developed a solid professional relationship as deputy minister and Minister of Energy, Mines and Resources, but later when he was at PCO, I asked him for advice and he turned me away, saying stiffly: "I serve the Prime Minister, as I once served you." His entourage of bureaucrats rose through the public service in his wake, proof of his "job jar," which he once explained gave key jobs to those men—rarely women—who performed well under his direction.

On Saturna in the summer of 1985, I received a call from Huguette Labelle, a PCO official, advising me that my new deputy minister of Energy was de Montigny Marchand.

"Who?" I asked. "De Montigny Marchand," Huguette repeated. "He's from External Affairs." Never heard of him. I was dismayed and apprehensive. We had a heavy Energy agenda and I counted on having a DM experienced in a highly technical industry. My dismay increased when I first met him a few weeks later on the frozen sands of my High Arctic stomping ground, Melville Island. I noted bleakly that he was wearing an ascot, not exactly the Arctic dress code. "Isn't it exciting?" I enthused, waving my arms at the sun-bleached sky, the khaki-coloured desert, ice piled on the shoreline like the arrested threat of winter.

De Montigny looked around at the orange ATCO units with their bunk beds and grey blankets and shared showers. "It seems very comfortable," he said glumly. My heart sank to the bottom of my seal-skin mukluks.

But Marchand became one of my favourite deputies, since he knew little about Energy and made it clear he didn't intend to become a techie. Instead, he reached down into the department and brought everyone to the ministerial conference table, where the Minister, in her hands-on way, could chat away happily about citygate prices and pipeline throughput with her best and brightest bureaucrats.

Marchand and I became good friends, and he was visibly shocked when Marcel Masse replaced me at Energy. Masse was equally taken aback, since the two had worked together in Communications and found the experience mutually miserable. After spending time in the PCO, Marchand was sensibly reassigned to External where he rose to the top job as Undersecretary.

My best working relationship was with Gerard Veilleux, Secretary of the powerful Treasury Board, one of the so-called central agencies of government. When I was named President of Treasury Board, Gerard came over to my office, kissed me on both cheeks, and said: "This is how we do things at Treasury Board."

It was true. Treasury Board was responsible for all government spending and ensured that the government's policies were followed, from the design on Canadian National's wheat cars to the plans for the CBC's new headquarters in Toronto. But Gerard and I perfectly understood when the rules could be bent to accommodate political needs, and when they could not be.

In contrast to Marchand's open-access policy, Gerry Shannon at International Trade had a chokehold on communications between the Minister and the department. Few were allowed through the door. My first ministerial briefing dealt with a pending Canada-Russia wheat deal. Two briefing officials showed up, sat down at the table, and peeled off a one-page briefing note. I scanned it as the officials waited expectantly. "Insufficient," I snapped. The officials parted with another page. I scanned that, too. "Not good enough," I said. Sighing, they begrudgingly provided the entire paper. Nor was the department open to new ministerial ideas that would rock the comfortable Euro-centred, Ontario- and Quebec-biased boat.

When BC pilot and businessman Ron Price came forward with the idea for an aerospace trade show to be held in British Columbia in conjunction with the famous Abbotsford Air Show, which outdrew the Pope, it took the department five months to answer my ministerial memo and even longer to find seed funding similar to that allocated to British and French aerospace exhibitions. By 2000, the BC version was North America's biggest and best aerospace show.

Shannon and I found each other abrasive, and our relationship was rocky at times. Mike Wilson, his sponsor, was angry at Shannon for giving me advice that trod on the Finance Minister's toes. Shannon informed me that tariffs were within my mandate as Trade Minister. Wilson claimed that Trade might set policy but Finance sets the tariffs. Mike won.

In one of his sulphurous eruptions, Wilson ordered me to keep my deputy in line. Shannon did not accompany me, his Minister, to Washington for the FTA negotiations but was assigned instead to supervise the documentation in Ottawa, a subordinate role, leaving me with only my assistant, the unflappable Janice Whitters, and trade policy advisor Chris Thomas, for ministerial support.

Luckily, Chris and External Affairs career bureaucrat Don Campbell and his colleagues, who had fought the softwood lumber wars with me, were up for it. Like many superb bureaucrats in International Trade, our trade officials often left my office at 9:00 p.m. at night for their own in order to have new proposals or briefing information on my desk at 8:00 a.m. the next day.

An Albertan, Don Campbell became Ambassador to Japan in 1993 and told me: "I didn't realize you were such a frequent visitor to Japan until I found your breakfast menu posted on the inside door of the kitchen cupboard." When I visited Japan as Chair of the Standing Senate Committee on Energy, the Environment and Natural Resources, Don ensured I received ministerial treatment: a car and driver, Scotch in the hotel room, lunch at the Residence. Solid and competent, Campbell was appointed deputy minister of Foreign Affairs in 1997, but later he left the department for the private sector.

Ministers depended heavily on their bureaucrats for information. At EMR, I learned about a new Canadian nuclear technology called SLOWPOKE during a departmental briefing prior to my trip to China to market our energy products, such as the CANDU nuclear reactor, which had encountered market turbulence with few export sales in sight. SLOWPOKE was described to me as a small, unmanned nuclear power generator, being developed by Atomic Energy of Canada Limited, designed to supply smaller communities with electricity at low cost. I thought of our northern communities with their high-cost diesel power generators, twinned so that if one broke down, community residents wouldn't freeze. I thought of China, where 90 per cent of the population live in 10 river valleys and the rest have little access to energy.

I took the bait like a steelhead in a West Coast salmon stream.

Entranced with the future possibilities of SLOWPOKE for both Canada and our export markets, I hustled it to fascinated Chinese energy officials through the interior of China, places such as Fushun, with its six-mile-wide open-pit coal mine, and Shangdong, in what was once Manchuria, as well as in Beijing, where energy bureaucrats worked in offices so cold that their long johns edged their trousers.

After our trip I asked a favourite EMR bureaucrat how many SLOWPOKE export sales our mission had produced. He looked uncomfortable. Actually, he admitted, none. Because, he added, there never was a SLOWPOKE to sell. The technology had not progressed beyond its development stage. In an attempt to justify Atomic Energy of Canada's huge government subsidies, the putative technology was hyped in the minister's briefing book and by a gullible minister!

A minister's political staff is there to protect him or her from such duplicity. A minister is only as effective as her staff, who serve as her interface with the public and the department. Our ministerial office was considered one of the best on the Hill. Given the pace of activity, only the best aides survived and I was ranked among Canada's Top Ten Toughest Bosses by *Report on Business* magazine, along with Calgary entrepreneur Ron Southern, auto-parts magnet Frank Stronach, and impresario Garth Drabinsky. A former staffer was quoted in the article as saying: "Before you brief her, you've gone over all the possible questions she might ask you. She expects everything you can give. You can't be mediocre, you've got to be good."[4]

My Chief of Staff at Trade and Treasury Board was Toronto lawyer Effie Triantafilopoulos, whose main asset, apart from her political and analytical skills, was the impersonal way she could coolly critique her boss, with deadly accuracy, in order to focus my efforts. I listened to Effie, whose political judgments were shrewd and insightful. She had worked for Joe Clark and later Industry Minister Sinc Stephens, who left the cabinet under a conflict-of-interest cloud. When the engaging Perry Miele left politics to return to the lucrative private sector, I offered Effie the Chief of Staff position while we waited for our luggage at the Toronto airport carousel.

I told her when we left International Trade that she would have the best client list in Canada. In fact, our daily schedule showed we had met with 657 private-sector people, 113 foreign ministers or ambassadors, and 63 media representatives. My senior policy advisor, Chris Thomas, a trade lawyer, was typical of a top ministerial aide: bright, expert, and committed.

Executive assistant Martin Green had also worked for Sinc. I met him when I served as Acting Industry Minister while Sinc recovered from a serious operation. When Martin first briefed me for Question Period, I thought him a cheeky, flip young man, very protective of his sick minister. I quickly learned to appreciate his superb political skills and his marvellous sense of humour.

Martin and another aide Mark McQueen would meet for drinks after work and mimic their minister, whose standard rebuke was: "Clearly I have NOT been well served by my staff in this matter." All aides mimic their ministers; only Martin would wittily recount it. I trusted Martin; if, deep in conversation at a reception, I accepted a second drink from a passing waiter, Martin would quietly remove it from my grasp. Or he would say: "Turn to your right. The PM is approaching."

When I left the Cabinet, Martin moved on to work with Environment Minister Lucien Bouchard. His experience working with both BC and Quebec ministers served him well when he transferred to the public service, serving with Environment, the Privy Council Office, and Industry. He and his wife Sheila are dear friends, and I am godmother to Savannah, and The Chopstick Lady to Veronica, their beautiful daughters.

Pierre Alvarez was a BC francophone from Trail who was my executive assistant in Energy and served as "wagon master" on our trips to China and Japan. Once, as we arrived at the New Osaka Hotel in Japan, I hopped out of our limousine and noted flags flying, red carpets spread, a receiving line of men in black suits and white gloves. I skipped up the stairs and into the elevator. "I wonder who that was for," I commented to my dumbfounded EA. "*You*, Minister," he hissed, furious. He made me go back down and do it up right.

Mijanou Serre, a beautiful Ontario francophone, had the daunting task of arranging my schedule and logistics in Canada, Europe, and Asia. A major concern was arranging access to swimming pools so that

I could manage my back problems. Between each stroke in the top-floor pool of the Hotel Bristol, I could see the roofs and chimneys of Paris in the sunrise. I swam in the marbled Mandarin Hotel in Hong Kong, the art-deco YWCA pool in New York, and planned an article, which I never wrote, on the world's best swimming pools.

Mijanou says her worst ministerial moment was in the Intercontinental Hotel in Geneva when, phoning the desk to find out when the pool opened, she found herself staring down at an outside, snow-filled pool some 14 storeys below. She and Effie managed to lose their luggage twice on trips to Europe. Happily the Ambassador's wife in Brussels outfitted them from her own wardrobe, an unpaid diplomatic spousal chore.

My administrator Betty Hill saved us all from a political crisis when she uncovered an ongoing theft of ministerial expense-account funds by a staff member. Something must have aroused my suspicions. On February 5, 1987, I recorded in my black book: "*Who* is charging *what* to my expense account?" After Betty had sleuthed out the evidence, she called in the RCMP and charges were laid and a conviction obtained. A high-level bureaucrat suggested that I drop the charges to save political face. "It's *my* financial obligation and *my* responsibility and *my* reputation," I answered him bluntly.

In the end, only one question was asked and answered in Question Period and the issue faded. An RCMP review of office procedures suggested no changes, since there is no real protection against office thieves. Betty also alerted me to the fact that my ministerial papers had been illegally destroyed after Crosbie took over the Trade portfolio, effectively obliterating my ministerial history, causing me a great deal of anguish.

Ministerial drivers know all the Hill secrets. Good drivers see and hear everything and reveal nothing. My trusted driver André Deschamps was my comfort zone, meeting me with my briefing books early in the morning and driving me home late at night. If my hours were long, his were longer.

When I left the Cabinet in 1988, he wrote in the blank books my staff gave me: "Many times, taking you from one place to the other or waiting for you to come out of meetings, I have had lots of time to ponder and think about what I saw around me . . . in my book, it takes people of immense courage to withstand the incredible pressures that come with a job like yours."

Some staff didn't measure up, and some couldn't work the hours. I sent sunny Cindy Boucher, daughter of the late columnist Charles Lynch, home to her husband, two young daughters, and a less demanding job with the National Capital Commission when we found her working 16-hour days during the softwood lumber wars.

As political minister, I had assistants like Ray McAllister, Donna Mackey, and Vicki Huntington to resolve conflicts and keep me informed of emerging political problems in the province and the riding. Most good ministerial aides do as well or better than their ministers when they leave the Hill for the public or private sector. Effie eventually joined Liberal John Turner's law firm. Martin and Cindy became senior bureaucrats. Mark McQueen joined a chartered bank. After a senior position with the Government of the NWT, Pierre was appointed President of the Canadian Association of Petroleum Producers.

Mijanou joined a public relations firm. Janice went to Farm Credit Corporation as executive assistant to the vice-president until the Crown corporation was moved to Regina and she rejoined me in the Senate. Steven Probyn, from our Energy era, went on to start his own energy company.

Many of my staff, including André and my serene secretary Wendy Waite, were retained by Kim Campbell when she was elected MP of Vancouver Centre after I withdrew from the 1988 campaign, crippled by an arthritis flare. Some staff members were still with her during Kim's short but exciting months as Prime Minister.

Serving as Chief of Staff to the mercurial Mulroney could not have been easy, particularly for Derek Burney, who fussed about the tulip beds on the National Capital Commission lands that adjoined his Ottawa home and was not prone to subservience.

Brian Mulroney was normally a sunny-tempered man in public, who held his caucus colleagues in the palm of his hand, blowing birthday wishes into bashful ears, joshing sullen caucus members out of their sulks, smoothing over election worries or scandals or bad polls or all of the above. But he could also flash anger that could boil up, spill over, and then dissipate like a spring shower, leaving sunny skies. I often watched Brian create a whole drama in his own mind, turning a random thought into a suspicion and then into a conviction, precipitating plans for vengeful reaction before the unsuspecting innocent walked into the Cabinet Room, his briefing books under his arm, unaware of the fiery fate that awaited him.

Marcel Masse was one minister who aroused the enmity of Mulroney for his casual assertion of cultural superiority over the rest of us cultural illiterates in Cabinet. Once the Prime Minister waylaid me on my way into the Cabinet Room in Centre Block. "Did you read what Marcel Masse said in the paper today?" Mulroney asked me. "No," I replied. "He told the *Toronto Star* he was the only cabinet minister with any appreciation of culture! I'll culture him, with his airplanes," said the PM, storming back into the Cabinet Room.

Once, at Whistler with my children on our annual spring-break skiing trip, and joined by my good friend, broadcaster Jack Webster, the phone rang in our tiny condo kitchen. It was Burney. The PM knew that Webster and I were close friends and his office had tracked us down.

The Prime Minister was concerned because the *Toronto Star* had quoted an uncomplimentary remark attributed to Webster, Burney informed me. Could I verify whether Jack had actually made the remark? I turned to Webster who was sitting at the table, reading the *Globe and Mail,* and repeated the remark to him.

"Did you actually say that?" I asked, knowing that the PM and Webster were fond of each other. "No, no, of course not," said Webster. "Well, maybe I did. Probably I did. It sounds like the kind of thing I would say. Tell him I'm sorry."

I transmitted an edited confirmation and apology to Burney, wondering why a trivial remark in a Toronto newspaper merited a country-wide telephone search, hunting me down during my family vacation—what good would it do anyone?—and then impulsively said to Burney: "I'm sorry you had to spend your time doing this." Instantly, he assumed his formal, attendant to God role, silently rebuking me for questioning the PM's action.

As the political minister for BC, in charge of the regional ministers' office, it was my job to coordinate our federal initiatives with provincial priorities and wish lists where possible and to get along with provincial and regional politicians. The first time I met Premier Bill Vander Zalm we discussed our mothers, who were both in their mid-eighties. We agreed that for us, home care for seniors was a priority. His private manner was light years away from his public "Fan*taaa*stic" approach.

One day Jack Webster phoned me to state, with great importance, that he had been invited to have Sunday dinner with the Premier and his family at Fantasy Gardens, the Premier's business venture that was modelled, more or less, as a European village with windmills and archways and such. We discussed the honour of the invitation and what he should wear.

Jack later recounted the event to me, his avid listener. At the appointed hour, around 6:00 p.m., Webster showed up at the entrance to Fantasy Gardens. He was directed to a shop, where Lillian was selling headbands. She directed him to another section of the Gardens, where the Premier took Webster through an exhibit of all the Stations of the Cross. Finally, they settled at a table in a dining hall where, Webster reported, a bus tour was being served supper, which was shared with the Premier's family and his guest. I think it was fish and chips. Webster was impressed at the Premier's thriftiness in offering his guest the tour group's special!

I felt better about my habit of offering Webster one of his favourite meals, bacon and eggs, regardless of the time of day.

Given our hectic lifestyles, and the media's relentless scrutiny of people in public life, our friendships and our private life are particularly important. It is a truism of politics that the friends you have after politics are the friends you had before politics. Of course, there are exceptions and the friends I made in politics have enriched my life and are by far the greatest benefit I have gained in more than 20 years in the political arena.

Barbara McDougall and I have been friends for more than half our lives, pre- and post-political. She and her husband, architect Peter, partied at our Lions Bay home when I was married to my first husband, newsman and lawyer Gordon Dickson.

Barbara and I had the rare luck to be mutually ambitious but on parallel paths. When we first met in the 1960s at the *Vancouver Sun*, where we were business writers, she wrote about investments and I wrote about economics and natural resources.

As senior ministers and members of the inner Cabinet, the Priorities and Planning Committee chaired by the Prime Minister, I was Minister of International Trade and in the next cabinet she was Secretary of State for External Affairs. Same department, but different interests. Her home hearth was a Nova Scotia farmhouse filled with African art over-looking the Atlantic Ocean, while my Chinese-decorated home was on the Pacific. Even our devoted pets died in our first terms as MPs.

When Barbara was first elected she came to visit me for a weekend in my Ottawa condo and stayed for a year. We were both in Mulroney's Cabinet and at the end of the day we would lounge, exhausted, on my twin Chinese red sofas in front of the fireplace and review cabinet discussions. This was great fun since we were banned from discussing cabinet matters with anyone not at the cabinet table.

In a world with few women mentors, we were each other's fans. I thought she showed guts when as Minister of State for Finance she coolly recommended to the Prime Minister over our kitchen phone that the plug should be pulled on a financial institution playing out of bounds. Some of her male colleagues lacked her backbone. When I negotiated the Atlantic Accord with Newfoundland, which resolved an acrimonious dispute over management of the offshore oil and gas resources, I returned home to a living room filled with colourful bal-loons. We agreed that except for our husbands and possibly a sibling, we couldn't share space as agreeably with anyone else. We shared an apartment for another two years when I returned to Ottawa as Senator for British Columbia in 1990 and she was Minister of Foreign Affairs.

One reason for our compatibility was that once again we enjoyed non-conflicting interests. One drank coffee and the other tea. Bathroom assignments were easy; one liked baths and the other liked showers. No conflicts in the kitchen; one liked early breakfasts and the other late din-ners. One preferred gin and red wine and the other Scotch and white wine. There were no outraged accusations of "who drank the last drink?"

And I understood her notes left on the kitchen counter: "Gone to Bosnia for lunch. Back by suppertime tomorrow."

We are very comfortable in each other's homes, although our styles are quite different. Once visiting her Nova Scotia farmhouse, I asked what I should wear to go antiquing with her in the countryside. "Just wear casual clothes," she said. When we met at the head of the stairs, we looked each other over, as women do. I was wearing West Coast casual—forest-green denim pants, aboriginal T-shirt, and sneakers.

She was wearing finely tailored woollen slacks, a long-sleeved silk blouse, and gold jewellery. Saturna Island meets Chester Basin.

When, at a Press Gallery dinner, my chauffeur appeared to tell me of a death in my family, it was Barbara, sitting at another table, who followed me out of the Parliamentary dining room to see what was wrong and made the arrangements to fly me to Vancouver.

Barbara was one of the few people who was a successful constituency MP, despite the fact she never had a chance to serve an apprenticeship as an MP before being elevated to the Cabinet. She served both her terms as a cabinet minister. But she has always had a knack for the personal touch, both in and out of politics.

A classic example occurred in June 1999, when Barbara accompanied me and my husband Paul White to hear his great friend, jazz pianist Marian McPartland, open the Toronto Downtown Jazz Festival. Marian, then in her eighties, finished her first set at the Montreal Bistro at about 9:00 p.m. and needed something to nibble on between sets. Unhappy with the host's offer of water and crackers, she said she would like a banana. Barbara disappeared into the street, appearing a few minutes later with three bananas that she had purchased at a corner grocer she remembered from her political campaign days. A grateful Marian ate one banana, between sets, for each night of her three-day gig.

One of my most gracious colleagues was Manitoba's Jake Epp. When we were MPs, Epp, mindful of his Mennonite background, "talked out" my private member's bill in the House of Commons, which would add sexual orientation as prohibited grounds for discrimination in Human Rights legislation. At the time, I despaired at his obstinate convictions. Yet in the early 1990s when he was Energy Minister and I was in the Senate, he invited me to a dinner celebrating the successful launch of the Hibernia offshore energy project, which was made possible by my earlier negotiations of the Atlantic Accord.

In politics, ministers—or even governments—rarely receive recognition for their efforts that pay off years later. Certainly his graceful gesture was not repeated by the Liberal government that cut the ribbon when the historic Hibernia project came on stream in 1997. The dinner was held the same evening that Justice Minister Kim Campbell briefed the Senate caucus on her abortion bill, and my absence earned me her hostility when I subsequently voted against it.

Kim Campbell's downfall was that she was unforgiving. In the end, neither the media or the voters forgave her for her own weaknesses. One of my longtime media friends, along with Fotheringham, is Joe Schlesinger. Viewers trust Joe, partly because of his engaging television personality but also for his diligent research.

During Kim Campbell's bid to succeed Brian Mulroney as leader of the Progressive Conservative Party in 1993, Joe came to Vancouver to check out her family background and much-vaunted credentials, including her claim to speak Russian fluently. I had arranged to meet him for a drink, although not to talk about Kim, who was my cousin Marg Campbell's stepdaughter and therefore off-limits. But when Joe came into the bar he said with amazement: "Kim doesn't speak fluent Russian at all!"

"How do you know?" I asked. I was aware that Joe did speak Russian, among his many languages.

"Because I asked her what she would say to [then Russian President] Boris Yeltsin if she was attending the next Summit meeting as Canada's Prime Minister, and she couldn't give the normal greetings correctly," said Joe delightedly. He reported the incident, launching the first media shot that deflated Kim's claims to graduate degrees and foreign-language expertise.

I had sympathy for Kim because the hectic schedule of a senior cabinet minister leaves little time for much-needed reflection. A glance at a random schedule from my days at International Trade shows that after an early morning swim, I had meetings from 8:30 a.m. until my plane departed for Washington at 9:00 p.m., arriving at my hotel around midnight. The day's events included meetings on a ports labour dispute, my Crown company Export Development Corporation, a review of my National Caucus presentation on trade issues, caucus itself, lunch with a ministerial colleague on disputed items, Question Period strategy meetings, QP itself, briefings with my deputy minister on the Washington trip, calls to provincial premiers on our negotiating position, a newspaper photo session, a party fundraiser in Rockcliffe, and shopping for new boots, sent over by a shoe store, in the airport lounge.

Arriving in Vancouver late at night, I would find the schedule called for a breakfast meeting at 7:45 a.m., followed by events all day and into the night. Whatever I did was never enough. Leaving one speech at 10:00 p.m., I would meet someone in the hotel lobby complaining:

"Why do you have time to address that group when your office says you don't have time for mine?"

By the summer of 1989, my body began acting strangely. My limbs flapped as if they belonged to a puppet and were pulled by unseen strings. If I took painkillers and anti-inflammatory medication, my mind was too drugged to take in important briefing details. If I didn't take them, I was dazed with pain.

Yet I could not foresee that when my staffers Martin Green and Mark McQueen took me to the airport one evening in August to fly to the West Coast on a government Challenger ordered by my ministerial colleague Bill McKnight, I would never return to Ottawa as minister. The milk-run flight through the prairies seemed endless. At least McKnight had Scotch on board, unlike the Prime Minister, a non-drinker who didn't care what his passengers drank in-flight as long as he had coffee.

In Vancouver, I attended the Abbotsford International Airshow with one of my favourite former Trade officials, Patrick Reid, who served as the popular Commissioner General of Expo 86. Exhausted, I could not focus on what the Mayor of Abbotsford was lobbying me about.

With an election expected in the fall, I listened as veteran Vancouver Centre campaign workers Lyall Knott and Don Hamilton, recognizing that I could not climb up and down porch stairs to knock on doors, discussed the possibility of driving an empty bus, plastered with my picture around the riding during the campaign. High risk, they concluded. To them, not to me!

Picking blackberries together on Saturna, my brother Jim cautioned me to listen to my deteriorating body. I went up to Pender Harbour where my daughter Jane marched me for miles around the village to build up my strength. My son John was flying the sked runs in the Arctic out of Resolute.

From the Harbour I called the Prime Minister to tell him that I could not campaign in my present condition. Mulroney was soothing and supportive. He could postpone the election call, he told me. Each Sunday evening I called him with the same message: "I'm better, but not better enough." September was slipping by.

Finally I realized I could no longer postpone my decision to withdraw. On Saturna Island in 1988 there was only one private telephone line and that was in the Department of Highways maintenance building.

I arranged with the highwayman to leave the door open one morning so I could use the phone to call Ottawa.

With my friend Jeannie McLean sitting on the doorstep to wave away strangers, I picked up the phone from the workbench and dialled the PMO. When the Prime Minister came on the line I told him I thought I should resign my cabinet post. "It is a great loss to the government and to me personally," the PM said. He acknowledged that my resignation was "the proper thing to do," adding that it would enable him to do what was required as he moved into an election. "You'll still be there to speak out on the issues."[5]

He ended: "I appreciate all your hard work and devotion. Mila passes on her love and best wishes. I'll never forget your historic role. God bless."

Well, he did, didn't he? Mulroney, not God. But as I hung up the phone and picked up my blackberry pail and joined Jeannie on the doorstep I thought how lucky I was in my friends and my real life of jam-making and family dinners.

I faxed Martin my letter of resignation to the PM. My black book records: "They smuggled my letter to the PM during Planning and Priorities. Paul Tellier (Clerk of the Privy Council) picked it up from Martin with a wink outside the cabinet door. I told Martin that the next time I called him I would be his ex-minister. 'You'll always be Minister,' he said. Nice."

The media was sympathetic at my somewhat weepy press conference. After outlining my cabinet achievements, I thanked the people of Vancouver Centre for the opportunity to be their MP, my volunteers, and my family, who had paid the highest price. My resignation from Cabinet was overtaken by the story that Canada's Olympic medallist Ben Johnson was facing disqualification for taking drugs.

It was hard to face my sombre campaign workers in our campaign office, with the posters of my smiling face, to tell them that I could not go the distance. But it was not so hard when my wonderful aide Suzanne Fournier pleaded: "But first, Minister, can you please shake the hands of our 400 volunteers?" I couldn't hold a pencil, much less shake hands! Muscular skeletal breakdown, the doctor said.

The fall was a blur of exhaustion. I was bedridden much of the time. My income was cut by three-quarters to my MP's pension. Thank

God for the much-maligned pension! Only two people—outside my family—called to ask how I was managing financially—Barbara McDougall and Jean Pigott's sister Grete Hale. After five months of hassling with the insurance company about whether my diagnosis of arthritis was covered, I started receiving small disability cheques.

In January 1989 UBC Commerce Dean Peter Lusztig, another Shanghainese, offered me the post of Executive in Residence. No pay, but the use of an office and a computer. I transcribed some of my black-book notes. Former Alberta Premier Peter Lougheed invited me to participate in a business seminar at Banff and split his own fee with me.

It took me a year to recover. When I first became ill, my northern buddies at Canadian Airlines International, chair Rhys Eyton, and executive Murray Sigler, who knew me in my Gemini North economic consulting days, asked me to undertake an Asia Pacific trade and investment study for the airlines. They waited 15 months until I was well enough to begin the 10-month contract. Speech requests continued to flow in, but this time they offered a fee.

Life moved on. After a time, I realized that I never, ever missed the political life. Not even a teensy, weensy bit. That phase of my life was behind me, I thought, and good riddance to it.

CHAPTER 17

Senator Pat

TRADE SECRET:
*When the tide and the wind are against you,
tie up to the side of the inlet and wait for slack
water and the turn of the tide.*
—Gordon Gibson Sr., former BC logger and politician

The ferry that runs from Port McNeill on Vancouver Island across Broughton Strait to the village of Alert Bay on Cormorant Island looks like a Walt Disney cartoon tugboat, with its large blue funnel, squat shape, and white-and-red markings. Five senators are crushed around the vinyl table in the upstairs lounge, listening to whale scientist Dr. Paul Spong plead for the continued preservation of the grey whale. Spong runs an orca research lab on Hanson Island near the northern entrance to Johnstone Strait, which protects Vancouver Island from the jumble of islands known collectively as the Broughton Archipelago on the map and the Mainland to the people who live in these bays and coves, shadowed by the snow-peaked coastal mountains.

Orca, the famous killer whales with their distinctive black-and-white markings, live in these inside channels. Aboriginals and early settlers called them blackfish. The grey whales are found in the inlets and ocean on the other side of Vancouver Island near Ucluelet and Tofino, on Canada's *west* West Coast.

Paul has travelled by boat to Alert Bay to tell the five senators that at an international conference in Nairobi the following week Canada should maintain its position to continue the moratorium on trade in grey-whale and minke-whale products. He believes that Canada's commitment to its position is weak and might be traded away under pressure from Norway and Japan, which want to allow people to kill whales in local waters as a first move towards the resumption of commercial whaling.

Pounding the table in his passion, Paul tells the senators that the recovery of the grey whale in the western Pacific from near extinction at the turn of the century to around 25 000 today is a "miracle of conservation" and should be continued despite pressures from aboriginal groups and commercial whaling interests. The senators, wearing windbreakers or fleece jackets and jeans, listen intently. Members of the Standing Senate Committee on Fisheries, they are on a fact-finding tour to learn the prevalent issues in fishing communities devastated by disasters, both natural and political. The senators include the chair, Gerry Comeau from Nova Scotia, Melvin Perry from Prince Edward Island, Ray Perrault and I from British Columbia, and former hockey star Frank Mahovlich, the Big M, from Ontario. In Ottawa, when committee members are bickering over West Coast and East Coast fishing problems, Frank skates clear of conflicts, saying: "I'm from Ontario; I play centre ice."

Our field trip started in Prince Rupert, the southern terminus of the Alaska ferry system. When BC commercial fishermen, upset at Alaskan over-fishing of Canadian salmon stocks, took an Alaskan ferry hostage in July 1997, circling it with their boats, Prince Rupert paid the price in tourism losses.

The 28 native and non-native communities located on tidewater from Prince Rupert 300 miles down the coast to Steveston, south of Vancouver, comprise the Coastal Communities Network and are as close to a constituency as I have as an unelected Member of Parliament in the Senate of Canada. For many people, our office in Ottawa is their communications link.

And they appreciate it. When the village of Zeballos on northern Vancouver Island forwarded documentation that the government had cancelled firm commitments to rebuild their fire-damaged wharf three times in 10 years, I found the senior bureaucrat who could authorize the funds again. "You don't have to fly home, Pat," purred a village councillor. "You have the wings of an angel."

The coastal communities have been hard-hit in the late 1990s by both natural and political disasters, a combination of low salmon runs and worse fishing policies that have decimated the community-based fishing fleets, replacing them with larger boats home-ported in the urbanized Vancouver area.

Andy Erasmus of Masset on the Queen Charlotte Islands wrote me the result. When the community fleet is tied up at the dock or sold, the fuel dock closes. Without fuel and ice, the crab boats leave, the recreational boaters whiz by, the store closes, and the community dies. "Is our society to be based on nothing more than the bottom line or business decisions?" he asked. "Being Canadian must mean more than that, and small communities like Masset contribute in a very real way to the fabric of our nation."[1]

It has taken two years for the Fisheries Committee to win approval for the field trip from the Senate's Standing Committee on Internal Economy, Budgets, and Administration, since transport costs on the Coast are high in the eyes of Ottawa pencil-pushers.

Chair Gerry Comeau accompanied me once to visit Kyuquot, a West Coast community of about 300 people that is accessible only by sea or by air, when the fog lifts. We drove over logging roads and rode the crew boat to the community, curled inside the northern lip of Kyuquot Sound where it enters the Pacific Ocean. Our boat skirted the sea otters, which raft up together on their backs in the mist, holding their babies on their chests.

Under government policies, many natives and non-natives in Kyuquot lost the rights to fish the salmon that swim past their shore, while American tourists zooming around in their powerboats can catch their limit. A grade six student in the schoolhouse built in the spruce forest tells us: "My grandmother has hardly any fish in her smokehouse because there is hardly any fish."

This is the part of my job as senator I like best—bringing forward the concerns of British Columbians who are too far out of the loop geographically to access Ottawa power brokers easily. I chose the designation "Senator for British Columbia" rather than for my former constituency, as some senators do, because it covers the whole province.

The first time I was asked to accept an appointment to the Senate of Canada, I was 35 years old and working as a journalist in the eastern Arctic. The messenger was a staffer from the Prime Minister's Office during Pierre Trudeau's first mandate. I called my brother Jim in Montreal and we discussed the ifs and buts and maybes. While we were doing that, the Prime Minister appointed Ann "Nancy" Bell of Nanaimo-Malaspina, who proudly told the media that she had been a Liberal since she was age two. We became good friends. She shared her birthday, May 26, with my twin brother Jim and me, and signed her notes as "the triplet," writing her congratulations for the "Home Team" when I was appointed to Mulroney's Cabinet.

Ann Bell stoutly defended BC's interests and split from her party during the Free Trade debate, which took courage, since defiance brings retaliation in party politics. British Columbia lost a valued crusader when she died in November 1989.

The second time the PMO phoned, in August 1990 during Brian Mulroney's second mandate, to suggest the Senate, I was deep in the Fraser Valley, negotiating for "Miss Emily," a brand-new, traditional-style wood stove for my Saturna home, where winter power outages are the norm. A few weeks earlier, sailing with Jim, we were tied up at the marina on Newcastle Island enjoying gin and tonics when we heard a radio report that my name was being bandied about. But there was no official word.

The PMO's call, left on my answering machine, presented me with a dilemma. The three-hour time difference between British Columbia and Ottawa meant the PMO offices would soon close. Should I continue to negotiate for Miss Emily, the only Canadian-made wood stove I could find, and risk the possible senate appointment, or leave the store to find a private phone and risk losing the stove? Miss Emily won.

When I finally found a private phone, the PMO switchboard put me through to Prime Minister Mulroney at Harrington Lake, his family's summer residence. "I want you to return to Ottawa to fill Ann Bell's seat in the Senate," he said, adding, "I know that it may seem a comedown after serving as an MP and a cabinet minister, but I need your help with British Columbia." Brian knew that British Columbia was the key to my heart. We both knew that the Senate would not be as hard on my health as the rowdy pressure pit of the Commons.

The clerk swore me in on August 30, 1990. That was a mistake, since the rules said I must pay back 30 days of my MP's pension in order to collect one day's pay as a senator; double dipping is not allowed. The whole Senate scene was a mistake, I soon realized, since one of the first issues on the parliamentary agenda was the Goods and

Services Tax debate, one of the most repellent episodes in Canadian parliamentary history.

Mulroney set the mood by appointing eight additional Conservative senators, as was his constitutional right, to force the tax through the Liberal-dominated Senate, which had already scuppered the Mulroney government's day-care legislation and whose threatened opposition to Free Trade had triggered the 1988 election.

But Mulroney's unorthodox tactics inspired retaliatory actions by the Liberal opposition under Liberal Senate Leader Allan MacEachen, a master of parliamentary obstruction. Such antics included the reading of the Bible, endless petitions, kazoo-playing, assaults on the Speaker's chair by Liberal Senators infuriated by the Conservative Speaker's ruling, and some debates notable mainly for their bathroom humour.

Canadians reacted with disgust and dismay to the Senate, an institution they like to revile but embrace with a passion when their personal interests are at stake. The mail was abusive, the atmosphere repulsive. Even our own Conservative caucus was derogatory, although at one meeting I reminded the jeering MPs (who don't like unelected senators sharing their elected perks) that it was *their* legislation on the GST we were reluctantly defending.

Sitting for endless hours in my orthopedic seat in the Red Chamber, underneath war artists' scenes from the 1914–18 battlefront, caused my arthritis to flare. I felt, as I told Ottawa author Charlotte Grey, that I was a candidate for a World War I nursing station, minus the blood and bravery. I was lucky to be living with friends from Saturna who were both doctors—Jim Farrow and his wife Sally Stansfield, in their Rockcliffe home. Travel home was difficult.

After almost three months, the GST legislation received Royal Assent. But by then I had discovered other unpleasant aspects of the Senate, including a male-chauvinist attitude left over from the 1950s and a general atmosphere of fading testosterone in the Red Chamber. An example was the Orville Phillips Whipping Society dinner, held in honour of our former Whip, where the trophy was a plastic horse turd and silly gifts were exchanged. When I found myself buying coloured condoms to gift the inoffensive Senator Jim Kelleher, I came to my senses and refused to go.

A story by Nova Scotia Senator Finlay MacDonald set the tone. A student wrote the Senate seeking information on senators by age and sex, recounted Finlay, who was much admired for his wit and amiable manner. He wrote back: "Sex isn't the issue. *Booze* is the problem in the Senate." It was enough to make anyone squirm.

There were a minority of women senators, 60 years after Ottawa housewife and welfare worker Cairine Reay Wilson became the first woman to be called to the Senate of Canada, in 1930. Except for Kim Campbell's 1991 abortion bill, which the Senate defeated, we rarely worked together. One female senator, the revered French-Canadian author Solange Chaput-Rolland, did teach me something I had not learned in my previous tenure in Parliament as an MP and cabinet minister: the Parliamentary restaurant serves martinis. We drank doubles during the GST debate.

Bored and angry, I called Prime Minister Brian Mulroney and told him I wanted to give up my Senate seat. He was sympathetic but soothing. He acknowledged that I could leave if I wished, but he would prefer if I waited until after the BC election in October 1991 so that the appointment of a new BC Senator did not become an election issue.

He had cause for his concern about senators selected by a province. In the spirit of the failed Meech Lake Accord, Mulroney named Quebec senators selected by then Liberal Premier Robert Bourassa, but he found that when the chips were down, their loyalties lay with the province, not with the national interest, when the two appeared to conflict.[2]

But the timing for my resignation was never right. An NDP government was elected in BC in 1991. By then, it had dawned on me that I had a government phone, fax, and office, and two able assistants to dedicate to British Columbians and their problems. As a Member of Parliament, I gave priority to my constituents. As a cabinet minister, my mandate was Canada-wide. But as a senator, my loyalties were to Canada's Constitution, minority interests, and my region, British Columbia.

Some British Columbians had already figured this out. Our mail bag was always full, partly because there were no elected Conservative MPs for Conservatives to turn to if they were wary of the other parties. Since I knew the province and had a high profile, British Columbians inevitably turned to my office. In response, we have always made our

Ottawa offices fully available to any BC group that needed a place to work or rest before the evening plane home to British Columbia.

I often read excerpts from the BC letters in our mailbag during my Senate speeches so that they become part of the parliamentary record. Now that the Senate debates are published on the Internet, feedback is fast. During third-reading debate on Bill C-9, the Nisga'a Final Agreement Bill in April 2000, I related the concerns of a voter who supported the widespread view that the treaty should be referred to the Supreme Court before it was implemented. Within 24 hours I received an e-mail saying simply: "Thank you."

Early in my Senate career, my assistant Fiona MacLeod took a phone call from a family in Fort St. John, who wanted to know whether their son was in jail in Dawson Creek in northeast British Columbia. The RCMP, citing confidentiality, wouldn't tell the parents. Fiona phoned the RCMP and confirmed that the son was indeed in jail. After reporting this to the parents, Fiona asked if there was anything else we could do. No, said the relieved parents. They simply wanted to know where their son was, so they telephoned "Senator Pat"!

I appreciated the fact that I was free to vote on bills without partisan or political pressures, although I believe that an appointed Senate should not overrule the elected House of Commons unless Constitutional, regional, or minority rights are involved, according to parliamentary precedent. Senators rarely overturn a bill. Our job is to correct, suggest, and amend after sober second thought. But sometimes we do vote against bills.

One example was the Liberal government's Bill C-68 (Firearms Act), complex, emotion-driven legislation, covering 193 convoluted clauses that proposed expanding Kim Campbell's gun-control laws in the aftermath of the December 1989 shooting of 14 female students at Montreal's l'École Polytechnique. Some 2873 people, mainly opposed and mostly British Columbians, wrote me their concerns about Bill C-68's cost, complexity, confiscation measures, and failure to address criminal violence—all elements of bad law.

When I was growing up in the Kootenays, I used firearms. My son-in-law carried a gun in his fishboat. Other family members, including my young granddaughter, who shot a moose on her first hunting trip, hunt for food. But as a woman concerned with violence against women I fully expected to vote for Bill C-68, until I walked into a Senate committee hearing on the bill in the Hotel Vancouver and heard four women voice their concerns.

One mother of teenage girls said the bill as written would destroy shooting competition, an Olympic sport. An aboriginal woman, a respected advocate for women and children who hunts to feed her family, said the bill would contribute to the breakdown of aboriginal culture, causing increased family breakdown and violence.

The third woman, who also hunts for her family's dinner, drove 11 hours from her rural community to tell the committee that the last five murders in her town involved a baseball bat, a bathtub, barbecue skewers, rope, and matches—not firearms.

And the fourth woman, a three-gun championship shooter, told the committee: "This firearm legislation is tearing our country apart. Is Bill C-68 good for our country, as a whole? Is it necessary? Is it equal or fair for everyone? And if so, why are so many people opposed to it?"[3]

These were tough questions that I couldn't answer. When the vote came, and the Senate clerk called for the "nays," I was on my feet. The legislation has since proved to be unenforceable, and full implementation has been delayed to January 1, 2003. The cost, originally expected to be $85 million, had escalated to $350 million and counting, according to a Library of Parliament report in April 2000.[4] That amount could support more police officers on the crime prevention programs.

Regional issues are priorities for our office because British Columbia generally is under-represented in Parliament, with only 38 seats in the House of Commons. There are only six senators for British Columbia, compared with 10 for New Brunswick, and three for Prince Edward Island. And coastal issues are my focus, since my husband and I live on a Gulf Island, Saturna. "Senator Pat is a local girl," smiled an aboriginal woman in far-off Nootka Sound.

I first met Paul Spong at a whale seminar in Maui, our favourite family vacation home. The seminar featured a film of Paul drifting in his kayak on a fog-veiled ocean, playing his flute to the killer whales. He was concerned with the pending closure of Pulteney Point Lightstation, built in 1905 on nearby Malcolm Island, reserved by the Dominion of Canada for Finnish immigrants, whose blond descendants still live in the fishing village of Sointula.

One of my earliest battles in the Senate was the fight to keep lighthouse families on the lightstations that protect one of the world's wildest coasts. The lightkeepers are more than a beacon of hope on storm-tossed seas; they give vital weather and sea-state information, search and rescue people from the sea, take water temperatures that help determine the El Niño presence and where the salmon will migrate, report environmental spills, provide first aid to tourists, and offer a human presence on a coast where there are no roads for hundreds of miles.

In the 1990s, Conservative Transport Minister John Crosbie and later Liberal Transport Minister Doug Young announced that the Coast Guard's West Coast lightstations would be "destaffed" and their function assumed by automated equipment. The whole coast protested—coastal communities, fishermen, recreational boaters, marine pilots who guide big ships through the Inside Passage, and aviators who fly their floatplanes into the small camps and communities in constantly changing weather and sea conditions.

Led by Cape Mudge lightkeeper Jim Abram, the lightkeepers themselves reported that automated weather equipment, such as a wave buoy, has a high failure rate, particularly in winter when it's most needed. They also explained how the staffed lightstations situated along the isolated coasts provide a "profound sense of the safety net" for all those who live and work there.

Armed with petitions, faxes, letters, and logged telephone calls of dismay, I delivered an emotional speech in the Red Chamber and won a unanimous mandate from my senate colleagues to establish a Senate committee, under the mandate of the Standing Senate Committee on Transport and Communications, to hear the concerns of coastal people.

After the hearings were advertised and the witnesses already en route from their distant homes, Senator Mike Forrestall phoned a warning: my own Tory colleague, Nova Scotia Senator Don Oliver, Chair of Transport, planned to kill the committee hearings under pressure from Liberal Transport Minister Doug Young, a maritimer, who publicly declared staffed lighthouses, like railway cabooses, relics of the past.

Horrified, I ran to the committee room, and watched while the bemused Liberal Senators, led by Tory Senator Oliver, voted to kill our West Coast hearings. When I returned to my Centre Block office I phoned Reform MP John Duncan, whose North Island-Powell River contained many key lightstations.

"I'm quitting," I told Duncan flatly. "Those Eastern bastards just killed our committee." The Reform MP replied: "Don't quit yet. We'll form our own parliamentary committee and hold the hearings anyway."

And we did, sitting as the Ad Hoc Parliamentary Committee on Lightstations, co-chaired by John Duncan and me. It was exhausting, because we had no Senate budget, but Janice and I, drawing on our Gemini North experience, set up the hearings in a Richmond hotel, a Nanaimo Canadian Legion hall, a Sidney scientific station, and in Campbell River's beautiful museum. Reform MPs John Duncan, John Cummins, and Bob Ringma, all committee members, paid the rental and coffee costs.

Senator Mike Forrestall came from Nova Scotia to help us. Public Service Commission language-training manager Hélène Irving, who sails with her husband, voluntarily provided French translation services at every meeting. Other volunteers transcribed hours of taped evidence from witnesses. And supporters packed the halls. They told stories about lives saved, dramatic rescues, and mundane-but-vital weather reporting:

These lightkeepers are important. These lightkeepers save lives. These lightkeepers help all of us working on the water . . .

One only has to look at the track record of the local automatic weather stations in the area that I fish. They play like a broken record all year long: Sartine unavailable, Solander unavailable. We hear this complaint all too often from other fishermen coast wide. The track record is scary to say the least . . .

The only reliable thing about the automated stations is their unreliability. . . .

We probably are contending with the worst flying conditions for VFR pilots anywhere in the world, and the reason we do it successfully is because we have those lighthouses out there giving us information . . .

I work on a fish packer and we pack fish up and down the coast from Vancouver to wherever, and if it wasn't for the lighthouse keepers we wouldn't even know the Coast Guard exists . . . They are going to take the lighthouses away and then there is nothing . . .

They are our eyes and ears on the water, which no machine or computer can take the place of . . .

Our motor wasn't strong enough to get us out of the tide. We were being swept out to sea. The lightkeeper at Race Rocks saw us and rescued us. I don't know what would have happened otherwise . . .[5]

Musician Kent Fiddy brought a guitar and a song he had written to sing at the Campbell River hearings:

In the 1880s the islands were in darkness
Storm-tossed, desolate as any coast could be,
Wracked by Gales, shrouded in deathly fog,
There was no refuge for a sailor on the sea. . . .

One hundred years later, things are much the same
The little men in Ottawa are pinching pennies again.
They wants to take away the keepers. "They're needed there no more."
But tell that to the families of those lost along the shore.[6]

In the end, the coastal people won the battle. The Coast Guard was moved over to Fisheries and Oceans, and in 1997 Fisheries Minister David Anderson announced that only eight of the 35 stations would be destaffed. Among the first to go was the lightstation on my home island of Saturna.

Pulteney Point Lightstation is not far from Alert Bay. As the ferry eases into the ferry slip at Alert Bay, we decide to write letters supporting Paul Spong's position that grey and minke whales should be protected from international trade.

When our bus drives off the ferry Chief Bill Cranmer of the Namgis First Nation, wearing a striking black-and-red vest decorated with Kwakiutl symbols, waves the way to the U'Mista cultural centre and long house. After a tour of Kwakiutl potlatch masks and other ceremonial artifacts, we meet with Gilbert Popovich, the popular mayor of the Village of Alert Bay who runs the fuel dock, and other First Nations chiefs over a lunch of wild salmon, halibut, clam fritters, crab, dried kelp, oolichans, bannock, and other finger-licking delicacies. We pay for the food; we are not freeloaders.

We learn that the village has lost 80 per cent of its fishing jobs and 50 per cent of related boat repairs and commercial business since federal policies reduced fishing opportunities by limiting fishermen to one area and one type of fishing gear unless they paid huge fees. Since little other work is available, unemployment among the largely aboriginal workforce is 10 times the national average.

With rare unanimity, the Tribal Council and the Village have signed an accord to try to diversify the economy by promoting eco-tourism in the area, already a popular destination for sailors, recreational boaters, kayakers, and others intent on seeing the killer whales cruise the inlets and rub themselves on the pebble beaches of nearby Robson Bight.

One fear is that the fish farms established on the inlets along the migration routes of the wild salmon will deplete the wild fishery through pollution, disease, and interbreeding. Atlantic salmon have already escaped from the farms, contained only by nets, and are being found in the ocean and spawning streams of the wild salmon as far north as Alaska.

Pat Alfred, president of the Kwakiutl Territorial Fisheries Commission, reminds us that the whales depend on wild fish for food. "If you drag the fish farms out of these migration routes, the traditional fishery would rebuild," he explains as we nibble on our smoked wild salmon. He adds: "It's our way of life." And the salmon provide food for the whales, which draw the tourists, the area's new economy.

Earlier that morning we heard similar warnings from whale researcher Alexandra (Alex) Morton, who raises her children in a floathouse dragged ashore in Echo Bay on Gilford Island, where majestic Knight Inlet sweeps down from glacial heights in the interior. When I am flying the Coast, I can identify Knight Inlet by the jade-green colour of the water.

Aboriginal settlement at Echo Bay dates back about 8000 years, judging from the red pictographs on the pale cliffs lining the small bay. The homesteaders, fishermen, and hand-loggers arrived around 1880, clearing their small holdings in the forest or living in their floathouses, building their shake mills, canneries, and salteries on shore. They have long since vanished, but the post office and schoolhouse remain. So does Alex, whose husband, an underwater photographer, died in the deep water as Alex and their son played on the beach a few metres away. From her Echo Bay home she tracks the whales, recording how the noise devices used by the fish farms to scare away predator seals also chase away the whales.

At our hearings in the basement of the Haida Way Motor Inn Alex outlines her case against the 26 fish farms in the Broughton Archipelago, also home to all five species of Pacific wild salmon and particularly the threatened chinook. She suggests that the farm fish are a lethal threat to the wild fish, showing us photographs of diseased Atlantic salmon caught in the area, escapees from a net farm, and warns of toxic pesticides used by fish farmers that could threaten the health of seafood consumers.

"The salmon farms belong in tanks, isolated from resources used by the public in the same manner as other animal feedlots," she maintains.

I have visited Alex at Echo Bay and met her again the night before our field trip, at the home of Bill and Donna McKay, who run whale-watching tours out of Port McNeill. I also knew Port McNeill when it was a new town in the 1960s, basically a hotel, beer parlour, café, and grocery store emerging out of the fresh forest slash to replace logging camp life.

Since then it has grown to around 2000 people trying to maintain their homes in the face of forest "fall down," or diminishing annual cut, and reduced fishing. "The coast is crashing," said Donna McKay. "People here are living on the edge of fear." But it maintains its small-town spirit. "Port McNeill is a hockey town, and they know the Big M is here," said the hotel clerk at Haida Way Motor Inn.

Before taking the ferry to Alert Bay we stop at Englewood Packing Company, located at nearby Beaver Cove, on the site of a former log-sorting ground. Logging debris still surrounds the plant. We watch as the gleaming Atlantic salmon are unloaded from the barges, which transport them from the net farms, and move down the conveyer belt to the processing line, where they are cleaned, filleted, and chilled by men and women wearing hair nets, white coats, and boots.

"Why is the flesh of these fish so red?" I ask. Farm fish are usually a paler pink. Only the wild red spring salmon and wild sockeye salmon are deeply red-fleshed. "They add red pigment to the fishmeal pellets," the plant tour guide explains. "The fish meal comes mainly from Chile. It's made mainly from anchovies and mackerel."

Feeding fish to fish does not appeal to me, although of course some wild salmon species, like coho, eat herring. Sockeye salmon eat plankton. But then again, I am not a fan of farm salmon. My daughter Jane and her husband Malcolm were commercial fishermen for years until declining returns forced them to sell their licences and leave the wild fishery. We prefer bumper stickers that read "Real fish don't do drugs" or "Real fish don't eat pellets."

But aquaculture is now a big industry on the BC coast. Our committee learns that farm fish is BC's largest agricultural export, after marijuana. At least farm fish is legal but, like pot, its production is growing rapidly. This fish plant alone produces tonnes annually for sale, mainly in North America.

At Alert Bay, as we nibble on the last of our dried kelp and oolichan, Chief Bill Cranmer is trying to keep us on schedule after welcoming us in his Namgis language. Several other of the assembled chiefs want to speak. In the interest of time, however, he cuts off three chiefs. Angry, Chief Charlie Williams and Fred Speck of the Gwawaenuk First Nation walk out of the long-house dining room.

I slip out after them. They are from Hope Town on Turner Island. Once about 10 000 Kwakiutl people lived on this stretch of the north coast. Now only three villages are left—Gilford Village, Hope Town, and Kingcome Village at the head of Kingcome Inlet, which winds its way down through the coastal mountains to Queen Charlotte Strait.

I have travelled upriver to visit Kingcome and watched a traditional Hamat'sa dance at Hope Town. I have also pushed my way through the wild berry bushes of Mamalilaculla on Village Island, where abandoned houses stand watch over the inlet and a ruined totem pole lies strangled in the long grasses below the silver skeleton of an old long house.

On one trip with museum curator Jay Stewart, her husband, anthropologist Peter Macnair, read us old Kwakiutl legends on the white clamshell beach. On another visit, the only people my twin and I encountered in this mystical, myth-shrouded place was a pod of American kayakers paddling up from Seattle to camp overnight on the beach.

Outside the long house at Alert Bay, I tell Chief Charlie Williams that I knew his mother Elsie when she lived at Hope Town and record his concerns in my notebook.

On the return ferry trip I use the committee clerk's cellular phone to call Jim Borrowman, a former sawmiller who runs whale boat tours out of Telegraph Cove, a tiny bay shaped like a fist and the site of the last boardwalk village on the coast. For years Telegraph Cove was known mainly to kayakers and Americans who canned their chinook salmon in their recreational vehicles parked in the trailer camp above the cove.

Then, in the mid-1990s, out of the dust, I encountered a Thomas Cook tour bus lumbering along the former logging road down to the cove. It was packed with European tourists, including a family that had flown in from Amsterdam for the weekend and a group of Germans who wanted to know when the whales showed up. Telegraph Cove had been discovered.

Jim tells me he recently remarried. For his wedding present, his wife Mary gave him the carcass of a whale, which was killed when rammed by a cruise ship in Johnstone Strait. With the help of the Coast Guard, the whale was towed back north, and now was lying on the beach until its skeleton could be converted into a whale exhibit.

When I married Paul in 1998, Jim sent a fleece vest from Telegraph Cove. But how can I possibly top a whale for a present? Mary can. For their first anniversary, she plans to helicopter Jim over to Nootka Sound where a dead sperm whale is beached. She has arranged to harvest a tooth from the carcass.

From the ferry terminal we drive back to Port Hardy and fly over Vancouver Island to Tofino in our twin-engined charter aircraft. We circled over the white-maned surf, pounding the sand at Long Beach, and land before dark at the airstrip, which has few navigation aids.

"It's a rainbow kind of day," says our bus driver, Lisa Brisco, as we drive through the gale-twisted forests of Pacific Rim National Park to native-owned Best Western Tin Wis Lodge on MacKenzie Beach. And walking the surf-splashed beach, admiring the sunset over the Pacific Ocean, I see a rainbow through the evening mist.

It is another rainbow day when we cast off the dock at Tofino and cruise past densely timbered Meare's Island to visit Bill Vernon's fish farm on Tofino Inlet, close enough that the employees can live in town, not in isolated camps. Bill farms chinook salmon, raised from hatchery eggs, producing about one million pounds of fish in each 13- to 18-month cycle, mainly for the Japanese market.

On the site, we watch as automatic feeders shoot pellets into the ponds; we peer through telescopes to view the fish, milling densely below the surface of the water. There are about 20 fish farm sites in the Tofino area; Bill says it takes four or five farms to supply one fish plant, which offers local employment.

Bill is frank about the sewage and pollution problems at the farm sites and bullish about his industry's ability to solve them. "Sure, there is some impact," he concedes. "Our job is to minimize and manage it." He suggests that leaving some sites fallow would allow them to recover. Some net farm opponents suggest that fish farms should be moved ashore. In Bill's view onshore fish farms are uneconomic. A few weeks after our visit, 30 000 farm fish smolts escaped when a fish packer's propeller cut the fish farm's netted pens. At least they were chinook, not Atlantic salmon.

On the return trip down the inlet, a giant grey whale rolls over in the sun and flaps its fin on the surface of the sea as it feeds on shrimp and plankton. It looks like a barnacled reef rock, I marvel, as our group fumbles for our cameras.

Other coastal snapshots flash through my mind:

Sipping drinks on the flying bridge of Jane and Malcolm's trawler, Sea Rebel, anchored at the head of Jervis Inlet, mountains ink-black against the night sky, admiring the yellow disc of a full moon and listening on the marine radio to two sisters bemoan the fact that the sister living in Jervis Inlet can't visit her sister in Sechelt because the helicopter pilot logging nearby won't feed her chickens while she is away . . .

Stuffing ourselves with prawns, fresh from the sea, cooked in boiling water for a few minutes and served with garlic butter and white wine in the Sea Rebel's galley. Eating oysters, bought from the oyster farm on Nelson Island, wrapped in bacon and barbecued while a red snapper, also freshly caught, lies on ice in the galley refrigerator. My kind of perfect day; birthday, Mother's Day, run-away-from-work day . . .

Sleeping on the sailboat, watching the night stars rotate through the hatch as the boat, at anchor, swings with the current. Fishing with my son off Boiling Reef near Saturna as a killer whale leaps out of the water, pursuing a coho salmon as it is reeled in by a neighbour standing in his blue rowboat, dwarfed by the snow-white cone of Mount Baker across the strait . . .

Watching the black bears that chase us off the oyster beach on the shores of a coastal inlet. Gossiping with Pat Kidder, who with her husband Ed and sometimes with their son Dean, keeps watch at the lightstation at Friendly Cove on historic Nootka Sound, where British explorer James Cook met Spanish explorer Juan Francisco de la Bodega y Quadra, and broke the Spanish domination of the Pacific, then known as a Spanish lake; their host was legendary Chief Maquinna.

I love BC's West Coast. It hurts to see it hurting. Some of the pain is visible in Ucluelet, where Councillor Dan Edwards, members of the Nuu-chah-nulth Tribal Council, and young experts from the environmental community are awaiting us in the Municipal Hall. Offshore, trollers are fishing for winter chinook.

In 1999, Dan endured a 57-day hunger strike, against my worried advice, to draw attention to the plight of the West Coast fishermen financially devastated that year when the sockeye run returning from the Pacific Ocean to spawn failed to show up. No one knows why.

Ottawa provided natural-disaster funding when the 1998 ice storm damaged the maple sugar–producing forests in Ontario and Quebec, and when a virus struck the New Brunswick aquaculture industry. Dan won a hearing from Fisheries Minister Herb Dhaliwal but no relief funds for fishermen. No one really knows why, either.

Ucluelet is the largest fishing port left on the west coast of Vancouver Island. Anger at government policies, which have reduced community access to fish by 80 per cent in five years, has drawn the community together—both young and old, native and non-native. "We've gone beyond our differences, way beyond," explained snow-haired Simon Peter, who was born in Nootka, where his father fished and his mother worked in a cannery. "Why fight with the people we live with?"

Their dream is regional aquatic management, where local people would be stewards of the fishery, totally involved in its management. A community trust would allocate community fishing licences to local people. In Alaska, local communities run their own hatcheries and control fishing and licensing policies.

Community licensing would also encourage added-value processing in the community. Dan's sister Julie served us a lunch of Tanner, or red snow crab, a delicious seafood caught in deep water. So far the Department of Fisheries and Oceans is reluctant to consider community management. "Fish swim," state DFO officials. Detractors argue, however, that the DFO simply does not want to lose its power.

All coastal communities are developing a range of seafood products. Prince Rupert is looking at scallops, oysters, even octopus. Port Hardy is raising sturgeon in the former settling ponds of a reclaimed copper mine; squawfish eat the "morts" or dead farm fish.

Ucluelet also has a hake processing plant, which manager Mike Buston sold to foreign owners to raise the money for new processing equipment to produce surimi, or artificial crab. Eventually Mike hopes to buy the plant back, although it didn't help when DFO allocated hake to offshore Polish fishing vessels. Like others in the community, Mike is committed to the sea.

We drive over to the Ucluelet East Band Hall to meet with the Nuu-chah-nulth Tribal Council, including aboriginal leader Richard Watts. The walls of the hall are used for a native language lesson. Some words look almost Hawaiian: killer whale/*kakaw'in*; deer/*muwac*; bird/*maa-maati*; canoe/*c'apac*; cat/*huupukas*; star/*t'at'uus*; flounder/*puuhuu*; ling cod/*tuskuh*; steamer clams/*hiicin*.

Treaty negotiations will likely allocate fish to natives, but treaties can't entrench rights for non-aboriginals, we're told as Richard listens intently; his views are key. So far the First Nations here are willing to share with the community. But I wonder how long such cooperation will last if the DFO keeps dragging its collective feet.

"We are all going to live together," says native fisherman Archie Little. "If we don't, we are all going to die. The non-aboriginals are not going to go away. We all have that tie to the ocean."

But that bond is weakening among young people who can't afford to buy the boats and pay the increased licence fees. Archie's 18-year-old son has never fished. "I'm probably the last person in my family to fish," notes Archie.

Aboriginals lost 400 licences by selling their boats in various government buy-back schemes, paying capital gains tax on the sales price. The licences are being bought up at exorbitant prices by investors who then lease them back to fishermen, a practice that many believe should be banned.

The aboriginal community is also worried about the impact of farm fish on the wild stocks. Simon Peter, in his evangelical way, explains why: "First, they told us the farm fish would never escape the net farms, but they did. Then they said the farm fish couldn't survive in the ocean, but they have been found as far north as Alaska, which bans farm fish.

"Then they said the Atlantic salmon wouldn't spawn in the wild salmon spawning streams. But they are. Now they say the farm fish won't drive out the wild fish. Why would we believe them?"

I leave Ucluelet depressed, flying over the mountainous spine of Vancouver Island to Duncan and more witnesses, with much the same story of unintended consequences of government action. In Richmond, we are shown a colour fan so that customers can preorder the tint preference of their farm fish; the Japanese like the deeper red colour, while other customers like a delicate pink.

What emerges is the image of a DFO riding off in all directions, leaving environmental and cultural disaster in its wake. Officials are advocating aquaculture, but we could find no government studies on the impact of farm fish on wild fish, although in countries such as Norway and Scotland aquaculture has decimated the wild fishery. Alaska bans aquaculture and Iceland permits it only in closed systems. The only study we are familiar with, by University of Victoria PhD candidate John Volpe, found Atlantic salmon in threatened Pacific steelhead spawning streams.

We could find no studies on how disease spreads from farm fish to wild fish or on how net farm sewage pollutes the environment. There are no labelling requirements to inform consumers whether they are eating farm fish or wild Pacific salmon, or to explain which antibiotics or drugs have been used to treat the farm fish. Who knows what Frankenfish we are producing?

People who live on the coast, aboriginal or non-aboriginal, have been left out of the ecological equation. So have the whales and the bears and the other wildlife that depend on the wild fishery for their existence. But if the coast dies, as some predict, who will be accountable? Not, apparently, the politicians and officials in Ottawa.

Back in Ottawa, the Fisheries Committee meets at night in the labyrinthine halls of East Block. The witness is the DFO's special advisor, aquaculture, policy sector, a bespectacled official who tells us that about 20 federal laws and an even greater number of regulations cover aquaculture activities. DFO wants to improve the public perception of aquaculture and to convince the fishery sector of its benefits.

"Why is your department avoiding the issue of conflict between having Atlantic salmon in net pens, escaping from their nets, and establishing themselves in the streams where Pacific wild salmon spawn?" I ask. "We were stunned to find how little research is being done on this."

The official spoke of "balancing environmental interests," adding: "As a matter of fact, the issue of siting aquaculture facilities, while respecting other uses of the aquatic resource, has come up. In terms of migratory birds . . ."

"We are not talking about birds," I interject. "We are talking about fish, salmon. We are talking about farm fish increasing and being established in wild habitat for wild fish. We are not talking about birds. Could you address the question?"

The official, blinking, replies: "That is not a question I can answer because I have not had a great deal of involvement in fisheries management issues and the efforts being made to integrate the decision-making with aquaculture and wild fisheries . . . it is not an area I am expert in."

Nor, it seems, is anyone else. Fisheries Minister Herb Dhaliwal tells the committee that protecting our oceans is one of his "number one priorities." But the location of fish farms is a provincial responsibility. When asked if he would support labelling to identify farm fish, he says: "I have no problem with comprehensive labelling. That is not my mandate. That is for the agriculture minister."

The Fisheries Committee adjourns.

At home on Saturna a few weeks later, I receive an e-mail from Paul Spong's orca lab. "Good news for grey whales! CITES has voted resoundingly against allowing trade in grey-whale products." Japan lost the vote 63–40 with six abstentions.

The bad news is the grey whale, a young male, lying dead on the sea-smoothed rocks of a Saturna beach, starved to death, said the scientist who came to examine him.

Why are the whales dying? Ocean pollution? Because trawlers are harvesting plankton from the Gulf to feed farm fish—plankton that might otherwise feed the grey whales? Or simply because there are now too many grey whales for the ocean to support?

Clearly more work must be done on this file. Others are ongoing; the Coast Guard is talking about silencing the foghorns. There is also Bill S-21, the Heritage Lighthouses Protection Bill, sponsored by

Senator Mike Forrestall and me, which would require public consultation before our heritage lightstations are "altered, sold, assigned, transferred or otherwise disposed of."

The polls show many Canadians want to change, elect, or abolish the Senate. But in the meantime, it is the only Senate they have. And Senator Pat is happy to help.

CHAPTER 18

Gender Politics

TRADE SECRET:
*Women have to prove their excellence over
and over as they move from one job to another,
while men take their credentials with them.*
—Hon. Justice Bertha Wilson, former Supreme Court Justice

The Treasury Board offices located at 140 O'Connor Street, plain and unpretentious, belie its power as one of the central agencies of government, responsible for all government expenditures, second only to Finance in economic clout. Until I was appointed President of Treasury Board in the spring of 1988, the portraits of past presidents lining the walls of the severe conference room showed dour male faces. I was the first woman president, and my picture broke the barrier. Other women have since been appointed president.

My appointment marked the highest level that a woman minister has attained in an economic portfolio; there still has been no woman finance minister, although both Flora MacDonald and Barbara McDougall have served as foreign ministers and Kim Campbell was briefly Prime Minister. Yet I learned more about government operations and the power of government at Treasury Board than in either Energy or International Trade.

Many women who have served at the highest level of political power in Canada, the federal Cabinet, are bitter about their experience. The history of women in Canadian politics, from the first woman cabinet minister, Ellen Fairclough, to Kim Campbell, reveals that they have been underestimated, ignored, ridiculed, or usurped by their male colleagues, many of whom have been quite content, as was John Crosbie on the free trade file, to take credit for women's work.

These women's experiences have been explicitly documented by author Sydney Sharpe in *The Gilded Ghetto: Women and Political Power in Canada*. The roll call of women ministers—Judy LaMarsh, Jeanne Sauvé, Monique Bégin, Flora MacDonald, Barbara McDougall, Iona Campagnolo, and other "regimental mascots"—is accompanied by the drums of alienation, isolation, feelings of inadequacy, guilt, depression, anger. It took many of us a long time to understand that our problems were cultural, not personal, and that we, as Sharpe writes, "are travellers in a strange and alien culture that was created by and for men."[1]

Nor is this culture limited to the political level of government. The bureaucracy is steeped in systemic discrimination against women. For this reason, as the first female President of Treasury Board, which is responsible for all government spending and the civil service, I set up a task force to identify the barriers to women in the public service. It became the most comprehensive survey of its kind, involving 20 000 civil servants, male and female, and interviews with "pathfinder women."

The impetus for the study came from my experience as a Mulroney cabinet minister in three senior cabinet portfolios—Energy, International Trade, and Treasury Board. Often I was the only woman in the room when I met with my senior officials. If another woman was present, she was often in an "acting" capacity, even though her expertise was superior to her male colleagues.

Whenever I asked where the women were I was told: "We have one, but she's not ready yet." Or even: "She's too young." Whenever I looked at the staffing levels, I found very few women in either entry-level or senior-level positions. Something had to be done. I invited some of the few female deputy ministers for lunch in my Treasury Board conference room to discuss setting up the task force. When they suggested that the chair should be Jean Edmonds, my former business-writing colleague, now a retired deputy minister, I felt life had closed a circle.

The Task Force reported in 1990, and its findings are still depressingly valid in the millennium public service. While the percentage of women executives has more than doubled in the 10-year period, from 12.3 per cent in 1990 to 26.9 per cent in 2000, women are still employed well below their potential as more than half of the population. The percentage of women in the lower-paying office jobs has remained stable at 81 per cent in 1990 and 82.7 per cent in 2000.[2]

The 1990 report, a model of rigorous research and analysis, organized its findings under three broad headings: stereotyping, corporate culture, and family responsibilities, providing a useful if painful focus for examining my own career through its successive phases of journalism, business, and politics.

Why take such a narcissistic approach? Because people ask me how I coped, working all my life in a masculine culture and male-dominated world. Women want to know what lessons I can pass on to them to help them achieve a balance between career and family life. And young men, who are the fathers of daughters, approach me on the ferry, on the street, to ask me what the future will be like for their children. I hope it will be easier for them than for my generation, when stereotyping—defined in the *Oxford Dictionary* as "to fix or perpetuate in an unchanging form"—was the norm, and when women's roles, achievements, and capabilities were often ignored.

When Canadian historian Desmond Morton explained to the media why I had not been invited to attend the McGill University conference on the FTA @ 10 in June 1999, marking the tenth anniversary of the implementation of the Canada-US Free Trade Agreement, even though I was the minister responsible for the negotiations, he said: "Frankly, no one thought of her."

The original conference program listed a plenary panel titled "The Making of the Deal." All the Canadian and US politicians and bureaucrats who had participated in the high-stakes negotiations in Washington and Ottawa in October 1987 had been invited to recap their roles, except for me. The conference program listing the "deal makers" showed John Crosbie in my place, even though the "Great Pretender" was not the trade minister until six months later.

Why was I surprised? For one thing, any competent historian may have noticed my signature on the original agreement. Then there were all those television, radio, and print media reports as the FTA negotiations unfolded, the moments of high drama, the near failure, the ultimate success as we signed the agreement just before midnight on October 3, 1987. As the minister with the mandate for the historic negotiations, I was difficult to ignore.

Yet Morton and his group of self-promoting chauvinists had no qualms about inviting John Crosbie to sit in my place on the panel.

Nor did Crosbie hesitate to usurp my role at the McGill conference, even though the media and the American panellists with whom I had worked knew he was sitting in the wrong seat. When I protested, Morton simply changed the name of the panel and offered me a role in a conference workshop on regional impacts, which I refused. Crosbie remained in my place on the plenary panel.

Even former Prime Minister Brian Mulroney, who had appointed me International Trade Minister responsible for the FTA negotiations, mis-led the media, saying that Morton's subsequent sop of the workshop offer meant I had been invited. He ignored the fact that I had originally discussed my exclusion with him on the telephone. And the media, including my former employer the *Vancouver Sun*, believed him.

No apology was forthcoming; indeed, my action in making my exclusion public was deemed to be the typical, belligerent, Black Irish behaviour expected of Carney, who once again had refused to play the role of submissive "little woman," content to walk in the shadow of The Big Guys.

First, a confession. We are *all* guilty of stereotyping people, men and women, gender-sensitive people and chauvinist pigs. Let me, to my chagrin, provide some examples of my own errors and omissions. Shortly after the 1993 election, which voted the Liberals into office, a young woman approached me on a flight to Calgary and breathed: "Oh, Senator Carney, I would so like to talk to you. Do you think we could arrange a meeting?" I looked at her appraisingly. Dark hair, bangs, open face, obviously eager. Probably an advocate for some consumers' group wanting to discuss free trade.

"Why don't you give me your card and I'll see what we can arrange?" I said from my seat. She handed me her card. It read Anne McLellan, Minister of Natural Resources, my former portfolio. "Yes, Minister," I said, jumping to my feet. "Of course, Minister. My office will be in touch with your assistant."

We never did have that meeting. She probably had other priorities!

Nor do we stereotype only women. Once I invited community development worker Jim Green to address my graduate class at the UBC School of Regional and Community Planning, where I have been an adjunct professor for a decade, teaching master's and PhD students the policy-planning process. Jim, one of the best community development experts in the business, looks like a graduate from the streets of Vancouver's Downtown East Side, which he is, with his barrel chest, burly complexion, and battered features. Obviously a school dropout, I subconsciously concluded.

At the end of his lecture on how to establish a bank for people who have no homes, no fixed address, and little income, but who need a safe place for their welfare cheques, I said to Jim: "Well, I can't award you a master's degree for your excellent lecture but I would like to give you this UBC sweatshirt instead."

"I *have* a master's degree, Pat, so I'm happy to accept the shirt," Jim responded deftly, removing the gift from my stunned hands, while my students giggled at the look on my face.

And those are not my only examples—just among the most embarrassing ones.

For women politicians, stereotyping by male colleagues, bureaucrats, and businessmen means that they often assume our ignorance about tough and technical issues. "In my time (1974–79), women were always incredibly underestimated as to our abilities, training, background, our talent for devising strategy or tactics,"[3] Trudeau-era cabinet minister Iona Campagnolo told author Sydney Sharpe.

Ten years later that view hadn't changed much. The energy bureaucrats who publicly fretted that their new minister seemed poorly briefed couldn't accept the fact that I already knew what our Conservative energy policy would be, because I had already drafted it with the approval of my Conservative caucus. Nor could they grasp the fact that, as a shadow cabinet critic in Opposition, I had already negotiated the Principles of the Atlantic Accord with Newfoundland Energy Minister Bill Marshall.

The bureaucrats' scathing criticism also reflects another stereotype—that ministers are helpless without them. On one occasion my deputy minister, Paul Tellier, came to my office and tried to brief me on "your government's energy initiatives," when, in fact, he needed a briefing from me, the author of the policy.

The final irony was the readiness of the media (and thus The Town, as Ottawa's mandarin circle is known) to attribute my western energy policy to my political aide, lobbyist Harry Near, who was not even in the room when negotiations between ministers were in their crucial phase, and whose major role was to set up my ministerial office and liaise with the energy industry.

Harry moved my long-time personal assistant Janice Whitters to another position working off the Hill and replaced her with his wife Lee's most brilliant secretarial pupil, Marie Menard, who was subsequently convicted of stealing thousands of dollars from my ministerial expense account.

Near never publicly claimed to have authored my energy policy, but his silence on the subject, and his failure to credit me with my own work, merely reinforced his media image as Mr. Energy. After I left the Cabinet I asked him why no company in the oil patch had offered me a directorship, considering that it was primarily my successful efforts, backed by Prime Minister Mulroney, that had freed them from the financial noose of the Liberal's hated National Energy Policy. "Because you're a dame," he said bluntly.

Near subsequently served as a director on the board of a Westcoast Energy Inc. subsidiary, Union Gas Ltd., in my former riding of Vancouver Centre. Westcoast's Chair and CEO at the time was Michael Phelps, former aide to one of the architects of the NEP, Marc Lalonde. In politics, the rewards often go to former ministerial assistants, not to former ministers.

A frustrating example of ministerial stereotyping occurred during the softwood lumber dispute with the United States, which threatened to take tough trade measures against the Canadian lumber industry in 1986 on the grounds that our Canadian stumpage system, particularly in British Columbia, subsidized our exports to the US market. This nasty dispute occurred prior to the FTA negotiations and threatened to derail them. The Canadian compromise included a 15 per cent export tax on lumber shipments to the US, keeping the money in Canada, in place of an American-imposed countervailing duty.

My frustration stemmed from the fact that none of the well-trousered lawyers and industry flacks seated around my conference table would concede the fact that I actually understood our BC stumpage system; in fact, I was probably the only person in the room who did. I could recite the formula for allocating the allowable cut and the stumpage, or economic rent collected by the provincial governments. I knew exactly whose ox was being gored, and I was not displeased to see the pain shared with an industry dumb enough to increase its market share to the point—somewhere over 28 per cent—where the Americans retaliated with trade weapons.

Among those who opposed the export tax was forestry executive Adam Zimmerman, then head of the Toronto-based Noranda forest products conglomerate, who made negative comments in the media about the minister and the export tax. This annoyed me, because I had run the proposed measure past the highly paid forest industry lobbyists who sat at my ministerial conference table, along with my staff, in Ottawa. They reluctantly agreed that the tax, for technical reasons, was less onerous than an American countervail, a draconian trade penalty.

The softwood dispute reached its peak around Christmas time. I wrote an angry letter to Zimmerman, outlining my reasons for the tax, and dispatched it to the front desk in the Pearson Building, home of External Affairs and International Trade, for pick up and delivery to Zimmerman.

The next day I received a puzzling call from Zimmerman's office. Did I know, the caller asked, that Mr. Zimmerman was a Christian? I neither knew nor cared, I responded shortly, true to my Anglican beliefs. Bothered by the query, I asked my chief of staff, Effie Triantafilopoulos, to investigate. She reported that the Pearson Building lobby was decorated with seasonal Christmas trees and menorah, the candelabra used for Hanukkah, the Jewish Festival of Lights. For some reason, my letter had been stashed on a menorah, and the messenger delivered both the letter *and* the menorah to Adam Zimmerman's office!

The lumber industry's hostile reaction to my revenue-generating export tax reminded me of my experience when, as a business columnist in the 1960s, I had suggested a bidding fee to end blackmail bids in timber sales in British Columbia. Even though the concept was adopted into law and ended the spiteful practice, lumber executive Peter Bentley put his hand on my elbow and walked me down the halls of the BC Legislative Buildings, chiding me for stepping beyond the bounds of journalism in devising the concept. Good reporters, particularly women reporters, did not tell the industry what it should do, he explained.

My experience in International Trade illustrates a point made by Bertha Wilson, the first woman justice appointed to the Supreme Court, whom I personally interviewed for the Task Force on barriers to women in the public service. The wife of a United Church minister, Madam Justice Wilson's appointment by Pierre Trudeau had been heatedly opposed by male cabinet ministers, according to author Sharpe, who argued that Wilson was not known among the intellectual (male) elite of jurisprudence. Over lunch in Ottawa, Madam Justice Wilson told me: "Women have to prove their excellence over and over as they move from one job to another, while men take their credentials with them." Considering my record when I moved from Energy to International Trade, I ruefully accepted her verdict.

"Because women's efforts are undervalued, there is skepticism regarding their credentials and experience, and a double standard imposed with respect to how they are judged," concluded the Task Force.[4] And the judge imposing the double standard was usually a male boss.

I experienced this "double standard" at the hands of Erik Nielsen, the Yukon MP who later served as Deputy Prime Minister in Brian Mulroney's government. One day in 1989 I took a call from Marjory LeBreton, Mulroney's deputy chief of staff. "How are you feeling?" asked Marjory, cautiously testing for Carney's flash-point temper. "Great," I responded. "Has the media called you about Erik Nielsen's book?" she asked. When I said no, she continued: "The Prime Minister says you are not to worry about Nielsen. The PM says he will write his own book."

Naturally, I raced to the bookstore to find out what the dour Yukon MP had written about me in his book, *The House Is Not a Home*. Unknown to us, before the 1984 election, Erik had prepared a report rating the Conservative shadow cabinet members who would be contenders for cabinet posts in the widely anticipated Conservative government. Ratings ranged from Unsatisfactory to Exceptional. My rating, as critic for Energy, Mines and Resources, was dismal on all fronts. Although I had negotiated the Principles of the Atlantic Accord with Newfoundland Premier Brian Peckford's government, my rating was overwhelmingly "unsatisfactory."

My deficiencies included failure to organize, control, direct; lack of industriousness, dependability, discretion, judgment, political judgment, maturity, performance under pressure, flexibility. Although I held a master's degree in planning and had developed our entire Conservative energy policy working with the industry and caucus, I was deemed "not fully satisfactory" in planning, knowledge, quality of work, initiative, tactfulness, loyalty, and working relations with superiors and colleagues. I was "superior" or "exceptional" in nothing. Nielsen's assessment concluded: "Pat is a person of overwhelming self-esteem which, while enhancing the quality of decisiveness, at the same time erodes discretion, dependability and judgment. . . . She would pose serious political problems in any future cabinet."[5]

Poor Flora fared no better. The only other senior woman in caucus, the former Minister of External Affairs in Joe Clark's 1979 government, she achieved "exceptional" status only in industriousness, failing miserably in all the key ministerial indicators. "She would be a persistent source of disharmony in any cabinet,"[6] wrote Nielsen. Unfair and untrue.

In contrast, MP Perrin Beatty, who held the relatively minor role of critic for National Revenue, was rated "superior" or "exceptional" in every category except tactfulness, where he was only "fully satisfactory." Nielsen added: "This assessment speaks for itself. He is obvious cabinet material at the middle or senior level."[7]

"Perfect Perrin," snorted Brian Mulroney, who was none too pleased with his own Nielsen rating. Although both Joe Clark and Brian Mulroney tried to avoid stereotyping their colleagues and associates, and in general did better than their predecessors, they still fell into the same trap. Discussing senior External Affairs bureaucrat Sylvia Ostry, one of the first female deputy ministers, Joe acknowledged her brilliance in a private conversation with me, but labelled her "difficult." Ostry was one of my top officials, in charge of our multilateral trade negotiations at the General Agreement on Tariffs and Trade talks, and highly respected by trade officials around the world. I never found her the least bit difficult and took every opportunity to learn from her. Yet she was often undermined by colleagues, such as Simon Reisman, who once cheekily wrote to the Geneva bureaucrats masterminding the GATT, usurping her mandate, which I, as minister, took pains to correct.

Ostry was reluctant to play the game of gender politics. Indeed, when I had the rare opportunity to head up an all-woman team to an international trade meeting in Europe, with Ostry, assistant deputy minister Jean McClosky, and my chief of staff Effie Triantafilopoulos, Ostry was diffident about showcasing the fact.

317

One of the worst cases of underestimating a woman minister was Mulroney's treatment of Flora as Communications Minister responsible for developing a made-in-Canada film and video distribution policy to increase the opportunities for Canadian-made films to be played in Canadian movie houses to Canadian audiences. When Flora took her policy to the subcommittee on trade, which I chaired, she presented it to her colleagues in her usual professional manner. Her stance was: "Here is what I was asked to do; what happens is up to you."

The policy was greeted by our male cabinet colleagues with enthusiasm and much macho chest-pounding about standing up to the Americans, who viewed Canadian distribution of Canadian films as a threat to their near movie monopoly. Joe Clark, who was in India, faxed his support as Secretary of State for External Affairs. But when US movie lobbyist Jack Valenti screamed retaliatory threats, Flora carried the can.

Prime Minister Mulroney launched a diatribe against Flora and "her" film policy that "threatened the FTA," during a conversation with me at 24 Sussex. I was stunned speechless by his accusation, remembering that after the film distribution fiasco I was removed as Chair of the Trade Committee, and replaced by Mulroney himself. To my regret, I did not correct him. But someone had conveyed that false impression to the Prime Minister, either his manipulative Chief of Staff Derek Burney, or a male cabinet colleague, or the male Clerk of the Privy Council, Paul Tellier. No one had discussed it with me.

My clear-eyed view of equality of men and women reflected my unique experience as part of an "equal opportunity" boy-girl twin set. My twin brother and I were always treated equally in the allocation of farm chores; normally, I milked the cow in the morning and Jim milked her at night. Our parents offered us equal opportunities for education and careers, even though the family budget was very tight. The only exception was dance and piano lessons for the girls, while the boys received priority for sports activities.

But sometimes women stereotype themselves. When I first joined *The Province* in the 1950s, the editor explained to me that women were paid the same as men, but received a lower pension, since they usually had husbands, but the men had wives to support. This approach seemed reasonable to me at the time.

A generation later, women still often diminish their work. Heather Martin, an intelligent young woman working on a project I was managing, complained I was paying her less than her male colleague and threatened to file a human-rights complaint. I told her: "You set the job specs, Heather, and you set your wage rate. You undervalued yourself." Heather had the grace to agree, since at that point neither of us could do much about it. Although not a Conservative, Heather later worked on my election campaign.

Stereotyping works both ways, sometimes proving advantageous. My career as a business columnist was initially possible because few people realized that Pat Carney was a woman. They were sometimes shocked at the reality. When, dressed in my pink pantsuit, I first stepped out of the aircraft and onto the frozen Arctic desert at Rea Point, the oil and gas exploration camp on Melville Island in the High Arctic, the geologist who opened the aircraft door said it all.

"Fuck," he exclaimed.

In the High Arctic oil and gas play, my experiences as a journalist were unique. Charles Hetherington, president of Panarctic Oil Ltd., issued strict standing orders for dealing with uninvited journalists who showed up at the company's Arctic islands drill sites. Author Tom Kennedy described them in his book, *Quest: Canada's Search for Arctic Oil*: "Any undesirable reporter caught was to be quarantined. No assistance of any kind would be rendered, and the offender was to be flown out on the next plane at his expense.

"No women, under any pretext, were to go north. Hetherington put them in the same category of undesirables and proscribed commodities as long hairs, bearded ones, hippies, and homosexuals and dangerous weapons, booze or dope . . . Panarctic staff failing to carry them out to the letter faced dismissal."

Panarctic's rules clearly disqualified me from going north. "Carney was patrolling the North the only way she could—in a hitchhiker style," Kennedy wrote, noting that my "convertible" first name had caused some confusion. "Once Carney had been pronounced female, she was declared *persona non grata*. The war of wits had begun."[8]

Panarctic's vice-president on the site, Bob Currie, could not prevent my plane from landing at Rae Point on Melville Island. "Carney, however, was not to enter the camp." Hetherington ordered me put up in the dark tool shed—"a noisy, stinking hovel"—next to the diesel generators until the scheduled southbound Electra flight the following day. "While in captivity, her stay was to be made as uncomfortable as possible. Once off the plane Carney was kept waiting outdoors in the sub-zero winter temperatures, circled by a pack of snarling huskies." Instead, Currie assigned me the floor of his office trailer. What neither Currie nor Kennedy realized was that it was not my first visit to Melville Island: I had stayed there earlier with my twin.

It was a different story 16 years later when, as Energy Minister, I returned to the High Arctic and the drilling site Bent Horn on Cameron Island to hand-deliver Hetherington the number one oil production licence for the Arctic islands, plus permission to drill two more wells, which had been denied him by the Liberals. "Hetherington had reviled Carney the journalist," wrote Kennedy. "He wanted to forget that once he had wanted to exile her to the freezing dungeon of the Rae Point tool-shed."[9]

The 1990 Task Force identified that corporate culture, or "that's how we do things around here," is another major factor in gender politics. The current masthead of my former journalistic base, the *Vancouver Sun*, lists five names. Three of them are women: Patricia Graham, Managing Editor; Shelley Fralic, Executive Editor; and Daphne Bramham, Associate Editor. The other two are men: Neil Reynolds, Editor, and David Radler, Chair of Pacific Press, which publishes the *Vancouver Sun* and the *Province* for Southam Co.

That's progress from the days when women where shut out of decision-making in the news room or editorial offices. Women reporters can and have become editors, publishers, and directors on corporate boards, but it's a relatively recent phenomenon. Television documentary producer Dawn MacDonald gives a delicious account of her experience as an editor of the now defunct, then upscale magazine *City Woman*, which was pitched to women who were moving up the management ranks in the booming 1980s. Her publisher and his associates decided her benefits should include a clothing allowance, since she was expected to represent the magazine's target audience. They wrestled mightily with the appropriate amount and finally announced she would receive the annual sum of $450; Dawn estimated that the cost of an appropriate wardrobe would be closer to $5000.

At their next meeting, Dawn plunked down two purses, two belts, and five pairs of shoes on her publisher's desk, in addition to a bill for $1200. She made her point: a male editor in her position, such as a television anchor, would have received a far larger allowance. But, in the end, she lost her editorship and her magazine career, and turned to television to build a new life.

I encountered the academic corporate culture when, flush with funds from my consulting company, I applied to UBC's Faculty of Commerce to enroll in the master's program in business administration. The admitting clerk refused me, on the grounds that my first-year math marks obtained 20 years earlier were too low. Since I had already run a profitable and productive business for seven years, negotiating contracts and directly employing up to 20 people, with no corporate debts, and money in the bank, I went public with this rejection.

When the resulting furor died down, I refused the hastily extended invitation from Commerce in favour of the School of Community and Regional Planning, working and studying part-time for three years, earning my master's degree in 1977. I returned to the School in 1990 to teach a policy-planning seminar as an adjunct professor for the next 10 years.

The academic corporate culture shows some improvement with the increase in the number of women enrolling in MBA programs across Canada. Most students in my planning seminar are women, who account for at least half of the enrolment in some academic years.

But despite the increasing number of women MPs and senators, Parliament is still very much a male bastion, from the appointment of senior cabinet posts, and bureaucrats, to the washrooms in Centre Block. The corporate culture is still urinal-dominated.

When I was first elected in 1980 as BC's first female Conservative MP, Flora and I were the only two women in the 101-member Conservative caucus, and chair Chuck Cook would always open caucus by calling the "gentlemen" to order. Flora and I would wave our hands and insist that he use the term "colleagues." This drew dark looks from our male counterparts, who were convinced that feminist Flora was now joined by Carney.

When I noticed that few women MPs were assigned to parliamentary trips and raised the issue with our whip Bill Kempling, he told me to stick to my riding meetings and women's groups, and count myself lucky that women MPs were paid the same as men. When the women MPs supported Speaker Jeanne Sauvé's efforts to establish a daycare facility on the Hill, one Conservative MP sputtered: "I don't want my secretary running downstairs to the daycare centre every time her child has an accident." To which we countered: "Would you rather she drove across town?"

In his Cabinet, coached by Flora and Marjory LeBreton and his wife Mila, Brian Mulroney tried to change the corporate culture of boards and commissions by insisting that at least one-third of the proposed appointees on every list brought to the cabinet table for approval be women. And he stood his ground, tongue-lashing one hapless fisheries minister who pleaded an absence of women in the fishing industry: "Don't tell me there are no women in the fishery. Pat's daughter is a fisherman." Although my daughter Jane was not appointed while I was in the Cabinet, the incident was not repeated.

Until the free trade issue arose, I found Mulroney's manner to his women ministers exemplary and even-handed. Only once did he ever push the limits, teasing Barbara McDougall at a cabinet meeting in a flirting manner that rang warning bells in my "feminine-alert" system. His private actions, however, lagged his public ones. He regularly asked his press secretary Michel Gratton, "What are the Boys saying?" in reference to the day's media comment.

Outside the Prime Minister's orbit, the corporate culture was often objectionable and discriminatory. John Crosbie, famous for his sexist attacks on Liberal MP Sheila Copps—"Pass the tequila, Sheila, roll over and love me again"—did not spare his female colleagues. In demand as a speaker, he once told a full-house audience: "I notice that we have with us tonight Minister Pat Carney and her friend, famous columnist Allan Fotheringham. The issue is whether Fotheringham has had carnal knowledge of Carney."

Much tittering and sly glances were sneaked at my buddy Allan and myself, and I was embarrassed. I approached John afterwards and told him his comments were in poor taste, and were offensive to both of us, and asked him to omit his "carnal Carney" comments from his repertoire. But Crosbie, a colleague with a vicious tongue, repeated them at the next opportunity, which was a Conservative Party whoop-up, the Gatineau Hills Gentleman's Club annual dinner.

Accustomed as I was to working with men in male-dominated fields, often as the only woman, I rarely encountered overt, up-front, in-your-face discrimination in Cabinet until I was appointed President of Treasury Board.

The operations centre of Mulroney's government at the time was the Operations Committee of Cabinet, chaired by the popular and reliable Don Mazankowski, then Deputy Prime Minister. The "Ops" committee met at 8:00 a.m. every Monday and reviewed the government's upcoming agenda. It was very informal—as far as I could discern, no minutes were kept—and few bureaucrats attended.

Membership was limited to cabinet ministers who chaired committees, such as social development, economic development, communications, as well as the Minister of Finance. Treasury Board is a committee of ministers—typically ones with non-spending portfolios to reduce "scratch my back and I'll scratch yours" exchanges of financial favours—and my predecessor as President, Robert de Cotret, attended Ops meetings.

After my swearing-in as President of Treasury Board, I waited for my notice of Ops meetings to show up in my ministerial mail, but no notice was forthcoming. I was aware that my deputy minister, Secretary of Treasury Board, Gerard Veilleux, attended the meetings and I raised the issue with him. Gerard, who was the best deputy I ever worked with, told me bluntly that The Boys liked the all-male atmosphere of Ops and planned to keep it that way. The language was rough and the atmosphere abrasive; deals were cut and no women were welcome.

I was in the same "no win" position faced by women executives in Calgary's oil patch when they were barred from membership in the all-important Petroleum Club, where land deals were made and exploration rights negotiated. As President of Treasury Board, I held the responsibility for government spending, but my exclusion from Ops meant I couldn't exercise it.

The impasse was resolved when Gerard, who developed his infighting skills as a tough little kid from a Quebec asbestos mining town, told the Ops committee members that he couldn't attend the cabinet meetings without his minister present. My notice of the meeting place and time of Operations Committee subsequently appeared on my ministerial agenda.

These two positions—President and Secretary—are among the most powerful in Ottawa, since some rule can always be found to disallow a spending decision approved by Cabinet or to bend the rules if necessary. My ministerial colleagues might not want me as minister at the Ops table, but it was impossible to proceed without the participation of the Secretary of Treasury Board, who prepared the agenda for our Board meetings. I admired Gerard for his stand, because many bureaucrats were happy to align themselves with the macho males in Cabinet who gripped the reins of power. Gerard later served as President of the CBC before returning to Quebec and private industry.

One way that women politicians fought the corporate culture was our refusal to give speeches and hold meetings in men-only clubs. When I interviewed Jeanne Sauvé, then Governor General, for the Task Force, she recited a litany of her experiences, excused herself to receive a new ambassador's credentials, and came back to recite more.

The Rideau Club, symbol of Ottawa Establishment, had finally ended its discrimination against women members in 1979, inviting former Tory MP Jean Pigott to join. The club burned down shortly after. Barbara McDougall once reached the very steps of her speaking venue, read the club name on the door, and turned around and left.

As Energy Minister, I refused to meet with the industry corporate elite in the Petroleum Club. In the end, compromise was reached, another venue chosen, and the Petroleum Club subsequently limited its men-only exclusivity to a small bar.

But private-industry corporate culture was not much better. When I worked in the North as president of a company specializing in socio-economic and transport studies, I found my clients happier to perceive me as a "sociologist" or "educator"—roles for which I was not qualified—than as a hard-numbers economist. Academics were the worst.

My experiences after I left the House of Commons in late 1988 illustrated once again the perils of being The Only. As the only woman on several boards, I often found myself ignored or invisible. For 10 years I served on the board of Airshow Canada, which sponsored North America's largest aerospace trade show at Abbotsford, British Columbia, and which was initiated with my backing as International

Trade Minister. The other directors were men from the aviation industry—hardly a hotbed of feminism—and retired military officers. Typically, my suggestions were ignored. But if they were repeated minutes later by a male director, they suddenly became audible. I eventually quit the board.

In contrast, serving for the last 10 years with other women on a Ted Rogers board, Rogers Media Inc., with nation-wide interests in radio, television, magazines, and the New Media, I have never encountered similar problems. A "critical mass" of women, usually one-third, magically seems to alter the climate and achieve a gender balance. This suggests that truly it takes fewer women to do men's work!

One aspect of the male-dominated corporate culture that I did not encounter in politics was sexual harassment, although my staff did. Overworked, experiencing "symptoms consistent with exhaustion," said one medical report, in pain from arthritis, often belligerent, I was not a likely candidate for such problems. But it was certainly an issue in my journalism and business careers. The presence of my twin Jim on my initial Arctic excursions defused any potential problems, so that when I travelled on my own I had already established an "off-limits" reputation. But periodically I felt it prudent to ask a male colleague to accompany me to an interview. A woman business writer in the field in all-male camps is a target for propositions, but I learned to fend them off; the power of the pen was a useful defence.

I had my worst harassment problems in running Gemini North, where some male clients—or prospective clients—expected me to provide additional services not included in the contract, or as a preliminary requirement for new contracts. This was a real dilemma, since I had a payroll to meet and employees depending on my success in closing deals. I was the main marketer in our three-person partnership.

One federal government official, a key player among our clients, bluntly offered me the position of northern mistress, following a precedent he had set in South America, where he had a similar arrangement. I said I would check it out with his wife, and the matter was dropped.

A Calgary client was so persistent that I threatened to report him to his president, a wild card, since the president was pursuing his own extramarital interests. One political appointee literally chased me around the room. I simply outran him to the elevator.

Did we lose contracts because of my elbow-in-the-stomach rejections? Probably. But we were efficient, experienced, and produced professionally for our clients. And I learned to avoid situations that could lead to trouble or to find a male mentor, usually happily married, who would provide no-nonsense cover. Pipeline executive Robin Abercrombie, a key contact in my business life, was such a person; I could, and did, go anywhere with him.

Today, women in business and politics have resources and laws to assist them against harassment of all kinds. And young men today tell me that they are now afraid of smiling at a woman co-worker, or making any personal comment, no matter how casual. Some balance must be found to provide a corporate culture in which both women and men can work together in confidence and comfort.

It will surprise no one that the third set of barriers to the advancement of women identified by the Task Force is family responsibilities. Although some men are happy to assume the main parenting role while their partners pursue demanding careers, other women either have no partner and thus no choice or don't wish to diminish their "homemaker" role while in the workforce. The issue then is how we cope and what we can learn from each other.

I admired Mila Mulroney for her skill in protecting her family's home life while exposed to harsh public scrutiny of her clothes, her hair, her office, and her public activities. Once, at Rideau Hall to meet the Queen and Prince Philip, I complimented Mila on her hair, which was tied back in a ponytail under her hat. Although we women politicians were unused to hats, which perched precariously on our heads, we were informed by protocol officers that hats were mandatory in audiences with the Queen until 6:00 p.m. Queen Elizabeth, wearing *her* hat, was outside on the lawn inspecting a black RCMP horse that was given to her, the usual purse over her arm. Mila laughed at my comment and explained that she had adopted the ponytail because she hadn't had time to wash her hair for her meeting with the Queen. One of her sons had fallen and hurt himself at school, and it was a choice between a shampoo or a school visit to comfort her son. Other mothers in her situation might have made a different choice but not Mila. She liked it when I told her my most impressive accomplishments were my wonderful children, my son John Patrick and my daughter Jane.

There is no doubt that single parenthood was by far the most difficult situation I ever faced. When I decided to end my marriage when my son was age two—my daughter was away at school—I knew it would be tough, but as a politician the strain is almost insurmountable. As the only Mom elected west of the Lakehead in 1980, I had no support base in Parliament, with the important exception of Speaker Jeanne Sauvé, who changed the travel rules, at my request, for MPs so that children could accompany their parents to and from Ottawa. The decision to end night sessions of the House, except for extended hours and emergency debates, made family life easier for all parliamentarians.

As a journalist who was constantly on the road, I had employed an array of live-in babysitters, including one so intimidating that it took all my courage to fire her. Life was much easier when I hired Frankie Martin, a red-haired graduate of a British nanny school, who taught my four-year-old son impeccable manners.

As a businesswoman also on the road when we lived in Yellowknife, I turned to the local YWCA, headed by Ruth Spence, herself a mother of five children, to supply native and non-native babysitters. JP particularly liked Inuit babysitters since, like him, they didn't care for vegetables.

One night I returned home from a client dinner at 11:00 p.m. to find six-year-old JP playing in the gravel outside our home in the pale sub-Arctic light. "Where's your babysitter?" I asked. "I sent her home," said JP. And she had gone! Ruth, a good friend, had the grace to laugh.

When I worked in our Yellowknife office, I walked my son to school and at noon he brought his lunch pail to my office for some "quality time." I relied on Ruth and the YWCA primarily for after-school care. My most difficult time was when JP developed hepatitis, which was too infectious for babysitters, and I somehow had to care for him and work at the same time. No work would mean no cheques from clients to pay the rent and meet the payroll.

Often I simply took JP with me on our trips to the Mackenzie Valley native settlements, enrolling him in the local hostel school with native children while I did my work, or tucking him into a bunk bed in Atlas Aviation's Resolute camp in the High Arctic. Once, flying with pilot Duncan Grant in the eastern Arctic, JP slept on the mail bags, wrapped in his red parka trimmed with yellow ptarmigan birds, while narwhals spouted in the ice-strewn Sound below and Dunc explained a "Weldy fix," or makeshift radio repair to me.

After he graduated in science from UBC and earned his commercial pilot's licence, JP returned to the North and flew as Dunc's co-pilot in the same twin Otters in which he had ridden as a child and on which I had hitchhiked rides across the Arctic as a journalist.

When I was first elected MP, JP was age 15, too old for babysitters and too young to live on his own. After trying various arrangements, which meant that he went to four schools in four years, I ended up relying on a series of "house parents" who lived in during the week. Most weekends I flew back from Ottawa, arriving exhausted. JP learned that a clean kitchen, with dishes in the dishwasher, ensured peace and harmony in the family.

On Mondays I put his dinner in the oven, turned on the oven timer, and flew back to Ottawa, leaving other "make-ahead" meals in the fridge, which he often ignored. My nephew Joe, 18 months older, came to live with us, but leaving two teenagers at home, admonishing them not to smoke pot in an MP's home, was a constant worry. I missed most school concerts, sports events, exam pressures—my son explained he was majoring in Hanging Out in the Parking Lot—but I defied a Three-Line Whip wielded by the merciless Erik Nielsen to attend his graduation.

My children were both older and attending university when I was re-elected and entered the Cabinet, but I still yearned for my role as Mom. Instead, my role as part-time parent was painful to us all. One lonely evening in my Ottawa apartment I reflected that as President of Treasury Board, and a member of the inner Cabinet, I was one of the most powerful women in Canada, but I would trade it all for the opportunity to just be Mom again. But it was too late. My birds had flown the nest. I strongly believe that women with young and teenage children should think twice before being coaxed to run for federal office, unless they live in the National Capital Region close to both home and work.

The number of women in politics has increased dramatically since I was first elected an MP in 1980. Then there were only 18 women, or 6.4 per cent of the House of Commons. In 2000 there are 60 women, or 20 per cent of a larger House of Commons. The number of women senators has increased from 10 in 1980, or 11.2 per cent, to 32 in 2000, or 20 per cent. But it is far from the equal representation that our share of the population warrants.

But Parliament, in its present structure, is not family friendly. The sessions are too long, and the distances between Ottawa and home are usually too great to allow family members to commute. Both families and constituents, who have limited access to their MP in the little time she has in the riding, suffer.

Over the years, my party has asked me to persuade women candidates to run, including one who had just adopted a street kid. She asked me what it would be like for the child. I told her she could leave her child in the riding when she was in Ottawa, or leave her child in Ottawa when she was in the riding. She declined the opportunity.

Then there was the potential candidate, a man, who would be running against his stepchildren's father. Don't, I advised. Not in this world, I told the young woman involved in a custody battle with her ex-husband. Maybe later, I told the prospective candidate whose wife's job wasn't portable.

And when a promising potential candidate told me that he was thinking of running because both his mother and mother-in-law thought he should be prime minister, I advised him: "Tell them to run instead."

The strain of work and personal responsibilities finally culminated in a severe attack of arthritis, which ended my career as an MP. And yet, my absorption with my family saved my sanity and maintained my sensitivity to the problems my constituents faced in their daily, often difficult lives.

I clung to my Saturna Island "Home Place" like a barnacle, absorbed in the details of small-community life, sustained by my friends who were largely uninterested in politics, attending our little church, shopping in the supermarket in town, travelling on the buses and ferries, and survived as a whole person.

Too many politicians—women and men—don't.

CHAPTER 19

Politics and People

TRADE SECRET:
In politics, keep your eye on the Leader
and your back to the wall.
—Jean Pigott, former Conservative MP

It is the opening of the Second Session of the thirty-sixth Parliament in the Senate Chamber, the last Throne Speech of the twentieth century and arguably one of the dullest. It will be tagged the "Drone Speech" by the media. The Throne Speech is being read by the new Governor General, Adrienne Clarkson, who is wearing a drab grey gown. She looks like a dust mop sitting in her red-and-gold Throne chair.

"Today, the representatives of the Canadian people gather to open the session of Parliament that will carry the country into the new millennium," she intones. It is a mystery to me why the former television journalist has chosen to wear such an unbecoming dress in her new role when her sister-in-law, Senator Vivienne Poy, is an exquisitely dressed fashion designer. Grey is not a Chinese colour, except for Mao followers, and examining Adrienne's outfit one can see why. It is almost as dumpy as the blanket she wore when she met the Queen.

The Governor General's husband, John Ralston Saul, sits by her side in his smaller, consort Throne chair. Not even he can pretend to be fascinated with every dreary line she reads on behalf of her government, and his eyes flit about the Senate Chamber, resting briefly on the nine judges of the Supreme Court seated in front of the Throne chairs in three rows of three, their red, ermine-trimmed robes trailing on the red carpet. They look like Christmas angels.

Justice Louise Arbour, the newest appointee, sits in the last seat of the last row. She is smaller than her media pictures indicate. In contrast, Justice Beverley McLachlin is tall and chic with her flashing eyes and white pageboy. In the airport the day before I mistook her for a top-level bureaucrat, possibly an assistant deputy minister, in her well-fitting black pantsuit. The third female justice, Claire L'Heureux-Dubé, has the round, lined face of a countrywoman. Except for Chief Justice Antonio Lamer, who limped in on his cane, the men all look the same.

On the floor of the Red Chamber, near the Governor General, sits Prime Minister Jean Chrétien. We are wondering whether this will be the last Throne Speech his government will produce before the next election or, in fact, if this will be his last Throne Speech before retiring. Although the PM has already told my husband Paul White, his former ministerial aide, that he is running again, he looks worn down.

Paul is attending the Throne Speech with me, greeting his Liberal friends while I smile at my Conservative buddies. After 20 years of Not Speaking when I became a Conservative candidate, my long-time love finally wrote me from his Calgary office, where he ran his mining engineering company. When Janice Whitters called me at Saturna, where I was recovering from a knee operation, to tell me about Paul's letter, she added: "I want to be matron of honour." She was, at our Saturna wedding a few months later.

When Paul and I were married, Prime Minister Chrétien sent a handwritten note, saying: "Dear Senator Pat. Congratulations on your marriage to Paul. Now you must follow Paul at the next election so we can beat the Reforms." His written English may be as mangled as his spoken English, but his political instincts remain sound.

Thirty years ago, my twin brother and I interviewed Jean Chrétien while flying over Great Slave Lake in a DC-3. The newly appointed Minister for Indian Affairs and Northern Development had never been north of Sept-Îles before taking over his portfolio. Informally dressed in a grey turtleneck sweater and slacks, Chrétien was electric with excitement about northern Canada and its challenges.

Socially, "it gives us a chance to build the kind of society we want, without repeating the mistakes of the past," he told us as I scribbled notes and Jim took photos. "Economically, we can apply North American technology to the North. Only Canadians can do that."[1]

Now, a complacent Prime Minister Chrétien, between rounds of golf, tells talented young Canadians that if they don't like Canada's tax system they should leave for the United States.

Former prime ministers usually sit behind the Supreme Court judges on the floor of the Chamber, although they rarely attend the Speech from the Throne, choosing instead to turn up for special events such as the speech by South African leader Nelson Mandela, a man so revered that when he addressed the Joint Session of the Senate and the House of Commons, half the Press Gallery, crowded into the balcony behind Commons Speaker Gil Parent, broke their code of invisibility and rose to their feet to join the sustained applause. Naturally, they never reported their break with convention.

Former Prime Ministers Pierre Trudeau and Kim Campbell were in their chairs to hear Mandela. Trudeau appeared gaunt and subdued. I remembered him once bounding up the marbled stairs of Rideau Hall, wearing a dashing hat and a black cape. "You look like Charles the Second," I admired. "As long as I don't look like Charles the First," he retaliated, referring to the Charles who lost his head. Kim looked the way Kim does without the makeup artist.

Kim Campbell caused one of the most chilling moments of my political life in her efforts as Minister of Justice to finesse her abortion legislation through the Senate. When Kim, whose stepmother Marg Campbell is my close Carney cousin, replaced me as the Conservative MP in Vancouver Centre, she was a Social Credit MLA, unhappy with the political company she kept in her provincial caucus. I had suggested her as a candidate because our ridings overlapped. I bequeathed her a campaign team, a campaign office, and $100 000 in the riding association's campaign funds. She won by 279 votes.

When the abortion bill was referred to the Senate in 1991, I had returned to Vancouver for therapy to treat my GST arthritis flare, serving as an advisor to Senator Lowell Murray, a former cabinet colleague and Leader of the Government in the Senate. But when I heard about the vote, I arranged to return to Ottawa.

There was no doubt as to how I would vote. In all three election campaigns in Vancouver Centre, where a member of my riding executive,

Betty Green, headed an active pro-life movement, I had told voters that, for personal reasons, I would choose not to have an abortion, but explained that this was my individual choice. I would not limit any other woman's right to make her choice.

As an MP I consistently voted against proposed abortion legislation, once flying back from the Coast on crutches. If asked, I told constituents that as a former Vancouver board member, I supported the stand of the YWCA, which was that the issue was "a private matter of conscience decided by a woman and a physician."

In particular, I believed that Bill C-43 dealing with abortion was a bad bill, poorly drafted to appease conflicting views in the caucus. In my mind, I had an image of a pregnant teenager in a remote northern town, who was far from medical or spiritual advice, and unable to gain access to medical services. She would be unable to choose because many doctors had written to senators that the legislation was so murky they were unwilling to perform the procedure. What real choice would she have?

As I was leaving my Vancouver condo for the airport, I received a call from my former secretary Wendy Waite, one of several members of my staff who had continued to work for Kim Campbell after her election. (Kim also took over my Ottawa apartment lease and furnishings, which suited us both; she needed a place to stay and I was too sick to deal with a household move.)

Wendy said that Kim wanted to speak to me, obviously about the abortion bill. I told her that I was en route to the airport and couldn't take the call. Wendy, who had created an oasis of serenity in my often-frantic office, agreed to call me at my Ottawa hotel the next day. When she did, I returned the call from my Senate office in Centre Block, since the bill was on my desk.

"Kim said [vote for the bill] or you'll hang me out to dry in the riding," my black book records. "I said that I had faced three elections [on the issue] and it could be dealt with. It was the best of all possible worlds— KC for, PC against." I told Kim that the Prime Minister had said it was a free vote. She replied: "I don't think a senator's free vote is as valid as an MP's because we have constituents." I was taken aback by her attitude.

But this, of course, is one reason we have an unelected Senate, so that members can take a sober second look at legislation, without pressure from either the electorate or angry political leaders who refuse to sign one's nomination papers. And a free vote is just that—a vote that one is free to make according to one's conscience.

When Campbell realized that I would not be swayed, she said, in a threatening voice that chilled me to the bone: *"You've been warned."* I sat frozen in my chair, aware from my past experience of the immense power cabinet ministers have to wreak havoc, should they choose to use it. "Heavy, heavy pressure," I noted in my black book.

Shivering with shock, for a fleeting moment I thought of giving in and voting for the bill.

When the Speaker called for the vote, however, most of the Liberal Opposition Senators stood in their place in the Red Chamber and voted No. I was the first senator on the government side to vote No, pushing myself up from my seat, Kim Campbell's warning ringing in my ears. It was only after the Speaker announced the vote was a tie that we realized Bill C-43 had been defeated, the first bill to be defeated in the Senate since 1961.

I returned to my office, still shaking, to have tea with Jean Pigott while Kim Campbell faced the cameras. Later we learned that Prime Minister Brian Mulroney was furious with other Conservative Senators, but not with me, since he knew I would probably vote against the bill. He was angry at the Tory Senators who had blindsided him.

Advised by Jean to keep a low profile, I returned to Vancouver to join External Relations Minister Monique Landry at a ceremony at the UBC Centre for Human Settlements. At my Vancouver home, I found a fax from Lowell Murray advising me that I had been removed from my position as a western senator on the important Special Joint Committee Amending the Constitution of Canada. My replacement was Senator Jim Kelleher, from Sault Ste. Marie. "Real west, the Sault," I noted in my black book.

When I called Lowell and asked him why, he responded simply: "Because you voted and left." I called the PMO—no answer. Finally, I called a friend, Nick Hills, editor of the *Vancouver Sun*, and went public with my "punishment."

Then the fat was in the fire. People phoned. They wrote. They thought Lowell's action was unfair. Senator Murray, who faces television cameras like a deer caught in automobile headlights, eyes shining, defended his position. And I defended mine.

The flap eventually blew over, but later I found malicious stories circulating in the media and in books, including Kim's own, that I had sprung a trap on the Justice Minister, announcing I was leaving town, then creeping back secretly to cast my vote, like some evil villain.

Kim and I have never discussed the vote, and, since it was taken, we have rarely discussed any issue. I did not support her successful bid for the leadership of the Progressive Conservative Party. Nor, serving as a commentator on the leadership race for the CBC, did I work against her. Cousin Marg and I have other family matters to discuss.

Back in the Senate Chamber, Madam's voice skips smoothly over the politically polished phrases. I wonder who "held the pen" or was principal author of the document, with its innocuous promises, and why, given the sheer drama of the event—the last legislative agenda before the end of the millennium, the final chance to create a vivid canvas of Canada 2000 with its multicoloured faces and grand vistas and powerful silent spaces—we get rice gruel instead.

Adrienne had called me at my Vancouver home when I was first nominated for MP to ask me why I was running. "I think it would be like being nibbled to death by ducks," she said, which was exactly what it *was* like. I was drawn to her because of her Hong Kong background and my Shanghainese birthplace.

She and John Ralston Saul once came to my house for dinner at my round table, Chinese style. I served them Malcolm's Chowder—the fish chowder that fishermen cook out on the fishing grounds—with green salad, white wine, and sourdough bread. Of course I was making a statement: this was a coastal Canadian dinner!

In case you're curious, here's the recipe for Malcolm's Chowder, named after my fisherman son-in-law. First, you peel and parboil good firm spuds, such as Yukon Gold, which have been chopped up. You then pour off about half the water, until what remains in the pot is slushy, and add chopped onions and cook for a few minutes. For consistency, throw in a "whoosh" of rice grains. If I had ever measured a "whoosh" it would probably be a tablespoon. Add some chopped-up white fish, such as cod or snapper or even sole, with a touch of dill and salt and pepper and cook slowly for about five minutes. Add butter and two cups or so of milk and heat to the simmer point, but not to the boil. Remove from heat and serve with a whoosh of Parmesan cheese if you like it or not if you don't, and serve.

Adrienne and John seemed to enjoy Malcolm's Chowder, spooning it down with little conversation. Twenty years later, when Paul and I went to Rideau Hall for the traditional reception after the Throne Speech, and went through the receiving line, John said: "Mmm . . . The best fish chowder!" Truly a tribute to Malcolm.

In the 1980s, after I was elected an MP, I visited my friend Dawn MacDonald, then editor of *City Woman* in Toronto, who was invited to dinner that evening at Adrienne's home. Adrienne sent word through Dawn that she would like to invite me to dinner, too, but she couldn't because it would disrupt her table, which was set up for six people.

I didn't mind the non-invitation but did puzzle over the explanation; in the West, you invited unexpected guests to pull up a chair and take potluck or you didn't mention dinner at all. Easterners certainly had peculiar manners.

Once I visited Paris while serving as an MP on a parliamentary committee during Adrienne's term as Agent General for the Government of Ontario and she invited me for dinner. I went round the corner from my modest Left Bank hotel and bought a bottle of wine from a small store and took it with me in its brown bag. Adrienne received it in her elegant residence with perfectly raised eyebrows; talk about carrying coals to Newcastle! The wine discreetly disappeared in the patronizing presence of a servant summoned to remove the offending item, making me feel very gauche, and we went out for dinner.

Adrienne ordered dinner in expert French and proved to be an engaging and interesting host with a clear grasp of her job and Ontario's trade interests, which included the need to counter the oppressive and overbearing presence of her counterparts from Quebec, who were draping the blue-and-white fleur-de-lis over Canada-France relations at every opportunity.

This aspect of Adrienne as a shrewd and knowledgeable diplomatic in-fighter, clashing rapiers with her Quebec colleagues in defence of her province and country, was unexpected. I realized many of us had stereo-typed her as a television personality with limited and shallow knowledge, gleaned in eight-minute interviews and ten-second sound bites. Wrong. When, as Minister of International Trade, I was grappling with arrogant

European politicians and Canada-Europe trade issues, I wished I had Adrienne on my team, but by then she had returned to her cultural career.

I also found Adrienne's nature warm and practical. When I worried that my then teenage son might be stranded in Paris, she sent subway directions to her place and served as den mother to several young Canadian sons and daughters who endured their parents' anxieties. It turned out my son didn't need her subway directions or hospitality, but Adrienne's response was a great comfort to his mom.

In the Red Chamber, the Governor General drones: "We stand before a new century confident in the promise of Canada for our children and grandchildren." I look around to see who else is present. The audience is similarly colourless, composed mainly of grey-haired senators and privy councillors, former ministers now working as lobbyists for corporations and special interest groups.

There is former Solicitor General Robert Kaplan, whom I once nailed to the wall over his comment that soliciting was good for the chip-wagon business in Lower Town because everyone knew that sex made people hungry.

Missing is former Liberal Finance Minister Mitchell Sharp, still working for Prime Minister Jean Chrétien as a dollar-a-year man, although at age 87 his stamina is fading. I was told of this by former House of Commons Speaker, Lloyd Francis, a spry 82 himself, who radiated the collegiality that former MPs share. As Finance Minister, Mitchell Sharp briefed me, then with the *Vancouver Sun*, on the budget priorities in advance of actual budget day, since I had travelled so far and had never broken a confidence.

Up in the Public Gallery are my guests, the Morrison girls, Jean Pigott and Grete Hale, daughters of pioneer Ottawa baker G. Cecil Morrison, both in their seventies and not looking it. Jean Pigott was my political mentor, a former MP who talked me into running for the Conservatives, when Joe Clark couldn't, by telling me the most whopping lies. She phoned me in my kitchen in Vancouver and said in her kind, confidential voice: "You don't know me, but my name is Jean Pigott and I'm an MP and I know you're worried about your son JP."

She told me that I could look after him in Ottawa because I would be excused from night House duty. I wasn't. She said MP Steve

Paproski's five children would babysit him. They never did. She said JP could go to Ashbury, an Ottawa private school where he would have hot lunches. JP liked public school and refused the hot-lunch option. But I loved Jean regardless.

Jean is one of those politicians who revere Parliament; she liked being an MP, and would have graced the Senate but had a short parliamentary life, defeated after serving less than a full term. But she became a political force for women in politics, whatever their party. We call her The Godmother.

"Keep your eye on the Leader and your back to the wall," she warned me as I nervously started my first term as a green MP. "Spend time in the House of Commons—it is the only way to learn the rules," she admonished. "Trust your instincts, your gut reactions," she said when the issues were confusing and the pressures were great. "They are what got you elected."

My favourite story about The Godmother came from the time when she was responsible for patronage appointments during Joe Clark's aborted government and had an office in the Langevin Building near the entrance where the RCMP were stationed. One day an RCMP officer told Jean there was concern about a letter written to the PM threatening violence, mayhem, and assorted mischief. Jean listened carefully. "What specifically did this person complain about?" she asked. The RMCP officer told her. "That's my cousin," she said. And it was!

In 1984, Queen Elizabeth read the Throne Speech in the Red Chamber, with Prince Philip in attendance in the smaller Throne chair. I met members of the Royal Family several times as a reporter and a politician and they sometimes had a faintly puzzled haven't-we-met-before look when I was introduced.

My favourite memory of them was of their trip to the Northwest Territories in 1970 to celebrate the Centennial of the date in 1870 when the young Dominion purchased Rupert's Land and the North-Western Territory from Britain for £300 000. I was commissioned to write a history of the Royal visit for the NWT government and trailed along behind the Royal Tour with the rest of the media. At Tuktoyaktuk, the Hercules aircraft transporting the press corps broke down and the

Royal plane took off for Inuvik without the news media, whose members spent an uncomfortable night sleeping on the floor of the gymnasium in the local school.

Meanwhile, I had slipped down to the local airplane dock on a channel of the Mackenzie River and hitched a ride on a floatplane chartered by retired soldier Major-General Richard Rohmer, returning to Inuvik across the channels of the delta in near white-out conditions.

The next day, I found the press corps had dwindled to Jake Ootes of the NWT government, a hungover Canadian Press reporter who had missed the press plane, and me. The delighted Royals toured Inuvik *sans* media, with the exception of the three of us skulking in the background.

They had a wonderful time. Charles skidded down the freshly waxed floors in Inuvik General Hospital, freed from snooping photographers. In the fur shop, located between the Eskimo Inn and the town laundry, Princess Anne swirled a muskrat hat on her finger and studied the effect in a mirror until her father told her to move on.

The Queen had a run in her stocking and her lady-in-waiting rode in a pickup truck. There was a sherry reception and community lunch in the gaily painted Family Hall, attended by Indian chiefs from neighbouring settlements and their wives, wearing print dresses and parkas and mukluks. One chief wore his treaty uniform, blue pants with a red strip and a jacket with yellow lapels.

The Royals were relaxed, smiling, happy. I was thrilled with my exclusive story, since the CP reporter had retreated to his bunk, until Commissioner Stu Hodgson got hold of my copy and excised every item that might appear un-Royal. No runs in Her Majesty's stocking for him!

As the Throne Speech drones on, I think of other members of the Royal Family I met in my political career. Vancouver's Expo 86 brought many dignitaries to Canada and since Expo was in my riding of Vancouver Centre I hosted many of them as a Canadian cabinet minister. It was great fun, and furthermore I had a chance to sleep in my own bed in my own home.

Prince Charles and Princess Diana, the featured guests, opened Expo 86. I served as Minister Escort to the Royal Couple at several functions. I was struck by how professionally they worked the crowd at

City Hall, each doing "walkabout" among the crowd on one side of the walk, then crossing over to work the other side, with a murmured exchange as they met in the middle.

Diana had the most beautiful ankles I have ever seen, rising from her slim feet like fluted sculptures. Jim and I escorted Charles and Di to a rock concert, where they clapped their hands in perfect time while Premier Bill Bennett, leg swinging awkwardly, managed to miss the beat. When we took them back to the Pan Pacific Hotel, Diana removed her Walkman earplugs from her ears in the elevator and said wistfully: "People expect me to like all rock music—but I don't!"

I accompanied Prince Charles to Gordon House, a neighbourhood house offering programs for street kids, seniors, immigrants, and others in Vancouver's West End. Charles sat in the daycare centre, looking very tanned and tailored, allowing young three- and four-year-olds to climb all over him. He told the ladies in the knitting circle that his grandfather knit, too; I realized, after a moment, that he meant King George VI.

But when he asked a group of teenage homosexual prostitutes enrolled in a construction course what they did, I held my breath, afraid one of the neon-haired kids would tell him. Whew!

The Queen and Prince Philip came, too. While Premier Vander Zalm and his wife Lillian were their hosts for the event, Jack Webster accompanied me on my Minister Escort duties. The six of us sat at the head table, with Webster next to the Prince, and the Premier and his wife on each side of the Queen. Sitting next to the Premier, I was so close to the Queen when she stood at the microphone to speak that I could admire the needlework on her pink dress.

It was about the time Fiji announced it was leaving the Commonwealth and the Queen was cross. When she got up from the table, her purse slipped from her lap and she ordered Philip in a sharp voice to retrieve it for her, which he did, since the Premier did not seem inclined to do so, and I was afraid to bend down in case I couldn't get back up.

When Jack and I escorted them to the door of their hotel suite in the Four Seasons, the Queen turned and murmured: "So kind." We heard Prince Philip telling Her Majesty: "Interesting chap. Says he's a sheep farmer from Salt Spring Island."

They later sent me a signed pair of photos of each of them encased in a blue leather folder. I wish I could remember where I put them.

One of my favourite visitors to Expo 86, although I didn't expect her to be, was Princess Margaret. When my sister Norah and I were little girls, the Royal Princesses Elizabeth and Margaret were our role models. Elizabeth was the grave and responsible older sister, just like me. Margaret Rose was saucy and sassy, just like my little sister.

My ministerial assistant Ray McAllister suggested a brilliant concept. Since Princess Margaret was known as a patron of the arts, we would invite the BC arts community, performers and patrons, to the state dinner I was hosting for her. The usual politicians were shuffled off into a side room, and a receiving line of actors, artists, playwrights, and musicians greeted the Princess instead. Since I couldn't imagine what Margaret and I would have in common, I asked Hugh Pickett, a well-known arts entrepreneur and friend of Ginger Rogers, Mitzi Gaynor, Marlene Dietrich, and others, to sit beside her at the head table.

I met the Princess at the hotel door and escorted her through the receiving line of assembled artists, all spiffed up for the occasion in black tie and formal gowns. Margaret appeared delighted with the opportunity to talk to them. During the first course, she was entertained by the charming Hugh on her right.

Then she turned to me on her left and uttered the fateful words: "Do you have children?" Well! The next course was entirely taken up with "my son the furniture maker" (hers) and "my son the physics student" (mine), and "my daughter Sarah" (hers) and "my daughter Jane" (mine). When we finished discussing the virtues of our children she asked about my family. I told her my father was a Canadian and my mother a fourth-generation South African. "I've visited that country," Princess Margaret commented, as if the whole world didn't know she had been accompanied on that visit by Peter Townsend, the man she gave up for duty and her royal prerogatives. "Of course, I can't return under the current *repugnant* regime," she added, referring to apartheid with revulsion and destroying the myth that members of the Royal Family don't make political comments.

She told me that on an earlier visit to British Columbia she had been given an island by the provincial government but added, wistfully, that she had eventually given it back. When I asked her why she had returned it—the island is now a park near Saturna—the Princess said candidly that it was too far away for her own use and that her uncle had been criticized when he sold his Alberta ranch. It took me a second to recall that her uncle was King Edward VIII, who gave up the ranch and the throne for Wallis Simpson. Clearly family property is an issue for the Royal Family as well as for ordinary Canadians.

We proceeded to discuss the upcoming wedding of Sarah Ferguson and Prince Andrew and other delicious happenings and when the trumpet blare ended the dinner we were both disappointed. It was the most enjoyable state dinner I ever attended. It was also the only one where the guests sent me thank-you notes, dozens of them, all thrilled with the evening. One of my favourite artists, Gathie Falk—I have one of her paintings—sent me an exquisite note illustrated with one of her own flower sketches. Right in the centre is carelessly stamped MINT, my ministerial registry stamp. As I stared at this desecration I wanted to write Gathie back. "Thank you for your thank-you note, but can I please, please have another one?"

British Prime Minister Margaret Thatcher also visited Expo 86 in Vancouver. I was her Minister Escort, assigned to accompany her during her visit. It was one of the most exhausting days of my life. I met her at the door of the Concorde, which had jetted the Prime Minister and her husband Dennis to Vancouver from London. She shook my hand enthusiastically, obviously briefed that I was not a "wet," her name for weak-kneed, lily-livered cabinet ministers who failed to show sufficient gumption in the exercise of their duties. "My dear," she exclaimed. "What a marvellous trip. We brought a plane-load of British businessmen with us. They paid for the trip, so it didn't cost Dennis and me a penny." Our housewifely souls thrilled to this small economy.

In the limousine to the Hotel Vancouver, she recounted how she had spent the morning riding in a crane bucket, dedicating a new construction site in the City. I gathered that she had ridden in one of those huge earth-moving shovels clearing a site in London's financial district. The thought of being swooped into the air by an earth-moving machine made me feel queasy. At the door of her hotel suite, she turned and asked: "Would you like to come in for a drink?"

I was startled. "Prime Minister, I have a protocol briefing book that covers every situation, but it doesn't say how I should respond to your kind invitation," I confessed, confused. Surely she was tired after her trip? Or was it rude to refuse? "Do come in," she waved me through the door. "I'm having one." So we did.

That afternoon, she gave a magnificent Rule Britannia–style speech. As she turned to leave the stage, a woman in the crowd below called out: "Mrs. Thatcher! I am one of your constituents." Instantly the Prime Minister turned, stooped down, and shook the woman's hand, holding up the line of dignitaries exiting the stage as she chatted with a voter.

I recognized the reaction. Once, during a fire alarm in a hotel in Newfoundland, as I escaped down the fire stairs in my flannel nightie, someone called out: "Pat, I'm from Vancouver Centre." I stopped and pushed past the guests fleeing down the stairs to shake my constituent's hand, too. Good thing the fire was a false alarm.

That evening I accompanied the Prime Minister and Dennis Thatcher to a performance of England's Royal Ballet, which she watched entranced, while Dennis discreetly snoozed and I watched the audience watching Thatcher. During the intermission I told her Princess Margaret had also visited Expo. "That lot," sniffed the Prime Minister. "It's her job."

After the performance she went backstage to thank the performers before returning to the hotel for the British formal reception. The Prime Minister stood at the door of the reception hall and shook the hand of every guest, which took a long time since she waited for the members of the ballet to show up after changing from their costumes into street clothes, while husband DT, as he was called, discreetly downed gin-and-tonics and discussed the energy business with me until security officers packed him off to bed.

Finally, exhausted, I found the Prime Minister chatting up her guests, gin-and-tonic clasped firmly in her hand, and implored her: "Prime Minister, as your Minister Escort I can't go to bed until you do. I am dead on my feet. Would you *please* call it a night?" She obligingly did. As we rode up in the elevator I calculated that she must have been up at least 24 hours. We said goodbye at her door. "If you come to

London, do come and have tea with me," she said graciously. I promised to do so, knowing it was unlikely. Prime ministers' schedules rarely permit drop-in guests from the Commonwealth.

President Ronald Reagan and Prime Minister Brian Mulroney were great pals. I was there the night they sang "When Irish Eyes Are Smiling." It was one of Canada's formula bilingual events. Thank Heavens they didn't sing their song in French. Some of us in the Cabinet poked fun at the President, with his dyed brown hair and his cue-cards, which he used when he met with us in the Cabinet Room, where the Prime Minister told jokes about Sir John A. and George Brown. Clearly the President didn't have a clue about either Canada's first Prime Minister or the famous editor of the *Globe*.

But Reagan gave a marvellous speech in the House of Commons to a joint Commons-Senate audience, much better written than the one we are hearing from Madam. And I felt remorseful when we learned that at the time he was suffering from the early effects of Alzheimer's.

Governor General Clarkson's script may lack excitement, but her performance is certainly more professional than some of her predecessors' in the role. Former Governor General Ed Schreyer was our Canadian High Commissioner in Australia when I paid a bilateral visit as Minister of International Trade in 1987. I was struck by how little he seemed to know about the country that he was appointed to serve as Canada's diplomatic representative. Once he accompanied me to the Parliament Buildings in Canberra to pay a courtesy call on Prime Minister Bob Hawkes. As we waited in the lobby, we heard a raucous debate on the audio system reporting the activities of Australia's legislative assembly. Anxious to know what parliamentary crisis faced Hawkes, I asked Schreyer what the uproar was about. "I don't know," shrugged our High Commissioner.

This is highly unusual; normally a Canadian minister is briefed on a country's issues from the minute he or she steps into the diplomatic limousine on the airport tarmac. On the plane from Canberra to Brisbane, where I was scheduled to visit the Expo 88 site, I looked out the window toward Australia's legendary interior and asked our High Commissioner: "What's out there?" Schreyer waved a dismissive hand. "Nothing," he said.

I had my turn at this game. When he accompanied me to the airport for my return to Canada, he asked me to convey his concern that he had not been notified of his next posting by Joe Clark, the Minister for External Affairs. I didn't tell him that Joe had told me he had nothing in mind for the ex–Governor General. The issue was not his patronage appointment by Trudeau, Joe said, but the assessment by his senior diplomats that Schreyer had performed his duties as High Commissioner in an undistinguished manner.

How do you greet an ex-politician whom you have formally met when he or she was in office? I faced that dilemma when I sat at a table in a London hotel, eating my breakfast, and realized that the man seated at the next table with his wife was Bob Hawkes, former Prime Minister of Australia. We exchanged one of those don't-we-know-each-other looks. Finally I approached him and said: "Prime Minister, I met you several times when I was in Prime Minister Brian Mulroney's Cabinet." (Actually, once, at a conference in the South Pacific, where I was head of the Canadian delegation, he asked me: "What's a pretty face like you doing here?")

Jumping to his feet, he invited me to join his wife and him for breakfast and we chatted about common Canadian-Australian concerns, such as BC salmon exports and lumber shipments. He had warm words of praise for Brian Mulroney. In turn, I praised Hawkes' trade policies, tactfully ignoring what diplomats call "bilateral irritants." He encouraged me to drop in on him when I next visited Australia.

The Governor General is now making promises she knows in her heart can't be guaranteed. "The Government is committed to prudent fiscal management. It will never let the nation's finances get out of control," she states flatly. She would never have accepted that statement without challenge in her former life as a television interviewer. I look up at the Press Gallery to see who is smiling.

As a journalist in the 1960s I looked down on the politicians from the Press Gallery above and behind the Speaker's Chair and wondered what on earth ever possessed grown men (there were very few women) to rant and rave at each other, waving their fists on the floor of the House of Commons. The Senate was not even on the radar screen.

I still keep in touch with many of my journalistic colleagues and write sporadically for newspapers and magazines. I also serve on the advisory council of the Sing Tao School of Journalism at the University of British Columbia, which offers a master's program in journalism. From time to time I have worked as a political commentator on television and radio, and I admire the on-air professionalism of television journalists such as Pamela Wallin, Peter Mansbridge, and Lloyd Robertson. Their ability to process, absorb, and analyze a steady stream of new information during election television reports is astonishing.

But in politics I am most often the interviewee, not the interviewer. The best print interviewer for overall balance is journalist Robert Hunter, co-founder of Greenpeace. As writers and columnists, Barbara Yaffe of the *Vancouver Sun*, Mark Steyn of the *National Post*, and Hugh Winsor of the *Globe and Mail* are usually a good read.

The best television interviewer I have ever had is Brian Stewart, because his intelligent questions coax intelligent answers from his guests. One of the most difficult is CBC's Hana Gartner, who gave me the impression that she was already thinking of her second question while I answered her first.

Viewers told me they liked my CBC commentary during the 1993 Progressive Conservative leadership convention that made Kim Campbell Canada's first woman prime minister. But my most listless performance was during the subsequent election, when I was assigned the role of western analyst for CTV. In that election, no Conservatives were elected west of the Lakehead and only two—Jean Charest and Elsie Wayne—won seats at all. I had precious little to analyze!

I see Elsie now behind the Bar, along with other Members of Parliament, at the entrance to the Senate Chamber, where I too stood to hear the Throne Speech when I was an MP. During the Speech from the Throne, elected MPs are unable to cross the barrier, symbolically separating the House of Commons from the privileged Senate, a tradition from the 1600s still in force as we prepare for 2000. Leaders such as Preston Manning and leadership hopefuls like Allan Rock crowd together.

Under the harsh television lights, the Governor General is coming to the end of her Throne Speech, saying that as Canadians we can look to our past with pride and to our future with confidence. "We will build the twenty-first century together," she says.

Canada's agenda for the beginning of the new millennium is revealed. As the old Peggy Lee song goes, "Is that all there is?"

CHAPTER 20

Canada: Whose Country Is It, Anyway?

T R A D E   S E C R E T:
*Much will have to change in Canada
if the country is to stay the same.*
—Political economist Abraham Rotstein

On the eve of our sixty-fifth birthday, as the final chapter of this book was written, my brother Jim and I separately visited the graves of our parents in the small cemetery located in the former schoolyard on Saturna Island. The original school had been sited by the simple expedient of having the schoolchildren walk from each end of the island toward the centre and building the school where they met. When the school was later moved down into the valley, the yard was recycled to its present and permanent use.

It is a do-it-yourself kind of cemetery. There is a small, unlocked shed containing a shovel (we dig our own graves, or at least those of our family members) and a plywood coffin for emergency use. The list of future occupants who have paid their five dollars for their burial lot, plus an unspecified donation to the Community Club for upkeep, is currently maintained by the baker, Jon Guy, whose farm and country bakery are next door. We have faith in this procedure; so far it has worked.

Standing beside our parents' red granite headstone, under a vigorous young fir tree, each of us whispered: "Thank you." For bearing us in the first place. For the toil and sacrifices paid by our Canadian grandparents and great-grandparents when they emigrated to Canada, some on the cholera-stricken coffin ships from Ireland. For our health, our wonderful children, our happy marriages late in life to his Brenda and my Paul, both longtime friends and lovers. But most of all, we gave thanks for that most precious gift, Canadian citizenship. The right to live and love and work and pray and achieve and contribute in a country so awesome in its magnificence, so generous in its opportunities, that we have been able to live in peace and plentitude ever since they brought us from our birthplace, Shanghai, to Canada, our home. Jim and I argued for the right to our Canadian citizenship and won it under the laws of the day. We were always the last shipboard family cleared through immigration, sighed my mother, South African-born, with three children born in China and a Canadian-born husband with a British passport.

Yet, as the new millennium begins, our most precious asset of citizenship appears undervalued and debased. Many Canadians, including my own family members, hold dual passports, retaining their citizenship in other countries as well as Canada. Canadian passports are bought and sold around the world, used to penetrate our borders, undermine our country, and attack our friends. As an adjunct professor I sign applications for legal passports, and I marvel at how easy it is to acquire this key that unlocks a treasure of a country.

The devaluation of Canadian citizenship is occurring within our own country and institutions, by our own actions. We permit illegal immigrants to abuse our proud record of providing refuge to people who face persecution in their countries of origin. We find ourselves unable to deport criminals and others to whom we have denied entry. We spend, according to media reports, up to $8000 a month in British Columbia supporting in detention the children of people who have defied our laws and landed illegally in Canada while other children, Canadian citizens, lack adequate food and shelter.

We ignore the real hardships faced by legal immigrants to this country as they struggle to adapt, to learn, to be accepted. One of the most moving moments of my political career came when, attending a Canadian citizenship ceremony, I heard social worker and citizenship judge Angela Kan, who immigrated to Canada, tell her audience of hopeful new Canadians: "I have stood in your shoes. I know what it is like to be homesick, to be without family or friends, to stand in a telephone booth with a directory written in a language you can't read, a language you must learn if you are to feel at home in your new country."

As an MP I was unable to explain to a tiny, weeping South Asian woman why her son, an unemployed taxi driver in Bombay, couldn't join her in Canada. Once my constituency secretary Marjorie Lewis and I worked long hours to ensure the entry to Canada of the wives and children of some Polish seamen who had jumped ship and claimed refugee status here. Eventually the families arrived, happy, exhausted, unsure of where they were. But one wife didn't come. Her husband stood there, dazed; he understood the cost of citizenship.

Canadian Caucasians—I'm advised that this is the politically correct name for those, like me, of bog Irish ancestry or European descent—often fail to acknowledge that other races may have arrived here before us, particularly in British Columbia, home to an Aboriginal, British, American, Scandinavian, and Asian population when it joined Confederation in 1871.

My longtime friend Diana Lam is a third-generation Canadian who resents having to tick off her ethnic background on Canadian census forms. Her grandfather, Fong Dick Man, arrived in British Columbia about the same time as my grandfather Carney did, more than a century ago. Grandfather Fong operated a horse courier service on the forest road between the towns of Vancouver and New Westminster. He attended the Chinese Methodist Church to learn English and eventually became a minister of the Methodist and then the United Church.

Diana's maternal great-grandfather was a governor of part of present-day Taiwan. He sent his six daughters to Hong Kong to learn how to read and write both English and Chinese, a remarkable feat in the 1880s. One of the daughters, Diana's grandmother Jenny, came to Canada, sending away to England for books for her own daughters to read. One of them, Diana's mother Anna Fong Dickman (the surname changed, as did Kearney to Carney), became the first Canadian-Chinese nurse in British Columbia. Her aunt Lavina was the first Canadian-Chinese teacher in British Columbia. A third sister, Diana's Aunt Esther, was the first Canadian-Chinese woman to graduate from the University of British Columbia, as did Diana, at about the same time as me.

Yet when the wave of immigrants from Hong Kong in the 1980s and early 1990s washed through Vancouver, it was not uncommon for BC-born Anna Fong Dickman Lam to find a real estate broker on the front steps of her elegant West Side home asking: "You speak English, lady?"

The question of who should have the gift of Canadian citizenship still has not been resolved in a manner acceptable to all Canadians.

Each immigration minister is besieged by events—such as the arrival of boat people—and lobbied by various ethnic groups to make changes. No other issue has a more constant place on the front pages of newspapers or in MPs' constituency offices in the major cities; in Vancouver Centre, immigration problems were 70 per cent of my MP caseload.

Another question now facing Canadians is equally troubling: Should Canadians have different kinds of citizenship, with different rights, laws, and institutions for different Canadians, depending on race, religion, or sexual preference? And if so, what should these be and for whom?

This again is not really a new issue. If citizenship is defined as the right to vote in a federal election for the governing party, Canadian women did not win this right until 1918 and were not deemed "persons," able to sit in the Senate of Canada, until 1929, when the Famous Five[1] took their case to the British Privy Council and won, reversing an earlier decision by the Supreme Court of Canada. Canadian Chinese did not have the right to vote until 1947. Canadian aboriginals finally won it in 1960.

Canadians faced this dilemma again with the 1987 Meech Lake Accord, which recognized Quebec as a "distinct society" in order to acknowledge the Quebec French-Canadian majority's sense of itself as a community, separate from the enveloping embrace of the Canadian national community. This was 148 years after Lord Durham, appointed by Britain as Governor General, described Canada as two nations warring in the bosom of a single state.

Meech imploded when both Manitoba and Newfoundland failed to ratify the agreement, which was signed by the 10 premiers. Whatever the history books say about white feathers in the Manitoba legislature or buck-passing in the Newfoundland and Labrador House of Assembly, many Canadians believe the Accord failed because Quebec used the Constitution's "notwithstanding" or "opting-out" clause in 1988 to reverse a Supreme Court decision upholding English-language rights in Quebec, protecting French-only language legislation instead. Canadians who were faced with bilingual signs on federal institutions outside Quebec were not prepared to accept different laws for Canadians in different parts of Canada.

Similarly, the smorgasbord of constitutional changes proposed in Joe Clark's 1991 Charlottetown Accord was rejected by a majority of

Canadians a year later, partly because different rights were proposed for different Canadian citizens. In British Columbia, where every riding turned thumbs down, main factors were the entrenchment of Quebec's share of national institutions, despite its declining French-language population, at the expense of growing provinces such as British Columbia, and undefined aboriginal rights, which had the potential to affect every community.

Important as these issues were, Canadians paid a high price for addressing them. During my years in both Houses of Parliament, no other issue, with the possible exception of free trade, has taken up as much management time and effort as constitutional reform (read the Quebec problem) at the highest levels of government, with few positive results to show for it. Prime Minister Mulroney was basically a one-issue person, focused on one major file at a time. When Meech Lake was on his mind, other Canadian problems, such as the national debt and the economy, became secondary. The essential issue of citizenship—some confuse it with the Canadian identity—was ignored.

Political scientist Alan Cairns raised the issue of the growing importance of citizenship before the Standing Senate Committee on Social Affairs, Science and Technology in April 1992. He argued that our *1982 Constitution Act* included the Charter of Rights in an effort to "create, via the Charter, a single uniform rights-bearing Canadian citizenship."[2] This, of course, reflected the view of then Prime Minister Pierre Trudeau, who strongly opposed special status for Quebec.

"The idea that the Charter was instituted just to protect Canadians from their governments is a mythology," stated Professor Cairns. "We would not have a Charter had Prime Minister Trudeau not thought that it was to be a fundamental institution of national unity and national integration. Therefore, he had a political, social theory of how rights could unite us and strengthen our conceptions of ourselves as belonging to a pan-Canadian community."[3]

This view of Canadians as equal was also reflected in the 1982 amending formula, which recognized the equality of the provinces, and thus the inherent equality of Canadians in terms of citizenship. During my political career, I have been a member of several parliamentary committees on the Constitution where academics argued that since many provinces entered Confederation on different terms, provinces are in fact *not* equal: tiny New Brunswick, which has 10 senators, has more votes in the Senate—and therefore more clout—than British Columbia, with its six senators. Tinier Prince Edward Island has four!

Generally, however, Canadians appear to have accepted the ideal of Canadian citizens having equal rights in common, notwithstanding "notwithstanding" clauses. The ideal of equality has been the single most powerful force driving my own political career, which has centred on "equal treatment" for British Columbians, be it access to federal decision-makers, federal funding, or representation in national institutions.

What, then, to do about aboriginal rights, an issue very much on the public agenda, with some 50 treaties under negotiation in British Columbia, aboriginal fishing rights creating waves in Nova Scotia, and aboriginals demanding renegotiation of existing treaty rights in other parts of Canada? Cairns warned: "We are heading towards a situation—and the numbers are a bit vague—where up to one million Canadians, and possibly somewhat more than that, will exist in Canada with some status somewhat different from the rest of us."[4]

Professor Cairns pursues his argument in his new book, *Citizens Plus: Aboriginal Peoples and the Canadian State*, where he suggests that multiple identities are both "possible and desirable."[5] Aboriginals can have it both ways, with one of several aboriginal identities and an identity as a Canadian, Cairns argues, noting that "aboriginal peoples are also part of the very communities with whom they are bargaining"[6] in the contemporary treaty process.

Aboriginal and non-aboriginal Canadians are dependent on each other, he says, quoting the high rate of intermarriage; by the mid-1950s nearly 37 per cent of all Indian marriages in British Columbia were with non-Indians.[7] Cairns concludes: "We are all part of one another, although not always harmoniously so."[8]

Not everyone would agree with this view; Canadians have largely rejected the concept of "multiple identities" for French Canadians and for other ethnic groups, despite our lipservice to multiculturalism. But few would argue with Cairns' argument that citizenship is a critical unifying force.

The concept of aboriginal rights and self-government was recognized but not defined in the *1982 Constitution Act*, which enshrined existing aboriginal rights and treaties and introduced a new phrase, the "aboriginal peoples of Canada," which included Indian, Inuit, and Métis people.

Cairns pointed out that this was a complete turnaround from the position of Jean Chrétien in 1969, when, as Minister of Indian Affairs and Northern Development in the Trudeau government, he introduced a "white paper" that suggested that status Indians be given equality, in terms of citizenship, by incorporating them into the general Canadian citizenry and abolishing Indian Affairs. "The goal was really a symmetrical citizenry, existing in a symmetrical federalism,"[9] Cairns explained. But the concept of equality of citizenship, of integration into the Canadian value system, was rejected by aboriginal Canadians, who had cause to fear the result.

Instead, they pressed to retain their own cultural values, and to create native institutions such as a separate aboriginal justice system. One problem is that with 10 distinct groups involving 50 languages spoken by Canada's Indians, and variations of a common tongue, Inuktitut, spoken by the Inuit, there is no common aboriginal culture. The new "talking" mace of the NWT Legislative Assembly recognizes that 10 languages are spoken in the Northwest Territories; non-aboriginal Canadians have trouble with two!

Land claims have been settled in Yukon, the Mackenzie Delta, and other parts of the NWT and form part of the new Inuit-dominated territory of Nunavut, whose leaders explicitly state their allegiance to Canada and to Canadian citizenship. It is less clear where the treaty process is taking us in British Columbia, where the Nisga'a Treaty, which came into force on May 11, 2000, establishes a Constitution, an aboriginal form of government, and the supremacy of Nisga'a law over federal and provincial law in 14 areas. These include Nisga'a citizenship; culture and language; property and lands; direct taxation; health, child, and family services; aboriginal healers; education from kindergarten to post-secondary education; wildlife, fisheries, and migratory birds management.

When the legislation was before the Senate, constitutional expert and former Supreme Court Justice Willard Estey warned that ratification of the treaty "could destabilize the legal framework on which the Canadian nation is built."[10] The treaty is facing court challenges on the grounds that it sets up a third order of government, which it is argued is unconstitutional. While negotiators claim that the Charter of Rights applies under Nisga'a, some aboriginal organizations are proposing that they have their own charters outside the Canadian Charter.

We may, at our peril, leave the issue for the courts to settle. It was the courts, or specifically the Supreme Court of Canada, that produced the 1997 *Delgamuukw* decision, which provided its first comprehensive statements on aboriginal title, or the right to the exclusive use and occupation of the land. The court said that to prove aboriginal title, a group must establish that it exclusively occupied the land in question when the British Crown asserted sovereignty over the land. For British Columbia, sovereignty runs from the time of the 1846 Oregon Treaty between Britain and the United States, which established the current Canada-US border west of the Rocky Mountains.

Legal experts say the Supreme Court's decision lacks clarity; no one really knows what it means. But when it applies to British Columbia, where land claims cover 95 per cent of the province, including major cities and transportation routes, the result is confusion, fear, and heightened expectations. Does *Delgamuukw* decree that almost all of British Columbia is under aboriginal lien, and that no development should take place for the decades it might take to negotiate treaties? What interim measures must be put in place to ensure that successful aboriginal claims will gain title to forests, fish, and mineral wealth, rather than clearcuts, ruined fish habitat, and mine tailings? Who pays the compensation?

When I was a journalist, the distinguished economist John Kenneth Galbraith told a UBC audience that all wars, essentially, were about real estate. I reported his speech in my business column in the *Vancouver Sun*. The desire for land was a driving force behind the Crusades, he explained. "The fact that Jerusalem was in the hands of the Infidels was a stimulant," said Galbraith. "But the Infidels had been in possession for some 400 years. It was not a matter of sudden urgency at the end of the 11th century."

Similarly, religious and real property conveyancing went hand in hand in the exploration of North America. "The Spaniards felt themselves commissioned by God to save the souls of the Indians and to take up land as their reward," Galbraith told the students. "The Catholics believed they had the right to rather large acreage, and the Protestants generally felt that religious merit lay with the hearth and the family farm."[11]

So, you might argue, we should return the land to the aboriginals, or pay suitable compensation for it. But others might argue that in a democracy with responsible government, this is a matter for the people and their politicians to determine, not for the courts to dictate. I believed politics was the prerogative of politicians until I met Chief Justice Antonio Lamer at Rideau Hall in 1998. We were attending a ceremony for the recipients of the Order of Canada, including my pal and former newspaper buddy Barry Broadfoot, author of many books about Canadians and their experiences.

I was uncomfortable because the ceremony was very formal, with black tie and long dresses, but I was in a business suit because I was on my way to the airport. The Chief Justice was seated in the first row in front of me. I noticed that he had trouble standing and had to be assisted to stay on his feet. Since I suffer from arthritis, at the reception after the ceremony I approached him, seated in a corner, to commiserate. He explained he suffered from a condition that made it difficult for him to stay on his feet for any length of time. Conversation trailed off. What do you talk to a Chief Justice about?

I thought of the *Delgamuukw* decision, which had greatly affected the treaty-making process in British Columbia. The problem was that nobody knew what the Supreme Court decision meant. So I said to the Chief Justice: "You certainly created some confusion with *Delgamuukw*."

"There was nothing confusing about it," he shot back. "We knew exactly what we were doing." Then he launched into a near tirade about the fact that the treaty process in British Columbia had been progressing very slowly and that both Bennett premiers, the father William and the son Bill, should have tackled the issue years ago instead of avoiding it.

I was shocked. In my view, any attempts by the premiers Bennett to deal with the treaty issue were purely political and constitutional. The Constitution of Canada before the *1982 Constitution Act* was the old *British North America Act*, a British statute, which asserts that responsibility for Indians lies with the federal government. Why would W.A.C. Bennett, Premier from 1952 to 1972, and later his son Bill, Premier from 1975 to 1986, take on such a controversial issue at a provincial level when, under the Constitution prevailing for most of the time, aboriginal affairs were a federal matter and aboriginal rights not yet recognized? The concept of aboriginal rights was not on the public mind when the Bennetts were BC premiers, although the issue had public advocates such as former Judge Tom Berger. Professor Cairns agrees that negotiating aboriginal treaties was not a public issue during the premiership of W.A.C. Bennett, and was barely being discussed when his son Bill was Premier, whatever the jurisdictional responsibilities were.

And what business was it of the Chief Justice anyway to assess what the provincial premiers do or fail to do in a field of federal jurisdiction?

In the face of such a forceful political attack from the Chief Justice, I did not know how to react. The Supreme Court is responsible for clarifying the law, not formulating public policy. The formulation of public policy is the role of elected governments that are accountable to the citizens. Writing laws is the business of Parliament. And Parliament did not have the issue before it in the form of legislation.

In 1999, the Supreme Court generously interpreted a 1763 declaration by the British government that the Mi'kmaq have the right to fish for a "moderate livelihood,"[12] overturning the decision of the trial judge who presided over 40 days of trial that reviewed 400 documents. This triggered a rush by Mi'kmaq fishermen to launch their boats and set out their lobster traps, despite federal government conservation regulations that left angry non-native fishermen tied to the dock and fishery conservation officers frustrated.

What's going on here? Who holds members of the Supreme Court accountable when their decisions cause social tensions and political upheaval without regard for parliamentary legislation or processes required to effect Court judgments? Who is setting the agenda here— an elected government, after debate in both Houses of Parliament, or nine judges sitting on the bench, serenely immune to the upheavals and anxieties created by their often arbitrary decisions? If Lamer and his colleagues want to change society by changing the laws, let them file their nomination papers, collect campaign funds, and run for elected office.

These Supreme Court decisions are splintering the concept of Canadian citizenship without consultation with Canadians. And in the kind of underhanded hypocrisy that pervades our legal system when it deals with gender issues, some of these laws may ensure that aboriginal women cannot acquire the equality rights that are due to them as Canadian citizens.

When the Nisga'a Treaty was before the Senate, I was consistently reassured by treaty negotiators that native women would have their rights protected because BC's Family Relations Act would determine division of matrimonial property on marriage breakup. But aboriginal women have told me that some male-dominated bands do not recognize women's property or inheritance rights; in many cases, therefore, there would be nothing to divide. When I ask for answers I receive no response. When aboriginal women ask the government for answers, they are referred back to their band councils.

Cairns told the Senate committee: "The creation of a single, uniform, rights-bearing definition of all Canadians has run into roadblocks in two communities . . . who think of themselves in national terms, the Quebec French-Canadian majority and the aboriginal peoples, although the aboriginal peoples are really many nations and it is misleading to speak of an aboriginal nation."

I would hasten to add that there is another community that has erected roadblocks to the equality concept of citizenship—the federal government itself. When West Coast native fishermen try to form coalitions with their non-native neighbours in order to manage the local fisheries on a community basis, they are cold-shouldered by federal Fisheries and Indian Affairs bureaucrats who are bent on implementing fishery policies on ethnic, or race-based, grounds.

Cairns said the issue we must face "is the nature of citizenship in a multinational Canada, which contains more than one set of peoples who think of themselves as being nations." He added: "What sense of community and what sense of sharing can survive or will survive a situation in which we have a fragmented citizenship, fragmented along the lines of different nationhood ways of thinking of ourselves? What kind of a nation state that wishes to care for all of us will survive?"

Some Canadian philosophers, such as John Ralston Saul, are focusing on the Canadian identity, or sense of self. Others emphasize that the land itself unites us. With respect, I disagree. My vision of Canada is a reflection of the specific places where I have lived and worked, including the frozen desert of the Arctic islands, the black-spruce valleys of the Kootenays, and the wild, witch-like forests of the Pacific Northwest.

It does not reflect the gentle landscapes of southern Ontario or the maritime provinces. However, I do have a sense of citizenship, of belonging, of being a Canadian, based partly on the inherited memory of my family's hard-won, toil-worn efforts to build their home here, partly on the companionship of other Canadians with their diversity of backgrounds, and always with gratitude for the opportunity to participate in the public life of a country that inspires such profound love among its people.

What kind of citizens will we be in the future? Splintered, or united? And can we overcome our differences to create a more compelling unity of purpose? I take hope from the experiences of my own province, formed from two separate maritime colonies, British Columbia and Vancouver Island, so hostile to each other that one imposed a head tax on the other, with a population described by British Governor Arthur Edward Kennedy as "those who are convicts and those who ought to be convicts."[13]

After an acrimonious union, British Columbia joined Canada in 1871, not for love, but for economic advantage and a railway, thus allowing five generations of my family to say, with great pride, that we are British Columbians and citizens of Canada, our Home Place.

Notes

CHAPTER 1—SHANGHAI

1 The name of the department was changed from External Affairs to Foreign Affairs and International Trade in 1993.

2 Some of this material is drawn from the memoirs of the author's mother, Dora Sanders Carney, *Foreign Devils Have Light Eyes: A Memoir of Shanghai 1933–39* (Toronto: Virgo Press, 1980); Additional material is excerpted from Pat Carney, "Pat Carney Goes Home to China," *City Woman* (September/October 1979) and published as an afterword in *Foreign Devils*.

3 Dora Sanders Carney, letters to her parents, circa 1936.

CHAPTER 2—MEI MEI

1 Byrne Hope Sanders, "My Point in Time," unpublished manuscript, circa 1970s.

2 Dora Sanders Carney, personal papers.

3 Sanders, "My Point in Time."

4 Personal journal of Richard Higham.

5 Sanders, "My Point in Time."

6 Dora Sanders Carney, personal papers.

7 Sanders, "My Point in Time."

8 Jolly Slasher, family newspaper produced by young Sanders and Highams.

9 Wilfrid Sanders, "Jolly Good Show: Early Ontario," unpublished manuscript, circa 1970s.

10 Sanders, "My Point in Time."

11 Dora Sanders Carney, "Great Harmony," circa 1980s, and "Merrily, Merrily," circa 1950s, unpublished manuscripts.

CHAPTER 3—HOME PLACE

1 O'Keefe's first wife was an Indian. His native and non-native descendants held their first family reunion in 2000, according to his granddaughter Eileen O'Keefe Giuliani.

2 Donald MacKay, *Flight From Famine: The Coming of the Irish to Canada* (Toronto: McClelland & Stewart, 1990), 14.

3 Jill Carney, personal papers of niece Jill, who has untitled newspaper clipping. Uncle Tom Carney's memoirs also provided insight into early Okanagan Valley life.

4 MacKay, *Flight From Famine*, 37.

5 As quoted in Dorothy Hewlett Gellatly's *A Bit of Okanagan History* (Kelowna: Orchard City Press and Calendar Co. Ltd., 1958), 5.

6 This material is from John James Carney's letters to his sisters from 1910 to 1976 and is now among Pat Carney's personal papers.

7 Newspaper clipping from the *Kelowna Courier* (undated), found among Catherine Carney's papers.

8 Dora Sanders Carney, letters to father Harry Sanders.

9 Bridget Carney's letter found in the personal papers of Leo Casey, son of Mary Monaghan who married Bridget's brother, Tom.

CHAPTER 4—YA YA

1 As quoted in Dorothy Hewlett Gallatly's *A Bit of Okanagan History* (Kelowna: Orchard City Press and Calendar Co., 1958), 5.

2 This story about my father's early life is gleaned from the personal papers of Dora Sanders and John James Carney, the author's parents.

3 *Kelowna Courier* newsclip, undated, among Catherine Carney's papers.

4 John James Carney, letter to his sister, Catherine, written 8 May 1917.

5 A reference to Canadian flying ace, Billy Bishop, a famous World War I hero.

6 John James Carney, letter to his sister, Catherine, written 8 May 1917.

7 *Kelowna Courier* newspaper clipping.

8 Dora Sanders Carney, "Merrily, Merrily," circa 1950s.

CHAPTER 7—JOURNALISM

1 Ian Macdonald and Betty O'Keefe, *The Mulligan Affair: Top Cop on the Take* (Surrey: Heritage House Publishing Company, 1997), 43.

2 The words are tremendous, hazardous, stupendous, and horrendous.

3 Pat Carney, "Anatomy of a Corporate Takeover," *Vancouver Sun*, 10 Feb. 1968, 6.

4 Pat Carney, *Vancouver Sun*, 13 Feb. 1967, 22. Sent to the author by Ainsworth Booksellers.

CHAPTER 8—GEMINI NORTH

1 Pat Carney, "Proposed Mackenzie Valley Developments and their Consequences," speech to Opportunity North Conference, sponsored by Northern Alberta Development Council, Peace River, Alberta, 28 Nov. 1975.

2 Gemini North Ltd. report reference, volume one, page one.

3 Ibid., front piece to chapter one.

4 Ibid., front piece to chapter one.

5 Ibid., front piece to chapter one.

6 Ibid., front piece to chapter one.

7 Hon. Nick G. Sibbeston, *Senate Debates*, Vol. 238, Issue 24, 8 Feb. 2000, 548.

8 Tammy Nemeth, letter to author, 21 Feb. 2000.

CHAPTER 9—NORTH POLE

1 Ed Cowan, letter to the author, 19 Mar. 1971.

2 Fridtjof Nansen, *Farthest North*, Vol. I (Westminster: Archibald, Constable and Company, 1897), dedication page.

3 Fridtjof Nansen, *Farthest North*, 1.

4 Stuart Hodgson, itinerary given to expedition members—High Arctic 1971.

5 Mike Randolph, "The Cold Truth is Out There," *National Post*, 19 Dec. 1999, B12.

CHAPTER 10—MACHO MEN

1 Eric Smith and Adam Cohen, "Business: The Male Bulimia: Psychologists Say Financial Media Inspire Purge-and-Binge Behaviour in Your Men," *National Post*, 20 Jan. 2000, A1.

2 Unless otherwise indicated, this and other quotations in the chapter were originally printed in the *Vancouver Sun* and other FP publications from 1968 to 1970 and are reprinted with permission of the *Vancouver Sun*.

3 Pat Carney, "Oil Firms Doing Good Job Keeping Arctic Clean," *Toronto Star*, 29 April 1970, 21.

4 Robert Service, "The Spell of the Yukon," *Collected Poems of Robert Service* (New York: Dodd, Mead & Company, 1907), 5.

5 Ibid., 5.

CHAPTER 11—CANDIDATE

1 As the Alaska Highway has been improved over the years, some Mile Post distances have changed.

2 Pat Carney, personal field journal.

3 *Handbook for Candidates* (PC Party of Canada, 1999).

4 PC Handbook, *The Candidate* (PC Party of Canada, 1979), 3.

5 Pat Carney, "New MP's Life Not All Beer, Skittles," *Vancouver Sun*, 1980.

CHAPTER 12—BLUE STAR

1 Pat Carney, "New MP's Life Not All Beer, Skittles," *Vancouver Sun*, 1980.
2 Madame Jeanne Sauvé subsequently ruled that all MPs were to be called Honourable Members.
3 The legislation was finally introduced and passed by the Mulroney government in 1985.
4 *House of Commons Debates*, Vol. XI, 16 Nov. 1980, 12 775.
5 *House of Commons Debates*, Vol. XI, 16 Nov. 1980, 12 832.

CHAPTER 13—MINISTER OF THE CROWN

1 Barry McVicar, former Canadian Petroleum Association executive, correspondence to author, 23 Dec. 1999.
2 Peter Foster, *The Blue-Eyed Sheiks: The Canadian Oil Establishment* (Toronto: Collins, 1979), 42; as quoted in Tammy Nemeth's master's thesis, "Pat Carney and the Dismantling of the National Energy Program," University of Alberta, 1997.
3 Personal interview with the author, 6 March 2000.
4 *Globe and Mail*, 29 Dec. 1983, as quoted in Tammy Nemeth's thesis, 58.
5 We were also developing the Canada–Nova Scotia Accord, Western Accord and Frontier Energy Policy.
6 Premier John Buchanan of Nova Scotia, Premier Peter Lougheed of Alberta, and Premier Brian Peckford of Newfoundland and Labrador.
7 McGrath was later named Lieutenant Governor of Newfoundland and Labrador by Prime Minister Mulroney.
8 Pat Carney, MP, constituency archival files, circa 1985–86.
9 Tammy Nemeth, 2.
10 Ibid., 2.
11 Ibid., 2.
12 Ibid., 5.
13 Ibid., 147–48.
14 Mellon's memo to file, 17 Nov. 1984, 6.
15 Tammy Nemeth, 159.
16 Mellon's memo to file, 6.
17 Tammy Nemeth, 159.
18 Stephen Rogers' letter to the author, 31 Oct. 1984.
19 Paul Schoenhals' letter to the author, 20 Mar. 1985.
20 *Oilweek,* 7 July 1986.

CHAPTER 14—FREE TRADE

1 An abridged form of this chapter appeared in *The Globe and Mail*, 3 June 1999, A17.
2 Transport Minister Don Mazankowski was later named Deputy Prime Minister.

3 Letter from Simon Reisman to William Macness, Senior Vice-President, Bank of Nova Scotia, 11 June 1987.

4 While researching this book I found that Simon Reisman and Peter Murphy had already identified the following nine areas for negotiation in this politically sensitive area of investment: right of establishment/national treatment; forced divestiture; performance requirements; investors' right to divest; expropriation; transfers; exemptions; coverage of states/provinces; and unique for US and Canada.

5 The fast track ran out on Sunday, October 4, 1987, but according to tradition, the President did not send a message to Congress on a Sunday.

6 In fact, we discovered that there were 99 wine stores in British Columbia alone.

7 My three other rules are: listen for what they really want, not what they are asking for; identify what each side must have in the negotiations; and finally, know when to close the deal!

8 Simon Reisman and I never did go into business together, but Gordon Ritchie asked me to join his consulting company, Strategico Inc.; however, my Senate appointment intervened.

CHAPTER 15—CABINET

1 Jean Chrétien dropped P&P during his Prime Ministership; the decision-making body was the PMO and full Cabinet.

2 In compliance with my Privy Council Oath, the events of this chapter have been fused to represent a collage of cabinet agendas rather than a report of any specific cabinet meeting.

3 Pat Carney, Report from Parliament, 1980.

4 Flora MacDonald, "The Minister and the Mandarins," *Policy Options* I, No. 3 (Sept./Oct 1980), 29–31.

5 Erik Nielsen, *The House Is Not a Home* (Toronto: Macmillan Canada, 1989), 296.

6 The seven main provisions of the Meech Lake Accord are: compensation; amendment by unanimous consent; amendments by Parliament; initiation of amendment procedures; amendments without Senate resolution; Constitutionalization of the federal-provincial agreements on the settlement of new immigrants in Canada; and Constitutionalization of the federal-provincial consultative process by requiring at least one First Minister's meeting to be held annually, and by requiring that the issues of Senate reform and the fisheries be discussed at those meetings.

7 Undated note from Elmer MacKay to the author.

8 Handwritten notes of meeting between Ambassador Bouchard and the author, 14 May 1987.

9 Personal telephone call to the author during the summer of 1989.

10 John Crosbie, *No Holds Barred* (Toronto: McClelland & Stewart Inc., 1997), 48.
11 Personal interview with John Fraser, 9 Feb. 2000.
12 A term used to describe diplomats who become co-opted by the countries to which they are posted.
13 Quoted from Jeffrey Simpson's review in *The Globe and Mail*, 8 May 1999, D10, of *Governing from the Centre: The Concentration of Power in Canadian Politics* by Donald J. Savoie (Toronto: University of Toronto Press, 1999).
14 PC Research, briefing paper PC-41/1, Oct. 1996.
15 Ibid., briefing paper states that the submission went to Treasury Board, bypassing the Economic Committee of Cabinet, in October 1986. Previous Supply and Services Canada Minister Stewart McInnes of Halifax concurred.
16 Pat Carney, personal notes from black book.

CHAPTER 16—POLITICAL LIFE
1 "Canada Changes Course," *Time*, 17 Sept. 1984, 10–15.
2 Ibid., 10–15.
3 From the Oath of the Members of the Privy Council.
4 Michael Salter, "Canada's Toughest Bosses," *Report on Business*, Dec. 1987, 83.
5 Pat Carney, personal notes from black book.

CHAPTER 17—SENATOR PAT
1 Letter to the author from Andy Erasmus, 1996.
2 Quebec senators almost defeated the Canadian Environmental Assessment Act in Committee to support Quebec's claim that environment was a provincial jurisdiction, although the Supreme Court ruled that it was a joint federal-provincial jurisdiction.
3 Pat Carney, *Vancouver Sun*, 1995.
4 Library of Parliament report, April 2000.
5 *Lightstations: People Want People on the Lights*, report by the Ad Hoc Parliamentary Committee on Lightstations, June 1995.
6 Ibid., "Penny-pinching Bastards," a song written and performed at the Ad-Hoc Parliamentary Committee hearings by Kent Douglas Fiddy.

CHAPTER 18—GENDER POLITICS
1 Sidney Sharpe, *The Gilded Ghetto: Women and Political Power in Canada* (Toronto: HarperCollins Publishers Ltd., 1994), 272.
2 Statistics supplied by Claudette Barré, Acting Director, Employment Equity Division, Treasury Board, 8 Feb. 2000.

3 Sidney Sharpe, *The Gilded Ghetto: Women and Political Power in Canada*, xiv.
4 Jean Edmonds, Jocelyne Côté-O'Hara, and Edna MacKenzie, "The Report of the Task Force on Barriers To Women in the Public Service," *Beneath the Veneer*, 70.
5 Erik Nielsen, *The House Is Not a Home* (Toronto: Macmillan of Canada, 1989), 298.
6 Ibid., 303.
7 Ibid., 296.
8 Tom Kennedy, *Quest: Canada's Search for Arctic Oil* (Edmonton: Reidmore Books, 1968), 61–62.
9 Ibid., 213.

CHAPTER 19—POLITICS AND PEOPLE
1 Pat Carney, "How, Not What Is Issue in Northern Canada," *The Winnipeg Free Press*, 26 Aug. 1968, 13.

CHAPTER 20—CANADA: WHOSE COUNTRY IS IT, ANYWAY?
1 The Famous Five were Nellie McClung, Emily Murphy, Henrietta Muir Edwards, Louise McKinney, and Irene Parlby. All from Alberta, these women fought to have women declared "persons" under the law, making it possible for women to participate in all facets of Canadian public life, including appointments to the Senate and federal courts.
2 Alan C. Cairns, "Citizenship and the New Constitutional Order," *Canadian Parliamentary Review* (Autumn 1992), 2–4.
3 Ibid., 2–4.
4 Ibid., 2–4.
5 Alan C. Cairns, *Citizens Plus: Aboriginal Peoples and the Canadian State* (Vancouver-Toronto: UBC Press, 2000), 109.
6 Ibid., 193.
7 Ibid., 204.
8 Ibid., 211.
9 Alan C. Cairns, "Citizenship and the New Constitutional Order," 2–4.
10 "Second Thoughts: Delay of Racially Based Nisga'a Treaty Would Serve Canada Well," *Calgary Herald*, Opinion, Final Edition, 24 Mar. 2000, A22.
11 Pat Carney, *Vancouver Sun*, speech by John Kenneth Galbraith to UBC audience, as quoted by Pat Carney, circa 1965.
12 Supreme Court, *R. V. Marshall* (1997) 3 SCR 533, Section 39: 28.
13 Margaret A. Ormsby, *British Columbia: A History* (Vancouver: Macmillan of Canada, 1958), 214.

Bibliography

Ajzenstat, Janet, ed., Paul Romney, Ian Gentles, and William D. Gairdner. *Canada's Founding Debates*. Toronto: Stoddart Publishing Co., 1999.

Ad Hoc Parliamentary Committee on Lightstations. *Lightstations: People Want People on the Lights*. June 1995.

Bain, George. *Gotcha!* Toronto: Key Porter Books, 1994.

Barré, Claudette. Statistics supplied by Claudette Barré, Acting Director, Employment Equity Division, Treasury Board, 8 Feb. 2000.

Bowering, George. *Bowering's BC: A Swashbuckling History*. Toronto: Viking, 1996.

Bregha, François. *Bob Blair's Pipeline*. Toronto: James Lorimer & Company, 1979.

Cairns, Alan C. "Citizenship and the New Constitutional Order." *Canadian Parliamentary Review*, Autumn, 1992.

Cairns, Alan C. *Citizen Plus: Aboriginal Peoples and the Canadian State*. Vancouver: UBC Press, 2000.

Calgary Herald. "Second Thoughts: Delay of Racially Based Nisga'a Treaty Would Serve Canada Well," 24 Mar. 2000: A22.

Campbell, Rt. Hon. Kim. *Time and Chance*. Toronto: Doubleday Canada, 1996.

Carney, Catherine. *Kelowna Courier*. Newsclip found among Catherine Carney's papers. Undated.

Carney, Dora Sanders. Letter to her father Harry Sanders.

Carney, Dora Sanders. Letters to her parents, circa 1936.

Carney, Dora Sanders. Personal papers.

Carney, Dora Sanders. *Foreign Devils Have Light Eyes: A Memoir of Shanghai, 1933–1939*. Toronto: Virgo Press, 1980.

Carney, Dora Sanders. "Great Harmony." Unpublished manuscript, circa 1980s.

Carney, Dora Sanders. "Merrily, Merrily." Unpublished manuscript, circa 1950s.

Carney, Jill. Personal papers.

Carney, John James. Various letters between John James Carney and his sister, Catherine, 1910–1976.

Carney, Pat. "Anatomy of a Corporate Takeover." *Vancouver Sun*, 10 Feb. 1968.

Carney, Pat. Article on gun control. *Vancouver Sun*, 1995.

Carney, Pat. Article in *Vancouver Sun*, 13 Feb. 1967: 22.

Carney, Pat. Constituency Archival files, circa 1985–86.

Carney, Pat. "Free Trade: The Making of the Deal." *Globe and Mail*, 3 June 1999: A17.

Carney, Pat. "How, Not What Is Issue in Northern Canada." *The Winnipeg Free Press*. 26 Aug. 1968: 13.

Carney, Pat. "New MP's Life Not All Beer, Skittles." *Vancouver Sun*, 1980.

Carney, Pat. "Oil Firms Doing Good Job Keeping Arctic Clean." *Toronto Star*, 29 April 1970: 21.

Carney, Pat. "Pat Carney Goes Home to China." *City Woman*, (Sept./Oct. 1979). Article published as an afterword in *Foreign Devils Have Light Eyes*.

Carney, Pat. Personal field journal.

Carney, Pat. Personal notes from black books.

Carney, Pat. "Proposed Mackenzie Valley Developments and their Consequences." Speech to Opportunity North Conference, sponsored by Northern Alberta Development Council. Peace River, Alberta, 28 Nov. 1975.

Carney, Pat. Report from Parliament, 1980.

Carney, Pat. "Royal Tour." *Tiara & Atigi: Northwest Territories 1970 Centennial*, Vancouver: Mitchell Press, 1971. Copyright, Canada, 1971 by the Government of the Northwest Territories.

Carney, Pat. *Vancouver Sun*. Speech by John Kenneth Galbraith to UBC audience, as quoted by Pat Carney, circa 1960s.

Clarkson, Her Excellency, The Right Honourable Adrienne, Governor General of Canada, "Speech from the Throne." Opening of the Second Session of the 36th Parliament. Ottawa, 12 Oct. 1999.

Cowan, Ed. Letter to the author, 19 Mar. 1971.

Crosbie, John. *No Holds Barred*. Toronto: McClelland & Stewart, 1997.

Department of Foreign Affairs and International Trade. *China Regional Report—Yangzi Delta*. Canadian Consulate General, Shanghai, China: Oct. 1998.

Edmonds, Jean, Jocelyn Cote-O'Hara, and Edna MacKenzie. *Task Force on Barriers To Women in the Public Service*. Ottawa: Queen's Printer, 1990.

Erasmus, Andy. Letter to the author, 1996.

Fairclough, Ellen. *Saturday's Child: Memoirs of Canada's First Female Cabinet Minister*. Toronto: University of Toronto Press, 1995.

Foster, Peter. *The Blue-Eyed Sheiks: The Canadian Oil Establishment*. Toronto: Collins, 1979.

Fotheringham, Allan. *Last Page First*, Toronto: Key Porter Books, 1999.

Fraser, Hon. John. Personal interview with the author, 6 Mar. 2000.

Gemini North Ltd. *Social and Economic Impact of Proposed Arctic Gas Pipeline in Northern Canada*. Books I-II, III. Calgary: Canadian Arctic Gas Pipeline Limited, 1974.

Gellatly, Dorothy Hewlett. *A Bit of Okanagan History*. Kelowna: Orchard City Press and Calendar Co., 1958.

Globe and Mail. Article dated 29 Dec. 1983. As quoted in Tammy Nemeth's thesis, 58.

Globe and Mail. "A Gloomy Future for a Futuristic City." 23 Feb. 1999.

Grey, Charlotte. "Women of the Year '85." *Chatelaine*, Jan. 1985.

Higham, Adrian. Personal papers and diaries of the Higham and Sanders families courtesy of Adrian Higham, Chichester, UK.

Higham, Richard. Personal journal.

Hodgson, Stuart. Itinerary given to expedition members. High Arctic, 1971.

Holland, Clive, ed. *Farthest North: The Quest for the North Pole*. New York: Carroll & Graf Publishers, 1994.

House of Commons Debates. Vol. XI, 16 Nov. 1980: 12 775.

House of Commons Debates. Vol. XI. 16 Nov. 1980: 12 832.

Kennedy, James R., and Howard S. Kennedy, and Donald E. Read. *St Patrick's Roman Catholic Cemetery*. Ottawa Branch, Ontario Genealogical Society. Publication: 78-8. Ottawa: June 1978.

Kennedy, Tom. *Quest: Canada's Search for Arctic Oil*. Edmonton: Reidmore Books, 1988.

Lee, Peggy. *Miss Peggy Lee: An Autobiography*. New York: Donald I. Fine, 1989.

Lethbridge, H.J. Introduction. *All About Shanghai: A Standard Guidebook*. Hong Kong: Oxford University Press, 1983. First published by University Press, Shanghai, 1934–35.

Library of Parliament. Report, 2000.

Lower, Arthur R.M. *Colony to Nation: A History of Canada*. Toronto: McClelland and Stewart, 5th ed. First published by Longmans, Green & Co, 1946.

Macdonald, Ian, and Betty O'Keefe. *The Mulligan Affair; Top Cop on the Take*. Surrey: Heritage House Publishing Company, 1997.

MacDonald, Flora. "The Minister and the Mandarins," *Policy Options*, Vol. I, No. 3 (Sept./Oct. 1980).

MacKay, Donald. *Flight from Famine: The Coming of the Irish to Canada*. Toronto: McClelland & Stewart, 1990.

MacKay, Elmer. Handwritten note to the author, undated.

Martin, Lawrence. *The Presidents and the Prime Ministers*. Toronto: Doubleday Canada, 1982.

Martin, Patrick, Allan Gregg, and George Perlin. *Contenders: The Tory Quest for Power*. Scarborough: Prentice-Hall Canada, 1983.

McVicar, Barry. Former Canadian Petroleum Association executive, correspondence to author, 23 Dec. 1999.

Mellon, Barry. Memorandum. 27 Nov. 1984.

Morten, Alexandra, and Billy Proctor. *Heart of the Raincoast*. Victoria: Horsdal & Shubart Publishers, 1988.

Mowat, Farley. *The Polar Passion: The Quest for the North Pole*. Toronto: McClelland and Stewart, 1967.

Nansen, Fridtjof. *Farthest North*. Vol. I, II. Westminster: Archibald, Constable and Company, 1897.

Nemeth, Tammy. "Pat Carney and the Dismantling of the National Energy Program," master's thesis, University of Alberta, 1997.

Nichols, Marjorie, with Jane O'Hara. *Mark My Words: The Memoirs of a Very Political Reporter*. Vancouver: Douglas & McIntyre, 1992.

Nicolas Davin. *The Irishman in Canada*. Library of Parliament #F5030 I GD 39, 1877.

Nielsen, Erik. *The House Is Not a Home*. Toronto: Macmillan of Canada, 1989.

Oilweek. 7 July 1986.

Ormsby, Margaret A. *British Columbia: A History*. Vancouver: Macmillan of Canada, 1958.

Pan, Ling. *In Search of Old Shanghai*. Hong Kong: Joint Publishing Co., 1982.

PC Party of Canada. *Handbook for Candidates*. 1999.

PC Party of Canada. PC Handbook, *The Candidate*, 1979.

PC Research. Briefing paper PC-41/1, Oct. 1996.

Randolph, Mike. "The Cold Truth is Out There," *National Post*, 19 Dec. 1999.

Reisman, Simon. Letter to William Macness, Senior Vice-President, Bank of Nova Scotia, 11 June 1987.

Ritchie, Gordon. *Wrestling with the Elephant: The Inside Story of the Canada-US Trade Wars*. Toronto: Macfarlane Walter & Ross, 1997.

Rogers, Stephen. Letter to the author, 31 Oct. 1984.

Romney, Paul. *Getting It Wrong: How Canadians Forgot Their Past and Imperilled Confederation.* Toronto: University of Toronto Press, 1999.

Salter, Michael. "Canada's Toughest Bosses." *Report on Business,* Dec. 1987: 83.

Sanders, Byrne Hope. "My Point in Time." Unpublished manuscript, circa 1970.

Sanders, Wilfrid. "Jolly Good Show—Early Ontario." Unpublished manuscript, circa 1970.

Sawatsky, John. *The Insiders: Power, Money and Secrets in Ottawa.* Toronto: McClelland and Stewart, 1989.

Schlesinger, Joe. *Time Zones: A Journalist in the World.* Toronto: Fawcett Crest, 1990.

Schoenhals, Paul. Letter to the author, 20 Mar. 1985.

Service, Robert. "Spell of the Yukon." *Collected Poems of Robert Service.* New York: Dodd, Mead & Company, 1907.

Sharp, Mitchell. *Which Reminds Me.* Toronto: University of Toronto Press, 1994.

Sharpe, Sydney. *The Gilded Ghetto: Women and Political Power in Canada.* Toronto: HarperCollins Publishers, 1994.

Sibbeston, Hon. Nick G. *Senate Debates,* Vol. 238, Issue 24, Feb. 2000.

Simpson, Jeffrey. Review in *The Globe and Mail,* 8 May 1999, D10, of *Governing from the Centre: The Concentration of Power in Canadian Politics* by Donald J. Savoie. Toronto: University of Toronto Press, 1999.

Smith, Dr. Eric, and Dr. Adam Cohen. "Business: The Male Bulimia: Psychologists Say Financial Media Inspire Purge-and-binge Behaviour in Your Men," *National Post,* 20 Jan. 2000.

Smith, Gordon, and Moisés Naím. *Altered States: Globalization, Sovereignty, and Governance.* Ottawa: International Development Research Centre, 2000.

Speech from the Throne; Opening the Second Session of the 36th Parliament, Senate Chamber, 12 Oct. 1999.

Supreme Court. *R. V. Marshall* (1997) 3 SCR 533, Section 39; 28.

Time, "Canada Changes Course." 17 Sept. 1984: 10–15.

Walker, Olive and Harry. *Carleton Saga.* Ottawa: Runge Press, 1968.

Index

United Nations, 268-69
United Empire Loyalists, 43
University of British Columbia, 26, 66, 80, 83, 85, 93-96, 101, 106, 112, 125, 129, 132, 177, 312, 321, 328, 349, 354
University of Toronto, 36
US Naval Arctic Research Station, 142

Valenti, Jack, 318, 352
Valpy, Mike, 200
Vancouver Art Gallery, 256
Vancouver Centre riding, 185-87, 192, 194-95, 197, 198, 206
Vancouver Museum, 200
Vancouver Sun, 52, 98, 99, 102-10, 112, 114, 151, 153, 173, 184, 189, 192, 252, 281, 312, 320, 334, 337, 346, 354
Vanderleest, Leo, 153
Vander Zalm, Bill, 244, 260, 265, 280-81, 340
Vander Zalm, Lillian, 340
Veilleux, Gerard, 254, 274, 323-24
Vernon, Bill, 302-3
Vézina, Monique, 264
Victoria, Queen, 177
Volker, Paul, 246
Volpe, John, 306
von Schellwitz, Mark, 182
Voortrekkers, 29-31

Waddell, Chris, 247
Waddell, Ian, 192
Waite, Wendy, 279, 333
Wallace, Pat, 97
Wallin, Pamela, 242, 247, 346
Wang Ching Wei, 15
Ward, Barbara, 110
Wardair, 156
Wardrup, Terry, 113
Warren, Jake, 228, 243
Wasserman, Jack, 93, 103-4
Watson, Hugh, 97, 100-1
Watson, Patrick, 102
Watts, Richard, 305
Wayne, Elsie, 346
Weber, Richard, 150
Webster, Hugh, 101
Webster, Jack, 99, 104, 132-33, 280, 281, 340

Webster, Margaret, 104
Westcoast Energy Inc., 314
West Coast fishery, 244, 289-90, 299-307, 357
West Coast lightstations, 295-98, 307-8
Western Accord, 220, 225
Western alienation, 193-95, 203, 207, 209, 211-12, 213, 223, 224, 244, 263
Whaling, 288-89, 298, 299, 307
Whelan, Eugene, 69
Whisky Whisky Papa, 135
White, Paul, 90, 91, 92, 112, 114, 151, 152, 163, 165-68, 172, 174, 196, 283, 302, 331, 336, 347
Whitters, Janice, 176, 183, 184, 187, 200, 207, 208, 239, 243, 275, 297, 314, 331
Wilde, Mary, 28, 29
Williams, A.R., 102
Williams, Andy, 174
Williams, Charlie, 301
Wilson, Bertha, 309, 315-16
Wilson, Cairine Reay, 293
Wilson, Michael, 198, 200, 202, 203, 204, 217, 221-24, 229, 232, 236, 239, 240, 242, 243, 244, 246, 251, 259, 262, 271, 275
Windsor, Duchess of (formerly Wallis Simpson), 342
Windsor, Duke of. *See* Edward VIII
Winsor, Hugh, 110, 346
Women, aboriginal, 357
Women, politicians, 309-30
Women's right to vote, 350
Woodstock Sentinel Review, 36
World Bank, 110
World War I, 10, 19, 41, 59-62, 63
World War II, 18, 19, 20, 33, 39, 63, 99, 108, 177
Worthington, Peter, 95

Yaffe, Barbara, 346
Yellowknife, 126-27
Yeutter, Clayton, 239, 242, 243, 246
Young, Doug, 296

Zabawa, Roseanne, 83
Zaozirny, John, 214, 215, 222
Zimmerman, Adam, 315